The Flavor
of
Wisconsin

*An Informal History
of Food and Eating
in the Badger State*

Harva Hachten

THE FLAVOR OF WISCONSIN

AN INFORMAL HISTORY OF FOOD
AND EATING IN THE BADGER STATE,
TOGETHER WITH 400 FAVORITE RECIPES

THE STATE HISTORICAL SOCIETY OF WISCONSIN

Madison: 1981

For

ELIZABETH and MARIANNE

affectionate critics of both my
culinary and my literary efforts.

Library of Congress Cataloging in Publication Data:
Hachten, Harva.
THE FLAVOR OF WISCONSIN.
1. Cookery, American—Wisconsin.
2. Wisconsin—Social life and customs. I. Title.
TX715.H12 641'.09775 80-26172
ISBN 0-87020-204-9
Printed and bound in the United States of America.

INTRODUCTION

ACCORDING TO MENOMINEE LEGEND, MAPLE syrup used to come out of the tree as sugar. Mä'näbŭsh, the primal folk hero who set life in order, was disturbed by the ease with which this delicious staple could be obtained. So he climbed to the very top of one of the trees and scattered water like rain over the maples to dissolve the sugar and make it flow from the trees as a liquid. This was necessary, he told his grandmother, Noko'mis, the Earth, so his people would have to keep occupied and work hard to make sugar. Otherwise they would get into bad habits by spending so much time in idleness.

Mä'näbŭsh succeeded in his purpose: idleness is hardly possible when converting maple sap into sugar. Nor is it possible when converting any of Wisconsin's bounty into food for any of the various peoples who have joined the Menominee to settle on this land. For, though Wisconsin has been amply endowed with fertile lands and a great variety of wild food plants and game, it has not yielded up its riches easily.

It is not recorded whether Mä'näbŭsh was responsible for Wisconsin's climate, too, but that certainly has been a reason—if not the primary one—for ensuring its citizens a life free of idleness. Though many things grow well and many others are available just for the taking, their seasons are short. Providing foodstuffs for the entire yearly cycle has always required planning, diligent organizing, and hard work.

But this never discouraged Mä'näbŭsh's people or any others. In the years since he sprinkled water on the maples, many groups have come to tap the trees and the other riches—Potawatomi, Oneida, Stockbridge-Munsee, Ottawa, Chippewa, Winnebago, Kickapoo, Illinois, and Eastern Sioux; French, Canadian, Yankee, English,

Cornish, Polish, German, Czech, Norwegian, Finn, Swede, Dane, and Swiss—the list is long. More than fifty different peoples have settled here; no one is sure of the exact number.

This book is about those who have come here, and particularly about the ways they set their tables. It is more than a recipe book. It is designed also to offer sample servings of the state's varied culinary traditions; how they were maintained, changed, or adapted to the realities of this particular environment; how they have formed the economic base for a society which, though still heavily concerned with food production, has diversified widely over the years. For we are what we eat in ways beyond nutrition. What we eat tells much about our climate, soil conditions, finances, transportation facilities, market conditions; how we eat, and when, and with whom, reflects family and community social customs.

This book offers some insights into these aspects of our heritage. It does not pretend to be all-inclusive. It is necessarily eclectic and in many respects serendipitous, limited by the availability of material.

*　　*　　*　　*　　*

The ingredients for this potpourri began to be assembled in 1971 when James Morton Smith, at that time director of the State Historical Society of Wisconsin, suggested an ethnic cookbook as a project for the Women's Auxiliary of the Society. Under the direction of the then president, Mrs. George C. Swart of Fort Atkinson, a great many ethnic recipes were gathered, mainly from secondary sources, and the literature on Indian foods and cooking was researched. When I joined the staff of the Society in 1973, the project was turned over to me, a journalist and author of a cookbook. In early 1974, the State Historical Society of Wisconsin sent out a news release inviting state residents of all ethnic backgrounds to contribute recipes and reminiscences about food and eating for a project then called the Wisconsin Heritage Cookbook.

And by the deadline—and beyond—the recipes poured in, as rich and varied as a cooking display at a county fair. Persons of all ages from all over the state (and out-of-state Wisconsinites) sent in recipes alone or accompanied by accounts of how mother, or grandmother, or great-grandmother (and sometimes father) fed their families in the old days.

A group of women in Parkview Terrace Nursing Home in Platteville spent several afternoons writing out long-used favorites they were no longer in a position to cook. A fourth-grade class in James Madison School in Manitowoc made a class project out of interviewing their mothers and grandmothers for old-time favorites. One woman sent in her recipe for Pear Bread together with a sample loaf of this Swiss specialty. In all, more than 900 persons stocked the larder of this project with close to 1,600 recipes. And, as in any well-supplied larder, there were many duplications. (The record for most recipes for a single dish would have to be shared by Potato Dumplings, Potato Pancakes, and Plum [Suet] Pudding.)

Not surprisingly, the contributions mirrored the state's ethnic makeup, with the largest number of recipes being of German origin, the fewest Armenian and Syrian. There was one Vietnamese recipe. And Potato Dumplings and Pancakes notwithstanding, about 25 per cent of the entries were for desserts of some kind, reflecting the way our culinary memory works: when asked about "best" or "most favorite" dishes we think of cake before cornmeal mush, though there were some recipes for the latter, too. I found it historically interesting that, on the other hand, not one recipe submitted fell into the category of appetizers.

In an effort to make the scope of this book more comprehensive, two student research assistants spent a summer canvassing and culling the Society's considerable archival and manuscript holdings, and combing through that mother lode of information about early Wisconsin, the *Wisconsin Historical Collections*. The result of the research and contributions was a mass of recipes and food lore surpassing anything we had envisaged at the outset.

The scope of the material thus gathered was necessarily self-limiting, for not all ethnic groups responded equally or proportionately to the call for material. And only the purest historical chance determines the range and representativeness of the materials that get saved over the years and then end up in the Society's archives, rich though that collection indisputably is. Furthermore, very little archival material by women—the ones most concerned with this subject—is extant; either their long, arduous days left them little time to keep diaries or write of their experiences, or else what they did record was not considered significant or worthy of saving for the historical record.

* * * * *

An interesting fact emerges from this harvest of materials. Historians and sociologists now question whether a distinctively American character was fused in the nineteenth and early twentieth centuries from varying foreign elements stewed up together in a great "melting pot." But to the extent that the pot did indeed exist, the different gastronomic ingredients added to it never blended together. No typically American cuisine has been distilled from our dazzling array of ethnic riches. The uniformity and blandness of franchise food chains and limited-menu restaurants, with their ubiquitous steaks, chops, and french-fried shrimp, have been spawned by our mass-consumptive society rather than our tasty ethnic traditions.

One might say that the cuisine that has evolved in America is more like a stew than a distinctively blended liaison like mayonnaise. What went into the pot was Italian, Greek, Scandinavian, French, Chinese, Mexican, etc., cooking. When it is dished out of the pot it is still clearly recognizable (occasionally altered a little, perhaps, by the simmering) as Italian, Greek, Scandinavian, French, Chinese, Mexican, etc.

Certainly this is true in Wisconsin. Unlike many other states, Wisconsin has come to be associated with the production of certain distinctive foodstuffs, of which cheese and dairy products, beer, and wurst are the most obvious. These delights, however, prove the point: they are legacies of our ethnic past, and their origins are still unmistakable.

Wisconsin's earliest nineteenth-century settlers, mainly Yankees and New Yorkers, did a little dairying (especially after their wheat crops began to fail) and started making cheese on their farms. (Those crossroads cheese factories came somewhat later.) Then the Scandinavians, Germans, Swiss, and even Italians soon were to give added impetus and distinction to the state's best-known enterprise. The Germans' thirst for economic advantage in a new land also fermented into our brewing enterprises, although Milwaukee's first brewery was in fact established by three Welshmen. When it comes to sausages, Wisconsin provides slices of all the major principalities of Germany, Poland, and Bohemia. Our wild rice, historically an inexpensive native American staple, remains an Indian enterprise (though recently it has pushed its way into the gourmet price class of Beluga caviar and saffron).

It is unlikely that we will ever homogenize a typically Wisconsin or American cookery. These days, citizens both old and new are showing renewed interest and pride in their own ethnicity. And few things are more culturally identifiable than the ways in which our ancestors combined ingredients and seasonings available to all into disparate and ethnically distinguished olfactory and taste experiences.

* * * * *

Making choices for the recipe section from this bumper harvest was difficult. A preliminary screening was done by a panel of home economists and food experts assembled by Rosalie (Mrs. Oscar) Mayer of Madison, who was the liaison for the Women's Auxiliary of the State Historical Society of Wisconsin for this project. The experts were asked to designate those recipes they felt were best, or most historic, or most representative of a particular ethnic group. They had, in short, the unenviable task of deciding whose Potato Pancake recipe was "better" than whose.

As the chef of this banquet, however, the final choices were mine, and I confess I did not always follow the advice of the panel. In making the decisions, I was searching for a menu that would impart the historical flavor of Wisconsin without taking up precious space with recipes that have become fixtures in ordinary cookbooks. This was not easy. How could I, for instance, compile a book of Wisconsin food lore without including Sauerbraten or Sugar Cookies? (The answer is, I couldn't.) Whatever errors of judgment, balance, fact, or omission that may have resulted are mine alone.

The recipes in this volume, then, were largely culled from the material contributed by many people to the Society's "heritage cookbook" project, seasoned here and there with items from the publications of church and social groups, the archives and manuscript collections of the State Historical Society, scrapbooks, newspapers, and the like. In most instances, the recipes were edited to conform to the modern standard style of listing ingredients first. Some rewriting or elaboration of directions was usually necessary, but, on the whole, I attempted to preserve the original literary flavor. Finally, I have accepted with only a few exceptions the contributor's word as to a recipe's ethnic origin and its title—though in some cases this involved more than a few minutes' puzzlement over a German, a Norwegian, even a Welsh dictionary. Not surprisingly, many ethnic recipes bore titles that were based on phonetics or European regional variations rather than conventional orthography.

This is a sharing cookbook, as much for reading as for using. These recipes have been tried and tested by years of use by those who sent them in, but not necessarily by me. In editing them, I have presumed a knowledge on the part of the reader of basic culinary techniques and terminology—for instance, that sugar means granulated sugar and flour means all-purpose flour; that brown sugar is always measured packed; that spices are ground unless otherwise specified; how to fold in egg whites; procedures for canning; and so on.

The feast is finally ready. Herewith the flavor of Wisconsin. *Bon appétit! Mahl Zeit! Håper det smaker! Smacznego!*
Enjoy!

HARVA HACHTEN
Madison, Wisconsin

CONTENTS

The Recipes:

The Flavor
of
Wisconsin

*An Informal History
of Food and Eating
in the Badger State*

COUNTIES AND COUNTY SEATS

Superior · DOUGLAS

Washburn · BAYFIELD

Ashland · ASHLAND

Hurley · IRON

VILAS · Eagle River

FLORENCE · Florence

WASHBURN · Hayward

SAWYER

ONEIDA · Rhinelander

FOREST · Crandon

MARINETTE

BURNETT · Grantsburg

Shell Lake

Phillips · PRICE

POLK · Balsam Lake

BARRON · Barron

RUSK · Ladysmith

LINCOLN · Merrill

LANGLADE · Antigo

MENOMINEE

OCONTO · Keshena · Oconto

DOOR · Sturgeon Bay

ST CROIX · Hudson

DUNN · Menomonie

CHIPPEWA · Chippewa Falls

TAYLOR · Medford

Wausau · MARATHON

SHAWANO · Shawano

KEWAUNEE · Kewaunee

PIERCE · Ellsworth

Eau Claire · EAU CLAIRE · Durand

CLARK · Neillsville

Stevens Point

WAUPACA · Waupaca

Green Bay · OUTAGAMIE · Appleton · BROWN

MANITOWOC · Manitowoc

PEPIN

BUFFALO · Alma · Whitehall

JACKSON · Black River Falls

WOOD · Wisconsin Rapids · PORTAGE

CALUMET · Chilton

WINNEBAGO · Oshkosh

SHEBOYGAN · Sheboygan

TREMPEALEAU

MONROE · Sparta

WAUSHARA · Wautoma

ADAMS · Friendship

Green Lake

Fond du Lac · FOND DU LAC

LA CROSSE · La Crosse

MARQUETTE · Montello

JUNEAU · Mauston

GREEN LAKE

West Bend · OZAUKEE · Port Washington

VERNON · Viroqua

RICHLAND

Baraboo · SAUK

COLUMBIA · Portage

Juneau · DODGE

WASHINGTON

CRAWFORD · Prairie du Chien · Richland Center

IOWA · Dodgeville

Madison · DANE

JEFFERSON · Jefferson

Waukesha · WAUKESHA

Milwaukee · MILWAUKEE

GRANT · Lancaster

LAFAYETTE · Darlington

GREEN · Monroe

ROCK · Janesville

WALWORTH · Elkhorn

RACINE · Racine

KENOSHA · Kenosha

CARTOGRAPHIC LABORATORY, UNIVERSITY OF WISCONSIN – MADISON

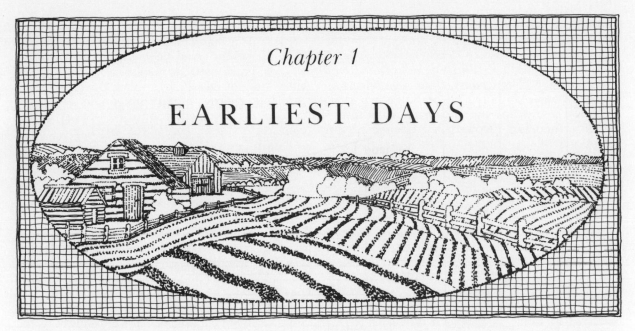

Chapter 1

EARLIEST DAYS

THE FINGERS OF THE LAST GREAT GLACIER OF the ice age poked well into Wisconsin, carving out the contours of the state, creating her many lakes, depositing new soils. Over the centuries, the conditions and climate left by the glacier evolved into an area of beauty, bounty, and great variety.

When Europeans first appeared, Wisconsin was dominated by a huge pine forest in the north, dotted with stands of spruce and hemlock, opening up irregularly at the southern edge into hardwoods pocked with bogs and marshes, and finally ending in rolling, oak-dotted meadows and flat prairies.

Sprinkled liberally throughout, like candy shots on a cake, was a great array of edibles—berries, fruits, nuts, greens, roots, game, fish, and fowl. The woods were chock-full of berries—sumac, bunchberry, blueberry, cranberry, chokeberry, sand cherry, blackberry, raspberry, strawberry, juneberry. Hazelnuts, black walnuts, beechnuts, butternuts, and hickory nuts carpeted the ground in their seasons. There were wild plums, crabapples, May apples, grapes. Wild rice choked lakes and rivers. The honey of wild bees

filled hollow tree stumps, and the maples flowed with sweet sap each spring.

Feeding on these riches (and on each other) were more than a hundred species of mammals and fowl—elk, moose, woodland caribou, bison, wolverine, cougar, deer, black bear, rabbit, squirrel, muskrat, woodchuck, beaver, racoon, fox, wolf, coyote, bobcat, lynx, skunk, badger, weasel, mink, otter, opposum, marten, fisher, grouse, quail, pheasant, partridge, prairie chicken, wild turkey, ptarmigan—to name only some. Migrant ducks, Canada geese, and passenger pigeons literally darkened the skies in their travels, so great were their numbers. Cisco, lake chubs, whitefish, smelt, perch, suckers, muskellunge, pike, bass, trout, sturgeon, crappies, bluegills, catfish, and bullheads teemed in the waters.

Pierre-Esprit Radisson, one of the early fur trader-explorers, traversed the Wisconsin country in 1659 and 1660, recording in his journal that Washington Island and the Door peninsula were places where "whatever a man could desire was to be had in great plenty; viz. staggs, fishes in abundance, and all sorts of meat, corne enough."

Even well into the nineteenth century, these

foods available just for the taking were still abundant and impressive. In 1837, William Rudolph Smith, one of Wisconsin's earlier publicists and historians, described the southwestern part of the territory: "The undergrowth is generally of small bushes readily passed over; the black currant, the furred and the smooth gooseberry, the red and the white raspbery, the blackberry, the cranberry of the vine, and of the bush; the haw, the wild plum, and the crabapple; all these indigenous fruits are found throughout the territory; the strawberry literally covers the prairies and the groves; . . . the hazel with its nut-laden branches is the most common bush in the country; acorns, black and white walnuts, and hickory nuts, are as plenty as hosts of swine may for ages desire."

The strawberry thickets must have been fabulous. A settler in Green Lake recalled years afterwards a walk taken in 1840 when "we snuffed a delightful odor—the smell of ripe strawberries. We followed it up and found a place as big as an eighty-acre lot, that had been burned over, all covered with ripe wild strawberries as big as any tame ones you ever saw, and so thick that you could not lay your hand down without crushing berries." (Smith, too, reported berries up to three inches in circumference.)

In this northern latitude, these bounties were seasonal, of course, so that sustaining life through the year was essentially a full-time, strenuous occupation for the first—and subsequent—peoples who settled Wisconsin.

Menominee, Winnebago, Eastern Sioux, Mascoutin, Potawatomi, Ottawa, Chippewa, Miami, Illinois, Kickapoo, Sauk, and Fox—all developed their own yearly provending routines during their varied periods of Wisconsin residence. Such annual rhythms helped give a purposeful order and stability to life. The routine differed from tribe to tribe, depending on the period and the foodstuffs available in the area in which it lived, but the seasonal Chippewa round of the 1830's and 1840's was more or less typical for the time.

During late spring in the Chippewa's northern areas, the Indians planted gardens, principally of corn, squash, and beans, in ground broken and cultivated with plows and hoes of wood or the shoulder blade of a large deer or, when available, moose. Metal implements also were coming into use, especially as missionary organizations provided agricultural instruction among some Chippewa.

Wild potatoes, blueberries, gooseberries, and juneberries were gathered, some to be eaten immediately, others to be dried and stored for the winter in birchbark bags (called mococks). Berries were usually dried whole on frames made of reeds. Chokeberries were ground, pits and all, after drying. Raspberries were first boiled, then portioned out onto birchbark to dry; the small cakes were stored stacked and tied up in little packages.

Spring also brought the migrating pigeons to help fill the tribal pots. They were caught by the men who strung long fish nets on poles and held them up in the path of the huge flocks. The pigeons were generally boiled with other meat and perhaps wild potatoes, or with parched wild rice, carefully processed and saved from the previous year's harvest.

There was fishing to be done—women's work all year except during the winter. The catch was eaten both fresh (boiled or roasted over the fire) and dried (on racks over a fire or in the sun). Men trapped smaller animals for food and fur.

Then it was early autumn, the season to harvest the food staple, wild rice. Rice was an immensely important commodity to the Chippewa as well as all other peoples who lived in the areas where it grew. Indeed, the Menominee took their name from the Indian word for wild rice: *manomin*. At harvest time, the entire village moved to its rice camp on the lake shore. Working in canoes in family groups, a man poled two women out to the family's special section. The women, armed with two sticks about twenty-four inches long, would bend the rice stalks over the canoe with one stick and knock off the ripe kernels with the other until the canoe was full. On shore, the rice was sun-dried or parched over fires, pounded, and winnowed.

The Jesuit missionary and explorer Pere Jacques Marquette, writing in 1673, described the Menominee handling of the rice: ". . . [T]hey dry it in the smoke, upon a wooden grating, under which they maintain a slow fire for some days. When the oats are thoroughly dry, they put them in a skin made into a bag, thrust it into a hole dug in the ground for this purpose, and tread it with their feet—so long and so vigorously that the grain separates from the straw . . . . After this, they pound it to reduce it to flour,—or even, without pounding it, they boil it in water, and season it with fat. Cooked in this fashion, the wild oats have almost as delicate a taste as rice has when no better seasoning is added."

Upon the Indians' return to their summer camps, the gardens were harvested, the produce dried. When it was time to move on to the winter camp, a large supply of food was ready for storing in pits dug near the village or in caves hollowed out of hillsides. These were lined with birchbark, cushioned with hay, covered with more bark and hay, and finally topped with wooden beams and mounded earth. The tasks of preparing and putting away the food were the women's responsibilities. George W. Feather-

stonhaugh, an Englishman who traveled in Minnesota and Wisconsin in the autumn of 1835, described the scene among some Sioux in Minnesota: ". . . I observed several women with [eighty-pound] bags on their heads and shoulders, appearing heavily laden, bent down, and not raising their faces from the path they were upon. I never saw individuals contend more with a load that almost mastered them than did some of these females. Following them a short distance to a place where they stopped, I found they were making a *cache* of the ripe maize of that season. A sort of cave had been hollowed out of the side of the hill, about eight feet in diameter at the bottom, and not more than two or three at the top . . . . Some very young girls were in the cave stowing it away."

In addition to the Chippewa's dried corn, rice, meat, fish, and berries, there were at least three other garden vegetables—squash cut into rings and dried; cranberry pole beans; and a special Ojibwe potato. The last was supplemented by several wild potatoes, including the creamy vetchling, which, like the Sioux corn, was stored in pits. There were also wild ginger, hog peanut, bearberry, and mountain mint for seasoning; smooth sumac berries, bog rosemary, wintergreen, catnip, and even hemlock for beverages; milkweed flowers, wild onion and wild leek, fern sprouts, marsh marigold leaves, dandelion, and a host of other plants for vegetables; and white pine lichen, red ash inner bark, and aspen inner bark, which were cooked into egg-like dishes.

Carrying only lightweight foods such as rice, dried berries, and dried pumpkin blossoms (for thickening), the village would move on to the hunting camps where the men spent the winter ice fishing and stalking game, especially deer. The former task was accomplished by cutting a two-foot hole in the ice and cleaning off the snow about twenty feet around the hole to permit light through the ice. Lying on a rush mat and covering his head and the hole with an old blanket, the fisherman would spear any fish lured to the spot with a wooden decoy fish jigged up and down on the end of a string. "They caught a great many sturgeon in that way and some very large ones," one white observer noted in 1837. The women spent their time preparing and partially drying the catch and kill on a rack over a huge communal fire. The final drying was done in the sun the following summer.

At the end of winter came the best—and busiest—time of all. After wrapping the dried meats tightly in tanned deerskins, all proceeded to the sugar camp to tap the maple trees and make syrup and sugar.* As with the rice, each family group had its own area to work, using birchbark utensils stored at the camp in lodges. The kettles boiled away day and night, reducing the sap to a thick syrup which was then strained, replaced in the kettles, and slowly reheated until thickened. Then it was poured into granulating troughs and worked with a paddle and the hands until granulated. For hard sugar, the thickened syrup was poured into birchbark cones or dishes and molds, some of which held twenty-five to seventy-five pounds. A particular delicacy for the children was hard sugar cones formed in small (three-inch) birchbark containers or in the upper mandible of a duck's bill. Children also made a taffy-like candy from the syrup, cooling it in the melting snow.

The products of the sugar maple were more than treats. Maple sugar was the primary seasoning for fruits, vegetables, cereals, fish, and meat, since Wisconsin Indians had no salt. And it made medicine more palatable to children. Some sap was allowed to sour into a vinegar—called *ci-wabo*—primarily used when cooking venison, which was then sweetened into a sweet-sour dish similar to such German specialities. Dissolved in cold water and sometimes mixed with sap of

*Some historians question whether converting the sap into sugar was an Indian art, since European explorers and missionaries did not mention sugar-making until late in the seventeenth century. Furthermore, the iron pots, later used for boiling down the sap, were European imports. Most agree, however, that whether Europeans mentioned it or not, Indians always used sap to make a form of syrup and sugar in one way or another, including dropping hot stones into sap-filled containers of birchbark or woven reeds.

other trees such as box elder, yellow birch, ash, red maple, and basswood, sugar maple sap or sugar made a refreshing summer drink.

As it was elsewhere in America, corn as an important staple for Wisconsin Indians. For example, the Winnebago ate corn hulled or in corn meal bread or porridge. Winnebago women made the meal in a wooden bowl with a large wooden pounder. They also used green corn, either roasting it or drying it by first heating large stones which were topped with husks on which the cobs were laid, then covering them with more husks and earth. After this cooking, the corn was cut from the cobs and sun-dried. This dried green corn, used for making soup, would keep for years.

The variety we call popcorn—*nanisa'pimin* in Menominee—was roasted or parched and pounded by them into meal. The Menominee frequently mixed this cornmeal with dried venison, maple sugar, or wild rice, or often all three for a nourishing, lightweight concoction carried by hunters and travelers, ready to eat dry or with the addition of water. This was a version of pemmican, a nutritionally well-rounded ration used by all Indian peoples in some form or other when traveling. Indian pemmican helped sustain early explorers and voyageurs. It was a basic food, for instance, for Alexander Mackenzie, a fur trader who knew the Lake Superior region, when he journeyed across Canada from the Atlantic Coast to the Pacific in 1793.

Not all the corn was dried. Jonathan Carver, an explorer and mapmaker who visited the Green Bay area in 1766, found that the Indians there made a kind of bread of fresh corn: "Whilst their corn is in the milk, as they term it, that is, just before it begins to ripen, they slice off the kernels from the cob . . . . and knead them into a paste. This they are enabled to do without the addition of any liquid, by the milk that flows from them . . . ." The mixture was formed into small cakes, wrapped in basswood leaves, and cooked in hot embers. "And better flavored bread I never ate in any country," Carver concluded.

All cooking was done over or beside an open

fire or in pits. Pit cooking was particularly convenient for the hard-working Indian woman, since it did not require watching. A Menominee woman who lived in the late nineteenth century is remembered to have heated stones to white-hot in a large hole, placed a pot or crock in it, then covered them with leaves and earth. Beans, for instance, were left to cook this way for twenty-four hours.

By custom and tradition, hospitality was a cardinal tenet of every American Indian tribe. Indians shared their supplies with family, friends, neighbors, and strangers; they entertained lavishly, even to the point of exhausting their supplies. As the New England Puritan Roger Williams noted in his 1643 *Key Into the Language of America:*

Sometimes *God* gives them *Fish* or *Flesh,*
    Yet they're *content* without;
And what comes in, they part to *friends*
    And *Strangers* round about.

From some white settlers' point of view, these customs and traditions must have appeared shockingly improvident—as when, for example, a Chippewa Indian would invite everyone to feast upon the first deer he killed annually, putting nothing aside for less abundant times.

Generosity of this sort among Wisconsin Indians is well documented. Jean Nicolet, probably the first white man to reach Wisconsin, for instance, was entertained at a series of feasts by the Winnebago chiefs at Green Bay in 1634, one of which, it is recorded, featured at least 120 beavers. And in September, 1688, the chiefs at Green Bay presented Louis-Armand de Lom d'Arce, third baron of Lahontan, with a repast that included whitefish boiled in water, boiled tongue and breast of roebuck, roasted woodhens (meaning, probably, grouse), bear feet, beaver tail, and a broth made from a variety of meats. For a beverage, which the baron termed "very pleasant," there was maple syrup beaten up with water.

The first explorers, fur traders, and voyageurs also profited by the Indian sharing customs and their guidance in using Wisconsin's native foods. Father Jacques Marquette and Louis Jolliet, who left on their historic journey to the Upper Mississippi in 1673 with supplies of smoked meat and corn, were treated frequently to sumptuous meals by the Indians they encountered. Jolliet also is said to have existed at one time upon two other favored Indian foods, wild onions and garlic. The explorer Nicolas Perrot described how these wild onions were handled by Indians of the Upper Great Lakes in the late 1600's: " . . . [T]hey first place the onions, covering them with a thick layer of grass; and by means of the heat which the fire communicates to them, the acrid quality leaves them, nor are they damaged by the flame; and after they have been dried in the sun, they become an excellent article of food."

Eighteenth-century French and French-Canadian voyageurs, criss-crossing the wilderness hauling goods and furs for the traders, became adept at supplementing their spartan ration. The ration, called "found," supplied by their employers as part of their pay, was standard well into the 1830's: one bushel of corn and two pounds of fat a month. The corn, which had been leached, washed, and dried, was like hominy; the fat was usually tallow, and the voyageurs felt well treated when it was the better salt pork, bear grease, or beaver fat. At meal time, each man would put a quart of corn and an ounce of fat into a communal pot, to be boiled in water with anything else available—berries, birds, eggs, game, fish, or, if luck was really with them, a beaver tail.

The latter was a real delicacy among the hearty voyageurs. In fact, any practicing Catholics among them maintained that a creature that lived so much in the water was really a fish and therefore not forbidden to them during Lent.

Bread was much rarer than beaver tails. On the few occasions when flour was to be had, a sort of pancake was made. If available, a bird's egg was used; but usually, according to one observer of the process, "a small hollow [was] made in the flour [while still in the bag], into which a little water is poured, and the dough is thus mixed in the bag; nothing is added, except, perhaps some dirt from the cook's *unwashed* hands, with which he kneads it into flat cakes, which are baked before the fire in a frying pan, or cooked in grease."

There were times, though, when game would disappear and supplies would dwindle, bringing hardship to the traders and voyageurs wintering in the wilderness, as well as the Indians. Captain Thomas Anderson, a Canadian fur trader who spent many winters in Wisconsin and Minnesota in the first decade of the nineteenth century, remembered the winter of 1807–1808 when he "had consumed every article I had of the eatable kind, including several packs of deer skins. I and my men roamed about in quest of game, without success. We set traps of all kinds, in which we caught wolves, fishers, martens, and minks,* all of which went to the pot, and I could take my share of all, except of the wolf. My cook said he would dress a piece, and dish it up so I would like it; so he cut off a choice bit from one just brought in, and put it into the bake-kettle, seasoning it with pepper, salt and mustard, adding some Stoughton bitters, and a glass of high wines to give it a taste of chicken. But with all this knowledge of refined cookery, I could not stomach what tasted to me like a mouse-nest; for when better food cannot be had, the wolves live on mice. The men, however, devoured it as voraciously as cats would their victims."

Anderson also recorded better times in his journal: "The men's practice in the culinary art was very simple, but good. The tin kettle, in which they cooked their food, would hold eight or ten gallons. It was hung over the fire, nearly full of water, then nine quarts of peas—one quart per man, the daily allowance—were put in; and when they were well bursted, two or three pounds of pork, cut into strips, for seasoning, were added, and all allowed to boil or simmer till daylight, when the cook added four biscuits, broken up, to the mess, and invited all hands to

breakfast. The swelling of the peas and biscuit had now filled the kettle to the brim, so thick that a stick would stand upright in it. . . . The men now squatted in a circle, the kettle in their midst, and each one plying his wooden spoon or ladle from kettle to mouth, with almost electric speed, soon filled every cavity."

When buffalo were to be found, as they had been in earlier Wisconsin times, the bone marrow was a special wilderness treat. Anderson described its preparation in western Minnesota about 1810: "The mode of cooking the marrow is to hold the bones over the fire until they are nicely browned; then break or split them in two with the tomahawk, and dig the marrow out. It is very nice, and does not clog the stomach like other fat, or congeal in the mouth like deer's. In fact, if we had salt, bread, or vegetables of any kind to eat with it, it would have been doubly delicious."

Anderson was particularly fond of venison fried in deer's tallow, though there were disadvantages to this dish: "These steaks I could not eat hot enough to prevent their congealing in their progress to my throat; consequently the roof of my mouth would become so thickly cased over with tallow as to necessitate the use of my knife to remove it."

Tallow, the melted and clarified fat from game, cattle, and sheep, was a versatile and essential wilderness (and later pioneer) commodity. It was a prime ingredient in candles and soap as well as the universal, albeit inferior, cooking fat. Anderson's experience with congealed tallow was not at all unusual. The superior lard—rendered fat from swine—did not become generally available until somewhat later, when the state became a settled agricultural community.

Wisconsin's first frontier communities developed around the fur trade. The French-Canadians who settled at Green Bay raised horses, cattle, hogs, fowl, and sheep. The growing number of inhabitants planted gardens in vegetables, potatoes, oats, and spring wheat. At Prairie du Chien, wheat, barley, oats, potatoes, and onions provided the French-Canadian set-

---

*Whites normally did not consider these ill-smelling fur bearers fit to eat.

tlers with surpluses for barter with the traders for goods or the Indian for wild game and fowl or dressed deerskins. The first gristmill was probably operated by Jacob Franks, who adapted his sawmill east of De Pere to handle grain as well about 1809 or 1810; four years later, one of the Grignons—an early Green Bay trading dynasty—built a mill west of the Fox River.

The Wisconsin area was off the main path of the westward settlement that followed the American Revolution. Only 651 white civilians were counted here in the federal census of 1820—361 around Prairie du Chien and in Crawford County, and 290 in Green Bay and Brown County, communities linked by the Fox-

Wisconsin river route. In addition, there were 131 soldiers, their wives, and children and servants at Fort Crawford, and 673 at Fort Howard in Green Bay. Undoubtedly some uncounted settlers were sprinkled along Lake Superior and on the route between the two communities.

But things changed rapidly after that. The peculiar American appetite for seeking new lands to cultivate began bringing Yankees and New Yorkers here. Mineral wealth in the form of lead brought Southerners from lower Illinois, Missouri, Kentucky, and Virginia plus the first sizable contingent from abroad. By 1825 the rush was on, laying the groundwork for the ways and means of setting the state's tables.

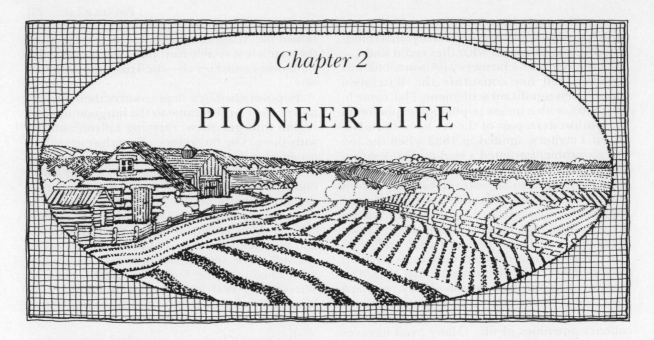

Chapter 2

PIONEER LIFE

THE COMBINED PROSPECT OF GOOD LAND, economic oppportunity, and the opening of mineral lands shifted the part of Michigan Territory that was to become Wisconsin from a fur trade center to one of the destinations of westward migrants in the early nineteenth century.

Yankees and New Yorkers in the 1830's tested the agricultural and industrial possibilities, particularly in the area along the Lake Michigan shore. Southport (later Kenosha) quickly became a thriving New York enclave. Many Yankees came directly from New England via the Great Lakes; others were already pioneer-wise, having broken new ground previously in New York, Pennsylvania, Ohio, Indiana, or Illinois. The casualness with which the peripatetic Yankee embarked on a move impressed a French traveler of the time: "Loading a wagon with a plow, a bed, a barrel of salt meat, the indispensable supply of tea and molasses, a Bible, and a wife, and with his ax on his shoulder, the Yankee sets out for the West."

There was a sack of flour or cornmeal and possibly a bag of beans in the wagon, too. The wilderness Yankee or New Yorker pioneer subsisted at first largely on salt pork and cornmeal, embellished perhaps with baked beans, as many garden vegetables as could be grown the first year, and whatever else the family's skill as traders, hunters, and gatherers might bring. The earliest arrivals had little trouble finding the ideal homesite; it was near a good water supply with both timber for building and fuel and meadow for rapid establishment of garden and commercial crops. If this felicitous combination was also close to existing or future settlements or good transportation to them, the settler and his family could more quickly forge a comfortable, though hardworking, life. They needed a nearby market to dispose of their surplus for profit or to trade for the goods he could not grow or make for himself. Naturally, the pioneer farmer's first concern was to feed his family and livestock. In fact, most people, in town and country both, grew their own garden produce. To be sure, the further one settled from village or town, the harder the life. But no one in those early days of the nineteenth century came to Wisconsin Territory expecting a life of ease, for these early arrivals had no way of knowing exactly what things would be like or exactly what they could find.

These dauntless farmers and town builders, however, did not constitute the Wisconsin region's first significant settlement. That came in the 1820's, with a minor population explosion in the southwestern part of the yet-to-be-born Wisconsin Territory, ignited in 1822 when the federal government granted a lead-mining lease on public lands to two Kentuckians. Up the Mississippi they came to the site of Galena, Illinois (population 800 in 1830), and from there fanned out into the rolling hills of southwestern Wisconsin, founding New Diggings, Shullsburg, Muscalunge, Mineral Point. Between 1820 and 1830, Wisconsin's census-counted civilian population increased by 2,350 (from about 650 to 3,000), most of it in the lead region. Many, perhaps most, were single men seeking their fortunes who managed without many of the physical or culinary amenities of life. (Many lived in caves they dug into the sides of the hills, thereby giving the nickname *badgers* to the future state.)

A few, however, brought their families and established homesteads in much the same way as the farmers soon would to the east. After the home was built, the tasks of the wife and daughters of the family were no different from those of other female pioneers, except that they were performed closer to neighbors instead of in the wilderness. They put in and worked the garden that provided them with much of their produce, raised chickens, collected the eggs, tended the livestock, milked the cows, churned the butter, ran the household, cooked the meals, and reared the children. In the mining communities, however, the housewife had to rely even more upon imported foodstuffs than her counterparts elsewhere. As late as 1835, a British visitor estimated that the lead region produced only one-twentieth of the food it consumed.

Most new residents in the lead region were American-born from Virginia, Kentucky, Missouri, Tennessee, North Carolina, Pennsylvania, Ohio, Indiana, Illinois, and New York. But the pull of the lead mines also reached to the other side of the Atlantic, into the British Isles, to draw the state's first sizable European groups since the Canadians and French—the Irish and the Cornish.

Impoverished by a depression in their own tin mines, the Cornish came to the burgeoning lead region to begin anew, carrying saffron and tea with them. On the ridges of southwestern Wisconsin they found plenty of rocks and stones to build cobbled houses reminiscent of their dwellings in Cornwall, and the means to buy or grow the ingredients of the foods associated with them: pasties, tea cake (a sort of biscuit), saffron cake, scalded cream, plum or citron preserves, and tea. Remains of those Cornish-built houses are still to be seen in southwestern Wisconsin, most notably at the State Historical Society of Wisconsin's restored Pendarvis complex at Mineral Point. And it is still possible to find places that serve the typical Cornish meal.

Nowadays it is easy to get a good argument going over what fillings in the sturdy pie crust constitute a "true" pasty (rhymes with *nasty*); whether for example, to include rutabagas or even onions. Actually, the transplanted Cornishman carried his midday turnover to the mine stuffed with whatever was at hand: meat and potatoes, plus greens, onions, carrots, or whatever. The Cornish housewife was just as resourceful in her new home as she had been in her old. And in the old country, Cornish women had the reputation of baking whatever they had into a pasty. (In neighboring Devonshire, people used to say that the Devil was afraid to cross the Tamar River into Cornwall for fear he would be baked into a pasty.) Pasty became a favorite of the American miners, too. As one explained in a letter home to Missouri, a pasty was a whole boardinghouse meal under one crust.

There is no argument about the fact that this hearty fare came in various sizes and in oblong and round shapes as well as the most usual: a single-serving round of pastry folded in half over the filling, to be eaten from the hand like a sandwich.

Though the thriving lead region accounted

for the modest growth of population in the 1820's, Wisconsin was still primarily a fur trade and military frontier in 1830. The next six years, however, brought even more significant changes. In July, 1836, a census taken by county sheriffs counted 11,683 persons between Lake Michigan and the Mississippi. This represented a nearly four-fold increase from 1830, and 70 per cent of this population lived wholly south of the Fox-Wisconsin portage. In those years, too, Milwaukee was established and grew to almost 3,000 inhabitants. Milwaukee was the latest boom city to be fueled by the Erie Canal, which, after its opening in 1825, made the Great Lakes one of the important immigrant routes West.

By the end of the 1830's, the new settlers had firmly set Wisconsin on the economic course it followed into the 1920's as primarily an agricultural state. And by then Wisconsin's pattern of development was well established, too. Urban centers grew up along the Lake Michigan shore, the main river routes, and the Military Road connecting Fort Howard at Green Bay, Fort Winnebago at Portage, and Fort Crawford at Prairie du Chien. Between the towns below the Fox and Wisconsin rivers, the farm lands soon became settled. The area to the north remained largely untouched. Thus a fairly sophisticated kind of agriculture developed fairly rapidly on the settled lands while the rest of the state was wilderness. Later arrivals, slowly moving northward to find new lands, experienced the same difficulties and privations as their predecessors had at a time when southern Wisconsin had moved from frontier to developed conditions.

Whatever the date, the first years were hard for just about everyone. Fish and game helped many a family over some rough times. Passenger pigeons, during their migrations and at nesting time, were unbelievably easy to come by, even for the greenest of frontiersmen. At sunset, huge flocks would settle in the oaks to roost; so numerous were they that often they piled upon one another until their weight would break the branches. They were most commonly netted, and often shot; but men would also walk through the woods and bring birds down with sticks.

Many people adopted the Indian method of covering a plucked and cleaned pigeon with clay, poking a few holes for steam release, and baking in the fire. According to some accounts many settlers didn't bother to pluck them, but simply skinned the bird, keeping only the meaty breast and legs. They were eaten fresh, meal after meal, during the spring and summer, and still there were plenty to salt or pickle for the winter.

There were fish, of course, and clams in some of the lakes and streams. And wild honey was a special treat.* John H. Fonda, a trader who traveled widely in the wilderness from 1820 to 1840, remembered the sweet delight of finding a tree filled with honeycombs. He and his partner filled the camp kettle with choice pieces and while his partner cooked a couple of prairie hens for supper, "I dipped into the honey—slightly. I have always been blessed with a good appetite, but on that occasion it must have been a little better than usual, for after eating my bird, and discussing a fair ration of dried meat and parched corn, I thought it better to fill the kettle again with honey, by way of dessert. That evening I got honey enough for a life-time."

The frontiersman had to be content with what he could find. Fonda wrote of another occasion when he dined on the Chippewa River on an animal he had shot. (He called it a hedgehog but it was probably a porcupine.) "It was cooked by throwing it into the fire whole, and after being perfectly roasted, taken out and all the quills and hair scraped off, and the entrails taken out. After it had undergone this process, it looked as nice as any roasted pig I ever saw, and with the proper seasoning, it tasted better."

It is no wonder that Fonda used pig as a measure of excellence, for pork, particularly salt pork, was in short supply in those early days, and was much sought after. A barrel of salt pork was a

*By then, wild honey was the product of European honey bees. These bees, a different and more productive species than the native wild bees that supplied Indians with honey, had been imported to the United States by Virginia colonists in about 1621 and soon had spread into Wisconsin. Apiarists are fond of saying that these honey bees were the first European settlers in Wisconsin.

standard item in a new settler's wagon, and usually it was expensive or difficult to replace once the barrel was empty. An early resident on the Rock River noted that his mother had brought such a barrel from New York and "people came as far as twenty miles to beg a little of it, so tired were they of fresh meat from the woods and fish from the river."

In those days when pigs were left to forage in the wild for their food, even something called "Hoosier pork" was welcome. Frontier tradition had it that Hoosier pork came from self-supporting hogs whose snouts were so long they could poke though a fence and root up the third row of potatoes. Apparently, however, that third row of potatoes was sparse; Hoosier pork was so lean that the settler's wife had to save fat from freshly caught fish to fry it in.

A bachelor resident of an 1837 Beloit boardinghouse recalled a time when news reached the cook that a barrel of pork was for sale at Rockford: "The solitary barrel contained a number of small lean hams covered with a generous supply of brine; price, thirty-one dollars. . . . The arrival. . . was expected to bring joy and gladness to its inmates; but when the cook reported that the pork was so lean that fish had to be fried with it to keep it from burning the bottom of the pan, their expectations were not so fully realized."

For most, the frontier diet was monotonous. "I often wonder," a pioneer later wrote, "how the present generation. . . would respond to viands set before them at meal time such as salt pork and cornmeal bread and possibly baked beans. Well this was the usual menu at most homes and there were no questions asked. It was eat it or go hungry."

Another early resident, who lived on the Bark River in Jefferson County, remembered the depression winter of 1837: "We caught sucker and red-horse. . . . boiled them into a sort of porridge, and ate them with nothing but salt. After a few such meals with nothing else, I was not particularly fond of boiled fresh fish. I have also eaten meals of nothing but boiled beans; also meals of potatoes and maple molasses."

As soon as a farm family was able, after clearing the land and bringing in the first garden crops, often including items like potatoes, cabbage, beets, onions, turnips, rutabagas, and the like, it would try to acquire a cow or two and a few hens. This would provide the family with homemade butter and milk and eggs. A milk house was built to store the dairy produce; it could be an underground room, preferably near a creek or spring, sometimes supported and insulated with logs. Limestone was the ideal flooring, and crocks were used to store the butter, cheese, and milk. Often the springhouse was built above ground, almost on top of a spring, and on hot summer days provided a cool place for the family to gather and relax.

But the refinements of the table—tea, coffee, flour, sugar, salt—could only be obtained in towns. In the late 1830's, pork at Milwaukee sold at from $30 to $34 a barrel and flour for $16 a barrel. Such purchases required money, itself a scarce commodity. Substitutes for tea and coffee were made of ground barley, peas, dandelion roots, etc.

Flour was another staple usually requiring a cash outlay. Even when a farmer had abundant wheat or corn, getting it ground required some doing. A trip to a mill could take three days or more over incredibly difficult roads and trails that for much of the year were rutted ribbons of ooze. The miller usually took a portion of the product as payment for his services. (In a pinch, coarse meal could be produced in a coffee mill.)

Life was not so hard for everyone, of course. The more neighbors you had and the older your community, the easier life became. In the earliest days, naturally, life in Wisconsin's first communities—Green Bay and Prairie du Chien—was relatively spartan, though relieved by the proximity of the residents and the presence of military forts. Most had lived so long on the fringes of civilization that a subsistence existence was the only way of life they had ever known.

Elizabeth Therese Baird, who grew up on Mackinac Island and married a pioneer Green Bay lawyer, described the work it took to achieve the niceties. Except for coffee, the women of Green Bay, unlike her sisters in the remote frontier, had the means on hand—slim though they may have been—to achieve culinary refinement when the occasion demanded: "For our own jellies and blanc manges we had to manufacture our own gelatine by boiling calves' feet. The wine jelly of those days was called 'calves foot jelly.' Everything had to start from the foundation. No fowls or game were ever sold dressed. Coffee was purchased unroasted. In fact, everything was in its raw state. The drinks for our parties were mostly home-made, such as currant wine, cherry bounce, raspberry cordial, etc."

Later, after stores appeared and goods were shipped more regularly, food preparation became somewhat less demanding in Green Bay and later in other cities, towns, and villages. Even so, whether on frontier farm or in frontier community, providing the nourishment to fuel the strenuous life was never easy.

As for parties and social events, they were there from the earliest days. Charles Reaume, whose appointment as justice of the peace in Green Bay in 1803 was the earliest evidence of United States control of the area, was excessively fond of the delights of eating. The menu of a wedding supper following the ceremony which he performed early in his tenure was planned with his tastes in mind: venison smothered in wild rice and maple sugar, stewed sturgeon, fat ducks, and a jug of strong drink.

Much of the early social life of Green Bay centered around Fort Howard. A commander in the early 1820's, Colonel John McNeil, built what became known as the assembly rooms—a sixty-foot mess hall with smaller rooms adjoining. These were formally opened with a large dancing party on December 18, 1822. At the Christmas party later, a hundred guests sat down at four o'clock to a feast of several varieties of fish from the bay, venison, bear's meat, porcupine, and other game then in season.

Twelve years later, when Daniel Whitney, one of Green Bay's early entrepreneurs, entertained the Reverend Jackson Kemper, later Episcopal bishop of the territory, and other members of his church in the summer of 1834, the sumptuous feast included a pitcher of lemonade; port, madeira, and champagne; roast pig, ham, venison, veal pie, salad, cranberry tarts, floating island pudding, cheese, raisins, almonds, walnuts, and filberts.

In La Pointe on October 8, 1838, Florantha Thompson Sproat, writing home to Massachusetts, noted: "I am expecting Mr. Ramsay Crooks [an important figure in the fur trade] and three or four other gentlemen to take tea with us this eve. I will tell you what I will have—pie of thimbleberries, a cake of whortleberries and cherries dried (a few were sent me in a box for company) and some warm biscuit." For the less affluent, entertainment menus were simpler. In Oshkosh in 1838, participants at evening parties and dances refreshed themselves with a big dish of cracked hickory nuts or sometimes doughnuts.

Some social occasions were more than merely recreational. "Donation parties" for widows were occasional events in the difficult, frequently hazardous new environment. At one held in the 1850's, practically no one could contribute money, but neighbors came with pork, flour, and vegetables; and the host family provided as much food and drink as it was able. It was a festive occasion, even though its moving cause was tragedy, and there were games for the children and adults alike. One such game played at a donation party in Cooksville was later described: "They filled a large pan with raisins, poured whiskey over the raisins and set fire to the whiskey. The game was to pick the raisins out of the burning whiskey with their fingers. One little boy remembered staying back of the crowd and getting the raisins that were dropped."

House raisings were also accompanied by feasting. A fortunate family that had money during the 1837 depression was able to set a generous table for the thirty or forty neighbors who helped raise its house at Prairie du Lac (now Milton) in 1838—boiled ham, baked beans, brown bread and white, all the vegetables obtainable, dried apple and custard pies, cakes, tea, and coffee. The usual culinary expression of thanks, however, was a very simple meal and a jug to pass.

In those days, strangers traveling through could expect to receive a hospitable welcome and an assist in their journey. Henry F. Janes, later the founder of Janesville, and his companion, lost, wet, and cold in 1836, had a typical experience after stumbling on a frontier homestead: "We were now snugly ensconced in a warm cabin, by a roaring fire, and soon had a stool placed between us, on which was a pyramid of potatoes, and a dish of pork swimming in a miniature lake of gravy, and each a tin cup of coffee. . . . How does your nonsense sink into utter insignificance when contrasted with the pure, genuine hospitality of the frontier adventurer."

Indians would also lend a hand to wilderness travelers, sharing or selling food and supplies to those in need. Nor was all hospitality dispensed in person. It was not unusual for travelers to help themselves to vittles in empty kitchens, usually leaving something behind in payment.

A good many of those pioneer meals were made by men, who outnumbered women in Wisconsin until well into the 1850's. (In 1840, there were eight men for every five women; by 1850, the ratio was down to six for five.) For persons inexperienced at this sort of activity, things were difficult in the beginning. "I commenced batching last Friday and guess you would laugh to

see what a horrid figure I cut," one 1849 novice wrote home to his sister in New York. "I have not been able to get any meat of any kind yet. So that makes it worse than it otherwise would be. My first batch of 'Irish Bannocks' (shortcakes minus the shortening) lasted me till this morning. I do not expect to see any butter this winter."

Whatever his previous training may have been, the single man on the frontier had to learn fast, and many became expert at dining well in the circumstances: "We drove back to camp, fed our oxen, and then ourselves on fried salt pork, flapjacks, cold baked beans, bread and butter and coffee, and then we felt more cheerful."

Culinary disasters naturally occurred. William W. Wright, one of the first settlers of Oshkosh, recalled an incident when some men were lumbering and taking turns doing the cooking. One of his companions set out a fine breakfast, but there was something unusual about the taste of the coffee. "At last one proceeded to investigate the contents of the tea kettle and discovered a well-cooked frog, hard-boiled and tender. . . ."

A small number of Wisconsin pioneers broke ground as members of groups seeking a better life through communal living and cooperation. In America during the 1840's, a number of social reformers put great faith in rural cooperative societies as means of curing poverty and other social ills. One of the first was an Owenite community, organized in England by the industrialist Robert Owen, who had founded a popular Utopian movement of the day. A group of English, mostly mechanics, was sent out to Spring Lake in Waukesha County to build what was known as the "Colony of Equality" or "Hunt's Colony." This 1843 Utopian experiment was short-lived, since the mechanics, ill-equipped for farming, soon sought employment elsewhere, mostly in Milwaukee.

The most popular Utopian and reform movement, however, was Fourierism. This was a blueprint for the better life drawn by a Frenchman, Charles Fourier. His ideas were adapted for the American scene by the journalists Albert Brisbane and Horace Greeley of the *New York Trib-*

une. Fourierites held that the solution to social problems was to reorganize society into associations of small, harmonious, cooperative groups, known as Phalanxes, that would work and live together for the betterment of all. The plan was communal, not communistic, for workers were to be paid according to the relative importance of their jobs and the quality of their work, the rights of private property were maintained, and capital was to earn profits.

The idea appealed to a number of the humanitarians and intellectuals at Southport (Kenosha) in 1844 who formed a Wisconsin Phalanx, sold stock, and bought a 1,000-acre site in Fond du Lac County (now part of the city of Ripon). A group of workers and farmers were recruited to make the actual experiment in associative living at Ceresco (named after Ceres, Greek goddess of agriculture). They were led by Warren Chase, a social reformer, politician, and later spiritualist who had settled in Southport in 1838.

Within a year, one of the residents could write to a friend that he was "now engaged in getting in the garden fixings. We have gathered 350 bushels of carrots and a whole heap of turnips and cabbage enough to make us all Dutchmen and I have just been to dinner—bean soup. We live on the fat of the land, no mistake—any quantity of game in these diggings—ducks, deers, and wild geese. . . ."

The Ceresco bylaws called for meals to be served at a communal table in the Long House (which still stands), but generally the menus were unappetizing, and the rules were soon revised to permit the resident members (180 at the community's peak in 1846) to make their own meals if they wished. In 1848, about sixty persons, mostly unmarried, were sitting down to the communal table. That autumn, a recent arrival, Charlotte Haven, described the meals in a letter home: "Our diet for the first three weeks was wholly vegetable. One evening as I entered for supper the atmosphere in the room was most savory, my eyes glistened and my mouth felt uncommonly grateful as I thought of stuffed turkey, but how my countenance fell or rather how I smiled when I perceived the savory steam arise from large pitchers of sage tea and bowls of onions. At the end of that time the teams returned from Sheboygan with tea, coffee, and other luxuries. Hogs and sheep have also been killed in abundance. Though I scarcely ever taste meat we are never without the most excellent bread, for there is a regular baker in the association and during the last week since two women besides the steward have been occupied in the kitchen, the fare is wonderfully improved, scarcely a meal without either pies or cake or some 'chicken fixen.'"

About the same time, her sister, Harriet, noted in her journal that an October Sunday feast, prepared in her living quarters, "lasted three hours. . . . during which time eight persons partook of baked squash (a standing dish here), toast, Johnny cake made by good Mrs. Bennett, a squash pie, milk, honey, and bread. This was fare preferable to the dining room fare, which consists of bread and milk on Sundays, occasionally rather too blue to be inviting."

Though it was an agricultural and economic success, Ceresco lasted only until August 28, 1849, when the members unanimously voted to disband. By then, Ripon had been founded and the value of Ceresco's property, which then totalled 1,713 acres, had increased to such an extent that many members wished to sell and take the profit. Many also found the social concepts too restricting and life uneventful; they felt a need to push on, westward. When Chase finally closed the corporation books in 1852, shareholders realized a profit of 8 per cent on their investment.

Two years after Wisconsin had attained statehood in 1848, the population numbered 305,390. Two-thirds were American-born; half the Americans hailed from the Northeastern states, and the 63,014 Wisconsin-born were mostly children. Of the 78,139 males who designated their professions or occupations for the 1850 census takers, at least 42,906 were concerned with growing, processing, or dispensing food and drink: 40,865 were farmers, 127 bakers, 233 butchers, 468 grocers, 588 innkeepers, forty-three boardinghouse keepers, 214 fishermen, 152 brewers, sixty-nine gardeners, eighty-five barkeepers, nineteen distillers, seven market men, and three wine and liquor dealers. And the list does not include any of the 11,281 laborers (some of whom worked on farms), nor any implement makers, nor any blacksmiths who kept machinery, oxen, and

horses in working order. Clearly, food was far and away the state's biggest business in 1850.

Of the approximately 106,695 foreign immigrants, there were people from England, Switzerland, Germany, Ireland, Wales, the Netherlands, Norway, Cornwall, and a host of other countries. So long was the list that the compilers of the census seem to have despaired, and lumped several countries into "other." The flow of persons from distant lands and cultures, which continues to this day, was well under way.

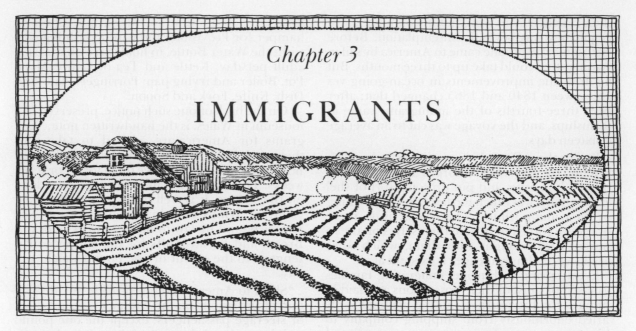

Chapter 3

IMMIGRANTS

WHETHER THEY CAME FROM ACROSS A STATE line or an ocean, new settlers in Wisconsin were spurred by a variety of motives. Some were consciously seeking a better life; others were buffeted by uncontrollable events like depressions, crop failures, famines, religious persecution, and revolutions; still others were merely swept along by friends, relations, and neighbors.

Whatever the reason, such a momentous move took courage and was undoubtedly traumatic, except for the very few with wealth enough to cushion the uprooting jolt. It was hardest perhaps for non-English-speaking immigrants. They not only had to cope with new customs, laws, money, and outlook—and economic survival—but had the added burden of learning a new language as well. Preparations for departure, the long and arduous voyage itself, and the first years in the new land—whether in the nineteenth century or in the first years of the twentieth—were heartbreaking, backbreaking, and terribly difficult. Many did not survive the hardships.

At mid-century, numerous new arrivals were men alone, either unmarried seeking their for-

tunes or married men preparing a home for the families that would follow. There were family groups emigrating on their own, others resettling under the auspices of church or emigration organizations (composed, for instance, of temperance advocates or out-of-work potters) into planned, staked-out communities. A number of Hollanders, for example, were organized by a Catholic priest, Father Theodore Van den Broek, for settlement in Little Chute. Groups of English were established in Racine County, Columbia County, and Dane County by three different English emigration societies. And the settlement of New Glarus in Green County took root and prospered even though the first emigrees from the Swiss canton of Glarus arrived before the advance party could make proper arrangements.

For those who took up farming—particularly the immigrants who came before mid-century—the first year was especially difficult because of the emigrating timetable, which precluded arrival in time to begin farming in the spring. The ocean crossing in a sailing vessel was difficult enough in the relatively reliable summer weather when violent storms were not uncommon; a winter journey was beyond contemplation. Before 1850, almost everyone came to America by sail in crossings that could take up to three months. But the dramatic improvements in ocean-going vessels between 1840 and 1865 changed that; after 1865, three-fourths of the immigrants came in steamships, and the voyage was cut to an average of sixteen days.

But in the sailing-ship era, it was at best late summer or early fall before a family arrived, found a homesite, and put up some sort of shelter. By then it was much too late to grow anything for the coming winter. The new arrivals, therefore, were forced to sustain themselves on the resources they brought with them, which were usually exceedingly meager if existent at all.

Every spring in Europe, emigrating families disposed of most of their possessions and laid in supplies for the journey. Eating arrangements varied enormously from shipping company to shipping company, from country to country, and from passenger class to passenger class. Cabin class passengers (who paid up to £25 Liverpool to New York in 1846) got more than they could eat. Steerage passengers (who paid £3 10s. Liverpool to New York and who accounted for 99 per cent of those on board) got just the barest of staples, but not enough to sustain life on the long voyage. Furthermore, shipping companies often cheated outrageously in the rations, so passengers seriously underestimated the supplies they were expected to furnish for themselves.

In Liverpool in the 1840's, one shipping company provided prospective passengers with a printed notice pointing out that water and bread (by law, one pound per day per adult) were always found on a ship, and that flour, oatmeal, rice, and potatoes usually were. There followed a list of items the passenger might wish to take: "dried beef or mutton; bacon, ham or tongue; herrings and dried fish; eggs and onions; vinegar and pickles; tea, coffee or cocoa; sugar, treacle, currants, raisins; pepper, salt, mustard, ginger; soap and a few candles; blacking and brush, senna, epsom salts or castor oil. (The ship has

however a full supply of Medicine); Chest or hamper for Provisions and cord to lash luggage with; the Water Bottle, to hold three quarts each adult per day; Kettle and Tea or Coffee Metal Pot. Boiler and frying pan; Porringer, Plate, and Dish, Knife, Fork and Spoon."

On the back of one such notice, preserved in a museum in Wales, is the handwritten note: "Emigrants for America are advised to take with them such kinds of Provisions they usually eat at home and sufficient to serve them for six or seven weeks. Though it is not likely they will be so long on the voyage, it is well to be prepared in case Contrary Winds or calms should prevail. The Ship is bound by law to have *ten* weeks stock of Bread, and Bread Stuffs for the Supply of Passengers, to the extent of one pound weight per day.

"Ships to America do not provide any description of provisions on the voyage to second cabin or steerage passaengers, except the one pound weight each adult of Bread or Bread Stuffs. Never engage to be found with *every* kind of provisions included with the passage money, but begin your own stock. If you buy them in Liverpool and *at the shops which are solely* engaged on supplying Emigrants, see that you are not overcharged. Some fresh baked loaf bread cut into slices and *rebaked* in the Oven will keep much longer than in the moist state and perhaps be more agreeable especially in the early part of the voyage than the Ship Biscuit Bread. For females and children a few of the very finest Flour Biscuits or a Currant Loaf not much too sweet. A Ham shank or a piece of dried Beef or Neats' [ox] Tongues boiled and ready for use will be found handy and lasting the first few days of probable seasickness. Also a few dried Herrings or dried Fish. Eggs properly packed for preserving and cream boiled with sugar and bottled up very tight are desirable.

"Take no spirituous liquors unless it be a very little Brandy, which may be useful as a Medicinal restoration. A few Lemons to squeeze into water; or Tamarinds to pour boiling water upon are very useful. Seidlitz Powders also. Exercise is needful to preserve bodily health, but as exercise cannot be had at sea to much extent, it should be substituted by mild aperients—Costiveness increases seasickness."

Letters from family and friends already in the new land helped some immigrants compile their shopping lists. William and Elias Williams, who settled in Welsh Prairie in the 1840's, wrote their emigrating brother: "For your sea voyage you will find the dried beef and ham take well. . . . [B]ring a lot of oat-meal along with you for you will be able to make cakes on the vessel. . . . Tea and coffee you will find very useful at sea; as for cooking utensils you will find a list of them at the emigrant office in L'pool. . . . Remember to bring a lot of pickles with you for the sea voyage. . . ."

Michael Rodenkirch, writing from the "State of Westkonsin" back to his family in Germany on December 26, 1846, advised: "For your sea voyage make your own 'Zwieback' and take along sufficient oatmeal and wheat flour. If you can obtain potatoes, use them for your vegetable. Also carry along ham, butter, brandy, spices, coffee, sugar, and whatever else you might like to eat on your trip across the sea, for on the sea your money will not buy anything. . . ."

Money could not buy anything on shipboard, but zwieback and other foods could. William H. Messerschmidt, who crossed the ocean in 1860, paid a Bohemian boy on board for a small, made-to-order wagon "in Zwiebach, to him a welcome coin at par."

On some ships, a cook was provided as part of the crew to prepare the basics supplied; passengers picked up their portions in the galley and carried them back to their quarters in their own utensils. On others, the raw ingredients were dispensed to be cooked by the passengers themselves, usually in crowded, chaotic communal kitchens.

One German immigrant described his shipboard cooking problems in 1848: ". . . [A]ll was not always too easy. Indeed, very often, the work was impossible. The kitchen was small. The stove had only four holes in the top for cooking, but one could also bake in an oven.

"Much patience was required to cook a meal, yes figuring too. The worst problem was to make a fire. Then we stood very crowded, the kettle in hand and figured and reckoned when our turn would come. Often there were collisions with kettles and pans. . . ."

Gastronomically, the sea voyage was usually a grim experience, whether the traveler relied on his own supplies or the ship's. One of the original settlers of New Glarus recounted his food experiences on the crossing in 1845: "The meat is all packed in barrels and so much salted that we have to wash it many times then parboil it and throw the water away until it was freshed, but even then it was hardly edible. We receive 2½ pounds per week to each adult person; those under 12 years were reckoned two for one. Hardtack we have sufficient but this is not a human food. The pigs that are kept on ship refuse to eat it; it is in ¼ pound pieces and of dark brown color inside and out, and so hard as to require a hammer to break it up in pieces; it is made solely of bran and only a wolf's stomach can digest [it]; it is calculated to kill by slow starvation. The rice is also of the worst quality, yet it is edible; each person gets ½ pound weekly. Beans and peas are fair. . . . Flour was gritty with sand and ½ pound per week was a portion for each. Potatoes were very bad, black, bad smelling and rotten, hardly fit for pigs."

Many voyagers complained of the excessively salty meat and fish—salted, naturally, to preserve it. But the primitive conditions of food storage sometimes made even salted foods decay. Worse, fresh water was in short supply, and salty food made passengers more thirsty than usual. One German immigrant, whose crossing by sailing vessel in 1848 took eleven weeks, reported that "the pork we ate had such long hair on it that we needed no forks to eat it with, and was so salty we could not eat it anyway." And John F. Diederichs, an 1848 settler of Manitowoc, once noted in his diary that "the meat this noon was not eatable on account of its stench, and the passengers threw their portions overboard. Upon my complaint to the captain he had the remaining supply inspected, when an entire barrel with decayed contents was found, which was quickly thrown overboard amid loud hurrahs and delivered as a welcome prize to the fish of prey."

After landing in New York, Diederichs summarized the journey's meals in a letter home: "The meals were most miserable; Sunday rice and salt beef, Monday peas and Bacon, Tuesday white beans, soup and beef, Wednesday peas, Thursday beans, Friday peas and Saturday pearl barley without meat. During the first 14 days some potatoes were mixed with vegetables, but later on we saw them no more, indeed during the later weeks we often were fed peas 3-4 times, 2 times sauerkraut with half herring, and evenings coffee or tea, and the former so undrinkable in the real sense of the word that to this hour all coffee still nauseates my wife. If you wanted to partake something in the evening you would save some of the noon meal and eat it cold, or, as the majority did, you took some dry crumbled black bread, put in a little butter and salt, poured some boiling water over it and this passed as bread soup."

Occasionally a ship would encounter a school of fish, and passengers and crew might land a few to break the monotony of the salt-cured provisions. On the Diederichs voyage, two hog-fish, the smaller weighing 100 pounds dressed, provided the passengers with welcome variety at one meal. John Remeeus, a Dutch immigrant to Milwaukee in 1854, recalled that "every passenger got a portion of the fish we had caught. We had to cut it in slices, beat it, and carve it. About the same way that you treat beefsteak. Then we fried it with a piece of ham and the whole including fried potatoes tasted very delicious." At times, immigrant ships would pass close to a fishing fleet, and the captain would buy fresh fish for the passengers and crew. When Isabella McKinnon crossed from Scotland in 1852, one such purchase made the deck resemble "a fish market. Every one crowding to get their share."

A few had happier food memories. A German doctor, Theodore E. Hartwig, who settled in Cedarburg at mid-century, became friendly with the crew members despite his status as a steerage passenger, and was invited to share their quarters and mess. The food "consisted alternately of salt pork, beef, peas, beans, potatoes, lentils, rice, rice dumplings always in the form of soup. This fare became so monotonous that I soon ate almost no dinner at all. . . . The Food on this ship was really quite good, only the variety which one has on land was missing."

But Hartwig's experience was not typical; more immigrants found, as did Diederichs, that "on the whole the meals were miserably poor; I would not complain if they were only eatable, but under the existing circumstances—well, it will all pass over and we will endure patiently."

Most did endure, more or less patiently. But on landing in New York, it was not unusual for new arrivals to seek out homes or establishments of landsmen to gorge to their financial limit at the first meal ashore. Dr. Hartwig remembered "the people had to serve us three times. I regaled myself particularly with beefsteak, salad, and potatoes, and for dessert I had rye bread and fresh butter." Others were starved for fresh milk and vegetables.

American eating habits and customs in the big city were viewed with wonderment, particularly the abundance of meat, eaten, many noted, not only every day but usually twice a day. (They also noted that hordes of New Yorkers made a living by cheating immigrants.) Coffee or tea at every meal was worthy of mention in letters home, as was the fine wheat flour used for ordinary bread. There were those, however, who hated American coffee. "Since the American only half roasts the coffee, it takes considerable time to get used to it," one German observed.

The three-meal-a-day pattern took some getting used to, also, for people accustomed to dividing their day's ration into numerous small repasts. Few Europeans were accustomed to the enormous breakfasts Americans packed away. "At seven in the morning one eats the same as in the evening. Roast, warm and cold, potatoes, usually fried ones, other like foods and coffee. . . . At first it seemed strange that one fills one self so full at seven in the morning that one can wait until noon, but one grows accustomed to everything."

Some English people found it curious that Americans did not always keep the courses separated. "They have apple sauce, preserves, meat and several kinds of cakes on the table at one time," Clara Chaney wrote home to her grandmother from Wisconsin in 1850.*

Most Wisconsin-bound travelers stayed in New York only long enough to arrange for the final leg of the journey by railroad or Erie Canal to Buffalo, then Great Lakes steamer the rest of the way; later in the century the trip could be made entirely by rail. Meals were available on these conveyances, or one could provide one's own. A noonday meal on one of the better Erie Canal boats could have included pike, bass, steak, bacon, sausage, ham, scrambled eggs, baked potatoes, boiled cabbage, squash, white and corn bread, wheat and buckwheat pancakes, sorghum, maple syrup, molasses, honey, coffee, tea, and milk.

A mid-century German settler recorded in his diary that he paid $2.50 to the canal boat steersman for board. He was pleased with the arrangement, since his fellow passengers "had to pay quite a price for milk and bread—their main dish—because the inhabitants of the canal know what money is and take it from the people whenever they can get it."

The Williams brothers advised their Welsh family to bring its own food: "Provide yourselves with some cakes to eat on the Railway and a jar of water and the least quantity of spirits in it as it will not be quite safe to drink it without. Or if you were to buy some water melons at Albany, they would quench your thirst on the road, and they are healthy and good."

The food served in the dining cars or salons was judged by what the traveler was used to.

---

*Placing an entire meal on the table at once was a custom dating from colonial times. Later, as the country industrialized and wealthier folk started vacationing in Europe, the new French custom of courses was imported into the U.S. Many resisted this "un-American" practice at first.

Emma Rendtorff Halasz, traveling from Germany to Sauk City in 1842, thought the Erie Canal boat meals were well prepared, but didn't like the confectionery because "they used nutmeg in everything." She thought the fruits to be generally small and sour, but commented on the deliciousness of "drinking water with a piece of ice in it."

Milwaukee was Wisconsin's primary port of debarkation. All summer long the population fluctuated as ships discharged new arrivals, most of whom then dispersed to establish new homes throughout the state. The New England writer and feminist Margaret Fuller, a Milwaukee visitor in 1843, wrote: "During the fine weather, the poor refugees arrive daily, in their national dresses, all travel-stained and worn. The night they pass in rude shanties, in a particular quarter of the town, then walk off into the country—the mothers carrying their infants, the fathers leading the little children by the hand, seeking a home where their hands may maintain them."

Perhaps she actually saw a family or two wander off in such an unplanned manner. The majority, however, followed paths marked by family, friends, immigrant guidebooks and pamphlets, church groups, Wisconsin information offices in Europe and New York, land speculators in Milwaukee, or, later in the century, books such as University of Wisconsin Dean William A. Henry's A Hand-book for The Homeseeker.

As was true elsewhere in the country, the new immigrants tended to settle together by nationality groups, stitching tight urban and rural communities with strong threads of language, custom, and the common experience of the wrenching transplantation. In some places, the immigrant settlers never found it necessary to learn English. Milwaukee's Germantown was old-country in every respect, as were Norwegian, Danish, Dutch, or Polish enclaves in the state. Indeed, in some small communities, German or Norwegian was the mother-tongue and language of instruction in parochial schools; a few continued the practice until the beginning of World War II. A few older folks too clung to their native dress, but most adhered especially to their familiar diet.

Setting a traditional table was usually not possible the first year or two for most new arrivals, particuarly in rural areas. Frequently plain survival was desperately difficult. It was not unusual for whole families to subsist over the winter on nothing but a few bushels of potatoes. As the state became more and more settled, particularly in the south, the game became increasingly scarce, making that basic source of food less available to many new arrivals, even if they had had skill, tools, or experience in hunting.

Hans A. Anderson, a Norwegian immigrant who became a judge in Trempealeau County, recalled his family's first grim winter in Wisconsin, 1867-1868, when he was about ten. The Andersons spent it in a decrepit cabin near Hixton in Jackson County, and their potato supply ran out: ". . . [W]e children dug in the cellar dirt one evening for potatoes and now and then found a small one which we immediately baked in hot ashes and ate. At this time the only food in the house was a small cube of pork about the size of a book of Common Prayer." Neighbors fortunately came to their aid the next week, "and we never again knew want for food."

America's depressions were particularly hard on immigrants. Belgian settlers in Door County suffered real hardships in 1855 because of lack of work, high prices, no money. Many of these families, unable even to make or buy bread, subsisted by foraging for fish, wild onions, and roots.

A Norwegian pioneer in Winneconne, Ole A. O. Birkeland, later wrote of the winter of 1857, when "we practically lived on potatoes and barley mush. I hated it and when we would give it to Rover, our dog, his lips would curl up in disdain, and I sympathized with him; but my wife and I had to make a pretense of eating it with gusto to encourage the children."

Another family—Germans living near Mayville, in 1851—could only manage to serve for breakfast "rye coffee, a piece of dry bread, and pumpkin syrup. Pumpkins were boiled, the mass strained, and the juice boiled down. It was not

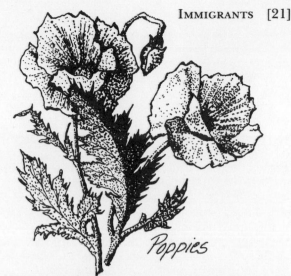

Poppies

very appetizing! For Dinner we had bean soup or potato soup; for supper only rye coffee and bread spread with lard."

John F. Diederichs, better off than most, could write with humor about his meager larder: "Potatoes, vegetables, or beef, are for the present not to be found with us, and just now mother reports that there is no more barley left, hence in the future we will have one course less, and the good housewife will have that much less trouble deciding what to cook."

In those desperate first years, the new arrivals would eat whatever they could get; but they returned to the familiar, old-world dishes as soon as economically possible. In fact, the appearance of familiar tastes and aromas was a tangible indication that their transplanted lives were successfully taking root and flourishing.

Kitchen gardens in town and country sprouted not only vegetables but all sorts of seasonings. *Schnittlauch* (chives), without which an omelet was considered barely edible, was planted in most German gardens. Poppies, grown for seed as well as for their ornamental value, were considerably rarer; but patches did appear in a few Pomeranian gardens in Dodge County and in Belgian and Bohemian gardens in Brown, Kewaunee, and Door counties. (No record has come to light of poppy cultivation by other groups that used them—Poles and Russians.) Helping mother gather the dried pods in the autumn and extracting the seeds was a yearly ritual for the children, a delectable chore since some of the pods were emptied into the mouth instead of the bowl.

Currant bushes were tended by those from the British Isles, Germany, and Scandinavia. Sage was grown particularly by the Scots and English, and dill by most middle and northern European groups, especially for pickles—and by the Russians for seasoning almost everything.

For the English, among others, a spring event was the digging of the horseradish; on a day with a moderate wind to blow the odor away, and thereby keep the tears from flowing, the root could be ground to provide piquancy to dishes all year long. (The root was also used whole, or ground when needed.)

Frequently, some of the family's meager cash resources were expended to buy the beloved tastes that were impossible to grow in Wisconsin. A kitchen redolent with cardamon and almond flavoring was usually, but not exclusively, Norwegian; with saffron, Cornish; with savory, laurel (bay leaves), and nutmeg, German; with caraway, Bohemian.

In those days, spices and herbs came in bulk, and a mortar and pestle were standard kitchen equipment for reducing seeds and leaves to powder. One woman, who spend hours as a child watching her German grandmother and mother grind spices for *Kringelin* and *Fuetjens*, later recalled "loving to watch them to do this—it seemed to me that there was an air of mystery and excitement in this ritual that I was too young to understand."

Bread was one of the sturdiest links with the past. Most immigrants marveled at and could appreciate the affluence represented by the abundance of white wheat flour, but few wished to embrace completely that manifestation of American life. For instance, I. O. Krohnke, who settled in New Holstein in 1848, wrote to his relatives in Germany that he intended to plant rye, though its persistence in fields made it an unpopular crop. "This does not stop me from sowing it, because the old dear black bread still tastes best,

and in spite of the fact that we eat wheat bread, I prefer the rye bread." And Michael Williams, a Welshman, felt gastronomically reassured when one member of his land-prospecting party in May, 1848, was able to provide fresh bread— perhaps the familiar Welsh oatmeal bread—for breakfast out in the "Indian land."

For those who could not afford to buy stoves and ovens at first, bread, familiar or not, took some doing to produce. *Bara Ceirch* (Welsh oatmeal bread) could be baked on a flat griddle or thick frying pan. Many rigged an oven, as did Torbjorn Wettleson's wife in her fireplace in a Norwegian area near Madison in 1845. She put her bread dough into a big, round iron kettle which was placed over glowing coals and topped with a frying pan filled with more coals. Some northeastern Europeans constructed the outdoor ovens familiar in their homelands, and they continued to do so well into this century.

"Our weekly baking was done in the out-of-doors oven," recalled a daughter of Peter Schuster, a German who settled in Dane County in 1850. "A weekly supply for our family consisted of about twelve large round loaves of bread, a goodly number of coffee cakes, and several pies. When the oven was properly heated, the coals and cinders were raked out, and the oven wiped with a dry mop. The raised bread, each loaf in a grass basket Grandfather had made for the purpose, was brought from the kitchen, taken from its basket, placed on a smooth wooden shovel, and tossed into the oven for an hour. The loaves filled about half the oven. Coffee cakes and pies were put in when the bread had been in thirty minutes."

Economics as well as old-world traditions determined the sort of facilities acquired for food preparation. As soon as possible, new arrivals obtained one of the American cookstoves which dazzled the European immigrant. John F. Diederichs, writing home to Germany in 1848, reported: "I bought a stove for 15½ dollars and must admit that one can't imagine anything more practical; there are four openings in it besides a bake-oven wherein we bake our splendid bread, and in addition we received, included in the above price, two iron pots, three iron pans, two tin pans for baking bread, one tin kettle holding four pails of water, one tin kettle, one tin skimmer and one dipper."

Some cooking utensils, both everyday pots and ethnically distinctive equipment, were brought from the old country. Norwegians frequently tucked into their baggage a *tvare*, a whisk made from the top of a spruce tree to stir *Romme grot* (cream pudding); special pans for items like the traditional stove-top pastry—Schleswig-Holstein *Fuetjens* or *Pfurten*, Danish *Aebelskiver*, or English *monks*—often added weight to trunks. Mixing and chopping bowls, wooden pestles, iron pots, china teapots, pudding molds, steamers—all were both tangible reminders of the old ways and the means of recreating them in the new setting. Other needed and reassuring items were easily made here, like wooden spoons or the simple wisks Swedish cooks made from the bark of willow branches tied together.

A cabbage cutter was indispensable in the kitchens of many ethnic groups; a crock or barrel of sauerkraut was sure to be put up each year by those from Alsace-Lorraine and most points east. In the fall, the women and children harvested the easily grown cabbages and sliced them until the barrel was full. The pickling liquid was added (spiced by some with caraway seed) and covered with a clean cloth, a board, and a heavy stone. Whenever some of the pungent contents was removed, the cloth was replaced and the board and stone washed. In many households, that removal was done on a regular basis, for example every Thursday, and the sauerkraut used for boiling spareribs, according to one traditional German recipe.

Other foods, depending on family tastes and customs, were virtual staples and fixtures in the larder. Salt herring, for instance, purchased in five-and ten-pound wooden kegs, was almost a necessity for many from Mittel-europa. One traditional procedure was to clean and cut up several herrings, cover them with a mixture of vinegar, onions, and spices, and let them stand for twenty-four hours. They were served with boiled potatoes and old-fashioned sour cream:

raw milk allowed to cool and stand until thick and slightly sour-tasting.

Most areas of Wisconsin provided ample resources to satisfy mushroom fanciers, particularly the Russians and Poles. Many considered the fall crop the best, gathered in late September on a warm and rainy day following a frosty night. (Those who added an unfamiliar variety to their baskets often relied on the now-discredited test for poison mushrooms: if a mushroom cooked with an onion turned the onion black, it was unsafe to eat.) The familiar fungi were cleaned and then mostly dried; some were packed in heavy salt, canned, or, in modern times, frozen. Drying increased the pungency of the mushroom, enhancing soups, main dishes, and vegetables in everyday cooking. A typical breakfast was eggs scrambled with caraway seed and mushrooms, accompanied by bread dipped in milk.

That precious gastronomic link with the past could be a variety of small, simple things: the earthenware crock ever-stocked with fried cakes by Danes and other northern Europeans and with ginger snaps or white sugar cookies by Scots, Irish, and English; or the pot of rice pudding perpetually setting at the back of Norwegians' or Swedes' stoves; the not-too-sweet tea cake as ubiquitous as the pasty in Cornish houses; the requisite *kova leipää ja korppuja* (hardtack and toast) found in Finnish kitchens. The latter staple once moved a devotee to rhyme:

No Friend have I
Except hardtack made of rye;
It is my faithful love
From cradle to heaven above.
Hardtack, thou art dearer than gold,
More priceless than blood, I needn't be told.
Superb—lovely—thou doth bewitch me,
With tears of joy I greet thee.

For some, a favored food could not be brought or duplicated in Wisconsin, so when the longing became overwhelming, precious funds would be dispatched to family or friends remaining in the homeland to send some.

Dulse, for instance. This is a dried seaweed that to the uninitiated tastes rather like cod-liver

Morel
Mushrooms

oil. But to eastern Canadians, Icelanders, and some Irish and Scots, it was—and still is—a sea-tangy treat. It was a seasoning for fish and chowders and salads; chopped and simmered in milk, smothered in butter, and served with crackers it was a main dish; or simmered in water until thick, cooled and dolloped with whipped cream, it turned into a dessert.

At least one cow headed the list of priorities of farmer immigrants from all ethnic groups, for she provided the family with nourishing milk and butter. How extensive a use was made of the milk for other dairy products or what forms they took depended upon the family's old-world traditions. Many pioneers had plenty of milk and all the good things that could be made from it. During dry periods, even when there was money on hand, there were those who decided to do without store-bought butter, cheese, sour cream, or buttermilk because they just did not measure up to what could be made at home.

Dasher, paddle, or crank butter churns could be found in most rural households, and were used at least once a week by the women of the house—though it was not unheard of to train the family dog to run a treadmill connected to the churn. After the milk was strained, cooled, and skimmed, the cream was put into the churn and worked until it solidified, then was washed, usually salted, and packed in wooden tubs or earthenware crocks to be stored in a cool place until needed. There were treats to be had during the process. "How well I remember how [in the 1880's] I used to come to mother with a slice of bread when she was churning butter and beg for a taste when the cream became very thick, shortly before turning into butter," recalled a Swedish Wisconsinite from Plum City. "This made a sandwich hard to equal."

In the days before widespread commercial dairying, when wheat was king in Wisconsin, those old-world traditions coupled with local agricultural conditions also determined whether or how quickly the cow barn would be expanded to provide surplus for barter or sale to markets in city and town. Some did not have to carry their excess any distance at all; on the frontier, Indian neighbors brought wild rice, corn, or game to exchange for dairy products.

In the earliest days, new arrivals from abroad frequently had trouble selling their butter and cheese because they did not conform to the Yankee standards of cleanliness. (Many immigrants themselves made note of the differences in housekeeping practices among various groups, and were dazzled by the spotlessness of even the poorest of Yankee and Yorker homes. This disparity was cultural; women from many European countries traditionally had complete responsibility for the barnyard, and were expected to work in the fields as well, so they had little time for interior sweeping and scrubbing.)

The story was told in Trempealeau County of a Swedish woman with a reputation for casual housekeeping who once found a mouse in the cream. She fished it out and went on with her butter churning. Taking the butter to the town grocer, she asked him to exchange it equally from his stock and sell hers, saying that what a buyer did not know could not hurt him. The grocer took the tainted butter, transferred it to another container, and returned it to the maker, reasoning that what *she* did not know would not hurt *her*, either.

Butchering time was one of frenzied activity, involving the whole family no matter what the ethnic group. It was also the time for making the various traditional sausages that appeared on the table throughout the year. A rural family was poor indeed if it did not have at least one pig to butcher in the fall; those more affluent slaughtered five or six or more hogs and perhaps a cow or steer as well. Hams were smoked, as was some of the beef, portions of which were also dried.

Every part of the animal was used—brains, kidneys, liver, heart, lungs, tail, fat. Even the cheeks, jowls, and ears that were not included in the sausage were utilized in some manner. The Germans, for instance, mixed them into *Knipp* ("snips") which were fried up like cracklings. Blood was also saved. Swedish immigrants would drain the blood into a dish pan, stirring until cooled to prevent curdling. If winter set in quickly, the blood could be frozen and kept for some time. The Swedes particularly enjoyed blood bread, which kept well for long periods in cold weather. If the bread got very hard, it could be cut into cubes and cooked in hot milk seasoned with salt and butter or in water and fat for a nourishing breakfast or supper.

The least favored job at butchering time was preparing the sausage casings from hog and beef entrails. The strong odors released in the process of emptying, washing, turning, and scraping them was a disagreeable memory some carried well into old age.

Every housewife had her own recipes for the mixtures that went into those natural casings or were packed into crocks or pans. These highly individualized recipes had roots deep in the old countries. Many Slovaks used some of the meat for rice sausage and head cheese; Norwegian favorites included *Sylte* (a hog's head cooked with spices, salted in brine, then packed in a cloth) and *Rull* (a loaf of strips of cooked and seasoned beef or veal flank).

Germans had a long repertoire of sausages, meats, and meat-based standbys for every meal of the day, like these staples in a single New Holstein household: *Eier Leber-wurst* (egg liver sausage, stored in a crock) and *Grütz-wurst* (made with steel-cut oats), which were sliced, fried in butter, and served sometimes with syrup, for breakfast; *Mehl Beutel* with apples (dumpling-like pastry or often made with blood at butchering time); *Sulze* (jellied meat or head cheese), or *Schwarz Sauer* (a sweet-sour pork dish darkened with blood) eaten for dinner or supper. Many of the sausages required smoking; householders without special smokehouses improvised with barrels.

Rendering the lard was as time-consuming a chore as the subsequent task of removing the film of grease from the kitchen surfaces. But it was an important job in a day when animal fat was an indispensable commodity not only for cooking but for soap and candles as well. For kitchen use, the large sheaves or slabs of leaf lard were rendered and stored in big stone jars. Some middle-European immigrants removed the thin skin of the fat and diced it especially fine. After rendering, the resulting fine cracklings were drained instead of being squeezed dry and were then added to pie crust as part of the shortening for added special taste and texture.

Other kinds of fat were rendered in the late fall and early winter. Germans and Jews, among others, prized goose grease, especially for holiday baking. It made a fine spread for bread, too, topped with a little salt. Or for a special-occasion spread, it was heated with a quartered apple or two and a small, cut-up onion.

Not all of the animal fat went into the rendering pot. Some chunks were put into the brine barrel for salt pork, an absolute necessity for many ethnic groups. It added fat and seasoning to many dishes or was served as the meat of the meal. French-Canadians, for example, dipped salt pork slices in beaten eggs, rolled them in cracker crumbs, and fried them golden.

Though butchering time was exhausting, the accompanying special treats were much anticipated and hugely enjoyed. Cracklings were nibbled as a snack or baked into biscuits which were then spread with fresh butter. Other delicacies were available only at butchering time—like sweetbreads for breakfast and the various blood dishes.

Butchering could mean a treat for city and village dwellers as well, for that was when freshly made sausages were available from the butcher. In turn-of-the-century Kohlsville, a hamlet in Washington County, one German settler recalled waiting in the shop until the butcher had finished boiling a large kettle of ring bologna to enjoy with hearth-baked bread and beer.

Another important fall activity was getting the potatoes out of the ground and into the cellar. Though many became heartily sick of potatoes after the first hard years, they remained a dietary staple—and a useful household item—for both native and foreign-born Wisconsinites.

Peter Leimerix, an early French-Canadian settler near Stevens Point, claimed to have grown the first potatoes in the area in the late 1850's. His unsubstantiated claim was set down in freeform spelling without punctuation by Simon A. Sherman in his diary: ". . . . [W]ell does he remember the 1st potato gron North of Stevens Point which he planted a few and how anxios he watched their growth and when they were about as large as his tumb of diging a few. Killing a pockupine which he made into a Soup and what a delicious feast he had out of it."

It was not unusual for potatoes to appear on the table three times a day—mashed, fried, baked, roasted, or boiled, or as potato pancakes, potato soup, hot potato salad, potato bread, potato dumplings. The boiling water was used for soups and sauces, or as the liquid ingredient in bread and rolls. Boiled potatoes, sugar, and hops stored in a jug provided homemade yeast for baking. And the starch that settled in the pans during various types of preparation was carefully saved and dried, to be used to stiffen dresses, aprons, petticoats, and shirts as fashion dictated.

Though so frequently served, potatoes could evoke pleasurable gastronomic memories years later. A daughter of Bavarian immigrants remembered the special taste of potatoes roasted in the bonfire at the celebrations marking the end of the harvest: "When the fire was almost burned to ashes, we put into the embers the freshly dug potatoes each wrapped in a thick coat of mud. No other baked potato can compare with such. We raised the Peachblow which were beautiful to look at, thin-skinned and fine tasting. I doubt if the Peachblow Chinese porcelain is more beautiful than were our potatoes."

Hard, precarious, and backbreaking as this period of transition may have been, things were better for practically everyone in the new, unfamiliar surroundings of Wisconsin than they had been in the old country. Those with some cash resources were struck by how cheap food was. "Father brought home for half dollar two pounds of sugar, quarter of a pound of tea, a pound and a half of coffee. This seemed a good deal to us for two English shillings," wrote Clara Chaney to her grandmother in England in 1850. And bartering was accepted business procedure: "Deio and I sawed pine wood at the end of the winter and the beginning of the spring, and we exchanged them for flour, pork, sugar, and tea," a settler wrote back to Wales in 1847.

The Swiss at New Glarus quickly overcame the dreadful first years. As early as 1850, William Streissguth, reporting on the colony, wrote: ". . . [O]f hunger days nothing at all is to be said. Flour, milk, potatoes, meat, butter, cheese, eggs, etc. are at hand in richest profusion. . . . And I can testify to the excellence of the tables spread and the keen, good appetites around the tables. One has but to look at the people in order to be convinced that hunger and want are not frequent guests in their homes."

A member of a Swiss family that settled in Sauk County—and experienced an extremely difficult first year despite being relatively well-to-do—remembered that "so far as material conforts went, we were soon as well off as at home in Switzerland. . . . The creek teemed with fish, which we considered a delicacy as we had seldom had any at home. . . . After the first year, we always had beef and pork—fresh, salted, pickled, or smoked—in good quantity. Chicken was a regular article of diet. Mother made butter and father cheese. He had to learn this from a book but soon mastered the art. . . . "

And later, in 1895, new arrivals were still extolling the spaciousness of the farmlands: "What a difference between [our] broad acres in Wisconsin and the small strips of land [we] had in Bavaria."

Though the transitional experiences were similar, each ethnic group experienced them separately. The border each group established around itself was almost as formidable as an Old World frontier. Commonality of the immigrant experience was usually shared just with landsmen. There was no crossing over even under the roof of a common religion, since services were frequently conducted in the mother tongue until well into this century. Marriage across ethnic lines was rare; when it did occur, the pattern was usually of a foreign-born man marrying a Yankee or a Yorker girl, since so many single men had come seeking their fortunes.

Gastronomically, such divisions were every bit as rigid. As happens today, new foods were approached with caution. Consider this Norwegian's reaction to the English mince pie he was served in the 1860's: ". . . . [T]his nondescript food was left to the last. I opened it and fled from the table. I did not call it by any particular name, for I knew none that would express its character as it appeared to me. What it was concocted from I know not, for it is probable that its ingredients were as unfamiliar to me as the name of this conglomeration was at the time. For years mince pie was absolutely safe from trespass on my part, and to this day I attack it with caution."

These common experiences were lived through by the various ethnic groups in different decades over a long span of time—right up to today. Now, however, though the experience is as wrenching as before, new arrivals have a somewhat easier time. Modern mass media, television particularly, and various social agencies help to cushion the transition and speed acculturation; and modern merchandising makes it possible for Wisconsin's newcomers—Cubans and Vietnamese in the 1970's and 1980's, for example—to buy foods they are used to.

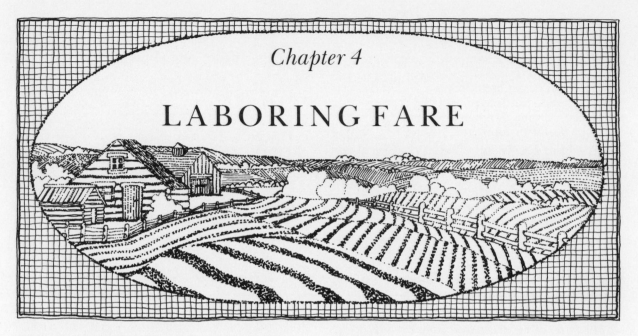

Chapter 4

LABORING FARE

IN THE PROCESS OF FORGING A NEW LIFE AND A new state in the last century, many tasks and economic endeavours had to be performed by large crews of men who often lived together as well. Such enterprises provided many single men with work and a place to live. There were married men in the crews, too, working for the grub-stake to reunite the family and settle down.

A few of these undertakings were performed in settled areas and served a social funtion be-sides—barn raisings, church raisings, and threshing activities at harvest time. They in-volved an equally diligent crew of women work-ing in the kitchen. Most, however, were exclu-sively male enterprises carried out on the edges of the frontier: railroad survey and building gangs, loggers, rafters, Mississippi steamboat crews.

Whether in community or in wilderness, the work was hard and long. Prodigious quantities of food were required to keep the laborers going, giving rise to a unique culinary tradition in fact and fable.

In one way or another, threshing time was one of the high points of the farm family's year. For the children, it was a gala event, a visit of near and far neighbors for at least one whole day. "When I was a small boy, there were three annual events in my life that I looked forward to with great eagerness. First there was the 4th of July . . . ; then Christmas . . . ; and third was the visit of the threshing machine." For the farmer, it was largely the economic matter of getting his crop in and assessing the success of the growing year. For his wife, it was a concentrated period of intense, hard work well larded with heaping por-tions of culinary competitiveness and pride. "It was no secret that the wives in the neighborhood vied with one another to see which could furnish the most satisfactory dinner," recalled a Madiso-nian of German heritage about his 1880's boy-hood in Sauk County.

Preparations began days before the threshing crews were expected. Some breads, cakes, pies, and puddings were made in advance; fresh meat was butchered and hung. While they worked, the women of the household no doubt prayed for good weather, for in the days before refrigera-tion, a rain meant postponing the threshing and the spoilage of much of the food.

Usually, neighbor women came to help out when the crews were working, but the primary burden, of course, settled on the farmer's wife. Her day (or *days* if the farm was large) began at 4 A.M. in order to get breakfast ready. Then there was a forenoon lunch to prepare and serve out in the fields, a dinner at noon, another lunch in the fields in the afternoon, and an evening repast when the day's work was done. The last pot and pan usually was scrubbed and put away about 11 P.M. Though the neighbor women helped, all food was prepared in the family kitchen on the family stove, which had to be kept going red-hot all day no matter how high the temperature outside. No doubt most shared the feeling of Mrs. Jane Kelly of Cottage Grove who noted in her diary on September 18, 1873, after four days of threshing (counting some lost time for broken machinery): "Finished Threshing today and I am so glad."

This threshing crew tradition (the term encompassed silo fillers, hay balers, harvest hands, etc.) lasted well into this century. From 1912 to 1916, Nellie Kedzie Jones, a pioneer in the development of the study of home economics, wrote a column for *The Country Gentleman* from her home in Marathon County, Wisconsin. In one of them, couched in the form of a letter to a mythological city-bred niece, who had married a farmer, she outlined the best way to feed a work crew: ". . . . I would begin my baking about three days beforehand with a big batch of drop cookies. At the same time the pie crust, if you want to use pie, can be mixed up ready for the wetting and set away in the ice box. Do the bread making the day before. At the same time boil and bake a whole ham. This will make your cold sliced meat. A big ham ought to boil at least four hours, and bake in a slow oven two more. The night before peel 'a heap' of potatoes; allow not less than four large potatoes for each man per meal and a few more for the dish. Set them away, covered with cold water.

"Just as soon as you can find out when the threshers will be getting into your neighborhood, even a week or ten days beforehand, I would make up some pork cake or some other moderately rich fruit cake. If you should not need it there will be no loss, for it will keep for some time. Better have too much than too little. Ice cream is one of the easiest desserts for a crowd. The mixing is practically nothing; one of the men will freeze it and pack it away hours before it is needed. It is easily served.

"Hot food promptly served makes more of a hit with a crew of hungry men than something so elaborate the service is slow and the food cold. However, I would have a cold sliced meat so that everybody could begin as soon as seated, for a dozen men are not served in a minute with the hot meat. They eat no more when you have two kinds than when there is but one; all would want a second helping anyway.

"A big dish of cabbage salad on each end of the table will be appreciated by all hands. By threshing time you will have ripe tomatoes. A big dish of these, sliced and covered with cream salad dressing, is easily prepared, and there is no serving, for the men will help themselves, putting them on their plates just as they do the cabbage salad.

"Put on three plates of bread and three plates of butter, allowing two slices for each man, and then watch the bread plates for further devourments. So, too, with the cofee. Have plenty. Plan at least two cups for each man.

"The hay balers, however, when the baling is done out in the meadow some distance from the house, can be treated differently. With the dew on the hay they will start late in the morning and so will work late at night, to get in a full day. They will need a lunch at four in the afternoon.

"The midday meal can be served in the field, picnic-fashion, to the real pleasure of the men, to the saving of their time and the lessening of your own work. I have served a mile and half from the house and got the dinner there hot. Really this serving in the field is easier part of the time than in the house. The trick of it all is in getting rid of the nonessentials. No frills but food fills the bill with the farm labor. The men and horses can better spend the time out of a short morning resting in the field than journeying to the house and back.

"The question of suitable drinks for the men in the field in hot weather is an important one. In the old days, grog aplenty was served with striking results, literally striking results, which were not at all on the program. That has most recently passed. Some like buttermilk, others could not be hired to touch it. There is oatmeal water, root beer or a harmless home brew, and so on, but I have found that canned fruit juice, properly diluted with well water—do not have ice water—and toned up with citric acid comes as near being universally acceptable as any drink that I know of. . . . "

The generosity of the tables set for threshing crews was fostered as much by the farmer's wife's pride in her reputation as a fine cook as by need. But even in operations that were purely profit-making, competitive enterprises, the importance of large, hearty meals was unquestioned.

On the Mississippi steamboats in the 1880's and 1890's, for instance, most companies and captains realized that the cook had a lot to do with keeping a crew. As Captain George Winas of the *Juniata* used to say, "I want to pay them well, feed them well, and then I want them to work like hell." In 1899, the *Juniata* budgeted 57 cents a day for each of eighteen men in the crew, a generous amount of money in those days. And that didn't include the cook's wages, which ranged from $80 to $90 a month, or that of the cook's helper.

On that budget the men sat down to a breakfast of fried potatoes, ham and eggs, pancakes, bread and butter, rolls, cookies, gingerbread or snaps, and coffee; a dinner of meat roast, mashed potatoes, two or three kinds of vegetables, and pie, cake, and ice cream for dessert; and supper, a lighter version of dinner, often with cold meat instead of hot. Fish—catfish, bass, and pike—provided fresh by fishermen who brought their wares to the boats, was served at least once a week. During the hunting season, there were ducks; in other seasons, foods like berries were bought in La Crosse and Trempealeau.

The cooks—universally men—were experts at stretching their food dollars and using leftovers. Harry G. Dyer, who worked on riverboats in the 1880's and 1890's, remembered a fine cook,

George Whalen, who once served a dessert of boiled rice and sauce. It didn't go over well, and there was plenty left. "The next morning it went into a big frying pan, then a big slice of ham or two diced, then a can of tomatoes; the diced ham, rice and tomatoes were then browned, seasoned quite highly, seasoned with a touch of red pepper, and then it was 'jambalaya' and fine for a hungry river man."

Sometimes, though, the cook went too far in his cost cutting. On one of Dyer's journeys, the cook kept serving butter so strong that it "was perfectly able to walk." It was still on the table on the return trip, and the cook informed the complaining crew members they would have to use it before they got any more. "Well, that night, 'the boys' used about five pounds of that butter to grease the door knobs in the cabin and about ten pounds more was used to decorate various kitchen utensils, drawer pulls, and anything else that they thought would look better with a coat of butter. The next day the clerk went ashore at Lake City to get some butter."

The ship's officers must have welcomed the fresh butter, too, since on most river boats all crew members customarily were served from the same pot. Chancy Lamb, head of the C. Lamb and Sons steamboat company, used to instruct the cook to "cut everything in two in the middle and send half of it each way," meaning that the officers ate what the men did.

But it was in the logging camps where the importance of a full belly was indisputable and the status of the cook exalted. Some cooks were better than others, naturally, and some logging companies more generous than others in providing a larder of greater quality and variety. But there was general agreement, as one logging manager noted, that "a good cook meant a contented crew and a contented crew meant a good cut of timber. Nothing disrupted a crew like poorly prepared food and a sloppy way of putting it on the table. A grouchy ill-tempered cook added to the dissatisfaction." And it was in the logging camps that food and meal traditions have been yeasted into the North Woods folk tales of today.

The gargantuan meals of logging folklore were well rooted in fact, for logging in those days was strenuous work, and the cook and his assistant (called the cookee) also worked mightily to provide them. Then, too, there was not much else to do in those all-male societies isolated in the wilderness except to work, eat, sleep, and think up practical jokes, so the quality and quantity of food assumed greater importance than in places where other diversions were available.

Consequently, the cook shanty was usually the best-constructed building in the camp, often in the early days before the 1880's accommodating the sleeping bunks as well. The shanty housed the stoves and the dining tables, the latter frequently set for more men that they could comfortably accommodate, so "with no elbow room, it was quite a trick to get an arm loose to spear a potato or a slice of bread." The food was usually served on well-scrubbed but bare pine-board tables set with tin bowls, plates, and mugs and bone-handled knives and forks.

The day for the cook and his cookee started about 3 or 3:30 A.M., preparing the spread required to get a lumberman going: buckwheat pancakes (begun the night before with sourdough starter and made on a griddle that covered the whole top of an eight-lid stove), oatmeal, hash, potatoes, fried salt pork, beans, blackstrap molasses, fried cakes, and lots of black coffee sweetened with brown sugar.

Cleaning up after breakfast merged with preparing the noonday meal, which was usually brought out to the men by the cookee carrying about an eighty-pound barrel-pack on his back. (When the cookee needed to rest, he would find a tree stump of suitable height, back up to it, and rest the pack for a spell.) The pack would have been filled, for example, with huge quantities of pork and beans, slabs of homemade bread, crusty sugared fried cakes, and molasses cookies. The cookee summoned the men to this repast by blowing on a tin lunch horn or into the neck of a whiskey bottle with the bottom broken out.

Dinner was dished up back at the camp: potatoes with brown gravy, fresh meat depending on the season, Red Horse (salted beef), pea soup,

stewed dried prunes or dried apples, rice pudding, the ubiquitous fried cakes, pie of dried apples, prunes, or raisins, and coffee or tea. And, of course, homemade bread, mixed up in pine troughs large enough for a half-barrel of flour at a time. Salt and pepper were passed in pint basins and sprinkled on the food with a knife.

The makings for all this were purchased in quantity. In 1884, for instance, the clerk for the Joseph Dessert Lumber Company of Mosinee recorded purchases of *18 pounds salt*, 24 cents; *14 pounds pork*, $1.12; *14½ pounds venison*, $1.02; *9½ pounds beef*, 54 cents; *4 pounds soap*, 20 cents; *5 pounds codfish*, 40 cents; *6 pounds steak*, 60 cents; *29 pounds butter*, $5.22; *6 boxes pepper*, 50 cents; *barrel of cranberries*, $5; *10 pounds veal*, 70 cents; *120 pounds wheat*, $1.50.

Flour, sugar, and rice came in barrels and were kept with root vegetables and dried foods in a small cellar under the cook shanty. In the cold of winter, storage of fresh meat was no problem; a small building set off from the warmth of the cook shanty was usually built for the quarters of beef, dressed hogs, lard, salt pork, and sausage.

The consuming of these enormous meals was as ritualized as the serving. Though there was considerable yelling, shoving, and pushing around the door before the meal horn was sounded, silence reigned at the table; there was supposed to be no talking except to ask for something. As one old-timer recalled, "If some one happens to laugh, the cook whistles or raps with a knife handle and we all know that means silence." Every man had his special place at the table; a change in seating ultimately required the cook's permission. Occasionally, a new man would sit in someone else's place, and would get just one warning before the laying on of hands by the rightful owner; it was considered cowardly to be driven from your place.

Like the atmosphere, table etiquette was rude. Most men, no matter what their background, "cast aside everything in the way of politeness and table manners. It's 'dog eat dog' if you get enough of what you want." But though all-you-can-eat was fundamental in logging camp dining, there *were* limits which if exceeded brought forth insulting references to porcine behavior. (One lumberman remembered a breakfast when a platter of six eggs was placed on the table and grabbed by a man who dumped all six onto his plate. A tablemate's comment was: "Well, I like pork, but damn a hog.")

Really epic eaters had to have tough skins to match their strong stomachs so they could withstand the reaction of their comrades. The story was told of a turn-of-the-century logger—described as a porcine cross between a Poland China and a Chester White—with a particular fondness for the weekly meat pies baked in six-quart basins. Each man was served a quarter of the pie, but the "hog" would "hurry and eat his piece, and then just to be friendly, would eat one more." The cook finally had enough and placed before him a six-quart meat pie with two large kitchen spoons neatly crossed on top. "The hog asked for a plate, but Ed [the cook] told him he was through feeding hogs from a plate, but that he ordered the wood butcher to make him a trough, and it would be ready for him for supper. That noon hour every one of us had some wonderful suggestions to make to the hog in regard to eating out of a trough. He could not

stand the gaff and packed his turkey and hit the grit."

On occasion, guests would be entertained at camp, enlivening the usual mealtime routine. At such "soirees," a better grade of coffee was sure to be served, and conversation was permitted. The spirited conversation, and perhaps an added course or two, promoted more leisurely dining.

When it was time to float the logs down the rivers, the culinary traditions of the North Woods went along with the raftsmen in the cook shanty affixed to a log raft. Breakfast and supper were served at the shanty, but, as he had in the woods, the cookee took the first and second lunches at mid-morning and mid-afternoon out to the men in tin hampers.

On the way to the mill towns along relatively sparsely settled stretches of river, shanties would be tied up at a bridge for a day or two for shopping forays to local farms, especially for chickens, which were "at a premium," and fresh pork. After the logs were milled, huge rafts of lumber were assembled, the cookstove put on board under a temporary shelter, and the trip to market at St. Louis or even New Orleans began. Cooks on these lumber rafts had the luxury of landing in river towns and cities for store-bought items like syrup, salt, dried apples, and flour.

Occasionally, these mobile provending practices were highly unorthodox. Raftsmen were fond of fish, but had no time to dangle a line and catch some. Their solution was to trail a drag line with a heavy iron weight from the back of the raft, thereby gathering in setlines strung across the river by fishermen on shore. From time to time, the drag was raised, the fish (which almost always included fine catfish) removed, and the hooks and setlines tossed overboard. "There were enough catfish for supper and some left over, which were sold in the next town."

While lumberjacks were generously packing the food away, railroad survey crews were tramping over difficult terrain throughout the state performing their arduous labors on a great deal less. Charles Monroe, a member of the crew do-

ing the Penokee Survey in Ashland County for the Wisconsin Central Railroad in 1881, wrote home to his mother in Ohio that "we live on bacon, ham, beans, potatoes, rice, canned tomatoes, with canned peaches and blackberries for variety occasionally, tea and coffee. Our cook makes very good bread, and there is generally enough to satisfy one of one sort or another. I am awfully tired of salt meat though. Yesterday we had some codfish. The cook has no stove, he bakes bread in open tin ovens, laid on the ground in front of a log fire, shaped so as to gather and intensify the heat."

Every once in a while, the crew would get back to the base station and stoke up on better meals, making the subsequent return to camp meals even more dreary. (This situation was made even worse when the regular cook was lured away by another outfit and Monroe and his companions had to share the cooking chores.) After a sojourn at the base, where he had a big supper on Saturday and then an equally big breakfast and dinner on Sunday, Monroe "came back, somewhat reluctantly, to camp Sunday evening. We had nothing in camp but salt pork, biscuit and coffee for a couple of weeks. My Thanksgiving dinner consisted of three biscuits and some coffee, and was eaten out on the line where we were at work. We shall fare better after this, probably, for we have just received a lot of supplies, and have got a new cook."

In the nineteenth century, compensation for many types of work in town and country included one or all meals. Lars Olsen, for example, writing home to his mother in Norway from Sand Bay in Manitowoc County in 1854, reported: "The lowest pay here is sixteen dollars a month and board, but the board is not rotten herring and gruel here as it is many places in Norway. Here we eat three times a day. In the morning we eat breakfast at 6:30 and begin work at 7, and for breakfast we have every morning fried pork, cold meat, coffee, wheat bread, butter and cookies, and for dinner boiled meat, pork, and potatoes and for supper at six o'clock we have fried pork, meat and potatoes, tea, bread and cookies."

Not all employers were so generous. For instance, Daniel Thomas, a Welshman, worked as a farm laborer and handyman in the Hartland area of Waukesha County after he arrived in Wisconsin in 1851. He noted in his diary the occasion when he was served turkey—"for the first time in twenty years"—or when given a very little bit of fish or a small piece of pork at butchering time.

Edgerton's brickyards in 1885 provided laborers with two lunch breaks—9 A.M. and 3 P.M.—and served warm meals which usually included hot buttered soda biscuits and coffee. And in a sawmill near Wittenberg in the 1880's, full board was provided.

Generally, the boardinghouse was a popular institution in the last century. According to some estimates, nearly 70 per cent of all Americans lived in a boardinghouse at some time in their lives for an average of three years. Such establishments provided living and eating accommodations for the many single men working in towns and cities, for newlyweds or couples or families in the process of arranging permanent living quarters, and for older people in retirement.

Whether it was a commercial enterprise run perhaps by a widow, or a private home whose owners were augmenting their meager income, the boardinghouse built its reputation on the skill of the cook. And the quality was extremely diverse. At the low end of the scale was Hans A. Anderson's poor experience in 1869 in Trempealeau County, where "during the two weeks I stayed there, every meal except one or two consisted of buckwheat cakes and pasty gravy." The 1849 fare at a boardinghouse in New Holstein was not much better: "Breakfast meant a wholesome meal soup, at noon pap or mush and milk, and evenings more meal soup with cinnamon and milk." The landlord's reaction to a complaint about the monotony of this diet was to butcher one of two cows that had helped provide the milk.

When Beloit was abuilding in 1837, meals at the first boardinghouse were limited after the original ten pounds of flour and six pounds of salt pork gave out. Since lack of money prevented restocking of the larder, the landlord relied on fresh fish, which were easy to come by. Each morning, the flume at the mill was closed and drained, and a generous supply of suckers weighing two to four pounds each was scooped up. The fish not eaten fresh were salted for future use.

Reaction to boardinghouse food, of course, depended to a great extent on personal tastes. A Blue Mounds visitor living a day or two with a Dutch family in 1850 heartily enjoyed her starchy diet: "I can have as much excellent milk and potatoes as I desire (without spice or fat, and potatoes in this country are my best food), as well as capital butter and bread."

In many places, there was no choice. Mrs. Barbara Elmer ran the only public boardinghouse in Black River Falls in the late 1840's where she fed about thirty men, most of whom were connected with the lumber industry. Salt pork and good, home-made bread was the staple diet, sometimes varied with bean soup and venison.

Later on, more choices became available throughout the state. Hotel dining rooms often offered full board to persons other than hotel guests, and the boardinghouse continued to thrive (and indeed exists to this day). Although meals are only rarely included in a salary these days, facilities for buying a reasonably nourishing repast during the working day are provided in many institutions and business establishments.

Chapter 5

ON THE ROAD

IN ANY NEW LAND, PRACTICALLY THE FIRST businessmen to appear on the heels of the first settlers were the keepers of taverns or inns. Indeed, the first arrivals perforce became involved in the business themselves; traditions of frontier hospitality included giving food and shelter to the wayfarer, though usually a monetary payment was demanded beyond the valuable emollient of contact with the outside world. In pre-territorial days, missionaries and traders opened their doors to and shared their tables with travelers. As towns were established, a tavern or hotel was often the first truly permanent structure to be erected.

Frontier hostelries were important, since not all pioneers came in wagons carrying eating and sleeping equipment; therefore many needed somewhere to stay en route and in the place they settled until they could make permanent arrangements. And as the new society enlarged, transients of various kinds—businessmen, tourists, drifters—followed hard behind. Taverns and inns served a social function, too, as gathering places where permanent residents could ease the isolation of the frontier, exchange local and national news, and even hold meetings.

So it was in Wisconsin. Judge John P. Arndt claimed to have established the first licensed tavern* in Wisconsin—in Green Bay in 1825—and his establishment enjoyed a reputation as a very comfortable house. By 1829 there were numerous taverns scattered from Green Bay to Galena, along the Fox-Wisconsin waterway, but rarely elsewhere. Shortly after statehood, 588 men told the census takers they were innkeepers and 468 listed themselves as owners of "groceries," which in those days meant a place to buy or drink liquor.

Unsurprisingly, the quality of these establishments varied, depending on the availability of supplies as well as the skill of the proprietor. Those offering decent food and passable accommodations enjoyed wide reputations. For instance it was said of Samuel Resique, who in 1835 opened the first tavern at Pike Creek (the first

* *Tavern* in the early part of the nineteenth century meant a place where travelers could find lodging and food. After 1840, the more elegant sounding *hotel* and *house* became increasingly prevalent. *Inn* was not widely used in Wisconsin. The sort of establishment now known as a tavern was then called *dram shop, tippling house, grocery,* and, later in the century, *saloon.*

name for Kenosha), that "few men knew better how to cater to the appetites of their guests. . . ; his table was provisioned with the best wild game the surrounding country could furnish; and the economy with which he was accustomed to stow away his numerous guests on a given area in his little garret, was truly astonishing." Word circulated equally fast about the places with bad food, meager drinks, and dreadful lodgings. But good or bad, the customers came. There was rarely a choice or an alternative.

When Morgan L. Martin went to Prairie du Chien in 1828 to act as prosecutor in the murder trial of Red Bird and several other Winnebago Indians, he put up at the home of fur trader John B. Brunet. "I remember that there was a French serving woman at this quasi-hotel, who had escaped from the Red Bird massacre," he wrote later. "Her daughter, a little girl of five or six, was going minus her scalp, and was shown to us as one of the curiosities of the place."

There was certainly no choice besides Rowan's tavern at Poynette in Columbia County. A traveler who stopped there in 1835 noted that when he was "ready to go to sleep, there was an unearthly squeal and grunt of hogs in the open space between the two rooms, only a partition of logs between our heads and them." The pig situation at Rowan's was well known, including the children's penchant for keeping them as pets. Governor James Duane Doty once stayed there and was poked awake by the current porcine pet. He managed uninterrupted sleep for the rest of the night by putting it under a loose floor board. Another guest, seeing the creature rooting through a dish of potatoes on the hearth, remarked to Mrs. Rowan: "Madam, I would like to be served before the pig."

Guests shared their quarters with other Rowan livestock as well. One traveler, after dining on hoe cake and bacon, slept soundly until aroused very early by several cocks crowing close to his bed, discovering at daylight that the footrail of his bedstead was the roost for Rowan's chickens.

Generally, the accommodations elicited the most complaints. "We can eat you better than we can sleep you" was the catch-phrase of the proprietors of frontier establishments. These earliest places (and the later ones out in the countryside) were usually just log houses with one huge room for sitting, eating, and cooking, and a loft or semi-finished space above for sleeping dormitory-style or in small cubicles. Some were merely family-sized houses, particularly when the proprietor became a tavernkeeper because the tide of settlement washed a busy road near his homestead; others were larger structures built with innkeeping in mind.

At Prairie Village (Waukesha) in 1837, a traveler put up at "the best house in town, which was a small log cabin, about fifteen feet square, and contained but one room and two beds." Though five or six guests were already there, he was taken in "as it was a standing rule of the country to entertain all travelers, regardless of accommodations, for necessity compelled it. After partaking of a very palatable supper, consisting of fried pork and bread, the two beds were properly divided among the crowd upon the floor. . . ."

Jams in the southwestern Wisconsin mining boomtowns were even worse, especially in the 1820's. The lone miner at the end of a long day was not particularly surprised upon returning to the hillside cave he had carved out for shelter to find "some weary prospector, who had, in his absence, there taken up his lodgings for the night," as one chronicler put it. "Having passed a pleasant night, they would separate in the morning, perhaps never to meet again."

At Mineral Point, the single men who came to work the lead mines constantly filled the town's several taverns to overflowing. One operating in 1836 had beds in what was described as a "capacious saloon" where the first to retire "might do so under the grateful delusion that he was to enjoy the comforts of a good bed alone; but before morning, would be most likely to find himself sharing his comforts with as many bedfellows as could possibly crowd themselves along side of him—some of them probably in a condition to render them entirely oblivious to the fact that they had 'turned in' without the usual formality of divesting themselves of hat, coat, pants, or boots."

Such conditions persisted on the frontier margins of the state. As late as the 1850's for instance, William Petit turned his one-room cabin at Sparta into an inn, sleeping his guests in a loft floored with loose, rough staves. As one account put it: "Travelers wrapped their blankets about them, and lay down on the uncouth floor, to be howled to sleep by the hungry wolves that often stuck their cold noses through the crevices, and snorted in anticipation of what a supper they might have."

Petit's dining facilities were little better, but even so, they frequently served forty persons at a time. "The small table would be set with the few dishes, and the few chairs put about it; then all that could get a seat, or a plate from which to eat, would satisfy their hunger; the remainder who were not so fortunate, standing around, meanwhile watching the progress of the others, and wishing for their own time to come."

On the frontier, the tavernkeeper and his wife needed the same talents and skills as the pioneer farmer, and many, in fact, combined the two enterprises. A good hunter and gatherer could take advantage of the area's natural abundance (while it lasted) to set a decent table—wild strawberries and other fruits that could be preserved (if sugar was available), wild nuts, game, fish, greens, maple syrup, wild honey. But unlike the farmer, the tavernkeeper had the financial resources (more or less) to buy supplies at the nearest commercial center. Most often, the problem was getting there; for much of the year, the roads were impassable for loaded wagons, and the occasional traveler had to be satisfied with meal after meal of only bread, bacon or salt pork, and something to drink. Coffee and tea frequently were unavailable luxuries, so the cup was filled instead with liquid brewed from wheat, rye, peas, beans, dandelion roots, or browned bread.

Sometimes not even bread was available. Probably hominy was most frequently substituted. As elsewhere, hominy was made by boiling corn in a lye solution until the hulls peeled off, then washing the corn and cooking into a mush. This was served as a porridge or allowed to set and then sliced and fried. Lye was readily obtained from the ashes from the open fireplaces where the tavernkeeper's wife did her cooking in the earliest days. Later, wood-burning stoves were possible, and some larger taverns added outdoor bake ovens for breads, pies, and cakes.

The prudent tavern operator was wise to start out with a goodly supply of food. When the Eben Pecks came to Madison in the spring of 1837 at the invitation of Governor Doty, the city's promoter, to provide facilities for the men who would build the city, they spent over $100 in Mineral Point to stock the larder of their crude log tavern. According to Mrs. Peck, "among the items were one barrel of pork, two of flour, one of crackers, one of sugar, half barrel dried fruit, one box of tea, and as good a sack of coffee as was ever brought into the State, . . . besides a half barrel of pickles, put up by myself, also a tub of butter and jars of plums and cranberries, collected from Blue Mounds' thickets. All these were carried to Madison when we moved [from Blue Mounds, where they also ran a tavern], besides a good load of potatoes. . . . "

Transportation and local resources were controlling factors in determining menus. Even taverns in towns depended on larger centers of commerce for some supplies. The story was told of a particularly bad spell of weather about 1839 that kept fresh provisions from Milwaukee from arriving in Janesville, Beloit, and the lead region. Finally, a farmer managed the trip and brought a quantity of bacon for the Bloods, who ran a tavern near Janesville. Mrs. Blood, whose reputation for cleanliness was well deserved, picked up a slab of the meat and slapped it onto the floor. "Thank the Lord," she praised, "there's a grease spot at last."

Transportation improvements and development of local farms occurred more quickly in some places than in others, of course, depending largely on the rate of settlement in the area. In 1846, for instance, southern Wisconsin was "civilized" enough for tavern landlords to advertise the "delicacies of the season." But at that time, the first tavern in Black River Falls was offering bread and fried salt pork for breakfast and supper and boiled pork, bread, and bean soup for dinner. And in 1856, at the Hotel Bennette on the Pigeon River, a guest found that the only food on the breakfast menu was well-cooked turnips. It was not until the coming of a railroad that an area could depend on some supplies or set a traveler to even thinking of complaining about limited or monotonous meals.

By the late 1830's and 1840's, Wisconsin was attracting tourists whose journals recorded the amenities of the early hostelries. In 1837, an Englishman, George W. Featherstonhaugh, visited Wisconsin on his return from *A Canoe Voyage Up the Minnay Sotor*. On his first night at Mineral Point, the overflowing taverns forced him and his party to seek lodging at a private home. "With difficulty, we procured a room to sleep in at the post-master's" whose brother, the town apothecary, fed them on "fried ham, coffee, bread and butter, and treacle, served up in a cleanly way . . . ." He was particularly grateful for the makeshift accommodations after looking into the taverns and being "thoroughly disgusted

with the dirty appearance of everything," including the motley collection of "ginnerals, colonels, judges, and doctors as were assembled there." He didn't like the "never-failing repast of coffee, rice, treacle, and bread and butter," either.

Featherstonhaugh stopped at the Peck tavern during its first year in Madison. If his recollections of the table Mrs. Peck set are true (she later said they were not, particularly regarding the coffee), he arrived after many of her original supplies were exhausted. (The Pecks arrived April 15; Featherstonhaugh, May 30.) "My first inquiry [wrote Featherstonhaugh] was, whether she had any fresh fish in the house. The answer was 'No!'. . . No fresh fish! no large, delicious catfish, of twenty pounds' weight, to be fried with pork, and placed before the voracious traveler in quantities sufficient to calm those apprehensions that so often arise in Indian lands, of there not being enough for him to eat until he falls fast asleep. 'Why, then,' exclaimed my alarmed companion, 'what's to be done?' 'I calculate I've got some salt pork,' rejoined our little hostess. 'Then, Madam, you must fry it without the fish,' I replied. So to the old business we went, of bolting square pieces of fat pork, an amusement I had so often indulged in, that I sometimes felt as if I ought to be ashamed to look a live pig in the face. Our landlady, however, was a very active and obliging person; she said she would make us as comfortable as it was possible for her to do, and 'she guessed' she had the little coffee, and would make us a cup of it. Whether it was acorns, or what it was, puzzled me not a little; it certainly deserved to be thought tincture of myrrh, and, as we drank and grimaced, dear Mrs. Peck, in her sweetest manner, expressed her regret, that she had no other sugar for our coffee, they having 'somehow or another, not brought any with them.' "

About the same time, a traveler heading west from Milwaukee sat down to a supper of fricasseed chicken, boiled potatoes, sour milk biscuit, dried apple sauce, and tea at Barstow's Tavern in Waukesha. (Waukesha County then had the most number of taverns for its size of any county in the state.) Later, at Childes on Rock Prairie east of Janesville, the party "had 'white bread and chicken fixins' for dinner. This was the usual manner of telling of a specially good meal for company. Otherwise it was 'corn bread and common doins.' "

In 1841, an Englishman arrived in the United States for a lengthy tour, recounting his adventure in unsigned articles for the *London Observer*. (These were later published as a book entitled *Life in the West: Back-Wood Leaves and Prairie Flowers: Rough Sketches on the Borders of the Picturesque, the Sublime, and Ridiculous*.) While in what is now Wisconsin, he criss-crossed the area from Green Bay to Janesville, Milwaukee and Racine to Madison, sometimes on his own, sometimes joining groups of other travelers. His accounts detailed not only the variety of the gastronomic offerings, but the conditions and the life styles of his various hosts, both tavernkeepers and friendly farmers and traders who put him up.

One night, for instance, en route to Milwaukee from Madison, he stopped at a farmhouse near the Rock River. "The farmers," he observed, "were flourishing like flaggers; they had fields of Indian corn and wheat, and oats, and pumpkins, and potatoes, and vegetables; in short, the farmers get on famously here; they have no roots and stumps to contend with, and the soil seems to be inexhaustible." The visitors provided the fixings of their meal which the farmer's wife prepared: "Breakfast upon a savory stew of the game we shot yesterday— snipes, prairie hens, quails, pigeons and robins, all stewed up together, so that the particular flavour of each bird was lost in this splendid soup a la Meg Merriles."*

And in Walworth County, on the way to Janesville from Racine, his host was a farmer and sometime tavernkeeper from New England who "from small beginnings is now the proprietor of five thousand acres of prairie land; he has enclosed several fields of Indian corn with ditches instead of rails—more permanent work— answering the double purpose of staying the prairie fire and keeping off cattle; he has sunk a well, and built stables, barn, and hog-pen, on a large scale, and, like a wise man, lived, up to this, in a simple log and mud cabin. I am really at a loss to know where the good people in this country— this out of the way place—find all the good things they set before travelers, especially the New Englanders; they seem to live better here than they do at home, and riot in pumpkin pies and all sorts of cakes and meats, savoury stews, &c.; and, to be sure, wine and strong drink is not to be found on the table, but rich cream, and excellent tea and coffee, fill up the vacuum, and invariably conclude a meal fit for an alderman. The trifling sum of twenty-five cents. . . is the moderate demand for all this . . ." (Many New Englanders who settled Wisconsin were fervent temperance people.)

Ardent sightseer that he was, he planned his itinerary to include one of the territory's first tourist attractions: the annual payment made by the United States government to the Menominee Indians for their lands, a week-long event of great ceremony and considerable revelry at the Lake Poygan paygrounds in the Winneconne area. And getting there was half the gustatory adventure.

En route from Green Bay at the tavern at Wright's ferry (Wrightstown), his supper was fried bacon, eggs, mush, maple sugar, wild plums, dried fish, and potatoes. At Augustin Grignon's well-known trading post at Butte des Morts he had an early snack of "a soup of Indian corn and wild duck. . . with some good bread" and then "at four, we sat down to a very savoury mess of stewed wild ducks, prairie hens, and vegetables; delicious bread, butter, potatoes, coffee, and plum pies." (From earliest times, the Grignons had enjoyed a wide reputation for their lavish hospitality. Pierre Grignon, Sr., for example, liked to entertain, at his home in Green Bay, the traders who came from the East each fall in the 1790's. His banquets featured, as one ama-

---

* A soup combining as many varieties of game as were on hand; named after a gypsy character in Sir Walter Scott's *Guy Mannering* who made such a dish.

teur historian put it, "all delicacies procurable in water, air, and forest" and good wine which "flowed freely.")

While at Grignon's, the Englishman witnessed the transporting of some of the payment and met an august chief. "Just as we sat down to supper, our ears were saluted by a loud, wild, discordant song, raised on the river by a large band of half-breeds and Indians who were pushing two heavy barges, full of flour, grain, and pork, to the pay-ment-ground; for part of the payment was to be made in flour, grain, and beef, pork. . . . Old Grignon went out and invited the head men in charge to come in to tea. Osh Cosh declined sit-ting at the table. He was served with wild-duck stew, tea, and cakes on a stool in the chimney-corner."

At the paygrounds, the Englishman managed to find tolerable food at the huge tent encamp-ment that drew traders, observers, tourists, rogues, and thieves in addition to the Indian and governmental participants. "Got some savoury stew for breakfast this morning," he noted one day, "down town at the sign of the 'Striped Apron,' which floated gracefully above six wigwams thrown into one, by a spirited New England pedler from the Bay. He has got to-gether sundry cooking utensils, and a barrel of flour, some pork, and, *mirabile dictu!* coffee. He thinks he will clear his expenses, and perhaps a little more, as he charges half-a-dollar a meal. The long wigwam is the rendezvous of all the tra-ders and loafers in the place, though the Indians seldom pass the threshold."

Six years later, in 1847, an article in the *Water-town Chronicle* described the dining facilities at the Indian annuity payment: "The gentlemen we have conversed with who attended the payment, speak in the highest terms of the accommoda-tions furnished by the three temporary taverns on the ground. These were all kept by Indians. The principal one, the 'Washington House,' was a one-story edifice, of rough boards, about 100 feet long and 20 wide. 'Mine host' was A. D. Dick, of the Brothertown tribe. His boarders were ex-clusively from the 'pale face' portion of the

crowd, and averaged 100 per day. His tables, we are told, would have done credit to the Astor, the Tremont, or the St. Charles. They daily groaned beneath every variety of wild game—deer, bear, raccoon, squirrels, wild geese and ducks, prairie chickens, partridges, quails, pigeons, & c., to say nothing of fresh beef, pork, veal and lamb. In the vegetable line his supply was ample of potatoes, turnips, onions, cabbages, beets, pickles, etc. So much by way of substantials; his desserts and 'trimmings' were of an order correspondingly magnificent. And all this was furnished at 75 cents per day, and a berth at night, under his tables, thrown in!"

Gastronomically, tavern and hotel keepers were more amenable than most to experiment. They, for instance, were quicker to recognize the worth of tomatoes, often called love-apples, which were regarded with extreme suspicion by a great many immigrants of various nationalities. (Many had the experience of biting into a to-mato, thinking it was an apple; the result was so distastefully memorable that it was recorded in diaries and journals.)

The anonymous correspondent of the *London Observer* carried on at great length about his en-counters with tomatoes while staying at the American Hotel in Madison, the second hostelry, after the Pecks', to serve the capital. ". . . [B]ut how he [Col. James Morrison, the hotelkeeper] had reduced himself and family to enjoy a to-mato, was beyond my comprehension. Tomato was the word—the theme—the song, from morning until night—from night until morning. The first morning I descended to the bar, there sat the colonel in his white and black chip hat, set jauntily over his round, heavy, swelled face, his crooked foot resting on one knee, his twisted hand resting upon that, [he had been crippled in a mine accident near Mineral Point]. . . and his expressive mouth full of a red tomato. That swal-lowed, he held up another love-apple tantaliz-ingly, to a feeble little child, and, mincing his voice, he would exclaim, 'Who'll have a tomato? Who'll kiss me for a tomato?' In truth, not I; hav-ing in the early part of my days looked upon that

grovelling fruit as poison, and never having tasted it even as a pickle with much gusto, I was not prepared to enjoy the tomato feast, at the capital of Wisconsin.

"The garden at the rear of the house seemed to produce no other fruit or vegetable. At breakfast we had five or six plates of the scarlet fruit pompously paraded and eagerly devoured, with hearty commendations, by the guests. Some eat them with milk, others with vinegar and mustard, some with sugar and molasses. I essayed to follow suit, and was very near refunding the rest of my breakfast upon the table, the sickly flavour of the flat-tongue grass, sour milk, and raw cabbage, being concealed under the beautiful skin of the love-apple I had the temerity to swallow.

"At dinner, tomatoes, *encore*, in pies and patties, mashed in side dishes, then dried in the sun like figs; at tea, tomato conserves, and preserved in maple sugar; and to crown the whole, the good lady of the hostel launched forth at night into the praise of tomato pills."

The writer and feminist Margaret Fuller obviously did not stop at the American Hotel during her 1843 trip (which took her to Lake Superior), for she complained about the lack of vegetables: ". . . [H]e whose affections turn in summer towards vegetables, should not come to this region, till the subject of diet be better understood; . . . of fruit, too, there is little yet, even at the best hotel tables; . . . the prairie chickens require no praise from me, and . . . the trout and white-fish are worthy of the transparency of the lake water." The lack of vegetables is evident from the Milwaukee House menu of December 31, 1843: roast turkey, goose, duck, chicken, beef, veal; boiled corned beef, tongue, ham, turkey; and venison á la mode, chicken pie, bird pie, chicken salad, boiled fish.

On the other hand, in the 1840's in Fond du Lac, James Ewen, landlord of the Lewis House, bought the first celery—called "decayed pie-plant" by some citizens—offered for sale in that city. And it was at such establishments that many later Wisconsinites first encountered other exotica: bananas, grapefruit, artichokes.

As the state became more settled and innovations like plank roads improved transportation in some places, more taverns, inns, and hotels were established, giving travelers wider choices. This, of course, meant that the places offering the best food and accommodations did the best business. A capable wife who was a good cook and a good household manager was virtually a necessity for success. Those without such an asset usually suffered the fate of two bachelors who in 1851 opened a tavern in Armenia township on the road along the Yellow River near Necedah. "[T]hey had to be both landlord and cook," an early resident recalled. "This, together with a kind of reckless way of doing business, soon caused the balance to show on the wrong side, and consequently they were unable to continue the business. . . ." Some tavernkeepers, however, succeeded without a wife, Ebenezer Brigham at Blue Mounds being one.

The Sheboygan-Fond du Lac plank road had numerous taverns offering sustenance and shelter on that busy highway. There were three taverns alone on the western end of the route, including Ehle Tavern, known as a very hospitable place, and the equally well-regarded Log Tavern. Halfway between the two pioneer communities was the Wade House at Greenbush, built in 1849 by Sylvanus Wade and opened to the public in 1850. Housed in a substantial, commodious building, this establishment was in continuous use well into this century. Restored to its nineteenth-century appearance, it may now be visited as one of the historic sites operated by the State Historical Society of Wisconsin.

Similarly, the busy traffic between Milwaukee, Waukesha, Watertown, and Madison contributed to Waukesha County's high tavern count. One of the well-known places on that route, Hawks Inn in Delafield, is also now a restored site.

Some of the hostelries of the past were known for certain culinary specialties. The Old Spring Tavern on the western edge of Madison was known for its cookies. And the oysters at Hawks Inn were considered an attraction. (Fresh oysters were widely available after the arrival of railroads to the state. They were usually shipped live from the East Coast, to satisfy the tastes of the peripatetic Yankees, in barrels packed with seawater-soaked oatmeal, which provided the mollusk with food and moisture for long periods of time.)

The increased competition caused proprietors to advertise, frequently stressing the excellence of their tables. The Tallmadge House in La Crosse advertised in 1854 that its "table is at all times furnished with the best the market affords." (That phraseology was a favored one of the day.) This flowery ad appeared in the *Mineral Point Democrat* in September, 1845: "The subscriber tendering his grateful acknowledgements to his friends and the public for their liberal patronage heretofore, begs leave to inform them that during the past winter he has made extensive additions to the well known 'Franklin House,' and is now prepared to entertain in a comfortable manner all who may favor him with a call. His house is one of the most extensive in the Territory, and he can furnish private apartments or suits of rooms to his customers at a moment's notice.

"His table will be furnished at all times with the best the market affords, and every attention will be given to rendering a stay at his house pleasant and agreeable."

Even ten years later, innkeepers were not promising more than the seasons could provide. D. S. Potter, who ran the Gem Saloon in Janesville, inserted this notice in the *Janesville Gazette* on March 10, 1857: "The Proprietor has the pleasure of informing his patrons and the public generally that he is now prepared to serve them with all the delicacies of the season in the line of eatables, such as the market affords. Having one of the best Saloon Cooks in the west, flatters himself he can give perfect satisfaction to all his guests."

The social function played by the taverns, particularly those in rural areas, cannot be underestimated. The top floors of many of them were ballrooms which were frequently used. Dancing parties and cotillions—usually including a dinner or supper—were favorite forms of social diversion. They were staged to mark holidays and community milestones as well as for no particular reason at all. When the Shanghai House in Black River Falls was completed in the 1850's, people came from as far as ninety miles away for the opening dance and attendant festivities. The Jesse Smith Cobblestone Inn at Big Bend boasted a ballroom with a "spring floor"—a floor laid independently from the walls so it bounced up and down when set in motion by dancers' movements.

Often, as the largest building in the area, the tavern was the meeting place for community gatherings of various sorts, for organizations like the Grange, and in some instances, for church services. The Milton House, built by Joseph Goodrich in 1844, is said to have been a station on the "underground railroad" for fleeing slaves prior to the Civil War. This interesting hexagonal building is also a museum today.

Larger establishments had a separate parlor for women and families, as the taproom was usually strictly a male preserve where the latest news and drink were dispensed. Wine, whiskey, or beer was an ordinary accompaniment for a meal despite the strong temperance sentiments in some parts of the state. Led by Yankee settlers, the temperance movement was responsible for an 1849 law making dispensers of drink liable for the harm their drunken customers might do. The rising tide of immigration from mid-century on, bringing such social institutions as the German *Biergarten*, washed away this early temperance legislation in 1851.

As towns and cities were established and grew, hotels were built, though in the earliest days only the name distinguished them from taverns in the area either in accommodations or as social centers for the community. Many of them used the term *house* instead of *hotel*. Daniel Whitney built the Washington House in Green Bay in about 1830. The Durkee House in Kenosha was the largest and most elegant hotel in the territory when it was completed in 1843. By 1845, a number of towns offered hotel accommodations to visitors, including the United States Hotel, the Milwaukee House, and the Fountain House in Milwaukee; the Madison Hotel and the American Hotel in Madison; and the Whitewater Hotel in Whitewater.

Later in the century, restaurants competed with taverns and hotels for the eating-out trade. Some promised home cooking; others offered more sophisticated fare and services. The Washington Market Dining Room in Madison, for example, advertised in the *Wisconsin State Journal* of November 29, 1873: "On the European Plan. Open from 6 A.M. to 12 P.M. Daily. Board $3 per week. Meals delivered at private rooms $3.50 per week. Regular dinner from 11 A.M. to 6 P.M.; only 25 cents. Cold lunches, with hot tea and coffee at all hours. Oysters a specialty."

Nowadays, hotels and taverns mean very different things. But hotels continue to provide meeting places for community functions. And though they no longer offer sleeping facilities, taverns continue to serve an important social function in many communities and rural areas; a few even keep up the old culinary traditions.

Chapter 6

KITCHEN MEDICINE

IN THE JACKSON KEMPER PAPERS AT THE STATE Historical Society of Wisconsin is a small note-book with yellowing rag-paper pages. The cover is gone and with it the precise identity of the com-pilers. But most of the elegant early nineteenth-century script, obviously written by several hands, is still legible, so it is readily apparent what the book was: a collection of recipes, handed down and added to by succeeding owners. At one end of the book are food recipes; but the larger portion at the other end sets forth cures for a va-riety of ailments, beginning with hives and rang-ing through the Kings Evil to dropsy to "An In-fallible Cure for the Ague."

That yellowing book in the Society's manu-scripts section is typical of the sort of personal collection an early Wisconsinite made in quest of relief from discomfort or pain. Some entries are annotated with the name of the contributor and the date received. One of the earlier is an entry of June 4, 1816, for Jackson D. Kemper's—later Episcopal Bishop Kemper's—"Receipt for the Rheumatism":

"Take 2 oz. [two ounces] Balsam Cassive, 4 scruples* Oil Sassafras, 6 drams Gum Guaiacum, 10 oz. Spirts Wine, 1 oz. Balsam Peru, 24 grains Salt of Tartar. Infuse them together for six days, let it be kept moderately warm and shook fre-quently when it is fit for use— 25 to 40 drops to be taken twice a day in White Wine."

Apparently the Kemper "receipt" did not re-lieve the compiler's condition, for numerous other rheumatism cures were hopefully re-corded, including rubs made of egg white, brandy, oil, and goose grease, or one that could be applied both inside and out:

"Take one ounce of gum Camphor, and put it into one quart of Spirits: put therein as much of the bark of Sassafras root as the Liquor will cover; let it stand 10 or 12 hours, and is ready for use. Take half a common wine glass on going to Bed, and the same as soon as you can in the morning, if possible an hour or two before break-fast, and even again at 11 o'clock, should the Rheumatism be very painful, taking care to rub the parts affected well with the same."

* A scruple is 20 grains.

Such collections of remedies, gleaned from friends and newspapers for the collectors' particular afflictions and designed to be mixed, brewed, or cooked in the family kitchen, tend to be highly personal, even idiosyncratic. Indeed, with the advantage of hindsight, it is easy to find humor in home-grown remedies for diseases which stubbornly resist the most modern vaccines, serums, antibiotics. But in nineteenth-century Wisconsin, doctors were rarely accessible to immigrants or families on the frontier; and when they were, their treatments for most illnesses—at least until the end of the century—were often not much more effective than traditional remedies dispensed from the family's medical compendium. At that time, the medical tree had many branches; apothecaries, homeopaths, and hydropaths legitimately practiced various forms of medicine, and surgeons were often regarded more as "sawbones" than as mystical saviors. (Those who specialized in botanical remedies were called Thomsonians, after Samuel Thomson who popularized them in the 1820's.) The importance of the man or (most frequently) woman with special healing gifts and a repertoire of salves, syrups, brews, tonics, and purges is well-rooted in both the fiction and the history of America's development.

The worth of some of these folk medicines was proved over the years, based as they were on common sense, knowledge of herbs and other natural substances, and insightful observation. Others were at best harmless, at worst downright dangerous. One wonders, for example, what injury resulted to those who followed this 1864 advice of *Mrs. Winslow's Domestic Receipt Book*, an annual publication intended to advertise Brown's Bronchial Troches and Mrs. Winslow's Soothing Syrup: "A new method of dressing wounds has recently been adopted in Belgium. A sheet of lead, one-fiftieth of an inch thick, is applied to the injured limb, and made by pressure to assume its shape. The lead is firmly secured by means of strips of adhesive plaster, and a current of fresh water is made to pass over the surface of the flesh once or twice a day."

And how disheartening must have been the results of the procedures prescribed in *A Helping Hand for Town and Country: An American Home Book of Practical and Scientific Information Concerning House and Lawn, Garden and Orchard, Field, Barn and Stable, Apiary and Fish Pond, Workshop and Dairy, and the Many Important Interests Pertaining to Domestic Economy and Family Health*, published in 1870: "A Preventive of hydrophobia is to take a white onion, cut it across the grain into four equal slices, sprinkle fine salt on them, and apply them to the wound, bandaged on, as soon as possible after the bite, when the onion will extract the poison; repeating every half hour with fresh slices until the onion ceases to show any discoloration. Then apply a healing plaster."

The compilers of *A Helping Hand for Town and Country* were not, as might be assumed, cranks or lunatics. They were Lyman C. Draper, famous collector of manuscripts and first secretary of the State Historical Society of Wisconsin, and William A. Croffut, a young Connecticut journalist whom Draper had elected to the Society's board of curators. Like many intelligent, well-educated people of his day, Draper was a Spiritualist, and he communicated not only with his deceased daughter Helen but also with the shades of American frontiersmen and Indian fighters.

A hypochondriac who suffered the agonies of the damned whenever he was faced with writing (as opposed to *collecting*) the histories of Revolutionary War heroes and battles, Draper had an abiding interest in medicine and the treatment of physical ailments. With Croffut, he hoped to compile a universal family encyclopedia of advice, remedies, and medical lore, and, selling it by subscription, to raise sufficient money to publish the great works of history and biography that he never quite finished. (Although *A Helping Hand* received polite notices, Draper and Croffut were cheated by their publisher, and neither ever realized a cent from the sales of their 800-page compendium.)

Whether the home practitioner used the Draper-Croffut volume or another such compilation, or relied upon a family scrapbook or simply upon stored-up folk wisdom, a well-stocked larder was a necessity. Many cures called for nutmeg, brown sugar, hog's lard, cabbage, horseradish root, milk, dandelion root, and bread dough. Bread dough, for instance, was mixed with hog's lard, "the older the better," then spread on a piece of white leather and applied to the diseased part—as a cure for cancer. Older-the-better hog's lard mixed with sweet spirit of vitre (vitriol—meaning sulphuric acid) in an earthern vessel was the *proved* cure for the Kings Evil (scrofula).

A reasonable supply of liquor was necessary for many such concoctions. An "Infallible Cure for the *Cholic*," in the old, yellowing notebook (which concluded with the notation *proved*) called for some "good old H[olland] Gin." Brandy was specified for the "Blackberry Cordial for Dysentery": "Put any quantity of Blackberries in a wide and deep pan, cover them with molasses, and let them stand several days, 'till they ferment and are apparently spoiled, then strain and boil it about half an hour, skimming it well. To every quart of juice add a pint of Brandy, and when cold bottle and cork it close." Other recipes required Madeira, St. Croix spirit (rum), and hard cider.

Occasionally, the requirements were minutely specific. The "Cure for the Quinsy, or sore throat" called for new milk which had to be put into a new red earthen pot as soon as it was obtained from a red cow. Other recipes, in this and similar collections, frequently specified new-laid eggs or just-pulled roots.

Two of the entries in the Kemper collection were clippings from an 1822 newspaper. One was a cure for "gravel" (kidney stones) communicated to the *American Farmer* by Mr. Washington Spencer of Baltimore: "Having been much troubled with the gravel, I was advised by a Mr. Zane of this city, to try a decoction of wild carrot, Daucus Carota. I made a tea from the stalks and seed, with a few watermelon seed, and drank about a quart a day; it is as palatable as China tea, when sweetened with sugar or honey. In less than a month from my first using it, I passed a stone 3/8ths of an inch long and 3/8ths circumference, of an egg-like form. I have ever since, when troubled with any pain in the region of the kidneys, taken a strong tea of it for my common drink, through the day, and always found relief. I take it with my children for breakfast, once a week—they make no objection to the taste."

The compiler must have suffered from lameness as well as kidney stones, for the other clipping offered "a most valuable experienced remedy for a lameness, proceeding from any fixed contraction of the parts affected—from the pen of a late celebrated English Surgeon.

"Many years ago, when I lived in Yeoville, in Somersetshire, my advice was desired for a poor man's child, a boy about 9 years old, one of whose legs was contracted more than when a person is sitting in a chair. He could not stretch it nor move it; neither could it be extended by any person without injury to the part affected.

"I prescribed a relaxing linament, of which currier's oil was the chief ingredient, and ordered the parts affected to be gently rubbed with it, but it was of little service.

"The probable just consequences of this boy's living without the use of that limb, very much moved my pity: and while I was considering what further might be done for his relief, it came into my mind that the glovers of the town brought lamb and kid skins which they dry, stiff and hard, to be soft and supple as gloves, by rubbing them with a liquor made of the yolk of eggs and water.

"Hereupon I reasoned thus with myself, viz:—since this egg liquor is so efficacious in removing contractions from the part of dead animal fibres, vessels, and membranes, by art made dry, stiff and hard, why may it not be effectual when sufficiently applied to living animal fibres and membranes in a state of contraction? And I resolved to try its efficacy in the case of this poor boy.

"I ordered the contracted part of his leg to be gently rubbed two or three times a day with the egg liquor, and by this means he easily recovered the perfect use of his leg.

"The egg liquor I advised to be made in the

following manner: Take the yolk of a new laid egg, let it be beaten with a spoon to the greatest thinness, then, by a spoonful at a time, add three ounces of pure water, agitating the mixture continually, that the egg and water may be well incorporated. The liquor may be applied to the parts contracted, cold or only milk warm, by a gentle friction for a few minutes, three or four times a day. This remedy I have since advised in like cases, and with the like happy success; and others to whom I have communicated it, have found the same advantage from it in like cases. . . . T. LOBB."

Lobb's story apparently received wide attention, for the notebook contained two clippings of the identical article from two different publications.

Newspapers were not an unusual medium for dispensing medical advice in the nineteenth century. On April 20, 1841, for example, the *Southport* (Kenosha) *Telegraph* republished a prescription for avoiding malaria, a disease widespread in pioneer Wisconsin: "Drink cold tea, or buttermilk diluted with water, but no whiskey. Go out of your ploughed and newly cleared fields before the sun is down, and the miasma begins to rise, and keep in doors in the morning until the sun had dispersed the same."

The instructions not to drink probably appealed greatly for political, if not medical, reasons to the *Telegraph's* editor, the temperance advocate C. Latham Sholes, and to his numerous, like-minded readers in the Southport area. But the rest of the advice was fairly practical and helpful. In those days, the relationship between mosquitoes and malaria was not understood. The illness was believed to be caused by a harmful miasma, or vaporous air (malaria means "bad air" in Italian), that materialized in late afternoon and early morning, the times when mosquitoes are in fact most active. The Draper-Croffut book presented an explanation: "Heat so rarefies miasm as to make it comparatively innocuous. Hence the coolness of the early morning and of sundown throw the miasm to the surface by condensing or concentrating it; while the heat

of the day of the Summer's sun so rarefied and lightened it as to send it upward to the clouds; and the great practical truth follows, that miasm exerts its most baleful influence on human health, as it ascends at sunrise, and descends at sunset."

For those who had to go outside during the dangerous period, they had a suggestion for avoiding "malarious diseases, such as diarrheas, dysenteries, and chills and fevers." This was to eat "a hearty and warm meal before entering upon the exposure. The philosophy of the matter is, that a hot or hearty meal, or at least a cup of hot, strong coffee, with milk, so excites the circulation and so invigorates the whole frame that it acquires the power of resisting the disease-engendering influences of the miasm."

Typically, the medical advice appearing in newspapers was dispensed in an evangelical, testimonial style, and attribution to a foreign doctor was the crowning mark of authenticity. Another personal recipe notebook among the Society's holdings, begun on January 3, 1864, by Ann E-liza Tenney, of an early Madison family, included among the home remedies and health aids two representative newspapers clippings about cures for cholera. One of them extolled the

formula of one Rev. Dr. Hamlin of Constantinople, who "saved hundreds of lives by the following simple preparation, during the terrible raging of cholera in that city, a few years since. In no case did the remedy fail, where the patient could be reached in season. It is no less effective in cholera morbus and ordinary diarrhoea. A remedy so easily procured, and so vitally efficacious, should be always at hand. An ordinary phial of it can be had for 25 cents, and no family should be without it over night.—The writer of this received the receipt a few days since, and having been seriously attacked with the cholera morbus the past week, can attest to its almost magical influence in affording relief from excruciating pain. He ardently hopes that every one whose eyes trace these lines, will cut this article from the paper, and procure the medicine without delay. Its prompt application will relieve pain, and presumptively save life:

"Take one part Laudanum;*
    one part Camphorated Spirit;
    two parts Tincture of Ginger;
    two parts Capsicum.†

"Dose.—One teaspoonful in a wine-glass of water. If the case is obstinate, repeat the dose in three or four hours."

Cholera was the term used for the whole range of severe stomach upsets, not only the killer variety. Consequently, any collection of home cures included many different formulas and procedures each with its proven testimonial. One of those listed in Draper's book may not have cured the affliction, but must have provided the patient with a pleasant glow to cushion the misery:

"Dr. P. B. RANDOLPH, the distinguished American author and traveler, while in Europe and Egypt, in 1861–62, had many cases of genuine Asiatic cholera come under his observation, and has known the following treatment tried with unvarying success:

"Best French brandy, one pint; cayenne pepper, one quarter of an ounce; sweet spirits of ni-

ter,* one ounce; fluid extract of Cannabis Indica,† half an ounce. Keep in tight, glass-corked bottles.

"When the patient is attacked, put him to bed instantly; give one table-spoonful of the mixture in a gill of sweetened warm water every half hour till the symptoms cease, which will be the case when the patient perspires freely. Then let him be towel-bathed in warm water, four quarts, in which a little soda-ash has been dissolved. If the disease has reached the second or cramp stage, increase the dose and shorten the intervals one-half. Pound some ice, roll it in a towel, and lay it along the spinal column, or backbone; or, what is infinitely better, lay a roll of cotton, steeped in chloroform, along the spine, instantly covering it with oiled silk, to prevent the least evaporation. In three minutes, if this be properly done, the patient will experience very peculiar, and, perhaps, unpleasant sensations. Let this be kept on ten minutes, and unless the symptoms abate, repeat it, both on the back and across the abdomen."

"Responsible men from neighboring counties in Maryland testify to numerous instances of the fat-bacon treatment with uniform success, while those who depended on medicines alone, had, in most cases, fallen victims to the disease."

Like everyone else at that time, the authors gleaned such information from newspapers, not medical authorities, and unquestionably the reprinting in a volume by a distinguished scholar gave the remedies a certain authenticity. A discomfiting procedure for curing hay fever they attribute to a September, 1868, issue of the *Cincinnati Commercial*. After the long, requisite testimonial came the prescription: "Take one quart of warm rain water, add a tablespoonful of salt; stir till dissolved, and by means of a 'nasal douche,' pass it through the nostrils, to be followed immediately by another quart of warm water, to which add zinc sulphate, six grains; morphine, two-thirds of a grain; pure glycerine, three drams; carbolic acid, fifteen to twenty-five

*Tincture of opium.
†Red Pepper.

*Sodium carbonate.
†Marijuana.

drops; stir well, and pass it through the nostril as before. The first quart should be passed through the nose under a high pressure, to remove as much as possible all poisonous secretions from the linings of the nose; while the last should be done slowly, to allow the medicine to act on the mucous membrane. This can be regulated by elevating or lowering the reservoir of the douche. Repeat the operation from four to six times a day. The salt and water should be administered some two weeks prior to the time of attack, as it is of great benefit in removing whatever the irritating cause may be. For sulphate of zinc can be substituted any astringent—tannin, sugar of lead, etc.—but morphine, glycerine, and carbolic acid are deemed indispensable." Surprisingly, perhaps, this treatment for hay fever was still being prescribed well into the present century.

Other advice in the Draper-Croffut book could have caused even greater harm. In cholera, which produces potentially fatal dehydration, for instance, they declared: "In this disease the thirst is often uncontrollable, *but if the patient drinks water he will die.*"

In general, they were highly suspicious of cold water, warning, in less sinister terms, against it while eating: ". . . [C]old water largely used, that is to the extent of a glass or two at a meal, especially in cold weather, attracts to itself so much of the heat of the system, in raising said water to the temperature of the body (about 100°) that the process of digestion is arrested; in the meanwhile, giving rise to a deathly sickness of stomach, to twisting pains, to vomitings, purgings, and sometimes even to cramps, to fearful contortions and sudden death; which things would have been averted had the same amount of liquid in the shape of simple hot water been used." Milk with meals was discouraged, too: ". . . [T]he considerable employment of simple milk at meals, by sedentary people—by all, except the robust—will either constipate or render bilious. . . . "

Actually, Draper and Croffut frowned on liquid in general with meals: "Too much fluid on the stomach dilutes the gastric juice, prevents its direct and immediate action on the food, and, consequently, retards the process of digestion till the fluids have been absorbed."

Onions played a prominent medicinal role in the Draper-Croffut dispensary. (Strangely, however, garlic is never mentioned, probably reflecting the authors' Yankee backgrounds; many continental European and Middle Eastern groups, beginning with the ancient Egyptians, ascribed curative and restorative properties to the aromatic bulb.) Besides its previously noted use in rabies treatment, onions appeared in a number of remedies among the six and a half pages of cures for colds, coughs, and consumption: "Take into the stomach, before retiring for the night a piece of raw onion, after chewing. In an uncooked state, this esculent is very heating, and tends to collect the waters from the lungs and throat, causing immediate relief to the patient.

Even more space in these collections was devoted to salves. Most nineteenth-century families had sworn-by formulas that soothed or cured cuts, bruises, burns, and assorted aches and pains. Many are well remembered; some are still in use to this day. Turpentine, pitch, rosin, beeswax, oils from various trees, herbs, camphor, methyl, and various kinds of fat were ingredients frequently specified.

In *A Helping Hand*, Draper and Croffut offered numerous blends: "A mixture of lard and Scotch snuff is very efficacious for fresh wounds. A salve for hurts caused by needles, pins, etc., may be made of rye flour, soap, and molasses; or the white of an egg beaten up with camphor. Sweet mutton tallow is an excellent healing salve.

"Take one ounce lard, two ounces white-pine turpentine, half an ounce beeswax, half an ounce resin, one ounce strained honey, and one-fourth ounce gum camphor made fine, when melted together, add slowly one ounce laudanum, stirring all the while until cold; if the laudanum were all added at once, it would cause the mass to run over. After taking some good purifying pill, this salve will cure salt-rheum, and other eruptions, or sores.

"Melt together four ounces of white-pine turpentine, two ounces each of laudanum, lard and honey, one ounce each of beeswax and rosin, and half an ounce each of gum camphor and sugar of lead. A valuable salve is made by adding about ten per cent of phenic or carbolic acid to butter or other fatty matter used for such purpose."

Of course, they included a recipe for the widely known Green Mountain Salve: "To five pounds of resin, and four ounces each of beeswax, Burgundy pitch, and mutton or deer's tallow; an ounce each of the oils of hemlock, red cedar, and origanum,* balsam of fir, Venice turpentine, and very finely pulverized verdigris.† Melt the resin, beeswax, Burgundy pitch, and tallow together, adding the oils, having rubbed the verdigris up with a little of the oils, and put in the other articles; stir well, and pour into cold water, working it like wax until cool enough to form into rolls. This is excellent for rheumatism, or local pain, or weaknesses."

The Rev. Father Cormac Dwyer of Milwaukee still has the formula for skunk oil salve made by Ann Coughlin, an Elroy luncheon shop and bakery owner who was known to everyone in town as "Grandma Coughlin": "One pint of rendered fat from a skunk. Let cool for a short time and then add: Equal parts of menthol and camphor crystals, oil of pine, eucalyptus and sweet birch. Mix well. Try for the strength you desire—mild, medium, or strong."

Grandma Coughlin used her skunk oil as a sure cure for lumbago or other rheumatic pains "in the loins and lower back," a cure sought by many people: "It was the secret sourdough pancake method and the skunk oil salve," Father Dwyer recalls. "The unsuspecting patient was asked to lie on the stomach on a cot next to the old wood stove and to bare the buttocks and loins. Grandma Coughlin would then grease the area well with 'skunk oil.' Then she proceeded to bake six or eight large sourdough pancakes on the top of the well-greased stove. When they were golden brown on both sides they were deftly flipped from the hot stove onto the bare skin, which was quickly covered with a flannel cloth and then a heavy blanket placed on top. Until it had cooled down the patient was to remain there on the cot. However, many leaped from the cot and ran or jumped around the room. Some swore they were completely cured, while others just swore. It was one of those kill-or-cure remedies, but still many came on the suggestion of others to take the secret treatment."

Then there were the tonics and elixirs widely recommended for that tired, rundown feeling. Many certainly must have made a person euphoric, laced as they were with alcohol in some form and drugs (now illegal, but then ordinarily available) such as Cannabis or Indian hemp (marijuana) and opium derivatives.

Draper and Croffut offered their readers a variety of mixtures for a variety of generalized complaints, including: "For general debility and chronic weakness, put an ounce of carbonate of iron in a pint of blackberry wine, and take a tablespoonful three times a day before meals. For a good tonic bitters, take a handful each of the roots of Indian hemp, bitter root, milkweed, lady-slipper root, and prickly-ash bark; bruise, and add a pint of boiling water; when cold, bottle and add a pint of good whiskey, and an ounce of carbonate of iron, and take half a wine-glassful three times a day."

*Wild marjoram.
†Acetate of copper.

Not all such brews were alcoholic, of course. Tea made from slippery elm bark was a popular and versatile home remedy. "Break the bark into bits, pour boiling water over it, cover it and let it infuse until cold. Sweeten, ice, and take for summer disorders, or add lemon juice and drink for a bad cold," advised the *Every-day Cook-book and Encyclopedia of Practical Recipes*, first published in the 1880's.

The same book suggested "Raspberry Vinegar" as a pick-me-up: "To four quarts red raspberries, put enough vinegar to cover, and let them stand twenty-four hours; scald and strain it; add a pound of sugar to one pint of juice; boil it twenty minutes, and bottle; it is then ready for use and will keep for years. To one glass of water add a great spoonful. It is much relished by the sick. Very nice."

Sulphur, too, was highly regarded, particularly to help "clear the blood" in the spring after the inactivity of winter. Mrs. Norman J. Gerber of Stoughton inherited this "Blood Medicine" from her Irish ancestors, basically the well-known sulphur-and-molasses tonic: "One-half quart syrup, two teaspoons cream of tartar, two tablespoons sulphur, and one teaspoon of salts and charcoal." The iron, calcium, and other minerals in molasses and syrup no doubt raised the energy level in the days before vitamin supplements, while the laxative properties of sulphur seemed to prove the blood had been cleansed.

Compared with similar volumes of the day, the Draper-Croffut prescription for good health and disease prevention and cure was fairly typical, mixing large doses of Christian morality and common sense with all the contemporary old wives' brews and other popular remedies and notions. Some of their advice reflected the newest theories. At a time, for instance, when bathing and fresh air were still highly suspect, the two urged regular baths in winter and summer and open windows for sleeping all year around. At the same time, they repeated some quackeries of the day, citing only the advocates as authorities, as in this rabies entry: "In large numbers of well-attested cases in our country, the poison from the bite of rabid dogs and rattlesnakes has been completely extracted by the application of the mad-stone—a porous stone, resembling the piece of lava used by painters. This stone, applied to the wound, adheres firmly; after two or three hours, it is taken off, soaked in warm water to divest it of the poison it has absorbed, and thus applied till the virus is entirely extracted, when it will cease to adhere, and the greenish poisonous matter no longer appear on the water. It is idle to ridicule the successful effects of this simple remedy of nature. Whether cupping, or some other powerful drawing remedies may not produce the same results, should be faithfully tested, as some substitute for the mad-stone, accessible to all, is greatly needed. Mrs. TAYLOR, of Terre Haute, and JOSEPH BAUGH, near Bloomington, Indiana, possess mad-stones which have for many years cured every case in which they have been used. A quarry of mad-stone is said to have been recently discovered by Rev. E. T. RITCHER, on his farm, a few miles from Indianapolis."

Furthermore, other procedures to which they devoted space must have been bizarre even then. In their Scarlet Fever section, for instance, Draper and Croffut included "The mode of treatment of scarlet fever resorted to by Dr. SCHNEEMANN, physician to the King of Hanover. It is as follows, and exceedingly simple: From the first day of the illness, and as soon as we are certain of its nature, the patient must be rubbed morning and evening over the whole body with a piece of bacon, in such a manner that, with the exception of the head, a covering of fat is everywhere applied. In order to make this rubbing-in somewhat easier, it is best to take a piece of bacon the size of the hand, choosing a part still armed with the rind, that we may have a firm grasp. On the soft side of this piece slits are to be made, in order to allow the oozing out of the fat. The rubbing must be thoroughly performed, and not too quickly, in order that the skin may be regularly saturated with the fat.

"A syrup made of onions has cured many a child of a severe cold, and saved many a one from an attack of croup or lung fever. To prepare the syrup, slice the onion in a tin basin, pour upon it half a tea-cupful of molasses, or, what is better, honey; add a bit of butter as large as a small chestnut. Set the dish in the oven, and simmer slowly for an hour."

Counter-irritants were also apparently popular treatments for some complaints in the nineteenth century, their effectiveness being based on the fact that the condition was less painful than the cure. One of the suggested treatments for diphtheria illustrates this theory nicely. One is advised to supply hot compresses on the throat and "at the same time use a gargle made of one teaspoonful of cayenne pepper, one of salt, one of molasses, in a tea-cupful of hot water, and when cool, add one-fourth as much cider vinegar, and gargle every fifteen minutes until the patient requires sleep."

Occasionally, Draper and Croffut sound modern. Mouth-to-mouth resuscitation, a method they note was successfully used by a French surgeon to revive patients given too much chloroform, is perfectly described. And one of their cough remedies is in the best of today's mind-over-matter approach: "Place a glass or cup of *pure soft water* within reach, and whenever inclined to cough, or feel an irritation or tickling in the throat, take a swallow or sip, with a determination *not* to cough. Continue this perseveringly and the most vexatious cough will be removed speedily."

Draper and Croffut had no inclination to question the current wisdom that damp or cold or wet feet were the root of many ills, or that warm foot baths would help cure such afflictions as colic, "green sickness," convulsions, typhoid, and inflammation of the skin.

And they were free with flat-out pronouncements, some of which clearly revealed their moral righteousness: "The victims of [heart] disease are generally persons of irregular or wandering habits, or addicted to strong drink"; or, "Exercise strict control over the appetites and passions, with a fixed abhorrence of all excess and all unlawful gratifications whatsoever."

Others, from this perspective, are charmingly quaint: "[Baldness] is caused by keeping the head too warm"; "No man after the middle age, if he hopes to keep his mind clear, should think of working his brain after dinner . . . "; "It is generally advised that it is better to sleep resting upon the right side."

And then there was the matter of directional placement of a bed. "A medical writer in the *Dublin Journal of Medicine* [wrote Draper and Croffut] contends for the old notion that people sleep much better with their heads to the north. He has tried the experiment in the case of sick persons with marked effect, and insists that there are known to exist great electric currents, always crossing in one direction around the earth, and that our nervous systems are in some mysterious way connected with this electrical agent. Dr. JULIUS VON FISCHWEILLER, a German physician, who died a few years since at the advanced age of 109, always slept with his head to the north, and the rest of his body as nearly as possible in a meridinal position; by which, he thought, the iron in his body became magnetized, and thus increased the energy of the vital principle, and prolonged human life. Without attempting to decide whether the electric current, or magnetic forces, maintain their equilibrium in the human body more perfectly during sleep, when the head is to the north, it can do no harm, and *may* do good, to have the beds all head toward the north pole. Many persons contend that they can never rest as well with their heads in any other direction."

And for them, tobacco was one of the abiding evils of mankind. "Never indulge in the filthy, disgusting, and enervating practice (now a general vice among all so-called civilized nations) of smoking and chewing tobacco, as no other cause is more prolific of deleterious effects upon both mind and body." Tobacco, they declared, could make the blood "too fluid." and cited instances and authorities that showed that "sudden deaths and tobacco, among men, were usually found together," that three young men died within two years after forming a smoking club, that the use of tobacco could cause insanity. "Tobacco has spoiled and utterly ruined thousands of boys, including a dangerous precocity, developing the passions, softening and weakening the bones, deranging the nerves, and greatly injuring the spinal marrow, the brain, and the whole nervous fluid."

Such an injunction was no doubt a bit extreme. But it is difficult to quarrel with the Draper-Croffut preachments for moderation in all things—diet, alcoholic consumption, exercise, ventilation. And who will argue against the soundness of one of the basic precepts of their prescription for good health: "Always keep the head cool, and the feet warm"?

Home remedies continued to be collected and recorded late into the nineteenth and well into this century, even in urban areas where medical attention was more accessible and after commercial preparations were widely available. Mrs. Charles Kendall Adams, whose husband became the sixth president of the University of Wisconsin in 1892, had quite a store, including two interesting cures for sore throat. A gargle of one ounce each of tincture of iron and glycerine diluted with water was to be used carefully: "Do not touch the teeth with the preparation as it is very injurious to the enamel." (How to manage this was not explained!) Mrs. Adams' "Excellent Remedy for Sore Throat" was: "Cut a slice of fat salt pork and let it stand a minute or two in hot vinegar. Sprinkle the pork with black pepper and apply it to the throat, as hot as possible. When relieved, remove the pork and bandage the throat with soft flannel."

Naturally, the nineteenth-century homemaker was interested in less dire health concerns as well. The home kitchen produced a wide variety of health and beauty aids: tooth powder and paste, mouthwashes, deodorants, depilatories, hand and body lotions, and cosmetics of every kind. Miss Tenney, for example, entered three or four mixtures for both powdered and liquid dentifrices in her notebook. And she apparently made her own eau de cologne by mixing rectified spirits of wine with oils of bergamot,* lemon,

*A citrus.

rosemary (for which neroli—bitter orange—could be substituted), English lavender, and oranges.

Draper and Croffut offered numerous recipes for colognes, and directed their attention to other beauty problems as well. Some of their mixtures clearly were beyond the capabilities of the average reader, requiring as they did ingredients not readily available. For instance, their mixture that would "dye the hair flaxen" read: "Take a quart of lye, prepared from the ashes of vine twigs, briony,* celandine† roots, and turmeric, of each one-half an ounce; saffron and lily roots, of each two drams; flowers of mullein#, yellow stechas,§ broom, and St. John's wort, of each a dram. Boil these together, and strain off the liquid clear. Frequently wash the hair with this fluid, and it will change it, we are told, in a short time to a beautiful flaxen color." (Why they included the recipe at all is curious since they made it clear that they did not approve: "It is always vulgar to try to change the natural color of the hair, for there is a correspondence between hair and complexion which is violated by such tampering.")

*A viny herb.
†Pilewort, a yellow flowering plant.
#A herbaceous plant.
§French lavender.

Freckles were a vexatious beauty problem in times past. One removal concoction seems typical of the many, equally futile, often disfiguring suggestions: "Scrape horseradish into a cup of cold sour milk; let it stand twelve hours; strain, and apply two or three times a day."

Men contributed to the recipe file, too. The famed Progressive governor and senator, Robert M. La Follette, who as a teenager worked briefly as a barber, kept his thick, leonine hairdo manageable with twice-a-day applications of a tonic made of eight ounces of cologne, one ounce tincture of cantharides,* one-half dram oil of English lavender, and one-half dram of rosemary.

Soap, of course, was also made at home. All wood ashes from the various household stoves were saved (in a hollow tree trunk by one Yankee family), and when soap was to be made, water was poured over the ashes and drained into a wooden tub or other container. The resulting lye solution was mixed in a large kettle with the animal fat and rancid lard saved for the purpose, then boiled and stirred constantly until the mixture was creamy. (The length of boiling determined the hardness of the soap.) After cooling, it was cut into bars or pieces.

*Dried beetles; also used as an aphrodisiac known as "Spanish Fly."

For beauty soap, scents and oils could be added. Miss Tenney's notebook contained a formula for Palm Soap which called for melting two pounds of ordinary soap in a double boiler and adding a quarter of a pound of palm oil and "three penny worth" of oil of cinnamon and boiling it for six or eight minutes.

In many places, soap making—particularly for everyday household use—was never a lost art; elsewhere it has been enjoying a revival as a craft, as has making cosmetics. Many, also, are taking another look at traditional folk medicine and grandma's old cures.

It is very easy to be condescendingly amused or to cluck at the quackeries or bemoan the ignorance when reading the medical advice offered in nineteenth-century books and recipe files. Few among us today worry about the directional placement of our beds. And yet . . . there are those who ascribe beneficial properties to pyramidal shapes, or sea salt, or fertile eggs. Quackeries are still with us—one day the uranium cure, the next day Laetrile—in spite of enormous strides in medical knowledge during the past hundred years. Perhaps the real difference between today and yesterday is that there now exist government agencies to protect us from ourselves in our never-ending pursuit of infallible cures, youth-restoring cosmetics, and fast, FAST, FAST relief.

Chapter 7

COOKBOOKS

NINETEENTH-CENTURY WISCONSIN HOUSE-wives enlarged their culinary horizons much as do cooks today—by reading cookbooks and newspapers, and by exchanging recipes with friends. For most, economic realities limited the number of printed volumes that could be acquired. (Today's cookbook explosion is a modern phenomenon.) But unquestionably, the cookbooks and omnibus "how-to" collections (which usually included a recipe section) that began appearing at mid-century were exceedingly useful in a new and growing state.

When the period of Wisconsin's major settlement began, cookbooks had already passed beyond the province of the wealthy in the United States and were being written for all who could read English. The first truly American cookbook was already forty years old when Wisconsin became a territory. Published in 1796, it was entitled *American Cookery* and was written by Amelia Simmons, who described herself as an American Orphan. Before that, American-published cookbooks were reprints of English works. If they were revised at all, it was merely to exclude ingredients unavailable on this side of the Atlantic, as

was the first ever printed in America: Eliza Smith's *The Compleat Housewife*, published in England in 1727 and issued in 1742 by William Parks, public printer of Williamsburg, Virginia. Twelve American-reprinted English cookbooks were available in the United States when Amelia Simmons brought out her volume. A poorly educated woman, she had to hire someone to put her material into proper form for publication. She was knowledgeable, however, in the ways of the American kitchen, and was the first to include distinctive New World ingredients in her recipes, which were couched in a straightforward, vernacular style. Five of her recipes—for "Johnny Cake or Hoe Cake," "Indian Slapjack," and three for "A Nice Indian Pudding"—called for cornmeal, the first time that typically American ingredient had appeared in a cookbook published in the United States. Other culinary Americanisms included were cranberry tarts, Jerusalem artichoke, two recipes for "pompkin" pie, watermelon-rind pickles, and pearl-ash (purified potash) for leavening (a precursor of baking powder).

For the second edition four years later, Miss Simmons added those New England specialties,

Election Cake and Federal Pan Cake, the latter being a stove-top version of Rye 'n' Injun. Election Cake, rich bread-dough embellished with fruit and spices, traditionally concluded town meetings, while Rye 'n' Injun was the standard New England daily bread made of rye flour, white flint cornmeal, molasses, and yeast. As Federal Pan Cake, the yeast and molasses were eliminated, and milk was added; the cake was fried with lard, and the molasses could become a topping.

American Cookery went through at least eleven editions in the thirty-five years following its appearance. In the 1820's, others entered the field, most notably Lydia Maria Child, whose *The Frugal Housewife* became *The American Frugal Housewife* in the course of its thirty-two editions over twenty-one years, and Eliza Leslie, whose *Seventy-five Receipts, for Pastry, Cakes, and Sweetmeats* in 1828 was the first of a dozen or so cookbooks she produced during the next thirty years. Her final effort, *Miss Leslie's New Cookery Book* (1857), she described as a "complete manual of domestic cookery *in all its branches*" and emphasized buffalo, venison, and game as well as Indian meal.

Copies of both Mrs. Child and Miss Leslie's early American works found their way into the state and were on sale in Milwaukee bookstores as early as the 1840's. Others came in the baggage of early Yankees, New Yorkers, and Southerners. And emigrants from abroad carried books with them as well. One very old one in the collections of the Milwaukee County Historical Society is entitled *The Cook's Oracle,* the oracle in this case being a man, William Kitchiner, M.D. An Englishman, Dr. Kitchiner was decidedly not a one-book author. His other volumes, listed on the title page of his cookbook, reveal an oracular expertise—real or fancied—in a number of subjects: *The Art of Invigorating Life by Food, The Housekeeper's Oracle, The Horse and Carriage Keeper's Oracle, The Traveller's Oracle, The Economy of the Eyes, and Rules for Choosing and Using Spectacles, Opera Glasses, and Telescopes,* and *Observations on Singing.* He was also editor of *The National and*

Sea Songs of England. His cookbook very likely outshone all others when it came to sales, for it was published in numerous editions in both England and the United States, even long after Kitchiner's death in 1827.

In *The Cook's Oracle,* Dr. Kitchiner promoted an idea that was ahead of its time in 1818, when it first appeared: "The quantity of each article being accurately stated," he noted on the title page, "by weight or measure." In the introduction to the 1831 English edition—obviously a reprint of an earlier version—he wrote:

"My Receipts are the results of experiments carefully made, and accurately and circumstantially related; the Time requisite for dressing being stated; the Quantities of the various articles contained in each composition being carefully set down in Number, Weight, and Measure. The Weights are *Avoirdupois*; the Measure, *Lyne's* graduated Glass, i.e. a Wine pint divided into sixteen ounces, and the Ounce into eight Drachms . . . .

"This precision has never before been attempted in Cookery books, but I found it indispensable from the impossibility of *guessing* the quantities intended by such obscure expressions as have been usually employed for this purpose in former works:—

"For instance, a bit of this—a handful of that—a pinch of t'other,—do 'em over with an Egg,—and a sprinkle of salt,—a dust of flour,—a shake of pepper,—a squeeze of lemon,—or a dash of vinegar, etc. are the constant phrases. Season it to your Palate (meaning the Cook's) is another form of speech; now, if she has any,—it is very unlikely that it is in unison with that of her employers,—by continually sipping *piquante* relishes, it becomes blunted and insensible, and loses the faculty of appreciating delicate flavors,—so that every thing is done at random.

"These Culinary technicals are so very differently understood by the learned who write them, and the unlearned who read them, and their *'rule of thumb'* is so extremely indefinite, that if the same dish be dressed by different persons, it will generally be so different, that nobody would imagine they had worked from the same directions, which will assist a person who has not served a regular apprenticeship in the Kitchen, no more than reading *Robinson Crusoe* would enable a Sailor to steer safely from England to India."

Unfortunately other cookbook writers of the period here or abroad did not follow Dr. Kitchiner's recipe for precision, and it was not until the end of the century that Fannie Farmer came along to standardize measurements in America.

At least one non-English, European cookbook provided menu ideas on Wisconsin's frontier. An 1838 edition of *La Cuisinière Bourgeoise* (which means "everyday cooking" and was first published in 1742) was part of the household of Hercules Louis Dousman, the fur trader and business entrepreneur of Prairie du Chien who became one of Wisconsin's first truly wealthy men. It was used by the cooks in Dousman's elegant "House on the Mound," which was built in 1843. (Later rebuilt and called Villa Louis, the home is now a historic site operated by the State Historical Society of Wisconsin.)

Quintessentially French, the book begins with a brief manual on household arts and duties, designed for someone just entering domestic service; or, as the introduction put it, to be read by the lady of the house "from time to time to your domestics and thereby save you the trouble of repeating the same things over and over . . . . This work is [also] indispensable to single persons, exposed only to inept domestics." From there, *La Cuisinière Bourgeoise* goes on to all categories of recipes (but interestingly, no breads are included), then to the storage and serving of wines, and concludes with detailed instructions for putting on an elegant company dinner (including where and how to receive the guests) with suggested menus for twelve-course and fifteen-course repasts.

Later in the century, German settlers were also preparing dishes from books brought over from the old country. One at the Milwaukee County Historical Society, printed in Stuttgart in

1858 (again, a later edition of a much earlier— 1804—work) was merely entitled *Kochbuch* and was written by a woman named F. L. Löfflerin. (Various cookbooks, whose authors were known as Friedr. Luise Löffler, F. L. Löfflerin, and even Henriette Löffler, issued from Stuttgart and Augsburg for more than a century. This alone suggests the surname might be a mere pseudonym, since *löffler* means "spooner.") The cookbook was volume one of a larger work called *Praktisches Handbuch on Haushaltungstunst* (Practical Handbook on Home Economics) which offered advice for work in "kitchen and cellar, house and garden, sick room and nursery for mothers and daughters."

But Henriette Davidis was a better-known name than Löfflerin in Wisconsin's nineteenth-century German community. Writing in Germany, in the 1860's, Frau Davidis produced a number of books on cooking and home making for women and children, including *Praktisches Kochbuch für die gewöhnuliche und feinere Küche* (Practical Cookbook for the Everyday and Gourmet Cook). The Milwaukee County Historical Society has a copy of what is labeled the "14th noted and improved edition," published abroad in 1869. Ten years later, an American adaptation, *Praktisches Kochbuch für die Deutschen in Amerika,* was published by George Brumder in Milwaukee with Frau Davidis' picture as the frontispiece. However, the American revision is credited to one Hedwig Voss of Chicago who, according to the title page, made it conform to American ingredients, weights, and measures, and included useful information for coffee and tea klatsches plus a "lesson in napkin-folding."

Henriette Davidis' popularity in Wisconsin resulted in an English translation of her work in 1897, published by C. N. Caspar of Milwaukee and including "an English-German and German-English vocabulary of culinary terms." In 1904 Caspar arranged for a rewritten version, *German National Cookery for American Kitchens.* The Davidis books were not the first such volumes to be published in Milwaukee, however. As early as 1856 a cookbook bore a Milwaukee imprint, although actual publication was probably in Boston with distribution by a Milwaukee branch of the publisher. The book was Mrs. Mary Hooker Cornelius' well-known *Young Housekeeper's Friend: Or, a Guide to Domestic Economy and Comfort,* copyrighted in 1845 and published in many editions. (The Milwaukee publisher or distributor was Abram Whittemore, who operated a small publishing house and stationery and book store from the 1850's through the 1870's.)

Of course, information on cooking and household management was almost always included in the omnibus how-to books written by men. The Draper and Croffut volume, *A Helping Hand for Town and Country: An American Home Book of Practical and Scientific Information,* included sections on Domestic Economy (furnishings, cleaning, preserving and canning, etc.) and The Kitchen and Dining-Room (nutrition and recipes). As with the home remedies and much of the rest of the book, the authors compiled their homemaking material from secondary sources. Other books and newspapers are cited with some items, but most of the information and recipes, on the other hand, are unattributed.

Draper and Croffut were familiar with William Kitchiner's works. The British doctor is quoted at the beginning of The Kitchen and Dining-Room section with the observation—hardly original even in those days—that "the stomach is the main-spring of our system; if it be not sufficiently wound up to warm and support the circulation, the whole business of life will, in proportion, be ineffectually performed. We can neither think with precision, walk with vigor, sit down with comfort, nor sleep with tranquility. It influences all our actions." They also reproduce tables on the times required to digest various foods and on the "per cent of nutriment" as compiled by the noted military doctor, William Beaumont.

Some of Dr. Beaumont's research into the digestive process was performed when he was stationed at Fort Crawford in Prairie du Chien. His subject was a Canadian, Alexis St. Martin, whose gunshot wound to the stomach in 1822 never fully healed, providing the doctor with a "window" into the stomach. Draper and Croffut went on to interpret the findings:

"Such a table may be studied with interest and profit. It will be seen that a dollar's worth of meat, at twelve and a half cents per pound, goes as far as fifty cents worth of butter at twenty-five cents per pound; and that three pounds of flour, at four cents per pound, furnish about the same amount of nutriment as nine pounds of beefsteak, costing twelve and a half cents per pound; and a loaf of good home-made bread, of the same size, contains as much nutriment as a leg of mutton."

The introduction also contains a long discourse on the high nutritive value of "fresh red meat" and the proper way to cook it, attributed to Mrs. Sarah J. Hale, who is not further identified. (As editor of *Godey's Lady's Book,* author of several cookbooks, and a novelist, Mrs. Hale probably did not require further identification in her day.) The authors felt compelled to comment on several of her statements in footnotes.

"It is an established truth in physiology," wrote Mrs. Hale, "that man is omnivorous—that is, constituted to eat almost every kind of food, which separately nourishes other animals. His teeth are formed to masticate, and his stomach to digest flesh . . . ." Draper and Croffut noted at this point: "Some determined advocates of the vegetable system maintain, that the teeth and stomach of the monkey correspond, in structure, very closely with those of man, yet it lives on fruits—therefore, if man followed nature, he would live on fruits and vegetables. But though the anatomical likeness between man and monkeys is striking, yet it is not complete; the difference may be, and doubtless is, precisely that which makes a difference of diet necessary to nourish and develop their dissimilar natures. Those who should live as the monkeys do would most closely resemble them."

In extolling the benefits of eating animal flesh, Mrs. Hale went on to note that rulers of nations almost invariably eat meat. "Whenever the time

shall arrive that every peasant in Europe is able to 'put his pullet in the pot of a Sunday,' a great improvement will have taken place in his character and condition; when he can have a portion of animal food, properly cooked, once each day, he will soon become a *man*."

On this, Draper and Croffut felt compelled to point out, in a comment that might have been made today: "There is danger in extremes. 'All medical men agree,' says MISS CATHARINE E. BEECHER, 'that, in America, far too large a portion of the diet consists of animal food. As a nation, the Americans are proverbial for the gross and luxurious diet with which they load their tables; and there can be no doubt that the general health of the nation would be increased by a change in our custom in this respect. To take meat but once a day, and this in small quantities, compared with the common practice, is a rule, the observance of which would probably greatly reduce the amount of fevers, eruptions, headaches, bilious attacks, and the many other ailments which are produced and aggravated by too gross a diet.' "

Draper and Croffut, as they had in dispensing

home remedies, made questionable statements with great authority. They found, for instance, unusual properties in fresh-fallen snow. Two tablespoons full of it, they declared, were a fine substitute for one egg "in any compound that requires lightness rather than richness." And in their view, it "is probably the most natural yeast ever used, supplying atmosphere wherewith to puff up the dough, whereas other methods only supply carbonic gas." Saleratus (baking soda) as a leavening agent, they said, "is unquestionably bad, very bad. Canker in the mouth, ulcerated bowels, weak stomachs, and bad blood are its ordinary effects." (But several pages further on, they include it in many of their biscuit and bread recipes.)

Occasionally, a sense of humor is displayed in a recipe; but whether this pinch of leavening was supplied by Draper and Croffut or the source of the recipe is impossible to tell. Take, for example, this formula for Wedding Johnny-Cake: "One pint sour cream, the same of sweet milk, half a cup butter, three eggs, table-spoonful of salt, same of soda, one quart of meal, one pint of flour, one pint of raisins, half pint of citron. This makes a very large cake, and is delicious; and if one does not marry more than once in a life-time he can well afford to make it."

Other recipes show their tenuous grasp of the subject: "*Steaks Maintenon.*—Half fry; stew them [mutton steaks] while hot, with herbs, crumbs, and seasoning; put them in paper immediately, and finish on the gridiron. Be careful the paper does not catch; rub a bit of butter on it first to prevent that."

And there are the usual pronouncements by foreign authorities: "In an able article by BARON LIEBIG, in the *London Popular Science Review*, it is asserted that 'tea acts directly on the stomach, whose movements sometimes can be so much augmented by it, that strong tea, if taken fasting, inclines to vomiting. Coffee, on the contrary, furthers the peristalic movement downwards; and, therefore, the German man of letters, more accustomed to a sitting life, looks on a cup of coffee, without milk, and assisted by a cigar, as a very acceptable means of assisting certain organic processes.' "

With few exceptions, most cooking books, whether foreign or American, presupposed a basic knowledge of methodology and procedures until well into the nineteenth century. Directions were extremely sketchy if they were given at all; ingredient amounts were inexact (except for pastry); and cooking times usually just specified "until done." It was not until mid-century that cookery in America began to become more precise and scientific and a subject for serious study. Catharine Beecher is credited as a prime founder of the homemaking movement in the 1840's with *A Treatise on Domestic Economy for the Use of Young Ladies at Home and at School* (1841) which advanced the novel idea that the household arts were proper subjects for systematic academic instruction. To further the "habits of system and order: in everything, including cooking," she published *Miss Beecher's Domestic Reciept-Book* in 1846. More than just a compendium of recipes, the book also provided guidance on cooking utensils, buying and storing food, use of ovens, child feeding, and the preparation of "temperance drinks." Miss Beecher continued writing and working for education in the household arts until her death in 1878. In 1869, with her famous sister Harriet Beecher Stowe as collaborator, she brought out *The American Woman's Home; or, Principles of Domestic Science*, and in 1873 revised it on her own as *The New Housekeeper's Manual*. That same year (she was then seventy-three), she produced a book of 500 recipes, *Miss Beecher's Housekeeper and Healthkeeper*. Sold door-to-door, these books, according to Catharine Beecher, were carried by salesmen to every state in the Union.

By the 1870's, the movement promoted by Miss Beecher's tireless preachments—coupled with the need, created by growing urbanization, for information and instruction in diet and nutrition and the handling of "boughten" instead of home-grown foods—resulted in the establishment of ladies' cooking schools in New York, Boston, and other large cities. The Boston Cooking School is the one best remembered today because of one of its principals, Fannie Farmer. The first edition of Miss Farmer's *Boston Cooking-School Cook Book* appeared in 1896 and substituted standardized measuring and precise instructions for the jumble of teacups, walnut-sized lumps, coffee and dessert spoons, gills, handfuls, and admonitions to "cook until done." This standardization, and the recipes, were worked out by the school's founder, Mary Johnson Bailey Lincoln, together with Miss Farmer, who believed "correct measurements are absolutely necessary to insure the best results."

But not all the cooking classes of this period were designed for genteel, middle-class ladies. About the same time, in the 1880's and 1890's, reformers and pioneer social workers were establishing courses and facilities to improve the dietary lot of the urban poor and the immigrant. (Often the pupils were not as willing or eager to embrace new foods and new ways as were the pupils in Miss Farmer's classes. One of the participants in the 1890's New England Kitchen experiment about the scientific feeding of working men is said to have told the director, pioneer home economist and social worker Ellen H. Richards: "I don't want to eat what's good for me; I'd ruther eat what I'd ruther.")

One cookbook that grew out of such organized classes is a Wisconsin work almost as famous as Fannie Farmer's: *The Settlement Cook Book, The Way to a Man's Heart*. This was the product of an energetic, indomitable Milwaukeean, Elizabeth Black Kander.

Lizzie (as she was known) was born on May 28, 1858, shortly after John and Mary Black moved to Milwaukee from Green Bay where her father had been a merchant since 1840. She grew up on Milwaukee's South Side, graduating from Milwaukee High School in 1879 in the days when not many girls went beyond grade school. In 1881 she married Simon Kander, a clothing salesman.

The Kanders never had children, and from the earliest days of her marriage, Lizzie channeled her considerable energy into good works through various organizations within the Jewish community. She served as president of the Ladies Relief Sewing Society, which met in the vestry room of Temple Emanu-El to "alleviate the sufferings of the poor and needy by furnishing them with clothings." The particular poor and needy the ladies had in mind were the increasing numbers of Jews among the rising tide of immigrants, particularly from Eastern Europe, in the latter part of the nineteenth century.

Mrs. Kander and a few other women in the Milwaukee Jewish Mission soon realized that clothing was not enough, and in the mid-1890's organized the Keep Clean Mission. Its goals were to help improve sanitary conditions, maintain school attendance among immigrant children, and help speed acculturation through recreation and skills classes in sewing, darning, mending, crocheting, embroidery, painting, and drawing. Shortly thereafter, the Milwaukee Jewish Mission and the Sisterhood of Personal Service established a social settlement house, known as The Settlement, in the heart of the immigrant Jewish district at North Fifth Street between Galena and Cherry streets. To the Keep Clean Mission program they added a night school, a cooking school, manual training classes, and playgrounds for babies and mothers.

Lizzie Black Kander was elected president of The Settlement, a position she held for eighteen years. In addition to her administrative and fund-raising activities, she taught the cooking classes. The neat, precise, lesson-by-lesson notebook she compiled for the first class in 1898 still exists among her papers in the Wisconsin Jewish Archives at the State Historical Society of Wisconsin. The recipes were obviously designed to provide maximum nutrition at the least cost; they were also completely Americanized recipes: hasty pudding, graham muffins, creamed cod, gingerbread, orange-banana custard, Boston browned potatoes.

In those days—long before the mimeograph and Xerox machines—a great deal of class time had to be spent copying the day's lesson recipe from the blackboard, time Mrs. Kander felt

could be better used in other ways. She decided to get the recipes printed, even though the meager Settlement funds could not provide the $18 needed. A friendly printer helped her and her committee solicit advertisements, and the result, in April, 1901, was a 174-page book containing her lesson recipes, augmented by recipes contributed by committee members and their friends, as well as European dishes from the students.

After classroom distribution, about 1,000 copies were left over. These were quickly sold out through a Milwaukee merchant for 50 cents each. A second edition in 1903 further increased the demand for the book, a demand that grew to such an extent that Mrs. Kander and her committee formed the philanthropic Settlement Cook Book Company that has shepherded the book through thirty-three editions—the latest expanded and enlarged in 1965 and published by Simon and Schuster—with total sales approaching two million. Proceeds from *The Settlement Cook Book* made possible the building of the Abraham Lincoln House in 1911; and in 1928 the Settlement Cook Book Company provided the $60,000 needed to buy the Milwaukee University High School building on North Milwaukee Street for the Jewish Community Center. It became quite an honor for a Milwaukee woman to be asked for a recipe for possible inclusion in a new edition. Mrs. Kander required that new recipes go through many testings by herself, relatives, and friends to determine if they met with her standards of taste and nutrition.

In the 1920's, Mrs. Kander served on the Milwaukee School Board and with the other two women members pushed through the establishment of the Girls' Trade and Technical High School. In the year she died, 1940, the twenty-third edition of her book was published.

Mrs. Kander's fund-raising with a cookbook was the most successful in Wisconsin, and, according to a national authority, perhaps the most successful in the entire United States. But it was not the first, either in Wisconsin or nationally. Such fund-raising projects began during the

Civil War (1861–1865) to raise money for battle casualties and their families. Just which was the first in Wisconsin is virtually impossible to determine. The earliest Wisconsin listing in *America Charitable Cooks* by Margaret Cook, the most complete bibliography of 1861–1915 fund-raising cookbooks, is *Our Cook Book*, produced by the young ladies of the First Congregational Church of Beloit in 1881. That same year, members of the Fond du Lac Relief Society, Home for the Friendless, compiled *The Fountain City Cook Book*, "reliable recipes from experienced housekeepers." *The Capital City Cook Book*, published by the Women's Guild of Grace Episcopal Church, Madison, came out in 1883, with a second edition in 1884 and a third in 1906.

Two more known to have appeared in the 1880's were the *Appleton Cook Book*, "compiled under the auspices of the Tuesday Night Workers, First Congregational Church, Appleton," and *The Good Cheer Cook Book*, put together by the Ladies' Aid Society of the Episcopal Church, Chippewa Falls.

Within twenty-five years, many other Wisconsin groups and organizations, mostly church-related, had published such books, often includ-

ing ads from local merchants to insure a profitable venture—the Ladies of the Charity Circle of Oshkosh, 1892; *The Milwaukee Cook Book* by Mrs. J. Magie for the benefit of the Wisconsin Training School for Nurses, 1894; the Ladies of the first M. E. Church of Menasha, 1899; the Christian Endeavor Society of the First Congregational Church, Madison, 1900; Ladies of the First Presbyterian Church, Wausau, 1900; Ladies' Society of the Free Baptist Church, Oakland Center, 1902; Ladies of Kingsley Methodist Church, Milwaukee, 1907. And a 1912 manuscript for a household hints-recipes book of contributions from members of the Wisconsin Political Equality League is among the papers of the famed suffragist Ada James. To this day, cookbooks are financing all sorts of worthy causes in the state.

The powerful appeal of recipes was not lost on those engaged in profit-making enterprises, either. Manufacturers of medical nostrums, food products, and kitchen equipment conveyed their advertising messages through the medium of numerous cookbooks during the last 125 years. One of the first was probably Caleb M. Bement's 1852 catalogue for his steam mill in Albany, New York, to which he added *Hints from Cousin Susan's Receipt Book*. This collection probably never enjoyed a readership very far from the area of Bement's mill, unlike the patent medicine cookbooks, published annually at least by 1864 and distributed widely.

Apparently revised every year, these books, about the size of pocket diaries, had an almanac-like quality, included calendars, and provided space on the back covers for local merchants' imprints. E. E. Barney of La Valle, Wisconsin, "dealer in dry goods, groceries, hardware, drugs, medicines, paints and oils" is immortalized on the back of an 1879 *Ransom's Family Receipt Book* now in the advertising ephemera collection of the State Historical Society. The recipes—including soups, desserts, breakfast dishes, and preserves—were offered with an advertising message that was probably not unsettling in its day: "If the 'receipts' make you sick, the medicines will cure you." The Ransoms, of Buffalo, New York, included a household remedies section which, unsurprisingly, promoted Ransom products: Dr. Ransom's Hive Syrup and Tolu, Dr. Trask's Magnetic Ointment, Dr. J. R. Miller's Magnetic Balm, Prof. Anderson's Dermador, and King of the Blood, a supply of which promised to take care of ailments ranging from croup to cancer. *Mrs. Winslow's Domestic Receipt Book* likewise promoted her famous Soothing Syrup, and at least one Wisconsin customer, Ann Eliza Tenney of Madison, pinned a page from Miss Winslow into her own recipe notebook.

Cookbooks, of course, were a natural promotional device for manufacturers of nationally distributed food products, a development of the 1870's and 1880's. In 1875, E. R. Durkee & Co. published the first of its many editions of the *Practical Cook Book,* and the Royal Baking Powder Company followed suit in 1878 with a collection of recipes by Guiseppi Rudmani of the New York Cooking School. Most of these cookbooks seem to have been offered as premiums, although some may have cost a nominal sum.

Around the turn of the century, housewives had the opportunity to add flour company cookbooks to their collections. *The Ceresota Cook Book* came out in 1898 and the *Gold Medal Cook Book* in 1904; both circulated widely. And many a treasured family recipe handed down to today's cooks originally appeared in one of the many editions of the popular Calumet Baking Powder Company cookbook.

In Wisconsin, the Malleable Iron Range Company of Beaver Dam, manufacturers of Monarch stoves, published the *Monarch Cook Book* by Helen Tomson in 1906; a rival stove company, Caloric, of Janesville, came out with the *Caloric Book of Recipes* in 1910. Included among the recipes and household hints in many advertising and fundraising cookbooks were culinary rhymes, or such coy items as the widely reprinted "Receipt for Cooking Husbands." This version appeared in the shellfish section of the *Milwaukee Cook Book* put out by the Kingsley Methodist Church group in 1907:

"A good many husbands are utterly spoiled by mismanagement. Some women go about it as if their husbands were bladders and blow them up. Others keep them constantly in hot water; others let them freeze by their carelessness and indifference. Some keep them in a stew by irritating ways and words. Others roast them. Some keep them in pickle all their lives. It cannot be supposed that any husband will be tender and good managed in this way, but they are really delicious when properly treated. In selecting your husband you should not be guided by the silvery appearance, as in buying mackerel, nor the golden tint, as if you wanted salmon. Be sure to select him yourself, as tastes differ. Do not go to market for him, as the best are always brought to your door. It is far better to have none unless you will patiently learn how to cook him. A preserving kettle of the finest porcelain is best, but if you have nothing but an earthenware pipkin, it will do, with care. See that the linen in which you wrap him is nicely washed and mended, with the required number of buttons and strings nicely sewed on. Tie him in the kettle by a strong silk cord called comfort, as the one called duty is apt to be weak. They are apt to fly out of the kettle and be burned and crusty on the edges, since, like crabs and lobsters, you have to cook them while alive. Make a clear, steady fire out of love, neatness and cheerfulness. Set him as near this as seems to agree with him. If he sputters and fizzes, do not be anxious; some husbands do this until they are quite done. Add a little sugar in the form of what confectioners call kisses, but not vinegar or pepper on any account. A little spice improves them, but it must be used with judgment. Do not stick any sharp instrument into him to see if he is becoming tender. Stir him gently; watch the while, lest he lie too flat and close to the kettle, and so become useless. You cannot fail to know when he is done. If thus treated, you will find him very digestible, agreeing nicely with you and the children, and he will keep as long as you want, unless you become careless and set him in too cold a place."

Several versified recipes received wide circulation. *The Capital City Cook Book* from Grace Church in Madison printed seventeen verses of "For the Kitchen." Draper and Croffut included all twenty-three in *A Helping Hand for Town and Country:*

Always have lobster-sauce with salmon,
And put mint-sauce your roasted lamb on.

Veal cutlets dip in egg and bread-crumb—
Fry till you see a brownish red come.

Grate Gruyere cheese on macaroni;
Make the top crisp, but not too bony.

In venison gravy, currant-jelly
Mix with old Port—See Francatelli.

In dressing salad, mind this law—
With too hard yolks use one that's raw.

Roast veal with rich stock gravy serve;
And pickled-mushrooms, too, observe.

Roast pork sans apple-sauce, past doubt,
Is "Hamlet" with the Prince left out.

Your mutton-chops with paper cover,
And make them amber brown all over.

Broil lightly your beefsteak—to fry it
Argues contempt of Christian diet.

Kidneys a finer flavor gain
By stewing them in good champagne.

Buy stall-fed pigeons. When you've got them,
The way to cook them is to pot them.

Wood-grouse are dry when gumps have marred
   'em—
Before you roast 'em always lard 'em.

To roast Spring chickens is to spoil 'em—
Just split 'em down the back and broil 'em.

It gives true epicures the vapors
To see boiled mutton, minus capers.

Boiled turkey, gourmands know, of course,
Is exquisite, with celery-sauce.

The cook deserves a hearty cuffing,
Who serves roast fowls with tasteless stuffing.

Smelts require egg and biscuit powder.
Don't put fat pork in your clam chowder.

Egg-sauce—few make it right, alas!—
Is good with blue-fish or with bass.

Nice oyster-sauce gives zest to cod—
A fish, when fresh, to feast a god.

Shad, stuffed and baked, is most delicious—
'Twould have electrified Apicius.

Roasted in paste, a haunch of mutton,
Might make ascetics play the glutton.

But one might rhyme for weeks this way,
And still have lots of things to say.

And so I'll close—for, reader mine,
This is about the hour I dine.

Draper and Croffut offered another rhyme in their collection of recipes:*

Sidney Smith's Winter Salad

Two large potatoes, passed through kitchen
   sieve,
Unwonted softness to the salad give.
Of mordant mustard add a single spoon—
Distrust the condiment which bites so soon;
But deem it not, thou man of herbs, a fault,
To add a double quantity of salt;
Three times the spoon with oil of Lucca crown,
And once with vinegar procured from town.
True flavor need it and your poet begs,
The pounded yellow of two well-boiled eggs,
Let onion atoms lurk within the bowl,
And scarce suspected, animate the whole;
And lastly on the favored compound toss
A magic tea-spoon of anchovy sauce;
Then, though green turtle fail, though
   venison's tough,
And ham and turkey are not boiled enough,
Serenely full, the epicure may say:
"Fate can not harm me—I have dined to-day."

*This culinary rhyme, attributed to a Reverend Sidney Smith and dating to Colonial times, is included in a collection of beverages and sauces of Colonial Virginia.

Cookbooks of another sort were found in many nineteenth-century kitchens: notebooks or scrapbooks filled with handwritten recipes from family and friends, and clippings from newspapers, women's magazines, almanacs, and farm journals. That notebook in Bishop Jackson Kemper's papers (referred to in Chapter 6) contains fifty-one pages of handwritten recipes. It also contains a single newspaper clipping in the recipe section "HOW A FARMER OUT WEST PRESERVES HIS EGGS.—A gallon pot is filled with eggs; and one pint of lime, of the consistency of common white-wash, poured in, and the pot filled with water. A board is then placed on the top, and the water, which is never changed, as well as the eggs, remains pure and sweet. This practice is the one most common in France, the inhabitants of which, to their love of frogs and soup, add also, it appears, a very commendable taste for eggs."

Ann Eliza Tenney, of the pioneer Madison family, started her recipe collection in a composition book on January 3, 1864. At the end of many recipes she carefully recorded the source: Aunt Evelyn, Mother, Grandmother Chaney, Mrs. Joel P. Mann, Abbie Noyes, Juliette P. Tenney, etc. As is the case with such collections, virtually all of her recipes were for cakes and other baked goods, jams, pickles, and the like—things requiring some exactitude of ingredients and which were not made every day. Apparently even novices in the kitchen or brides didn't need to write down the ordinary, everyday dishes they had observed being made or had helped to prepare all their lives.

This was true for immigrant women as well.

Many wrote down the sort of family recipe associated with treats or special occasions. Mrs. Anna Zwicker Hochstetter of Madison had begun just that sort of copy book when she lived in Germany before her marriage in about 1910. Afterwards, she and her husband lived in Switzerland, where she continued the book. When she came to Madison in 1913, her carefully written collection contained forty-three puddings, cakes, jellies, tortes, and candies. Later additions included more ordinary dishes, many with New World ingredients such as turkey, corn, and cranberries. Most of the additions made in her new home were also handwritten, but some pages were interleaved with clippings from the German-language newspaper, *Milwaukee-Herold,* and from the magazine *Die Hausfrau,* also published in Milwaukee. (Her son Ernest continues to cherish the foods his mother made, and has preserved her cookbook.)

After World War I, more and more printed information about food and new and old recipes became available. Increasingly, newspapers started or expanded women's pages, the circulation of new and established women's magazines climbed steadily, and new cookbooks proliferated. Church groups and service clubs revised old fund-raisers or issued new ones. The *Milwaukee Journal* periodically published hard-cover collections from their pages, as did other newspapers. The Stout Institute (since grown into the University of Wisconsin—Stout) in Menomonie published *The Bride's Cook Book* in 1925. The appetite for such books has been and continues to be insatiable, as the thousands of titles published since Wisconsin became a state testify.

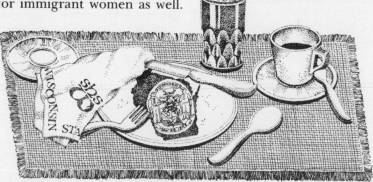

Chapter 8

THE CORPORATE KITCHEN

Throughout the united states, certain comestibles are immediately identified with Wisconsin. Beer and sausage, cheese and butter are the first that come to mind. But other state products also make significant, though often anonymous, contributions to the nation's larder—and to the gross state and national products. Over the years, for example, Wisconsin has ranked among the top states in production of potatoes, cranberries, honey, maple syrup and sugar, and freshwater fish. Wisconsin is one of only five states that produce spearmint and peppermint oils; and some of Wisconsin comprises a large section of the valley of the Jolly Green Giant. In other times, wheat growing, flour milling, and the sugar beet were important elements in the state's economic picture.

So marvelously diverse have been Wisconsin's food products that no single published account does them justice; likewise the industrial advancements in machinery and processing that have had such an impact upon agriculture remain a largely untold story. Many aspects of this story are beyond the scope of this book, but no discussion of Wisconsin's dietary riches would be complete without some glimpses (highly selective and non-inclusive) into the business end of food.

Wisconsin's commercial food industry began, of course, with the Indians who bartered meats, fish, and garden and woodland products, along with furs, to the earliest Europeans who traversed this land. By the late 1700's, they had added maple syrup and cranberries to their merchandise. In fact, without Indian help with foodstuffs, Wisconsin's first white settlers would barely have survived.

But with the arrival of significant numbers of non-Indians in the 1830's, that situation changed rapidly. Wisconsin became a farmer's territory and state, and for many decades farming dominated the working day of the majority of state residents. (Not until about 1930 did urban dwellers outnumber rural people in Wisconsin.) The 1850 census listed 40,865 farmers—more than all other occupations combined. And the processing of the fruits of the harvest quickly became an important occupation of the state's growing population.

Before the Civil War, wheat was king in Wisconsin, which ranked eighth among the states in production in 1849, reached the second position in 1859, and was first in 1860. Farmers long remembered 1860 as "the golden year," when production reached between 27 and 29 million bushels, compared to 4.3 million bushels ten years earlier. The state's preeminent position that year was due in part to a partial crop failure in Illinois, which invariably led in other years.

A happy combination of circumstances accounted for wheat's early supremacy in Wisconsin: excellent water routes by way of the Great Lakes and the Mississippi River, so that getting the wheat to populous areas was not a problem; recent improvements in plows and harvesting machinery, so that preparing virgin soil was not the task it once had been; and the virgin soil itself, for growing superb first crops. But subsequent plantings of wheat depleted the soil, so Wisconsin's production began to fall.

Nevertheless, throughout most of the 1860's, Wisconsin stood second only to Illinois in wheat production—close to 20 million bushels a year. That figure remained fairly stable in the 1870's, but Wisconsin's rank slipped steadily from second, to fourth, to tenth, until finally by 1893, Wisconsin wheat production slipped below ten million bushels, and the state's standing to seventeenth. Except for a brief flurry during World War I, Wisconsin's wheat production has hovered between one million and three million bushels in modern times. (In 1977, for example, Wisconsin farmers produced 3,075,000 bushels of wheat, ranking thirty-fourth among the states.)

Though records of the wheat harvests have been carefully kept and recounted, the history of milling in the Badger state has fared less well. No one has chronicled the thousands of mills which used to dot Wisconsin waterways. Mostly they were geared to supply a local market, and often, in earliest days, the proprietor also did sawmilling or some other pioneer craft like tin- or black-smithing. Not until the Civil War ended did a few Wisconsin cities emerge as commercial milling centers: Milwaukee, La Crosse, Racine, Superior, Neenah, Menasha, Appleton, and Janesville—all towns with advantageous water power or transportation resources.

Milwaukee soon dominated, vying with St. Louis for national preeminence. Milwaukee's output climbed from almost 100,000 barrels a year in 1850 to about 200,000 barrels in 1862, to a million in 1883 and almost two million in the 1890's. But Milwaukee flour milling declined as rapidly as it rose, superseded by Minneapolis, which was closer to major wheat states. In 1913, Milwaukee production averaged little more than 625,000 barrels, and by 1977, apparently no wheat flour for household use was milled in Milwaukee or anywhere else in the state.

Today, Wisconsin's important past position in milling enterprises lives only in the history of one of the giants of the industry, the enormous multinational corporation known as General Foods. The capital and entrepreneurial foresight of Governor Cadwallader C. Washburn of Wisconsin was responsible for the founding of the company that gave rise to General Mills, the Gold Medal Flour company. When Washburn died in 1882, notables from Minnesota and Wisconsin came to his funeral.

The state's once-flourishing industry is occasionally the subject of feature stories that now and then appear in newspaper feature sections, often in stories about one of the many mills now converted to making animal feeds. But no more can householders stop off at the local mill—as they could in 1891 in Alma—and pick up a bag or barrel of Little Hatchet, Toboggan, or Extra Straight flour. The labels and empty sacks for such fancifully named local brands survive only as collectibles for museums and private collectors.

Even during wheat's heyday, the more far-sighted Wisconsin agriculturists knew that the boom could not last. Almost immediatly they identified dairying as a logical alternative—one which would take advantage of Wisconsin's ability to cultivate grasses and grains, its transportation network, and the practical experience that so many immigrants brought with them, especially from the state of New York and from Scandinavia, Germany, and Switzerland. Dairying and its prospects were mentioned more than twenty times in the State Agricultural Society's first volume of *Transactions*, published in 1852. Four score and seven years later, in 1939, anyone who spotted a Wisconsin license plate knew that it had become America's Dairyland—proclaimed that very year by state statute. Supremacy, however, had occurred by 1910, when Wisconsin's cheese output alone (148 million pounds) was first in the nation, with New York (105 million pounds) finally taking second place. (1978 production was 1.3 *billion* pounds, or 38 per cent of the nation's output, with Minnesota second at 450 million pounds.) This was in addition to butter, condensed milk, non-fat dry milk, ice cream, and—not to be forgotten—milk itself. Wisconsin has had a significant impact upon national and international markets, as well as upon dairying and milk-processing technology.

In 1839, the first year for which any agricultural statistics are available, the value of dairy products in Wisconsin Territory was a mere $35,677. Settlers—most of them from the New England states and New York, with a few from Illinois and Missouri—usually brought along a cow or two, or soon acquired one. The Scandinavian and German influx had likewise begun, and these newcomers certainly continued to pursue familiar dairying practices in their farm operations. (These cattle were not the first in the state, however. French-Canadians had raised cattle for milk and meat, and the lead miners of the late 1820's and early 1830's also imported livestock.) However, all of these early cows mainly supplied milk, butter, and cheese for the farmers' own tables.

Tending and milking the cows and making dairy products were women's work, and the descendants of one such housewife, Mrs. Anne Pickett, have claimed for her the distinction of operating Wisconsin's first cheese factory. Whether the claim is valid is a matter for historians to sort out. Her "factory," begun about

1841 on the family farm near Lake Mills, was not a full-time operation; furthermore, in a time and place where neighborly cooperation in all things was standard and necessary, the cooperative plan developed by the Picketts and their neighbors could not have been unique. Be that as it may, as James G. Pickett, son and helper in the cheese undertaking, told the story years later, the Picketts pooled the milk from their own three or four cows with that from ten others rented from neighbors at five dollars a head. "The milk from these cows my mother made into very good cheese," he recalled. The following year, the neighbors decided they wanted a share of the cheese instead of a flat rental fee. "My mother suggested to my father that she could take the milk of all these cows, weigh it separately, and return to the owners the amount of product belonging to each. The plan seemed feasible, and so an arrangement was made . . . . . I believe the milk of some over twenty cows was made into a very good quality of cheese, which was properly divided and sold at a very good price."

By 1849, Pickett and other Wisconsin farmers were producing 400,300 pounds of cheese and 3,634,000 pounds of butter. This was still the output of a cottage industry, however, and merely a sideline to the raising of wheat and other crops. Furthermore, it was the only way to store and preserve bulky and easily spoiled milk. Yet the quantities indicate that a market outside the home, and perhaps outside the state, had developed. Spoilage of butter and cheese, on the other hand, was not the problem that it often is said to have been. Even by 1800, according to a recent study, Americans were making butter "that remained edible for up to three years without refrigeration" and that was even exported to China—"a trade that required two crossings of the Equator." By 1854, so much butter was exported eastward from the port of Milwaukee (305,500) pounds), that the *Milwaukee Sentinel* claimed a shortage in the city. Not all of it, of course, met the three-year standard; much Wisconsin butter was inferior and was used as grease for everything from axles to the backs of sheep. Obviously, most Wisconsin butter and cheese were consumed close to home, where they could be kept in springhouses or other cool storage, and a good deal of it was bartered at the local general store.

Cheese made it out of the home kitchen and into the commercial factory two or three decades before butter graduated to the creamery. Cheese transformation began moving from farm to factory in the 1860's among Wisconsin dairymen, many of whom had come from western New York where commercial operations date from the 1850's.

The Wisconsin figure usually credited with the first authentic cheese factory in the state was Chester Hazen, who came from New York in 1844 and opened his establishment in Ladoga (Fond du Lac County) in 1864. Hazen had been dairying as early as 1850. He and some others in Wisconsin also had started working at scientific breeding and feeding of dairy cattle—a movement also begun before in New York and New England and, even earlier, in Europe. Hazen's factory, which he patterned after those in New York, processed milk from his own herd and those of several neighbors, some 100 to 200 cows in all. By 1873, he was using milk from 800 cows, and had established another factory at Brandon, supplied by an additional 200 cows. His total production that year was 297,630 pounds, and the cheese was of exceptional quality. At the Philadelphia Centennial Exposition of 1876, Hazen's

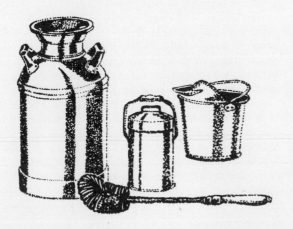

cheese won first prize, one of many awards he garnered in the 1870's and 1880's.

Hazen's success inspired others, many also New Yorkers, to start cheese factories. And so did many immigrants. Germans in the east-central region began marketing cheese early. The Swiss in New Glarus and elsewhere were shipping their Swiss and Limburger cheese to eastern markets out of Monroe by the 1870's. (In those days, cheese was transported in open wagons, giving rise to an early form of air pollution. An ordinance is said to have once been proposed in the Monroe common council to ban he pungent Limburger from the streets of the town.)

But even as late as 1870, many, if not most, Wisconsin farmers continued to look on butter and cheese making as a woman's chore, and somehow only incidental to the real moneymaking aspect of farming. Nor did dairying in general concern many farmers, who disliked the idea of being "tied to a cow." Census takers in 1870 counted only twenty-five Wisconsinites who identified themselves as dairymen or women, and only fifty-four cheese factories in the state producing slightly more than half the state's cheese. Wheat was still viewed as the money crop, even though yields had been steadily declining. But it became increasingly evident within the following few years that soil depletion, disease, the chinch bug, and competition from newer and better wheat lands west of the Mississippi had completely eroded the wheat foundations of the state's agricultural economy. Gradually, Wisconsin farmers came to realize that being tied to a cow had its rewards, as did cheese and butter making. By the 1890's, the diversified dairy farm emphasis of Wisconsin's agricultural future was clearly established.

Wisconsin's preeminence as a milk, cheese, and butter state was attained through the efforts of many people of many ethnic backgrounds. But one of the most important contributors was a failed hop grower: William Dempster Hoard of Fort Atkinson, editor and publisher of the *Jefferson County Union*. Hoard was convinced that

Wisconsin's future lay in dairying. He was quick to perceive that the potential could not be realized without the scientific breeding of cattle, the imposition of product standards, and the businesslike development of markets. All these causes he vigorously promoted in his newspaper, and later in *Hoard's Dairyman*, which he founded in 1885 and built into a world-renowned agricultural journal.

In 1872 Hoard was a primary moving force in the formation of the Wisconsin Dairymen's Association—Chester Hazen was its first president—and was instrumental in the association's efforts to improve the quality of the state's cheese and butter, and to get them to market efficiently in the refrigerated railroad cars that appeared in 1871 and 1872. Within a year, Wisconsin cheese was to be found not only in the stores of the eastern United States but also in England.

Establishment of standards for dairy products however, did not progress so quickly. By the late 1880's, though the factory system of cheese making was well established, the reputation of Wisconsin dairy products had declined so badly that the export market dried up. This was quite a comedown from 1876, when the cheese and butter in the Wisconsin Dairymen's Asociation exhibit at the Centennial Exposition had won more medals than any other state or country. One problem was that so much "filled cheese"—cheese made partially with lard or vegetable fat instead of butterfat—was being produced. Also, the conditions under which much of the state's cheese was being made were hardly conducive to quality production. Grimy walls, swarms of flies, and maggots in the whey tanks were not unusual in the cheese factories of the day. The Wisconsin Dairy and Food Commission noted that "at least one thrifty cheese maker kept a tame duck at his factory which, at the right time, he would pick up and put into the cheese vat filled with milk and allow it to swim around and gather flies from the surface of the milk."

The Dairy and Food Commision had been established in 1889 during the administration of William Dempster Hoard, who served as governor from 1889 to 1891, and slowly was able to impose standards of quality and sanitation. The commission's efforts were but one aspect of the Wisconsin cheese industry's success story. The educational and research activities of the University of Wisconsin were another. Two research advances especially assisted cheesemakers in standardizing and improving their products: the Wisconsin curd test of 1895 to determine unreliable milk, and the cold-curing process (34° F to 36° F) of 1903, which improved the stability of cheddar cheese under the extreme effects of temperature changes in storage plants and retail shops. Knowledge of these accomplishments was spread through such University of Wisconsin institutions as the agricultural Short Course (begun in 1885 and a turning point in the careers of hundreds of young farmers), the Extension Division (begun in 1891), and farmers institutes (the first being held in Hudson on November 24 and 25, 1885). This combination of research, education, and quality standardization helped the state's cheese industry to regain its reputation. By 1909, Wisconsin accounted for 46.5 per cent of national cheese production, usurping New York's lead. Wisconsin has held its position as the number-one cheese-producing state ever since.

Butter making remained in the kitchen far longer than cheese. It was not until the 1890's, after two important technological advances, that the great growth of creamery butter production took place. The first was the cream separator, developed in the 1870's for factory use, then (in 1885) adapted by the De Laval Company in smaller hand-operated versions for farm use. No more would farmers have to make daily deliveries of whole milk to creameries, and no more would dairymen have to wait for gravity to provide cream and skim milk in old-fashioned pans set in water in a springhouse.

The second key development was a Wisconsin contribution: the butterfat test developed by Stephen Moulton Babcock at the University of Wisconsin in the spring of 1890. Before then, farmers usually were paid by the pound for milk they sold to cheese factories and creameries, regardless of quality. Some cheated and watered their product; others provided superior milk, high in butterfat. This inequitable pricing discouraged many of the better farmers from improving their herds, to the detriment of dairying generally. Several chemical tests for butterfat appeared in the 1880's, but none was wholly successful. Then in 1890 three new tests were developed, including the celebrated invention of Stephen Moulton Babcock. It was the simplest of the lot: add acid to milk to liberate the fat, then whirl the mixture in a glass bottle with a percentage scale on its neck, to measure the butterfat content. The test took only fifteen minutes, and those factories that adopted it reaped dividends quickly, since their products commanded higher prices. Several years passed, however, before this Wisconsin-developed test became *the* standard in its home state. Now, no history of the state is considered complete without a paragraph of homage to Babcock.

The impact on the butter industry was remarkable. In 1889 only 23 per cent of the state's butter was being made in less than 300 creameries; but by the turn of the century, more than 1,000 were producing 58 per cent of the state's total, and in 1909, factory production accounted for 79 per cent. The Wisconsin Buttermakers' Association was formed in 1902, and in 1909 Wisconsin became the nation's leading butter producer (replacing Iowa) as well as the leading cheese producer. The percentages, however, were quite different: 8.1 per cent of the nation's butter as opposed to 46.5 per cent of her cheese.

Today, Wisconsin leads the nation in production of milk, butter, cheese, and nonfat dry milk. (It no longer leads in evaporated or condensed milk, and several other states' output of ice cream far exceeds Wisconsin's.) Almost half the nation's American-type cheeses alone carry a Wisconsin label. In 1976, the state had eighty-five processors of fluid milk, twenty-three makers of creamery butter, 361 makers of natural and process cheese, sixteen makers of ice cream and frozen desserts, and thirty-eight processors of condensed and evaporated milk.

Statistics, however, only imperfectly tell the human side of the story. They tell little about the work of countless individuals, especially those farmers who milk their herds twice daily, no matter what the weather or their state of health and mind. Joseph Schafer, a famed Wisconsin agricultural historian of the 1930's, credited the "newly-arrived"—Germans, Scandinavians, Swiss, Bohemians, Poles, and all the rest—with the state's dairying achievements. Unlike American-born farmers, the immigrants had no qualms about being "tied to a cow." Milking chores, after all, "interdicted summer vacations, day and night fishing excursions," and visits to friends. Immigrants, Schafer maintained, "craved no vacations aside from the usual holidays," were open-minded to new ideas, and "were generally thrifty." Thus, their success. While he may have slighted Americans and English-speaking immigrants, Schafer probably was generally correct in attributing dairying success to the human factor in Wisconsin's unusual ethnic stew.

Contrary to popular belief, and to frequent published comment, milk cows do *not* outnumber people in Wisconsin. In the late 1970's, there were about 1,810,000 cows being milked, while the population stood at about 4,700,000. And even though the cow census was close to a million head higher in the late 1940's, people still had the numerical edge. When counting all cattle, including animals intended only for slaughter, then animals and people were nearly neck-and-neck from about 1890 through the 1950's, with bovines losing in 1910 (2.31 million to 2.33 million people) but winning in 1940 (3.4 million to 3.1 million people).

Such substantial figures meant that the state has had a thriving slaughtering and meat-packing industry, although it has not since the 1860's and 1870's been in serious competition with Illinois to the south or Iowa to the west. Beginning in territorial days, local butcher shops supplied meat and fowl for urban dwellers, but rural residents usually did their own butchering.

Many of those local butcher shops were also important in the development of Wisconsin's substantial meat-packing industry. (The phrase "meat packing" derives from the seventeenth-century practice of salting pork, then packing it

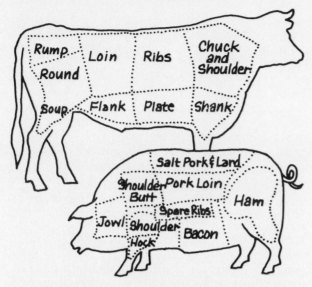

in shipping barrels. Refrigeration brought an end to this method of preservation and packing, but not to use of the term.) So was the tanning industry, which processed animal hides and exported leather; the meat went northward to lumber camps and eastward to urban markets, even in the days before the Civil War. It was a small business then: only 8,000 barrels of meat, mostly pork destined for New York, were shipped from Milwaukee in 1850. Racine exported greater quantities in that period, but within a few years was eclipsed by Milwaukee.

Expansion began in 1851 when Thomas and Edward Roddis erected a packing house in Milwaukee, then enlarged it the next year to accommodate 125 head of cattle and 300 to 400 hogs daily. That same year, 1852, Milwaukee butchers Frederick Layton and John Plankinton formed their famous firm, the forerunner of Chicago's giant Armour and Company. By 1859 the Roddis brothers and Layton and Plankinton together dominated the other ten Milwaukee outfits, handling 95 per cent of the cattle and 60 to 70 per cent of the hogs. In 1863 Plankinton invited young Philip D. Armour to become a partner in the enterprise. He proved to be a man with a vision, quickly perceiving Chicago's transportation

and geographic advantages over Milwaukee. In 1867 Plankinton and Armour opened a Chicago branch under Armour's personal direction. When Plankinton retired in 1888, his firm was taken over by the Cudahy brothers. As part of a larger conglomerate, it is still in business today.

From the outset, Milwaukee's meat-packing success was based upon pork. Beef, which enjoyed a flurry during the Civil War, declined after 1865; but by 1871 Milwaukee stood fourth among the nation's pork-packing cities.

The state as a whole, however, was among the top few leaders in the industry in the last century. In 1880, Wisconsin stood eleventh among thirty states in the value of animals either slaughtered or processed or both, and twenty-five years later was twelfth in capital invested in meat packing. Between 1905 and 1972, however, the situation changed, and the state's large meat packers in the Milwaukee area boosted its ranking to number five in terms of value added to the meats prepared in Wisconsin. In 1972 there were seventy-three establishments in the state—a number that placed Wisconsin only twelfth nationally. But those relatively few firms did enough business to rank them fifth in terms of the value their processing added to the meats they sold. Clearly, industry leaders like Patrick Cudahy, Inc., of Cudahy, the Hillshire Farm Company of New London, Jones Dairy Farm of Fort Atkinson, Oscar Mayer & Co. of Madison, and Stoppenbach, Inc., of Jefferson have helped to demonstrate that meat packing no longer is the centralized industry it once was, dominated by a handful of railroad centers.

That the list of meat packers includes several which are better known for their sausages than for fresh meats should come as no surprise to Wisconsinites, who for generations have feasted upon a wide variety of these gustatory specialties. One authority has called Wisconsin the sausage capital of the nation in both production and consumption. While the latter claim may be true enough, unlikely as it may seem, Wisconsin does *not* make more sausage than any other state: it stood ninth in 1905 with 12,621,837 pounds, and sixteenth in 1972 in terms of value added to the products used in making sausage. Forty-one plants made sausage in 1972, putting Wisconsin tenth on the list—and indicating that the state possesses a large number of sausage makers who produce relatively small quantities of their specialties.

Actually, sausage making in Wisconsin was first practiced by the native Americans. As did people elsewhere in the world, America's Indians discovered that meats could be preserved by drying or salting and, mixed with other ingredients for bulk or seasoning, be kept for long periods. Their pemmican—which was meat, corn or wild rice, herbs, and berries kept in bags of animal skins—was a kind of sausage.

Sausages enabled our frugal ancestors to use up every bit of a meat animal: blood, organs, entrails, fat, and the other scraps and snippets left over after butchering. The fall ritual of slaughtering beef or pigs for winter eating included sausage making for pioneers and early settlers, and, as urban settlements developed, for meat-market operators as well. "Home-made" sausages are still a tradition with many butcher shops in the state, and some also specialize in custom sausage processing of venison for hunters.

Probably most of the bigger commercial operations in Wisconsin—and the nation—started out as butcher-shop enterprises. And in this culinary category, too, emigration from Germany, Bohemia, Poland, and other Middle European principalities was a factor in the development of the speciality. Starting around mid-century, butcher shops in Milwaukee, Sheboygan, Jefferson, and Watertown, to name but a few, gradually became known for the special ways they combined various meats and the basic seasonings of salt, pepper, and sugar. They then created endless variety with combinations of other spices, herbs, and flavorings: garlic, bay leaf, parsley, cumin, mustard and dill seeds, paprika, nutmeg, mace, sage, cloves, celery seed, marjoram, thyme, fennel, ginger, allspice, lemon rind, wine, pistachio nuts, and all members of the onion family.

Sausage goes by many names, each with a flavoring all its own: braunschweiger, blutwurst, goettinger, Laona bologna, nurnberger, mettwurst, saucisschen, mortadella, hildescheimer, landjaeger, presskopf, lachsschinken, gansebrust, goteborg, thuringer, cervelatwurst, arles, calabrese, genoa salami, soppressata, kielbassa, krakauer, weiner, frankfurter, bologna, bockwurst, bratwurst—to name some but by no means all of them.

More than a few of those nineteenth-century establishments are still in business today, locally, regionally, and, several, nationally. Usinger's in Milwaukee was started by Fred Usinger, a Frankfurt apprentice sausage maker, in 1880, at the same address on North Third Street where it continues to dispense about seventy-five different types of sausages to fifty states and some countries abroad today.

Three years later, Oscar F. Mayer and his brothers, Gottfried and Max, started a small retail market on Chicago's north side. The popularity of their Bavarian-type sausage soon expanded beyond that city's German community. In 1919, the company purchased a plant in Madison which became its headquarters after World War II. By the end of the 1970's, it had grown to one of the nation's leading meat processors, selling one-third of all the sliced meat consumed in the country, with nine U.S. processing plants and three abroad.

An exception to the butcher-shop beginning is Jones Dairy Farm of Fort Atkinson, whose pork sausage business had an almost-too-good-to-be-true start. It really did begin, however, storybookish as it may sound, in the farm kitchen of Milo C. Jones as an adjunct to the dairy, cheese, and butter business the family had founded in Jefferson County during territorial days. Jones had been ill in bed for seven years, and getting involved in making sausages—like those his Vermont-born mother had made—helped to restore his health. The first batches were turned out in 1889–1890 and were sold locally. As the operation expanded, it moved from kitchen to modern factory, and sales were for many years confined to direct mail purchases by consumers. Now, Jones's "little-pig sausages," as they were characterized in a 1914 biography of Milo Jones, are found in markets through the country.

Not all of Wisconsin's food specialties have had the staying qualities of dairy products and sausage. Some of the state's culinary reputation has been built on highly specialized items that were mere decimal points in the state's income totals over the years, not all of which have lasted to this day. Stuffed—or noodled—goose was one. The center of the industry, if that is the proper word, was Watertown, which was known at one time as the goose capital of the United States. (One of its bridges even commemorates the bird in cast-iron relief panels along the sidewalk.) Like several other Wisconsin food enterprises, it had its roots in German immigration, in this case Germans from Pomerania and Alsace who settled in Jefferson and Dodge counties. They brought with them the old-country tradition of stuffing—that is, force feeding—geese to both fatten the bird and produce the prized enlarged liver.

While Germans throughout Wisconsin practiced stuffing geese for their own tables and limited local sale at holiday times, the first record of truly commercial goose stuffing in the Watertown area was in 1886 in nearby Johnson Creek. (Some sources credit a farmer named Louis Stchert as the man who started it all; others refer to a family named Steems or Stiehm—possibly the same name spelled several ways.) Soon many farmers in the area added stuffed geese to their list of profitable seasonal crops. At the height of the enterprise, more than 150,000 pounds of stuffed geese were shipped annually from Watertown, mostly to the East and South where they were prized by gourmets and elegant restaurants. (There was a demand for the birds for three holidays—Jewish high holidays in early fall, Thanksgiving in November, and Christmas in December.)

A great deal of time and the labor of wives and children as well as the farmer were needed to produce these succulent birds. The process was called "noodling," the term deriving from the feed the bird got in its last three or four weeks of life—a noodle, made by the farmer's wife, of equal parts of corn meal, ground wheat, and wheat flour mixed into a thick paste and put through a sausage stuffer. The one-inch-diameter noodles were cut into three-inch lengths, boiled, and then force-fed to the goose.

The authenticated record weight* for a Watertown goose is thirty-eight-and-a-half pounds; the weight of that bird's liver is not known, but it was probably close to four pounds. Legend has it that a Watertown goose sent to President William Howard Taft—himself a trencherman of renown—weighed forty-eight pounds; but poultry experts believe that the weight of Taft's goose was exaggerated to match the president's proportions.

Watertown geese were marketed well into this century, but as a commercial venture the practice was a victim of the Depression. In the mid-1960's, only one family, Mr. and Mrs. Fred Rumler of Watertown, was still noodling geese for long-time customers, including New York's famed German restaurant, Luchow's, which had a standing order for 300 each holiday season. During their last year of operation in 1974, the Rumlers noodled only about ten geese for gourmets in New York, Ohio, and California, who paid $1.65 a pound for the delicacy.

Vastly more adaptive than the Watertown stuffed goose industry has been Wisconsin's sizeable fishing enterprise, which persists even today despite ever-changing problems and conditions. Variations in species available, introduction of contaminants and pollutants, new fishing technologies, and regulations involving sport fishing—all have riled the industry's economic waters. The constants throughout have been the fishermen—who from Wisconsin's earliest days have set forth in boats to gather a commercial fish harvest—and the waters in which

---

*Meaning its weight plucked but not drawn. A non-noodled goose, by contrast, might weigh twelve to sixteen pounds.

they plied their trade—principally Lake Superior, Lake Michigan, and the Mississippi River.

From the time of the first European incursions, Indians found it profitable to sell fish (and other foodstuffs) along with pelts to explorers and fur traders. However, the first large-scale attempt to exploit the Lake Superior fisheries was made by the American Fur Company, in an undertaking that was also an early example of corporate diversification. In 1834, John Jacob Astor sold his famed firm, and Ramsay Crooks became its new president. Crooks decided to expand into fishing—and into the building of boats and barrels to carry the cargo—as a means of keeping his men occupied during the fur trade's off-season.

With La Pointe at Madeline Island as headquarters, fishing stations also were established at Sault Ste. Marie, Grand Portage (Minnesota), Fond du Lac (now the southwestern section of Duluth), and on Isle Royale. On August 3, 1835, the 112-ton schooner *John Jacob Astor* was launched in Lake Superior, and even though most of its crew was inexperienced at fishing on that scale, the company recorded a fair catch. During 1836, about a thousand barrels of whitefish, siscowet, trout, herring, and pickerel were shipped to the Sault, then portaged to the company's brig *Ramsay Crooks* for the trip on the lower lakes to Detroit. From there, the fish were marketed to points in the East and along the Ohio River.

The peak year was 1839 with about 5,000 barrels. But the company could not create a large enough market for its fish harvest, particularly in the country's depressed economic state following the panic and recession of 1837; indeed the company itself failed in 1842. Its efforts, however, had proved the point: Lake Superior's fish were well worth commercial attention. By 1850, local fishing settlements were scattered here and there along the south shore. Most of the catch, however, was consumed locally until the 1870's. Then steam-driven vessels, the canal at Sault Ste. Marie (opened in 1855), and a ready supply of ice enabled expansion. By the end of the decade, about 300 Wisconsin men made their livings

fishing in Lake Superior, and, together, with their companions from Minnesota and Michigan, they harvested 68.7 million pounds of fish, with whitefish and herring accounting for more than half the amount.

The fishermen were largely French-Canadians, many of them having some Indian blood. But there were also some Swedes and Norwegians and Indians. The dealers, on the other hand, were described as Americans, and nearly all of them worked in sailboats out of Bayfield or Ashland. Wisconsin supplied only about a fourth of the fishermen from the three Lake Superior states, and its production in 1885 accounted for about a fifth of the fresh fish and about a fourth of the salted fish. (Both Ohio and Michigan had many more persons fishing Great Lakes waters than did Wisconsin.) The rail lines that linked Bayfield with points south in 1883 made it possible to ship fish year around.

That may have been a boon for business, but it worked a hardship on the fish population. Even in the 1870's, Lake Superior fishermen found certain species in short supply, and they had to search farther and farther to find them. Yet the catches rose in size, and the introduction of steam-powered winches in the 1890's made even larger hauls possible. Whitefish production then began to fall, and continued to decline until about 1920. Herring production rose dramatically, reaching almost 12 million pounds in the years before World War I. The lake sturgeon, however, was nearly wiped out, until that giant and spectacularly ugly fish—prized for its caviar and its swim bladder out of which isinglass was made—is rarely encountered today. (Both sturgeon and whitefish suffered, too, from polluting lumber, pulp, and paper industrial wastes.) The lake trout yield, on the other hand, remained fairly stable throughout until the late 1950's. A banner decade for all Lake Superior fish was the 1940's, when catches reached about 7 million pounds a year.

Introduction of new species into the lake, however, changed the picture dramatically in the 1950's and 1960's. The sea lamprey nearly wiped out the lake trout industry and managed to make inroads on the whitefish before it was brought under control through use of poison in its spawning areas. Another newcomer—smelt—competed successfully with the herring, which also appears to have suffered from overfishing, possibly because of more effective nylon nets. Fishermen adapted to these changes by adding smelt to their line and by concentrating on chubs, which had been available before but were not as desirable as trout and whitefish. Catches, however, plummeted—a million and a half pounds in 1974, scarcely a million pounds in 1977, or only about a fourth of the total fish taken altogether from the American waters of Lake Superior. The figure was about the same as it had been 140 years earlier, but experts are not particularly pessimistic about the status of Lake Superior's fisheries. They believe that fish populations are recovering, and that, if they do, commercial fishing may once again thrive.

Periodic declines in the pounds of fish caught in Lake Michigan have not been as dramatic. In fact, there has been an over-all increase: from 7.7 million pounds in 1940 to more than 47 million pounds in 1974. But the increase is due wholly to the lowly alewife, which did not even figure in the catch until 1957. Now it is a staple of the pet food industry and a source of fish oil, which has an extraordinary number of industrial applications. The alewife, however, does not make its way to American tables as a culinary item, and when it is eliminated from fish statistics, then the Lake Michigan picture is about the same as Lake Superior's: production has declined from 7.7 million pounds in 1940 to 3.5 million pounds in 1977.

Lake Michigan commercial fishing by non-Indians dates back to the same period as Lake Superior's: the 1830's. In 1837, Captain J. V. Edwards sailed from Green Bay and around the Door peninsula to cast his nets between Manitowoc and Two Rivers. Edwards, his thirteen-year-old son Henry, and two other men hauled in ten barrels of fish, a bountiful catch that prompted Edwards to build a fishing shack on the beach at

Two Rivers. At the trading post there, the rendering of fish oil became an important activity.

Edwards soon had competition from J. P. Clark and his crew of twenty men. The two fishing captains quickly became partners, and tradition has it that just one of their catches of whitefish, trout, and herring yielded enough to fill 175 barrels—worth, in 1838, $12 a barrel in Detroit. (Each barrel held about 200 pounds.)

In the years that followed, commercial fishing at Two Rivers and Manitowoc continued to be an important though not a primary component of the area's economy. The fishing fleet continued to grow, and by 1868, when a barrel of fish was selling from $5 to $8, the *Manitowoc Pilot* noted: "From a point seven or eight miles north of Two Rivers south to this place there are no less than one hundred men, who with their families are dependent on this branch of industry [fishing] for a livelihood."

The rich fishing grounds became so crowded in the 1860's that they spawned numerous quarrels and disputes of such seriousness that a law

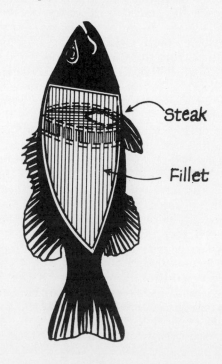

Steak

Fillet

was passed enabling Lake Michigan fishermen to stake claims to specific segments of the lake. Fifty claims were filed between 1864 and 1866, couched in such nineteenth-century legalese as: ". . . that said monument is a Birch stake driven into the ground and having a pine board nailed or attached thereto on which is painted or printed the name of the undersigned and the true date of its erection as follows, 'C. Schoch, March 17th, 1864'—for the purpose of perfecting a claim or right to fish at said locality in the water of Lake Michigan with a trap or pound or pond net."

Fishing was also important to the communities lining the shores of Green Bay, and to a lesser extent, those along the rest of the Lake Michigan shore line south of Manitowoc. Green Bay was known then and now for some of the richest fishing in all of Lake Michigan. The favorite from the outset was the whitefish, which were extremely abundant near shore. By the 1870's, though, Wisconsin fishermen began to complain about its scarcity. (In Michigan and Illinois, the complaints had begun even earlier.) Still, the pursuit of fish occupied about 270 Wisconsin men living along Lake Michigan in 1880, who daily set an estimated 400 miles of nets. These men represented great cultural diversity. (Fifteen hundred men altogther fished Lake Michigan.) In the community of Green Bay, only about twenty-five men earned their living wholly from fishing, but they included English, French, Americans, Norwegians, Germans, Poles, Swiss, Belgians, and Swedes. The French-Canadians, however, dominated in the Two Rivers area, and one village near there even bore the name Canada.

The total Lake Michigan catch was immense— 23 million pounds, nearly half of it whitefish, with trout, herring, and sturgeon making up almost all the rest. The sturgeon catch was large enough to support briefly a small isinglass and caviar business at Oconto, until that species was quickly fished into obscurity. Whitefish yields declined quickly, too, but the total catch did not, since there were increases in the catch of trout, herring, cisco, perch, suckers, and (to a lesser extent) walleyes. Total production even jumped, thanks to the herring, and averaged 41.2 million pounds in 1893–1908, and there was a corresponding increase in the number of fishermen— about 2,500 in 1890, with about 900 of them from Wisconsin.

The herring catch declined abruptly between 1908 and 1911, but other species that had been introduced into Lake Michigan, principally carp and smelt, found a market. So total production figures stabilized from 1911 to 1942 at an average of 23.6 million pounds annually.

Since then, tremendous changes have taken place among the species in Lake Michigan. Pollution; cyclical imbalances among commercial and game fish, predators, and rough fish; disputes between commercial fishermen and sportsmen over the freshwater salmon—all have contributed to varying perspectives on the future of the Lake Michigan fisheries. There is no end to change, nor to the commercial fisherman's ability to adapt. In fact, more and more fishermen took to the waters in the late 1960's and early 1970's, and upwards of 300 commercial licenses were issued in 1975. Thus, despite all the problems, things are looking up for Lake Michigan—and for fish fanciers who long have valued the culinary delights of the Great Lakes.

Commercial fishing has not been confined to Lake Michigan and Superior, however. Even in territorial days, inland lakes and streams as well as the Mississippi River provided at least sporadic employment for some. As unlikely a stream as the Pecatonica in southwestern Wisconsin, now known more for flooding than for fishing, in 1837 yielded wagonloads of buffalo fish and catfish, brought to Mineral Point for sale. Such undertakings were probably casual efforts on the part of area farmers, and they assuredly extended throughout Wisconsin. Until well into the nineteenth century, most fishing on the Mississippi River was done to augment a family's food supply or to sell in the immediate area.

Commercial quantities of fish were there, but high transportation costs on steamboats and trains, the necessity for refrigeration, and the low prices commanded by a plentiful commodity all delayed commercial development of the Mississippi. By the 1870's, however, commercial fishermen were harvesting the river from its junction with the St. Croix all the way to the Illinois border. Their activities, however, were largely uncontrolled at first. On numerous occasions, so many boatloads of fish converged on St. Louis that more than half the shipments were simply dumped back into the river. In 1876, the fish commissioner of Iowa called for a law to protect fish in spawning season, citing instances of catches of from 30,000 to 80,000 pounds that were marketed "covered and reeking with their own spawn."

Among the species hauled in were yellow walleye, sheepshead, sauger, yellow perch, white and yellow bass, catfish, buffalo, and sturgeon. (In those days, most of the sturgeon was discarded after its eggs were taken for caviar—the meat was not considered tableworthy.)

In the last quarter of the century, carp were added to the list. Carp, which are not native to Wisconsin waters, were planted in stocking programs in the 1880's, and by 1900 the commercial carp poundage exceeded that of any other fish in the Mississippi (more than 3 million pounds out of a total of more than 11 million pounds). Plenty of carp, of course, were loaded into the first refrigerated railroad car of fish that went from the Midwest to New York in 1896. Eastern markets have traditionally been the biggest purchasers of carp, which is the main ingredient of that Jewish speciality, gelfilte fish. Nowadays, the demand for carp has diminished, reflecting the decline in the number of women willing to spend the time boning and preparing such a complicated dish.

However, carp has continued right up to the present as the upper Mississippi's top commercial fish (2.7 million pounds in 1976 out of a total Wisconsin catch of 4.3 million pounds), but buffalo, sheepshead, and catfish are all in the half-million-pound range. In 1976, nearly 1,300 Wisconsin fishermen took out commercial licenses for the Mississippi, an increase of almost 500 from ten years previously.

Tributaries of the Mississippi and the Great Lakes also produce carp, and the state of Wisconsin contracts with many commercial fishermen to remove them—along with other rough species as well—from inland lakes and streams. State-owned-and-operated vessels also engage in the harvest. Between 1970 and 1979 more than 56 million pounds of rough fish were removed from such places as the Wisconsin River in Sauk County, Lake Winnebago, Lake Koshkonong in Jefferson and Rock counties, and Lake Puckaway in Green Lake County. Those fish taken in the Mississippi River basin are added to the catch for state-to-state comparisons, in which Wisconsin regularly leads in the total catch of fish from the Mississippi.

Compared with other states bordering the Great Lakes and Mississippi River, Wisconsin's commercial fishing industry has fared well over the years. Wisconsin stood third in the nation's freshwater fishing industry in 1880, surpassed only by Ohio and Michigan. It was still number three fifty years later; but in the mid-1940's Wisconsin began to surpass Ohio, as Lake Erie became increasingly polluted. Wisconsin overtook Michigan in the 1960's, and in the 1970's led all other states handily. With the emergence of commercial fish farms, it likely will maintain its top ranking in the statistics. Thus, while "fishing in Wisconsin" will forever conjure up the vision of a lone angler casting for musky in the shallows of a North Woods lake, there remains another equally significant (and economically important) side to the harvest from Wisconsin waters.

But it was on dry land that Wisconsin's primary food riches were to be had, and the state's advantages for cash crops were recognized early.

An early booster, William Rudolph Smith (who in 1838 followed his own advice and moved to Wisconsin), observed that potatoes, "of a quality and size superior to any I have ever tasted," could be grown in southwestern Wisconsin, 300 to 500 bushels an acre; "and with regard to this vegetable, I venture to predict, that the time will arrive when the Wisconsin potato, *par excellence*, will become an article of trade in the best demand in the southern markets."

Smith was not far from the mark: Wisconsin did become a major potato producer, but the achievement was forty years in the making. Potatoes topped the list of Wisconsin cash crops in 1840 (420,000 bushels). In 1850, more than 1,400,000 bushels were dug out of the state's soil, with Dodge and Washington counties contributing the most, but Wisconsin ranked only fourteenth among the states that year. Its position steadily improved, however, so that by 1872 it stood seventh (5,226,000 bushels), and in 1880, second (13,552,110 bushels) after New York and just ahead of Pennsylvania. That year, sixty-six carloads of potatoes left Waupaca for Chicago; in 1912, the same community shipped out 2,200 carloads, indicating how the industry grew in the three intervening decades.

The growers eventually received encouragement from the University of Wisconsin, especially through promotion and scientific education. The University helped sponsor potato exhibit trains between 1905 and 1912, when display cars toured communities on the Soo Line throughout the northern counties. The potato growers formed a statewide association after the 1912 tour, and its work has continued to the present.

The center of the industry has shifted northward over the years to Portage and Langlade counties; and Wisconsin's ranking has slipped (in 1978 it stood sixth in fall potato production, at 1,732,500,000 pounds, compared to rankings of second or third between 1900 and 1912), but the crop sold for more than $76 million in 1978, demonstrating the potato's importance in Wisconsin's economy.

The potato's slice of the vegetable industry overshadows other significant species—peas, sweet corn, snap beans, beets, lima beans, cabbage, cucumbers, and carrots. Wisconsin farmers grow important quantities of all these vegetables, which in recent times have meant $100 million annually in the state's coffers. In monetary terms, California, Florida, Texas, and New York all surpass Wisconsin's vegetable industry. But in terms of acreage, Wisconsin for years has cultivated more vegetable land than any other state. (Double-cropping in the West and South, and better soils elsewhere, account for the different yields.)

Compared to the dairy industry, vegetable cultivation is a recent phenomenon. Its star began rising, with the earlier exception of peas, during the first two decades of the twentieth century, and the growth during World War II was astonishing—nine million cases of peas canned in 1938, for example, compared to almost sixteen million in 1945 and fifteen million in 1946. As these figures indicate, most of Wisconsin's produce reaches market in canned or frozen forms. So without parallel growth in the canning industry, Wisconsin never would have landed on the vegetable map. This marriage between agriculture and the vegetable canning industry has been a happy one: for decades Wisconsin has produced more canned vegetables than any other state, and it regularly accounts for a fifth to a fourth of the entire national industry's output.

While canning may be a relative newcomer, interest in vegetables is as old as Wisconsin itself. Back at the beginning of the territorial period in 1836, Milwaukee entrepreneur Byron Kilbourn offered three-dollar prizes for the largest turnip, potato, beet, and radish presented at his office. One winner toted in a twenty-three-pound rutabaga; the largest radish tipped the scale at four pounds, five ounces.

Until the 1870's, however, most Wisconsin-grown vegetables graced only Wisconsin tables, with only a relative few finding their way to nearby urban markets. In 1860, for instance, Wisconsin ranked twenty-first out of the thirty-four states in pea and bean production. Then

canning made widespread export possible. (Canning actually had been around quite a while. The process was first made practical in Europe around 1810. It reached the United States about 1820, was given a boost by the Civil War, and finally took off technologically and economically in the 1870's.)

The industry appeared in Wisconsin in the person of Albert Landreth, who came to Manitowoc originally to grow seed peas for his family's seed company in Pennsylvania. In 1883, he began experimenting with the canning of green peas. The following year he produced his first commercial pack in the kitchen of the hotel his mother-in-law owned. Then, three years later, Landreth built a canning plant and began producing under the Lakeside label. The impact on Manitowoc County and Wisconsin agriculture was startling. In 1889, Wisconsin stood third among the nation's pea states, and although its position had slipped a notch by 1899, Manitowoc County was far and away the leading pea producer among the state's counties, and was among the leading counties in the nation. Manitowoc County still grows significant amounts, but has been superseded by Dodge and Fond du Lac counties, the current leaders.

The state's climate and some of its soils are favorably (if not perfectly) suited to certain vegetables. Furthermore, many farmers in dairying and diversified crops could add them as a sideline on small portions of their acreage. Peas particularly were a good rotation crop which helped to restore nitrogen to depleted soils. There was also Wisconsin's central transportation location. All these factors contributed to the establishment of canneries throughout the state. And since the season for peas is short, many canneries were equipped to handle other crops for which Wisconsin has become known.

By the turn of the century, there were twenty-one canning operations around the state—in Cassville for corn, tomatoes, pickles, and kraut; in Sauk City for peas; in Randolph for tomatoes, corn, peas, and pickles; in Platteville for corn and tomatoes; in Kewaunee for peas; in Burlington for corn and tomatoes. In the first year of the new century, seven more canneries started operation. By 1931, 170 plants were providing seasonal employment to students, housewives, teachers, and others. The number of plants declined during the Great Depression, though the peak year for production came in 1945 when, to meet the requirements of the armed forces, output was four times as great as in 1931. That record still stands, so far as can be determined, despite increases in population and production of some vegetables. (Exact comparison is not possible, since the 1945 figures were based on case-lot statistics that no longer can be compiled state by state.) The inroads of freezing make it likely that 1945 will stand as Wisconsin's banner canning year for many years to come. In 1978, eighty-three canneries in forty counties contributed to Wisconsin's consistent leading rank in the American canning industry.

Peas and sweet corn deserve much of the credit for this success story. At first, in the late nineteenth and early twentieth centuries, the canners themselves raised many of the peas they required, since farmers did not care to meet the special demands imposed. But when they saw the profits, thousands changed their minds. Peas for canning became a Wisconsin specialty even before World War I, and Wisconsin has led much of the time since. The state of Washington now grows many peas for freezing, and some years noses out Wisconsin as the leading state. But in 1979 Wisconsin was number one with 177,550 tons—almost 30 per cent of all the peas grown in the United States.

In the sweet corn sweepstakes, Wisconsin's competition is its neighbor Minnesota, and for the last several years Wisconsin has trailed. In 1979, state farmers, especially in Columbia, Dodge, and Fond du Lac counties, grew 129,300 tons of sweet corn (22.7 per cent of the national output) for canning, and about 400,000 additional tons for other kinds of processing. Sweet corn's importance dates from World War II. So short-handed were the canneries in that era that the federal government stepped in and supplied hundreds of German prisoners of war to fill the gaps.

Within the last five years, Wisconsin—with Waushara County accounting for almost 40 per cent of the acreage—has surged ahead in growing snap beans, replacing Oregon as the leader. As with corn, snap beans became a popular Wisconsin crop during World War II. In 1979, production reached 212,500 tons, or almost 28 per cent of the national total.

Somewhat earlier—in the 1920's—beets began emerging as a profitable canning crop, and now two states—Wisconsin and New York—grow more than 80 per cent of the nation's supply. New York leads Wisconsin more often than not, but in 1979 Wisconsin was ahead with 104,170 tons—about 42 per cent of all the beets grown in America for processing. Dodge, Walworth, and Washington counties together grow almost half of Wisconsin's beets.

Equally impressive is cabbage grown for sauerkraut, of which Wisconsin produces nearly a third of the nation's supply. Its preeminent position might be considered another by-product of Old World immigration. The state's large German and Middle European population made kraut for home consumption, of course, but demand for commercially made sauerkraut gradually grew as well. Racine, Kenosha, Milwaukee and Outagamie counties are especially suited to cabbage growing, and Wisconsin consistently ranks second to New York in total production.

The state's share for its other important vegetable crops is less remarkable: about 10 per cent of the nation's cucumbers for pickles, 10 per cent of its total cabbage, and 9 per cent of its lima beans—but each crop is worth several million dollars to the state nonetheless. A fairly new Wisconsin success is the carrot for processing. Relatively unimportant forty and fifty years ago, carrots (especially in Jefferson and Marquette counties) were worth $4 million in the state's economy in 1978, and Wisconsin farmers grew 72,050 tons of them, exceeded only by California and Washington.

Such hefty statistics, success stories, and flourishing canning activity tend to disguise one important negative development: the decline in popularity of canned foods as the frozen food industry has expanded. The state did not get its first frozen food processing plant until 1964, when Libby, McNeill and Libby opened one in Darien. By 1979 there were ten frozen food plants in the state—some of them quite small, and nothing like the large numbers of operations in other major vegetable areas.

Another agricultural newcomer, though not for canning, is mint—both peppermint and spearmint. In 1948, the first year for which information is available, only a hundred acres were planted. In recent years, the acreages have varied between about 5,000 and 11,500, and the output has been sold for between $4 million and $8 million annually. Muck land is most hospitable to these aromatic herbs which need loose, wet soil. The plant is harvested for its oil, which is used for candy, gum, seasonings, and medicines. Most of the mint crop is processed where it is harvested, then shipped elsewhere. The quantities vary considerably from year to year. In 1970, the peak year for actual production, some 11,000 acres were harvested, yielding 611,000 pounds of oil. But in 1972, only 4,500 acres were harvested, and the yields per acre declined, so that production reached only 135,000 pounds. In the late 1970's, however, acreage mounted again. Peppermint is the more popular of the two mints, and Wisconsin yields of it average two to three times those of spearmint. Only five states— Idaho, Indiana, Oregon, Washington, and Wisconsin—grow mint commercially, and Wisconsin usually ranks last or next-to-last among them. Within the state, Marquette County well exceeds all others, although Walworth, Dane, and Columbia counties, too, produce valuable quantities.

What muck soils are to mint, bogs are to cranberries, Wisconsin's leading fruit crop. The cranberry started as a wild crop, several varieties of which grew naturally and abundantly, especially in Waushara and Wood counties. This marsh berry was well known to most Wisconsin Indians, usually as a food (often dried and on occasion mixed up by the Menominee with corn), and by the Chippewa also as a source of tea as a remedy for nausea. (White settlers are said to have made more medicinal use of the berry than Wisconsin's Indians, for immigrants found that the leaves made a good diuretic and that the berries prevented scurvy.)

Since the leading cranberry lands closest to areas of settlement were among the last in Wisconsin ceded by any Indian tribe, Indians—in this case the Menominee—considered the crop their own until well into the 1850's. As the *Berlin Courant* observed in 1861: "In former years, . . . the natives used to consider cranberry gathering one of their regular harvest[s], and an unusually prolific season a god-send; but the never-satiated progress of the settlers has steadily encroached upon their domain, until the once powerful tribe of Menominees will have to seek the headwaters of the Wisconsin . . . to find a scant supply of the delicious fruit that they were wont to gather in such profusion. . . ."

Most accounts date the first commercial use of cranberries in Wisconsin to January, 1829, when Ebenezer Childs took eight "loads" of them (probably picked by Menominee Indians) from Green Bay to Galena, Illinois, trading them for provisions to feed shingle makers who were at work in the unsettled regions along the Wisconsin River in Juneau County. Indians—along with settlers in the following decades—descended on the marshes in September and October each year to harvest the crop, bartering or selling most of it in an expanding market. Beginning in 1849, the *Milwaukee Sentinel* gave almost annual reports on the state of the cranberry crop, though domestication of it was more than a decade off.

Settlers in the Berlin area, especially in the Town of Aurora in Waushara County, were among the first to buy cranberry bogs. Some, like James and Dick Carey in about 1850, fenced their best bogs to prevent unauthorized picking. But true systematic development awaited the arrival of Edward Sacket from Chicago to examine land he had purchased as a speculation. He came to Berlin in the fall of 1860 to see his 700 acres of (in his words) "shaking bog covered with marsh grass and many Wisconsin plants including cranberry vines." Copying methods used in Eastern marshes, Sacket had it ditched in 1861, "so that it can be drained at pleasure, thus allowing him to keep the vines flooded" and preventing frost damage. By 1865 (only a few months before Sacket's death) 938 barrels of cranberries from his marsh sold for more than $13,000 in Chicago. Sacket's neighbors and his sons followed his lead in cranberry cultivation and soon were making huge profits. "The owner of a cranberry marsh has a better thing today, than an oil well or a gold mine," the *Berlin Courant* noted in November, 1866, "because his 'mine' grows better the more it is worked."

The Sacket and Carey successes set off a boom in Berlin cranberry lands, and speculators soon cast their eyes towards other known cranberry areas, such as those in Wood, Juneau, and Jackson counties. In 1870, Sherman N. Whittlesey visited his father in Berlin and got the fever. He left for Wood County, which he later described as "a vast uninhabited wilderness of level wet marshes of spongy peat, ten to twenty feet deep, interspersed with islands of two to 200 acres of higher sandy land, covered with pine, tamarack, and tangled bush, shading off to spaces of open marsh where patches of wild cranberries could be seen with their crop of red berries awaiting the coming of adventurous, fortuitous pioneers such as we."

Early frost was a particular hazard in pre-radio days. In 1868, frost losses around Berlin ran as high as four-fifths of the crop; in 1871, frost again was a severe problem. Growers set out huge iron pans filled with flaming tar to provide some protection. Improvements in ditches and dams eventually enabled them to control the level of water in the bogs for easy flooding as protection against both frost and insects. But when to prepare for frost? By the middle 1880's the Weather Bureau could telegraph warnings to the Berlin area. And some enterprising growers in Wood County in the 1890's arranged to have railroads post frost signals in the windows of trains passing through.

Particularly severe fires in 1893 forced growers in the Wood County area to rebuild their marshes. By starting from scratch, they actually improved the marshes considerably and accelerated the plant selection process that had begun years earlier. From the start, growers had nurtured their best vines as their growing stock; but even today all commercial cranberries are merely wild berries cultivated assiduously.

The same steady progress marked the growth of the industry in the state. In 1900, about 1,200 acres were under cultivation. Twelve years later, the figure had risen to 1,800 acres, and at the outbreak of World War II it was 2,400 acres. The wartime demands for fruits and postwar expansion enabled Wisconsin to overtake the second-largest grower—New Jersey—at about that time. Now Wisconsin and Massachusetts vie for leadership in the industry, each producing close to a million barrels a year. (Wisconsin's acreage has grown to about 7,000, while Massachusetts harvests 11,200 acres, so the production figures are a tribute to Wisconsin scientific management of its crop.) In 1978, the crop sold for about $17.5 million—Wisconsin's leading commercial fruit crop.

Other commercial fruits have thrived in the state, though on a much smaller scale than cranberries. From about 1800, settlers had planted apples in their gardens, and they are found in every county in Wisconsin. Significant commercial orchards were started in the 1840's, though only $27 of commercial orchard products were reported in the census of 1840. By 1853, enough farmers were producing apples and other fruits to found an organization—the Wisconsin Fruit Growers' Association—which held its first exhibition in Milwaukee the following year. (The association exists still as the Wisconsin Apple and Horticultural Council, Inc.) More than a hundred varieties of apples were displayed. Historically the organization has paid a great deal more attention to apples than to any other fruit. An index of its transactions from 1859 to 1918 contains sixty-six pages of listings about apples but only seven pages about cherries, and a little more than two pages about cranberries.

In the nineteenth century, apples were often grown from seed rather than from grafts, giving rise to numerous new varieties. From Wisconsin there came the Northwestern Greening from Waupaca County, the Wolf River from Winnebago County, and the McMahon White from Richland County. Lesser-known strains with Wisconsin roots were the Pewaukee, Windsor Chief, Gem City, Milwaukee, and Newell.

Despite this lively interest in apples, the quantity grown in Wisconsin has never been very significant nationally. Washington has been the leader for years, followed by New York, California, Michigan, and Virginia. Wisconsin's ranking has improved somewhat in recent decades, from twenty-first in 1928–1932 to eighteenth in 1976 and sixteenth in 1978.

In the middle and late 1970's, owners of about 8,500 acres of commercial apples in about forty of the state's seventy-two counties sent between 52 and 66 million pounds a year to market. The Gays Mills area of Crawford County, and Door County, account for something less than half the crop. Ozaukee County ranks third; Bayfield and Trempealeau counties also produce significant amounts. In 1978, the crop sold for almost $8 million. While some is processed into cider and sauce, the bulk is sold on the fresh market.

For cherry pies, Door County's tart cherry varieties have been nationally recognized for decades. Beginning in 1896, tart cherries were added to Door County's commercial orchards. Their phenomenal success attracted publicity, and according to the chronicler Hjalmar R. Holand, "a boom in fruit growing was created which lasted many years. Huge wagonloads of two-year-old fruit trees were to be seen in springtime on every road. They were often planted with the aid of dynamite, shattering the underlying rock stratum into fragments, and sometimes they were rammed into a crevice with a crowbar." The heyday was from 1924 until 1945, when the county averaged about a seventh of the nation's total pie cherry crop—but the total was never enough to make the state the nation's leader; New York and Michigan have that honor. And while in 1950 there were about a million cherry trees in Door County—more than in any other

county in America—by 1974 the number had declined by two-thirds, owing to economic problems and growing conditions. Recent Wisconsin production has amounted to between six and twelve million pounds of cherries annually, depending on the weather, but nothing like the banner year of 1941 with its 69.3 million pounds.

Finding convenient sweeteners for those tart cherries and other purposes amounted to a culinary and industrial struggle in nineteenth-century America. Sorghum, honey, and maple sugar were adequate (even delicacies by today's standards), but cooks then had visions of convenient and manufactured refined sugars dancing in their heads. Earlier, the crowned heads of Europe sought a suitable northern crop that would substitute for expensive and unavailable cane sugar, and one was soon found: the sugar beet. But the beet resisted refinement into a standardized product. Finally in 1802, in the German province of Silesia, the trick was turned, and Germans thereafter held sway in the sugar beet industry.

The first American factory—not wholly successful—appeared in Massachusetts in 1838 and prompted William Rudolph Smith to recommend Wisconsin for the sugar beet as well as the potato. Smith's predictions, however, were thirty years ahead of their time. Not until 1868 were any real experiments made. Then Andrew Otto, a forty-three-year-old Prussian with seven daughters, appeared in Fond du Lac and undertook a sugar beet enterprise in company with Augustus D. Bonesteel, a New Yorker whose roots reached well back into Wisconsin's territorial soil. (Among other things, Bonesteel had been an Indian agent on a Menominee Indian reservation, a two-term mayor of Fond du Lac later accused of embezzling $10,000, and promoter of an oil well at Appleton in 1865.) Despite fanfare and expensive copper machinery imported from Germany, their refinery lasted only a year.

By 1870, Bonesteel and Otto were building another near Oakland, California, using the same machinery. It, too, failed. In 1873, they doggedly hauled their machinery to Soquel, California, where their efforts again failed. Eventually Claus Spreckel, the California sugar king, managed to open a successful plant at Soquel, and it is often said, quite erroneously, that Bonesteel and Otto's enterprise was the source for it. (Bonesteel died there in 1874, and what became of Otto and his seven daughters has never been determined.)

Their ill-fated Wisconsin labors inspired a great deal of publicity and local boasting, since theirs were among the earliest, somewhat successful sugar beet efforts in the United States. According to the historian Frederick Merk, "Other companies were induced to follow the example thus set, and between the years 1869 and 1871 approximately a dozen beet-sugar companies were organized in the southern and eastern counties of the State." The Wisconsin legislature even granted a ten-year tax exemption to them. But to no avail. "It was impossible," Merk concluded, "to compete successfully with the cheaper and better southern product, and after one or two years of discouragement all these pioneer companies disappeared."

There was proof, however, that Wisconsin was well-suited to growing the sugar beet, and in the 1890's the industry was reborn. Again the manufacturing processes proved troublesome, and first efforts in 1893 at Menomonee Falls were plagued with setbacks. But new capital and new equipment solved the problem, and in 1899 some 233 tons of beets were grown on just eight farms, ranking Wisconsin thirteenth among the then fourteen sugar beet states. An astonishing increase occurred over the next five years in refined beet sugar production nationally—329 per cent—and Wisconsin farmers were near the head of the parade in growing the boom crop. By 1909, more than 4,300 state farmers planted about 12,588 acres to sugar beets. Wisconsin then ranked third among sugar beet states. Dane, Dodge, Racine, Waukesha, and Washington counties led the way in growing; factories blossomed in Janesville, Madison, and Green Bay, as well as in Menomonee Falls. Beet sugar became Menomonee Falls' first million-dollar industry, and from 1910 to 1918 over fifteen million pounds of sugar were produced there each year.

Even during the boom itself, Wisconsin never led the nation in sugar beets. Michigan easily topped the list in the early days, and soon the mountain states—Colorado and Utah—took over. From third place in 1909, Wisconsin slipped to eleventh out of twenty by 1924, and by the 1940's, sugar beets had become decidedly less popular. Refining ceased when the Menominee Sugar Company of Green Bay, for years the last plant operating in the state, closed down in 1964. Towards the end, the company had to import beets, for Wisconsin farmers had stopped growing them two years before.

No similar decline affects Wisconsin's leading natural sugar crop—honey—in which the state often ranks from number four to seven in the U.S. And unlike many of today's agricultural products, which are grown on a massive scale by relatively few persons, honey has somehow escaped this high degree of specialization. (Only 61 per cent came from major farm operators in 1974, for example.) But for hundreds of persons, honey is a full-time business, not a sideline.

Small operations characterized apiaries from the beginning. In early days, settlers and Indians collected honey from hollow trees where the bees swarmed. Later, farmers started capturing and keeping a few swarms in a wide variety of contraptions, including hollow logs and overturned baskets, thus guaranteeing not only a supply of honey but also the pollination of their crops. To get the honey, they would kill (often by smothering) the bees in the fall and crush the comb. Even this inefficient system produced 131,000 pounds of honey and beeswax together in 1850. Twenty-five years later, such haphazard and wasteful methods had largely given way to scientific, commercial bee culture, and the profession of apiarist had come into being. For that development, historians credit four men: Moses Quinby and J. E. Hetherington of New York, John S.

Harbison of California, and Adam Grimm of Jefferson County, Wisconsin.

Born March 25, 1824, in Bavaria, Adam Grimm emigrated early in the spring of 1849 to a farm near Jefferson. His father had kept bees, and Adam followed suit. By 1860, he was producing 500 pounds of honey—the most by far of anyone in his neighborhood and by far the most important product of his 200-acre farm. (He was also one of the few in the vicinity who had a market garden.) By 1863, he had more than sixty colonies of German black bees, and the following year was one of the first in Wisconsin to start using the movable-frame hive invented in the 1850's by the Reverend Lorenzo Lorraine Langstroth of Philadelphia. Langstroth's design had several kinks in it, and one was worked out by another Wisconsin figure, James Forncrook of Watertown, who in 1879 devised a means of making a one-piece section for the Langstroth hive. The improved Langstroth hive is still in use, and enables beekeepers to extract honey from small combs, rather than large masses. Bees still have to be subdued before they will relinquish their combs.

Like beekeepers everywhere, Grimm had his troubles with the black bee, which was ill-tempered and given to a marked and unpredictable tendency to lie down on the job. Beekeeping literature of the day was filled with discussions about the merits of the Italian honey bee, which was relatively better-tempered and more productive. While most others were debating, Grimm acquired some Italian queens by 1865, and within a year and a half had satisfied himself about them, "so much so, that I have given an Italian queen to every one of my 440 colonies but two." He soon began selling them, and in 1869 sent 449 colonies to Utah beekeepers (now the Beehive State), keeping about the same number of hives to begin the 1870 season. His 1869 production was 22,725 pounds—10 per cent of the entire honey crop of the state. His work with bees prompted Grimm to reduce the size of his farm, and by 1870 he maintained only ten acres, earning a handsome living from bees—so handsome

in fact that he was able to co-found Jefferson's Farmers and Merchants Bank.

When Adam Grimm died on April 10, 1876, he had 1,397 colonies of bees in seven or eight apiaries around Jefferson, and by some reckonings the descendants of the Italian queen bees he marketed pollinate 80 per cent of the nation's crops today. His success, like that of his associates in New York and California, had attracted nationwide notice. Grimm was instrumental in proving that bees could provide a livelihood, in testimony to which his family had his tombstone adorned with a relief sculpture of an old-fashioned straw beehive or skep.

In the years since Grimm's death, bee culture, though excessively dependent upon weather, has grown into an important agricultural enterprise. In the 1880's, production topped a million pounds annually, and in 1929 it reached more than five million pounds—second only to California and reflecting the impetus that World War I and its accompanying sugar shortage gave the industry. World War II had the same effect. In the years following 1948, Wisconsin honey production boomed, peaking in 1955 with more than 18.5 million pounds valued at more than $3 million. In 1961 and 1963, production also ran high, then began to taper. In recent years, the average has been closer to ten million pounds a year, but the net worth of the crop to apiarists has risen since 1970 from about $2 million a year to almost $5 million.

Not all Wisconsin honey producers rely entirely on their summer output. Quite a number pack up their bees with the first frost and "over-winter," as they say in the trade, in Florida, Texas, and California. There, they rent out their hives for pollinating and get extra crops of honey in the bargain. California particularly suffers from a shortage of bees which are essential to the pollination of many fruit and nut trees.

Maple sugar and syrup share honors with honey for persistence as a Wisconsin product. But while honey production keeps advancing, maple products peaked in 1860, then declined until the twentieth century. Since the 1950's, however, production has more or less stabilized. Much of the crop was consumed by the maker in the early days, but even then a goodly proportion found its way to market. Between 1839 and 1849 (when census takers first gathered such statistics), production went from 135,288 pounds (mostly from Milwaukee, Brown, and St. Croix counties) to 610,976 pounds from all but eight counties. Ten years later, the figure had reached 1,584,451 pounds of sugar and 83,118 gallons of syrup—number seven among the states. (A gallon of maple syrup equals eight pounds of sugar.) Thereafter refined sugar imports made maple sugaring much less crucial, and the introduction of Wisconsin beet sugar in the first decade of the twentieth century saw sugar production drop drastically to 27,199 pounds in 1910. Meanwhile, syrup took over from sugar, until it now accounts for virtually all of the state's maple sap, completely reversing the earlier pattern. (In 1955, only 1 per cent of the maple sap gathered in America was made into sugar. All the rest became syrup.) Recent Wisconsin production has varied widely—anywhere from 56,000 gallons of syrup in 1971 to 130,000 gallons in 1977. Still, it is a million-dollar enterprise or better, being sold by the maker for gourmet prices: about twelve dollars a gallon, compared to $4.80 a gallon in 1955 and $1.30 a gallon in 1916. Vermont and New York well outdistance Wisconsin in maple products, but since 1955 Wisconsin has moved ahead of Pennsylvania, and annually ranks between third and fifth in the nation.

While gourmets may treasure traditional maple syrup, everywhere in America the man-in-the-street knows that Wisconsin is synonymous with lager beer. The art of brewing and its historic association with German immigrants, the neighborhood saloon, and a day at the ballpark has had far-reaching impact on the social, cultural, economic, and political aspects of both state and nation.

Since beer and Milwaukee are virtual synonyms, it is logical—but incorrect—to surmise that Wisconsin breweries originated there. They did not. Like so many other Wisconsin institutions, brewing traces its origins to the lead region in the southwestern corner of the state. Just who got things going there has not been determined, but by 1840, when census takers made their rounds, there were two breweries* in Iowa County with a total output of 11,200 gallons. (Barrels of beer contain thirty-one gallons, so the annual output was a modest 361 barrels—probably insufficient to the demands of thirsty lead miners.) The beer they made was assuredly one of the heavier malt liquors—ale, stout, or porter—then popular everywhere in the United States and among English-speaking people generally. These were potent, "top-fermented" products, not like the lighter, less potent, "bottom-fermented" lager beer favored by Germans. (Lager gained wide favor in 1850's, and soon dominated the American market.)

This English or American brew also was the first to flow from a Milwaukee brewery, although it was followed within months by German lager. Credit for being first in Milwaukee belongs to Richard Griffith Owens, a Welshman, not a German. In June, 1840, he and two partners set up operations with homemade pipes, tubes, barrels, and a wooden box they lined with copper to form a five-barrel brew kettle. With 130 bushels of barley purchased in Indiana, they began making Milwaukee Brewery Ale in July. Their product found an immediate and enthusiastic local market. Within a year, Owens had acquired a proper twelve-barrel, copper brew kettle from Chicago and added stout, porter, and distilled Scotch whiskey to the brewery's line, though ale remained the principal product until the plant closed in 1880.

By 1845, Owens had changed the plant's name to the Lake Brewery (other Milwaukee breweries had entered the field, making nomenclature confusing) and was using more than 12,000 bushels of barley a year for his brews, which sold throughout the territory and as far south as Chicago for seven dollars a barrel. Within the next

---

*There were also three distilleries in Wisconsin Territory in 1840—one each in Rock, Iowa, and Walworth counties.

five years, he had bought out his partners and built the first pier on Lake Michigan to accommodate the ships unloading grain for his operation. He invested the profits of his successful business in Milwaukee real estate, especially along the city's main street, Wisconsin Avenue.

Hard on Owens' heels came Wurtemberg-born Herman Reuthlisberger, who was in business only briefly when his operation was taken over by creditors. It continued successfully thereafter until it was absorbed by the predecessor of Pabst in 1870. By 1844, three firms were making beer; five years later, ten. Seven of them were German-owned, and some of today's beers can trace their lineage to those times. Jacob Best, Sr., moved from Rheinhessen in 1844 at the behest of one of his sons, and together with the four of them set up the business that his grandson-in-law, Captain Frederick Pabst, took over twenty-two years later. Two of the boys—Phillip and Jacob, Jr.—stayed with the firm; the other two, Charles and Lorenz, helped in 1850 to found the Plank Road Brewery, later (1855) bought by Frederick Miller. Thus the Bests can claim to have founded today's two largest Milwaukee breweries. In 1849, August Krug began brewing, and soon hired Joseph Schlitz as his bookkeeper; and Valentin Blatz took over the City Brewery in 1846 upon the death of its founder, John Braun.

Those ten breweries in 1850 turned out about 20,200 barrels and 70,000 bottles of beer (a figure which included some bottled soda) worth more than $85,000. Seven years later, twenty-five Milwaukee breweries produced an estimated $700,000 worth of beer. By 1872, the seven leading Milwaukee brewers alone were making almost 200,000 barrels, and the Pabst operation had grown from about 5,000 barrels in 1864 to more than 90,000 barrels in 1872–1873, making it the second largest brewery in the country after Seipp and Lehmann of Chicago.

"Such an increase," wrote the historian Thomas C. Cochran, "could be due neither to Milwaukee nor to Wisconsin alone. Diligently as the Germans of the Cream City might have consumed, a town with only 70,000 inhabitants in 1870 had its limitations, and rural Wisconsin was not a heavy beer-drinking area." According to Cochran, the increase came from sales outside Milwaukee and Wisconsin, with as much as half going elsewhere. The trend towards exporting had begun in the late 1850's, when lager beer's popularity soared. The early trickle became a flood in the years just after the close of the Civil War, and nationwide beer consumption increased 140 per cent between 1864 and 1873. By 1872, the Milwaukee Chamber of Commerce could boast that "the relatively small city of Milwaukee had overtaken such great brewing centers as New York, Philadelphia, and St. Louis, as the greatest beer exporting center in the nation," an attainment aided by a 44 per cent boost in total sales when many Chicago breweries were destroyed in the great fire of 1871. (The state as a whole, however, was far from making the most beer—eighth in 1871 with 218,544 barrels, compared to New York's 2,305,145. In total production, Wisconsin did not become number one until the 1950's.) Brewing had become big business in Milwaukee—larger even than flour milling in value of product and in capital invested, and in some years it even exceeded the city's iron foundries as the city's largest money maker.

Politically, beer was controversial from the beginning. Many Yankee and Yorker settlers were staunchly prohibitionist, and vigorous, though unsuccessful, efforts were made to incorporate temperance provisions into the state's constitution. Almost wholly an Anglo-Saxon, Protestant crusade, the temperance movement contained undercurrents of agitation against foreigners and the social and economic problems that accompanied rising immigration. In 1849, the legislature passed a law making saloonkeepers responsible for damage done by their inebriated customers and required the posting of a bond to assure payment. Germans, who were already disregarding the Sunday laws on the books since territorial days, immediately began agitating for repeal of this law. Instead, it was strengthened in 1850 with the support of Milwaukee legislator John B. Smith, a former head of the state chapter of the Sons of Temperance. Three or four hundred angry Germans expressed their disapproval of Smith's efforts by marching on his house and smashing the windows. The law was replaced the following year by an ordinary licensing act.

Outright prohibition was an issue in state elections in the 1850's. The newly founded Republican party's espousal of the cause left it open to accusations of nativism, and contributed to its defeat in the 1855 campaign, though historians agree that slavery was a more important issue. Periodically throughout the rest of the century, and especially in the 1880's, the issue was revived. Organizations like the Woman's Christian Temperance Union and the Anti-Saloon League, the latter an umbrella group for most temperance societies, were formed in the late nineteenth century. By the early 1900's, they were something of a political factor in Wisconsin.

With brewing Wisconsin's eighth largest industry in 1919, the Eighteenth Amendment to the U.S. Constitution was greeted with something less than universal enthusiasm. Prohibition forces had played their political cards effectively, and there was no doubt in anyone's mind that the Wisconsin legislature would approve the amendment. But when it did (passage was completed on January 22, 1919), the action had little impact: more states than necessary already had passed it. The succeeding dry decade was a grim one for beer-drinking Wisconsinites, though here, as elsewhere, "prohibition" simply meant clandestine rather than public revelry. As soon as they could, Wisconsinites joined the movement for repeal, and on April 25, 1933, in a special session lasting only forty minutes, the legislature cast unanimous ballots for repeal—the second state to ratify.

The drinking of beer was well laced into the fabric of German culture and the customs of other European groups. The *biergarten* bore only a passing relationship to the drinking establishments of America's earlier Anglo-Saxon settlers. Rather, it was a place where families relaxed evenings and weekends and enjoyed singing, instrumental music, drama, companionship, and lively conversation—in addition to golden, frothy brew. Steins of beer also eased the exertions of strenuous gymnastic exercises and intellectual and philosophical discussions at the *Turnverein*. *Gemutlichkeit*—which translates as good, warm feelings and fellowship—appropriately describes the atmosphere of the traditional German *biergarten* or the local *Turnhalle*.

Such establishments were to be found in all parts of the state where Germans settled, not just in Milwaukee. And it was not just Milwaukee beer that was sold. At one time or another at least 242 Wisconsin towns and cities had their own brewers and breweries—including such crossroads places as British Hollow, Francis Creek, and Tirade.

At one time in the late nineteenth century, 300 breweries were active in Wisconsin. One even made a non-alcoholic beer: the New Era Brewing Company of Kenosha turned out 10,000 barrels a year of "temperance" beer between 1883 and 1889, and sold from branch offices in Milwaukee, Philadelphia, and Jacksonville, Florida. Seventy-three breweries survived prohibition by making ice cream, cheese, near-beer, and soft drinks. But by 1956, only forty-one remained. The decade of the 1960's was very hard on these local breweries. Some went bankrupt; others were bought out by bigger outfits; many closed down, including Fauerbach Brewing (founded in 1848) in Madison; the Fountain Brewing Co. (1885) in Fountain City; the Kingsbury Breweries Co. (1847) in Sheboygan; and the Rahr Green Bay Brewing Corp. (1886). Six more dried up in the 1970's, among them Oshkosh Brewing Co. (1866), Potosi Brewing Co. (1866), and the George Walter Brewing Co. (1880) of Appleton. In 1979, eight companies were still pasting labels on Wisconsin brew. The three in Milwaukee—Pabst, Miller, and Schlitz—were national and international concerns; Heileman in La Crosse was multiregional, distributing in forty-one states under its own and the Blatz label; and three were regional: Point in Stevens Point, Leinenkugel in Chippewa Falls, and Huber in Monroe. Only

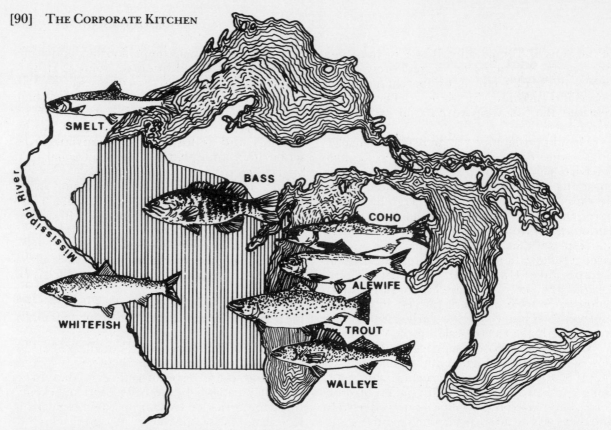

SMELT

Mississippi River

BASS

COHO

ALEWIFE

WHITEFISH

TROUT

WALLEYE

John Walter & Co. in Eau Claire survived as an example of a local brewery.

From the beginning, then, Milwaukee was indisputably the commercial beer center of the state—and among the leading producers in the nation.* Milwaukee's malt liquor preeminence was due in no small measure to the rapid and creative growth of advertising and promotion, stimulated by intense competition. Between 1870 and 1890, for instance, advertising and promotional activities helped increase annual sales of Milwaukee beer alone from 108,842 barrels to 1,809,066. Such promotion was costly. In 1891, the Pabst company spent $162,000 promoting its products in the U.S. and abroad, a large sum for the time and almost double its 1890 expenditure.

The leading brewers established beer gardens, restaurants, and occasionally hotels where their products were sold exclusively. In addition to numerous small beer gardens or saloons in Milwaukee, Schlitz built the fashionable Schlitz Hotel and Palm Garden in 1889, and Milwaukeeans were offered a variety of amusements—from sports to opera—in Schlitz Park. Captain Frederick Pabst also had his name on outlets in Milwaukee, and at one time he controlled nine hotels or restaurants in New York, Chicago, Minneapolis, and San Francisco. The Pabst Hotel* in New York was a hostelry for bachelors; many of the guests no doubt visited Pabst's Loop pavilion at Coney Island or ate at the Pabst Harlem, which was the largest restaurant in America when it opened in 1900. Pabst was fond of hiring matinee idols to go

---

*But not even in the boom days of the late 1880's and early 1890's was it the city's leading industry when compared, for example, with all iron products, or with the leather industry.

*Opened on November 11, 1899, it was razed only three years later to make way for a subway line.

around to his establishments, buy beer for the house, and drink the health of Captain Fred Pabst, "Milwaukee's greatest beer brewer."

The giants of brewing were also skilled at getting their product into the picture of momentous or well-publicized events. Admiral Robert E. Peary was said to have found a bottle of Pabst (empty, to Peary's disappointment, or so the story goes) near the North Pole; Schlitz made good on his offer of a reward of 3,600 bottles of Schlitz to Admiral George Dewey and his men for the capture of Manila; and Schlitz beer was among the supplies Theodore Roosevelt took on safari in Africa.

As for advertising, the distribution of words and symbols accelerated in proportion to beer production. Schlitz began using its famous line, "The Beer That Made Milwaukee Famous," which it is said to have purchased from another small brewer for $5,000 after the Chicago Fire.* (Later, Pabst started saying that "Milwaukee beer is famous—Pabst has made it so," a phrase that was dropped in 1898 after Schlitz threatened legal action.) Advertising stressed brewery symbols and logos as well as slogans. By 1903, the Schlitz globe, Pabst's blue ribbon, the Blatz triangle, the Gettleman thousand-dollar reward label, and the Miller girl on a crescent moon were recognizable all over the country and numerous points overseas.

In modern times, the number of Wisconsin breweries has diminished, corporations have consolidated or have been absorbed by conglomerates, and beers bearing Milwaukee company labels are no longer necessarily brewed in the state. Fewer breweries, however, have not meant less beer. In 1949, the first year that Wisconsin's output exceeded New York's, Badger breweries made 12,192,295 barrels; in 1966, the figure was 15,345,303; and in 1977, it was 24,059,542 or about 14 per cent of the national total—figures that would have staggered the imagination of Jacob Best in 1844.

When all the economic balances are totalled, Wisconsin no longer can be considered primarily an agricultural state. Comparing agricultural and food industries with Wisconsin's other endeavors (manufacturing, wholesale and retail trade, service industries, government, and all the rest) is of course a bit like comparing apples with oranges. Nonetheless, a glance at personal income figures shows that agriculture more than holds its own in Wisconsin today, and that it has been growing at a faster rate than other sectors of the economy. Sheer numbers of farms and farmers may have been dwindling, but total personal income derived from farming in Wisconsin leaped 116.9 per cent between 1970 and 1977—a far greater jump than that enjoyed by any other group except those employed in agricultural services, forestry, and fisheries.

Unquestionably both the growing of things to eat and drink and the processing of foodstuffs continue to play an important role in the economic well-being of the state. Even more vital is the reliance of state and nation upon agriculture for the physical well-being of their citizens. Farmers and food processors have proved again and again over the past 150 years that they can adapt to changing times and increasing demands, and American agricultural progress has become the envy of the world. A good deal of that envy has been aroused by a dwindling band of Wisconsinites whose roots reach into the soils of many lands. All credit to them from all corners of the globe!

*According to some historians. The official Schlitz version is that it evolved out of conversations between Baron Alfred von Kotzhausen, president of the lithography company that made the Schlitz label, and a Schlitz employee, Ernest Bielefeld.

Chapter 9

LEFTOVERS

ALL FEASTS PRODUCE LEFTOVERS—TIDBITS TOO good to throw away. They are usually set aside for later snacks, or even to provide another meal or two. So it is with this smorgasbord of Wisconsin's culinary heritage: the research for this book produced numerous morsels of information that could not be stirred into the preceding chapter courses. But they are too good to toss out, and they are served here for the reader to savor at odd moments.

* * * * * *

Mosquitoes have plagued Wisconsin farmers and livestock from earliest times. One farmer's son remembered how the mosquito problem was solved in the late 1850's at milking time in the open cow yard: "A smoke was first made by firing a bunch of farmyard litter, then turning down the blaze by putting green grass upon it. This made a dense, strong-smelling smoke, and the cattle would crowd into it."

* * * * * *

Syrup and molasses pails were saved as lunch pails for schoolchildren. Bread with butter or sorghum syrup, an apple, and some pastries made a typical hearty noon repast for a rural youngster in the late nineteenth century.

* * * * * *

Commercial frozen foods may be a twentieth-century invention, but Wisconsin's pioneer housewives discovered the principle for themselves in our deep-freeze winters. Cupboards built into the north side of a house, areas under the eaves, attics, closed porches, and separate storage sheds were perfect for keeping foods over the long winter. Some froze milk in pan molds to use in cooking. French-Canadians often baked huge quantities of their pork pie specialty, *tourtière*, and froze the surplus tucked up under the porch eaves out of reach of wild animals. And most logging camps had a separate storehouse for keeping meat.

* * * * * *

"The large *BEAR*, belonging to Gov. *FARWELL* which has been so often visited and admired by many of our citizens, was slaughtered this morning, and the meat is now in the market of Messrs *CONLEY* & Co. The animal is very large and fat, and any person desiring choice bit for *Thanksgiving*, will have to call early this evening, when it will be cut up and distributed. We understand that this animal had become rather cross and troublesome of late on which account he has forfeited his life."

—Item in the Madison *Wisconsin State Journal*, November 23, 1853.

* * * * * *

For much of his adult life, Governor and Senator Robert M. La Follette suffered greatly from digestive disorders. He found relief in a diet that today would be described as faddish. In response to a 1905 letter from former Governor William R. Taylor, La Follette described his daily fare:

"Breakfast: two granose biscuits (Battle Creek Sanitarium)* with cream and maltose (a Battle Creek Syrup made of grain).

"Lunch: plenty of zwieback (a Battle Creek bread which can be bought at any grocery) with butter. Two glasses of milk, and from six to a dozen English walnuts eaten throughout the meal from start to finish with the zwieback, and thoroughly masticated.

"Dinner: same."

La Follette's letter concluded: "I do not know how this would agree with you; it has certainly agreed with me."

---

*The Battle Creek Sanitarium was until 1906 a Seventh Day Adventist vegetarian health center run by Dr. John Harvey Kellogg. (Kellogg was excommunicated in 1906, but retained the sanitarium.) With the assistance of his brother Will Keith Kellogg, Dr. Kellogg developed numerous nut and grain products including corn flakes. Granose was a flaked wheat cereal. W. K. Kellogg founded the company that marketed his corn flakes nationwide.

* * * * * *

The gargantuan meals packed away by late-nineteenth-century Americans who could afford them have been much written about, especially the banquets, restaurant meals, and important family celebrations. And it was not only males who measured the success of a festive occasion by the degree of that stuffed feeling.

In 1883, the fourth biennial convention of Kappa Kappa Gamma sorority was held in Madison's Park Hotel. At the banquet, the young women sat down to offerings of raw oysters, tomato soup with rice, baked stuffed whitefish with port wine sauce, boiled chicken with parsley sauce, corned beef with young cabbage, chicken salad, celery, lobster salad, roast baron of beef with horse radishes, mallard duck with game sauce, young turkey with English dressing, prairie chicken with jelly, fried oysters, sliced prairie chicken with olives, tenderloin of beef with mushroom sauce, broiled snipe on toast, baked sweet potatoes, stewed green corn, stewed tomatoes, baked mashed potatoes, assorted cakes, lemon pie, vanilla ice cream, champagne jelly, mixed nuts, California pears, apples, raisins, oranges, grapes, and French coffee.

* * * * * *

When the Green Bay land sales office was selling the newly platted communities of Milwaukee and Navarino in 1835–1836, the ladies of the town marked the occasion with the first church fair in the community and possibly the state. Women of all denominations got together to raise money, although the fair was under the auspices of Episcopalian Christ Church, which had been incorporated in 1829. Numerous articles were collected and sold, including a miniature wigwam that brought $40. There was a supper of great quantity and much variety. Another culinary feature, which fetched a large price, was generous helpings of floating island, a kind of custard.

* * * * * *

No public occasion on a community's social calendar during the nineteenth century equalled the festivities of the Fourth of July. This was the big celebration of the year, with parades, oratory, public picnics, and fireworks displays in the evening.

In 1839, when Madison was a-building, the residents welcomed the Fourth as a chance to vary their usual diet of bacon and fish with a fat steer. The men washed this down with what they called Peckatonica and Rock River. (The names of southern Wisconsin rivers, not always spelled as they are now, were used to designate various grades of whiskey.)

Liquor, however, was not a part of every community's observance of July Fourth. In 1854, the *Wisconsin Temperance League* (a weekly newspaper published in Milwaukee) carried this account of the day's festivities in Baraboo: "The dinner, for variety, deliciousness and abundance, was probably never equalled in so new a place . . . . The tables were loaded with upwards of forty different varieties of food, well prepared and tastefully arranged . . . . We know by the tickets collected at the table that twelve hundred persons dined with us on the occasion . . . . No drunkenness was seen about the town during the day or evening; and with very few exceptions no profanity was heard. What a change there will be [elsewhere] in our Fourth of July celebration when rum is outlawed."

A northwestern Wisconsin resident recalled a memorable Fourth in the early 1880's when a cut-down pork barrel was used to make lemonade for the picnic. There was no ice, since the relatively new settlement had not yet progressed to the icehouse stage, and the water had to be carried from the creek under a July sun: "It was warm lemonade, but it was good, it was a treat, and it was free!" For entrees, "I suppose there were baked beans and homemade bread and butter sandwiches." And for dessert, "In those first few years it was only at Christmas time and on the Fourth of July that folks had pie or cake, so I suppose we did have a taste on the first Fourth celebration."

In another developing part of the state, at least one businessman promoted a Fourth of July celebration as much for profit as patriotic reasons. Dave Stewart, who owned a mill near Wittenberg in Shawano County, decided in 1889 to "have a Fourth of July celebration at the Saw Mill," as one of his employees later wrote. "He thought that way he would hold the Mill People and they would not go away for the Fourth of July and that the mill would start that much sooner after the Fourth of July. The men clubbed together and raised $32.00 for the Fire Works and the Ware House was cleaned out for dancing and the Brush was cleaned out of a piece of woods east of the Lumber yard for the afternoon celebration. A Methodist Minister from Clintonville was there to speak about the Fourth of July and our Liberty from England.

"I was cookee and so was Ovy St. Clair, and Albert Fitzgerald was the cook. He baked many Strawberry Pies, cookies, Doughnuts, cake, and so forth and we had a Big Supper for all. The outsiders paid for supper but the Boarders had theirs free. At 8 P.M. the Fire works were set off on a Hill across the road East from the Orchard and they were fine. After that was over every one went to the Ware House to Dance. The music was fine; they danced until 4 A.M."

* * * * * *

During the periods when the milk cow went dry, families had to go without. In 1874, the *Palmyra Enterprise* carried this helpful advice: "In early spring, when many cows are dry, and milk scarce, the housekeeper has a chance to show her skill in 'getting up' a variety for the table without the almost indispensable 'quart' or 'cup' of sweet or sour milk. In many dishes, water can be used instead of milk and few if any could tell the difference. Very nice bread puddings can be made with water by using one or more eggs and a little more butter and suet."

* * * * * *

When E. C. (Ed) Berners, owner of a modest ice cream parlor in Two Rivers, died on July 1, 1939, he rated a front-page obituary in the *Chicago Tribune*. He is credited with being the first man ever to make an ice cream sundae.

In 1929, when Berners himself recalled that historic day in the summer of 1881 for an interview in the *Two Rivers Reporter*, he gave full credit for the idea to George Hallauer, a Two Rivers native who became a utility executive in Illinois and who was a regular summer-vacation customer.

"One night, Hallauer dropped in and ordered a dish of ice cream," Berners said. "As I was serving it he spied a bottle of chocolate syrup on the back bar, which I used for making sodas.

" 'Why don't you put some of that chocolate on the ice cream?' he asked.

" 'You don't want to ruin the flavor of the ice cream,' I protested. But Hallauer answered, 'I'll try anything once,' and I poured on the chocolate. Hallauer liked it and the ice cream sundae was born."

Chocolate-topped ice cream became the rage at Berners' store, and Berners began experimenting with other flavors. His delicious concoctions carried fanciful names like Flora Dora, Mudscow, and Chocolate Peany, which contained peanuts. A generous slurp of apple cider was also a popular topping.

However, the name "sundae" originated in neighboring Manitowoc. According to Berners, George Giffy began serving the embellished ice cream dish on Sundays in his establishment. But one weekday, a little girl ordered a dish of ice cream "with stuff on it." When told he only served it on Sunday, the child is supposed to have said: "Why, then, this must be Sunday, for it's the kind of ice cream I want."

Giffy gave it to her, of course, and henceforth called the dish a *Sunday*.

How the spelling evolved into *sundae* is not known. But word of this new dish spread quickly. Hallauer, an Illinois resident, passed the news southward, and soon both Evanston and Rockford laid claim to its origin. (Ed Berners always felt the fame of the specialty was spread by glassware salesmen who, quickly realizing the possibilities, had fostered the design of the canoe-shaped, footed bowls known as "sundae dishes" that were fixtures in most every ice cream parlor in America by the end of the century.)

In any event, in researching the origin of the word *sundae* for *The American Language: Supplement I*, H. L. Mencken found claimants to the idea in Ann Arbor, Michigan, Ithaca, New York, Norfolk, Virginia, and Washington, D.C. He rejected them all in favor of Two Rivers, Wisconsin—and rejected as well one suggestion that the confection was named after the famous evangelist Billy Sunday.

Ed Berners, who never tried to capitalize on the treat that became an American fixture, continued to operate his candy store and soda parlor at 1404 Fifteenth Street for many years and was well-known in the community as a colorful personality. He always served his patrons in an immaculate white jacket, was rarely without a cigar (which he never lighted), and favored derby hats when outdoors.

The State Historical Society of Wisconsin recognized Two Rivers as the birthplace of the sundae with a historical marker erected in 1973.

* * * * * *

Before glass canning jars were widely available, foods were preserved in stone jars which were sealed with cloth dipped in wax made of resin and beeswax, or with home-made corks topped with melted resin.

* * * * * *

Swedish immigrants to turn-of-the-century Pierce County followed the Old World custom of setting one day aside for neighborly gestures. When calling on new or sick friends, the woman of the house and her older daughters brought along baked goods. If there was a new baby in the house, fruit soup was the traditional offering.

* * * * * *

Door County's famous culinary specialty, the fish boil, is believed to have originated with the early Scandinavian settlers, whose cuisine is replete with boiled fish recipes. In Wisconsin, they found plentiful supplies of whitefish and lake trout as well as hospitable soil for potatoes and onions. Those settlers included many loggers, and boiling dinner in one large pot out of doors was an efficient way to prepare a meal for the work crews. As a tourist event, however, the boil is of fairly recent origin, dating from the 1960's and proving that not all traditions are old traditions.

* * * * * *

One thing Wisconsin has always produced in great abundance is ice. And for about twenty years at the end of the nineteenth century (and to a lesser extent for the first two decades of the twentieth century), massive ice harvesting was the basis of a profitable food-related business.

Communities and individuals had long harvested ice for local commercial needs and family ice boxes and storage cellars and sheds. But then the burgeoning industrialization of Wisconsin and the Midwest, coupled with improved transportation facilities, created a huge demand for this commodity.

By the 1880's, Milwaukee brewers, for instance, required almost 350,000 tons of ice annually to keep their beer cool. In fact, there were those who credited the availability of natural ice for Milwaukee's brewing ascendancy over older and more southerly cities in the country. Even larger were the needs of the meatpacking industry in Chicago. It was Gustavus Swift who, in the 1870's, took the most successful advantage of refrigerator cars developed a decade earlier. Carloads of meat packed and shipped in ice were sent daily from Chicago to distant markets. Fruit and vegetable marketers, too, adopted the practice.

Wisconsin ice, almost always twelve to fourteen inches thick, was ideal for the purpose.

Furthermore, unlike the increasingly polluted waters closer to Chicago, the state's rivers and lakes were clean, and their natural currents produced a clear, bubble-free product, unlike the Chicago area's cloudier, more porous substance. Icehouses blossomed on Pewaukee Lake, in the Green Bay area, in Madison, and in McFarland. The ice was measured off, then cut with special saws, picks, and chisels. The cakes, weighing 200 pounds or more, were then floated down pre-cut channels to the icehouse where they were dragged onto steam-driven conveyor belts that hauled them up to storage lofts. Or the ice could be placed directly in sawdust-insulated railroad cars for shipment to Chicago or Milwaukee. As many as 300 freight cars could be loaded at the Armour ice facility at Pewaukee, which operated day and night when there was an ice shortage to the south.

At century's end, the ice business began to melt away. Mergers of Chicago outfits created what appeared to be an "ice trust" in the eyes of politically progressive Wisconsinites. And the economically minded saw in ice a possible source for school revenue. So the state legislature in 1901 imposed a 10 per cent state tax per ton on ice cut for shipment elsewhere. (Two years later, it repealed the measure.) Chicago regulations, too, hurt the trade. In 1895 and 1896, it adopted clean-ice standards; by 1908 most Madison lakes failed to meet them. (Lake Wingra, however, made the grade.) More importantly, technological advances began to make artificial ice production increasingly practical.

Ice continued to be cut for outside markets until the unseasonably warm winter of 1920–1921, having enjoyed a revival during World War I. Then massive harvest for export all but ceased. Local outfits, however, continued, since Wisconsin, as no resident need be told, still produces ice each winter. The Junction City Fire Department, for example, in 1977 was still harvesting ice on Mill Creek for its summer picnic and to sell to other picnics as a fund-raising enterprise.

* * * * * *

Stoughton lays claim to being the originator of one of America's most revered institutions—the coffee break.

It started because Stoughton was among Wisconsin's important tobacco towns. Back in 1880, the story goes, the many tobacco warehouses in the labor-short community began hiring Norwegian-born housewives to sort and grade cured tobacco. These workers needed periodic breaks to return to nearby homes to check on their children and the progress of slow-simmering meals. While at home, they naturally took some time out to pour a cup of coffee from the ever-present pot at the back of the stove. Thus the coffee break.

Stoughton residents consider it natural that the institution should have originated in their town, for Norwegians have always been known to require lots of coffee between meals to keep themselves going. Even today, Stoughton, which bills itself as the Norse Capital of the United States, claims to drink more coffee per capita than any city in the country.

* * * * * *

In some of the more remote rural areas, and more often in the developing areas of the cutover region, getting to market in the winter was difficult even as late as the 1910's and early 1920's. Many women ordered their staple groceries from the Montgomery Ward and Sears catalogues. And the grocery wagon was not an uncommon sight in places. As one man remembered it: "The Great Atlantic and Pacific Tea Co. was not a chain of food markets in the 'nineties. In our country seat city [Lancaster], one man drove a one-horse cart from door to door, taking orders and delivering tea and spices. The cart was small and enclosed and equipped with shelves and drawers for the numerous small packages of the products sold. There was barely enough room on the sides for doors and the name and design of A. & P."

* * * * * *

Weddings were noteworthy social events even when the guests came away hungry. A Prairie du Chien resident recorded in February, 1895: "We attended two weddings this week . . . . There was a big blow made about Nelda's, it was quite a high-toned wedding. They served supper on a napkin on your lap and if you were very hungry you could not satisfy it to a great extent as there was not enough passed to satisfy a very hungry man. The bridesmaids wore low-necked dresses."

* * * * * *

Pere Jacques Marquette, the seventeenth-century missionary and explorer, was much struck by a fish he found in the Mississippi River: "When we cast our nets into the water we caught Sturgeon, and a very extraordinary Kind of fish. It resembles the trout, with This difference, that its mouth is larger. Near its nose—which is smaller, as are also the eyes—is a large Bone shaped Like a woman's busk, three fingers wide and a Cubit Long, at the end of which is a disk as Wide As one's hand. This frequently causes it to fall backward when it leaps out of the water."

He was describing an unusual fish indeed: the paddlefish, found only in the Mississippi River system. Its scientific name is *Polyodon spathula*, and its sole relative resides in China's Yangtze River. Today the paddlefish is an endangered species.

* * * * * *

In describing the varieties of fish found in Wisconsin, early explorers often listed carp. They were probably referring to the buffalo fish or carp sucker. Carp is not native to this area, but thrived in state waters after being planted in lakes and streams during the latter part of the nineteenth century.

* * * * * *

Wild ginseng, an ancient herb much prized by Orientals, grew abundantly in Wisconsin, but not all Indian tribes used it either for medicine or as a seasoning. The Forest Potawatomi were one that did. They found medicinal uses for the root, which they pounded for a poultice to cure earache or soaked to produce an eyewash. It was also added to other medicines and cures as a seasoner or to mask unpleasant tastes.

The Forest Potawatomi and other Wisconsin tribes, however, harvested ginseng roots for sale, along with their furs, to traders. Many tribes were familiar with the plant's characteristics. The Chippewa, for instance, knew that it required five or six years of growth to produce both the seed-containing red berries and a large, mature root. When harvesting, they lopped off the fruiting top and dropped it into the root hole, firming the earth on top. That way, they were assured of another crop.

Early white settlers also were aware that the ginseng root was highly valued, and for many people in the areas where it grew—largely in well-drained forests—digging, drying, and selling it made a real difference in the family's ledgers. "Seng diggers," armed with a ginseng mattock (with a pick at one end of the head and a hoe at the other), would comb the forests in late August and September and on a good day find up to five pounds. In the drying, the roots lose from one-half to two-thirds their weight. Even so, the poundage added up to a valuable figure in Wisconsin, whose exports were said to have been worth $40,000 in 1858 and $80,000 in 1859. To this day, diggers comb the woods for their botanical prey, but now they must purchase licenses in Wisconsin, since wild ginseng is in danger of eradication.

Such a valuable crop naturally attracted agricultural attention, and in the 1870's American farmers attempted commercial cultivation. Their efforts failed at first, but eventually some New York experiments managed to repeat Mother Nature's processes, and commercial plantings began yielding by the 1880's. "How-to" publications appeared in the 1890's, after which various Wisconsin growers entered the field, especially in Marathon County, where in the first decade of the twentieth century, several interested farmers joined the National Cultivated Wild Ginseng Growers' Association. Today, Marathon County grows almost 95 per cent of the commercially cultivated ginseng in the United States. (The export value of the entire U.S. crop was almost $12 million in 1979.)

Besides export, ginseng served as the basis for a Wisconsin-made product. From 1906 until about 1930, the Ginseng Company of Menomonee Falls was cultivating the plant and then processing it into Pfabe's Ginseng Drink. (Hugo Pfabe was one of the company's owners.)

This drink was promoted as a "beneficial beverage which now takes the place of harmful liquors," as a "nerve tonic with soothing qualities," and "an energizing beverage with no harmful effects." The wording was designed to contrast Pfabe's beverage favorably with Coca-Cola, which replaced the cocaine in its formula with caffeine early in this century.

Ginseng has been long regarded in herbal pharmacology as an aid in treating weakness, bronchitis, asthma, tuberculosis, diseases of kidney and spleen, cold hands and feet, nausea, diabetes, diarrhea, arthritis, gout, high blood pressure, fatigue, ulcers, insomnia, leprosy, smallpox, weakness after childbirth, colds—and that is only a partial list. It is not, as some like to believe, an aphrodisiac. The scientific name for the plant is *Panax quinquefolium*. *Panax*, in Latin, means panacea.

More and more farmers have joined the ranks of ginseng growers. In 1978, Marathon County estimates were that two or three hundred farmers cultivated it on plots ranging from a quarter-acre up to a hundred acres. Ginseng is difficult to grow and requires a considerable investment. Profits, of course, make the work and risk worthwhile. In 1890, fair ginseng fetched $2.40 a pound, while the best—an old root resembling the body of a man with head and limbs—brought $4 a pound. A successful harvest in 1978 brought $45 to $60 a pound, as increasing demand in America and Europe added to the traditional Far Eastern market kept boosting the price in the decade of the 1970's.

* * * * * *

The large, warmly commodious kitchen and the giant of a stove that dominated it remain a vivid remembrance of things past for many Wisconsinites still living. Some stoves were of plain black cast iron, but others were lavishly embellished with shiny chrome or nickel. Plain or fancy, they were intricate and efficient constructions of lids, fire box, warming oven, baking ovens, water tank, storage shelves, movable grates, and ash chest. The manipulator of this marvelous machine was very adept at controlling the oven temperatures and utilizing the surface's hot and cool spots to achieve the results desired.

There were a number of ways to test the proper heat for baking in a wood or coal stove oven. Being able to keep your hand in the oven for a moderately slow count of twenty was one. Another was to throw some flour onto the floor of the oven; if the flour caught fire, the oven was too hot. (The proper temperature browned the flour slightly after a few seconds.)

The flour might also be placed in a dish in the middle of the oven; in that position, the correct browning time was one minute. And some relied on the white writing paper test. If a sheet of it burned, the oven was too hot. If the color turned to yellow or buff, the cake or bread could go in.

On the surface of the stove, there were usually pots and pans setting at all times on the hot and cool sections, with foods in various stages of preparation: the coffee or tea pot always at the ready, the bowl of sweet cream slowly souring, the pudding simmering, the bread rising.

* * * * * *

Nineteenth-century letters and memoirs are sprinkled with references to what are regarded today as curious ways to avoid illness. In 1882, for example, a Norwegian immigrant noted that many of his fellow workers in a railroad camp got sick "from the alkali water. I was not affected, perhaps because I seldom drank, even in hot weather, and when I did, I always drank water mixed with oatmeal."

At about the same time, a St. Croix Falls mother handed her children a bottle of Brown's Jamaica Ginger when they left home for a spell. " . . . [Y]ou take care of that bottle, for some of the boys might have a stomach-ache," she was quoted by a son seventy years later. "And sure enough, because of over-indulgence in good food or some other causes, you were the victim, and Brown's Jamaica Ginger was promptly applied."

Then there was this recipe for what was delicately called "female weakness" in Lyman Copeland Draper's book (see Chapter 6): "Take a handful of hollyhock blossoms, three pints port wine, a quarter of a pound of loaf sugar, and a grated nutmeg. Take a wineglass every morning before breakfast."

* * * * * *

Wisconsin's abundant wild strawberries provided numerous pleasant memories for early settlers. Richard Dart, one of several children in the family of Anson Dart who settled near the south shore of Green Lake in 1840, recalled years later a memorable treat in June, 1843:

"[We] found a place as big as an 80 acre lot, where the fire had burned over in the fall or spring, covered with ripe strawberries . . . . The next day we took the ox team [and] pails, pans, wash-tubs, etc. —everything we had to carry things—and all went over . . . . We boys picked all day and mother staid by the plum trees and hulled the berries as we picked so as to take home the more . . . . When we got home we were glad to find company . . . . We were ready for them . . . . We took part [of the berries] and hung them up in a large linen cloth or bag and put in a half-bushel at a time and squeezed out the juice and treated our friends to strawberry nectar. We had a gallon or so fit for gentlemen to drink."

* * * * * *

Non-English-speaking immigrants encountered many difficulties in their first days in the state because of the language gap. Not all of them were unpleasant. One Danish settler, who arrived in 1892, recalled the night he spent at a hotel in Thorp.

"In the morning, when we got up, [he wrote] we still had some butter and bread in our satchels, which we ate at that time. When we came downstairs a fellow asked us if we wanted breakfast. Of course, not being familiar with the English language we did not know what breakfast meant, but told him in good Dane, that we would like a cup of coffee. The landlord being as familiar with the Danish language as we were with English, rushed us into the dining room, and soon a young lady came with pancakes, two or three different kinds of meat, coffee and so forth. There was no use for us to protest and tell her that we already had our breakfast at our room, because she did not understand our language, so we decided the best we could do was to eat all we could out of it, in order to get our money's worth."

* * * * * *

In these days of dwindling energy supplies, fireless cookers could return to the popularity they enjoyed in the first quarter of this century. The 1924 *Calumet Baking Powder Cook Book*, a popular product cookbook of the time, described how to make this precursor of the modern slow cooker or "crockpot," but one that required little energy to operate:

"The use of the fireless cooker is spreading rapidly on account of its saving in fuel, time, work, and worry. It consists of a box or chest packed with a good non-conductor of heat, into which a kettle containing food heated to a boiling point is placed. The lid, consisting of the same non-conducting material, is closed, and heat cannot escape, consequently the water in the kettle remains at the boiling point to cook the same as if it were on the stove. These cookers are now being manufactured by many firms. Some of them, however, are not as good as home-made ones.

"A fireless cooker can easily be made by packing excelsior in a square box or bushel basket tightly around the kettle to be used and on removing the kettle, cotton cloth can be placed over the excelsior and tacked to remain. A cushion of excelsior should be left solid at the bottom, and the sides of the box lined with newspaper, before putting the excelsior therein. About 4 inches of excelsior should be left between the kettle and the sides of the box, and the same kettle should always be used so as to fit snugly in its own nest.

"In the fireless cooker there is no evaporation. All the goodness and flavor of the food are retained by this slow and thorough mode of cooking. Onions and cabbage may be cooked without the odor permeating the house. While doing the dinner dishes, you can cook what you want for supper. Put the kettles in the fireless cooker and attend to other things, or go out, without the slightest anxiety, and at supper time find it hot and deliciously cooked. You can cook the oatmeal, or any cereal, for 5 minutes after supper, put it in the fireless cooker, and find it thoroughly cooked and hot at any time in the morning as needed. You can cook a boiled dinner on a hot summer day, without any odor or heat in your kitchen. All this can be done on a fireless cooker."

* * * * * *

In many Wisconsin communities, particularly the smaller ones, the school picnic was, as one immigrant from Sweden put it, "the big social community event of the year." Around the turn of the century, he recalled, "All parents, children and others in the community met in a shady wooded area for a day of fellowship, games, and feasting. There was everything that you could imagine in foods—home-made breads, pudding, cakes, pies, ice cream, lemonade, and coffee. The children amused themselves with their games while the adults would sit around and visit, or join in a tug-of-war, baseball game, or other sports."

* * * * * *

In the late summer of 1773, Peter Pond, a fur trader and adventurer, spent a memorable day fishing on the Mississippi River at the mouth of the Wisconsin. His enthusiasm was undiminished as he wrote of the day's angling years later in his autobiography:

"We Put our Hoock and Lines into the Water & Leat them Ly all nite. In the Morning we Perseaved thare was fish in the Hoocks and went to the Wattr Eag [water's edge] and halld on our line. Thay Came Heavey. At Lengh we hald one ashore that wade a Hundered and four Pounds—a Seacond that was One Hundered Wate—a third of Seventy five Pounds. The Men was Glad to Sea this for thay Had not Eat mete for Sum Days nor fish for a long time. We asked our men How meney Men the Largest would Give a Meale. Sum of the Largest Eaters Sade twelve men Would Eat it at a Meal. We Agread to Give ye fish if thay would find twelve men that would undertake it. Thay Began to Dres it. The fish was what was Cald the Cat fish. It Had a large flat Head Sixteen Inches Betwene the Eise. Thay Skind it—Cut it up in three larg Coppers Such as we have for the Youse of our men. After It was Well Boild thay Sawd it up and all Got Round it. Thay Began and Eat the hole without the least thing with it But Salt and Sum of them Drank of the Licker it was Boild in. The Other two was Sarved out to the Remainder of the People who finished them in a Short time. Thay all Declard thay felt the Beater of thare Meale Nor did I perseave that Eney of them ware Sick or Complaind."

* * * * * *

Maple sap could be processed to provide piquancy to food as well as sweetness. As was noted in the 1849 diary of an early German settler near Sheboygan: "I went to boil sugar, however I did not make sugar or syrup today but vinegar, which has to evaporate. We collected some more sap from the trees and did evaporate as much as necessary, except the last portion which I let boil when I went home at night."

* * * * * *

In 1839 a doctor in Spring Prairie, Walworth County, got more than he bargained for when he decided to enliven the social scene with a "Pumpkin Pie Ball." The guests gathered in the doctor's two-story log tavern, ate the pies, and were enjoying the dancing when, as a later chronicler recounted, "one after another were taken sick . . . . among the throng, recently so happy and joyous. The strange sensations of the guests led to the suspicions that poison had, in some way, been administered, and the doctor began to search for the cause. He ascertained that the pies were seasoned with allspice; a specimen of which was brought for his inspection. He saw at once that his family had used a quantity of Lee's pills [a laxative], which he had brought with him from Indiana, and which were carefully laid away in his pantry. Being small and hard, they had been mistaken for allspice, and used, by the pastry cook, in preparing the pies, this producing the disasters of the evening."

* * * * * *

The early explorer Jonathan Carver described in his travel account one of the Green Bay area's native plants, which he noted on September 13, 1766:

"Near the borders of the lake grow a great number of sand cherries, which are not the less remarkable for their manner of growth, than for their exquisite flavor. They grow upon a small shrub, not more than four feet high, the boughs of which are so loaded that they lie in clusters on the sand. As they grow only on the sand, the warmth of which probably contributes to bring them to such perfection, they are called Sand Cherries. The size of them does not exceed that of a small musket ball, but they are reckoned superior to any other sort for the purpose of steeping in spirits."

Sand cherries were much favored as a flavor enhancer of whiskey—"the best I ever yet saw to put into spiritous liquor," Carver wrote.

* * * * * *

Christmas was a special time to men working in logging camps in the remote north woods, just as it was to farm and city folk. "For two weeks before the great day, things took on a brighter hue," recalled Otis W. Terpening years later. "At least they seemed to. The lads were better natured than usual. And why shouldn't they be. Some had left their families and kiddies early in the fall, with the understanding that at Christmas they would all be united again. While others thought of the sweetheart back in the settlement. Then we had a kind with us that I can't describe in this up to date language. But us Jacks called them lushers: a class that was shunned by the better class of Lumberjacks. For the only thing they seemly thought of getting out of life was a big drunk and and a feed of ham and eggs. As there was no drinking allowed in camp, it was real hard on them.

"And they [all] seemed to hail Christmas as a time of getting out of their bondage. As the day drew near the real Christmas Spirit seemed to prevail. And in the snatches of song that we would hear in the woodland during the day there was a real ring of joy in them. And in the voice of the Jacks on Christmas morning as they wished one another Merry Christmas. And to hear one Jack say, 'Thanks, pal, I hope you live forever and I live to see you die.' We seldom ever worked on Christmas, but the day was spent in visiting, darning our socks and mittens. While some spent their time in playing cards and listening for the cheerie sound of the dinner horn, saying come and eat, eat. The cook would always have something extry, and a plenty of it."

No one could deny there was plenty: "There was roast beef, brown gravy, good home-made bread, potatoes, shiny tins heaped with golden rings called fried cakes, and close to them a pumpkin pie baked in a ten-inch tin, about one-and-a-half-inch deep, and cut in four pieces. Any other day to a Jack it was one piece, but today it was Christmas. It only came once a year and help yourself, if you wanted a whole pie you was welcome. And rice pudding black with raisins, dried prunes, or the old-fashioned dried apples for sauce. Black coffee sweetened with brown sugar. And tins full of sweet cookies. They were white and had a raisin in the center of them. Did we eat, I will say we did! I have eaten many a Christmas dinner in camp. And some here on the farm, but the best was in camp. Just one more with a jolly crew, and I would be willing to say, 'Life is now complete.' "

After Christmas dinner—which was served at noon—the loggers relaxed until it was time for supper, which was almost a repeat of the main repast. Then, Terpening continued, "Some would get out the old greasy deck of cards and climb into some pal's top bunk for a quiet game of poker, while others took to the old-time square dances. The 'ladies' had a grain sack tied around their waist so we could tell them from the gents. And woe to the one that stepped on a lady's toe, and did not apologize. And do it quick. Or it would be one quick blow and a Jack would measure his length on the floor. Then it was the first two gents cross over and by the lady stand. The second two cross and all join hands. And we had to have a jig every set."

* * * * * *

Comestibles had other uses beyond nourishment. Ann Eliza Tenney's notebook had this formula for washing silk: "Take ½ pint of gin, four ounces soft soap and two ounces of honey well shaken. Then rub the silk with a sponge upon a table and wash through two waters in which first put two or three spoonfuls of ox gall, which will brighten the colors and prevent their running. The silk should not be wrung, but shaken smooth and ironed."

If less ambitious, Miss Tenney could avail herself of a "clothes scourer and renovator," the mid-century phrase for clothing care professionals, many of whom already were dry cleaning clothes with camphene in the 1850's. The first such cleaning process had been discovered in France in the late 1840's, and soon was practiced in larger American cities, including Madison and Milwaukee.

* * * * * *

That old saying about a woman's work never being done is vividly illustrated in excerpts from the diary of the Yankee grandmother of Mrs. Dale I. Hanson of Stevens Point.

"September 7, 1907—Clear, warmer. Did up the housework. Finished the ironing. Shelled beans. Canned 6 qts. peaches, 2 qts. tomatoes, 4 qts. crab [apple] pickles, 2 qts. crab sauce, 1 qt. cucumber pickes. Made a batch of white cookies.

"January 9, 1909—Cloudy, cold. Did up the housework. Baked a large pan of white biscuits. Baked a layer cake and 3 pans of coffee cake and 1 loaf of sweet bread. Made potato salad, baked beans. Washed up the kitchen floor. Had Rev. Morrison and wife here for supper. Got Conrad a book for his birthday.

"June 11, 1909—Clear, hot. Did up the housework. Did a washing, washed 1 quilt. Baked a mincemeat pie, a white layer cake, and a batch of white cookies. Did most of the ironing. Washed up the kitchen floor. Baked 2 pans white bread.

"September 8, 1909—Cloudy, rainy. Did up the housework. Baked 4 pans bread and a molasses cake. Washed up the kitchen floor. Canned 2 qts. crabs. Fixed and canned 6 qts. grapes.

"October 7, 1911—Clear, pleasant. Did up the housework. Churned. Baked 2 pumpkin pies and 2 pans oatmeal cakes. Swept the sitting room. Washed up the floor. Washed up the kitchen floor. Gave Orma and Dorothy each a bath. Picked off the lima beans. Canned 1 qt. ground cherries and made some sauce."

* * * * * *

Indians did not always skin before eating small game animals like rabbit. As the American-born sons of German immigrants in the town of Dane observed in the 1850's: "The Indians wrapped the animal as shot in wet clay and put the package over the fire. The clay hardened on cooking and the Indians peeled off the clay and the hair came with it. Then they ate the meat."

* * * * * *

A usual schoolboy activity in earlier times was collecting pitch from tamarack and pine trees to make chewing gum. Jennie D. Cate, in her recollection of growing up in Auroraville (Waushara County) in the 1850's, mentioned that her classmates—"our larger boys"—often foraged for pitch in the tamarack swamp a half-mile from the schoolhouse, not always getting back in time for class: "We also made gum from the pitch that oozed from the ends of the pine logs and stood in drops. By cooking it, we could have a plentiful supply of white pine gum. The sticky process could not have been pleasing to our mothers."

* * * * * *

Many Wisconsinites, looking back on their growing-up years, remember admiringly how their parents and grandparents provided for their families outside the cash economy. Pastor Lloyd C. Denzer of Wild Rose, for instance, sent this observation along with his recipe contributions for this book:

"As I recall my boyhood days back on the farm [at Denzer in Sauk County], I think of how our wants were supplied, almost entirely without the use of money. How my grandmother made our own soap, ground roasted rye for coffee, churned our butter, baked all we needed from flour raised on our farm and ground at the nearby mill. We made delicious ice-cream—with real cream. We had our chickens which provided our eggs and meat. We packed our own ice—for the ice-box during the summer. We made our own maple syrup in the spring. Our farm was blessed with running springs for water, for man and beast. A good variety of nut trees, butternuts, hickory nuts, hazel nuts, walnuts. Wild blackberries, gooseberries, apple orchard. We made our own sauerkraut, packed the dill pickles, made apple cider, butchered beef and pork, much of it put into sausages, fried down meat in lard, smoked the hams, dried the beef and sausages. What more could we ask for? We were rich! Now I know it."

* * * * * *

There was no mill readily available at first to the earliest settlers adjacent to Green Lake in 1840, so the job had to be done by hand. As one resident later described it, "we made a huge mortar by boring out a hard white oak log, and with a big heavy hickory pestle we ground our corn. The mortar held about two quarts at once. By rising at four o'clock we could get enough pounded for a breakfast of Johnnie cake. The coarser part we boiled as samp for dinner, and had corn-meal fry for supper. No milk, no butter."

* * * * * *

When in 1847 John Diederichs worked on clearing land he had just acquired near Manitowoc, he left his family in Milwaukee. In a letter written months later to German relatives he charted his progress and his limited diet: ".... Partook of half baked or half burnt, sour, dry bread and black coffee without sugar, for breakfast; at noon dry bread and black coffee again with turnip soup, and the same in the evening . . . ."

* * * * * *

A number of Wisconsin's wild foods show up regularly on the state's tables today. But other edibles that helped sustain the Indians and early explorers are rarely, if ever, used.

Acorns are one. Indian cooks in most Wisconsin tribes first had to rid the acorns of red or white oak of their bitter tannic acid. (The Chippewa, however, maintained that white oak acorns did not need this treatment.) This required soaking in quickly prepared lye, made by mixing the hardwood ashes of camp fires with water, followed by numerous hot-and-cold water washings to remove the lye. After sun drying, the acorns were ready to grind into a meal for cooking. Acorn meal was often cooked by the Menominee in a soup stock of venison or made into a mush with bear oil for seasoning.

Milkweed—shoots, buds, and flowers—found its way into numerous Indian dishes. The first sprouts of spring were used as asparagus is today, while the bud or young bloom was made into soup combined with deer broth or fat, or could be added to cornmeal.

The land around springs and in boggy marshes produced the groundnut, a species of wild potato. Nicolas Perrot, the seventeenth-century French explorer, wrote that some were "as large as an egg, others have the size of one's fist, or a little more. They [the Potawatomi] boil these in water by a slow fire, during twenty-four hours; when they are thoroughly cooked, you will find in them an excellent flavor, much resembling that of prunes—which are cooked in the same way in France, to be served with dessert."

And in times of extreme hardship or famine, the climbing bittersweet kept many alive. Pierre Esprit Radisson recorded that during his 1659–1660 Wisconsin expedition the earth was "frozen 2 or 3 foote deepe, and the snow 5 or 6 above it." His party followed the Indian example and cut "the stick some 2 foot long, tying it in faggott, and boyle it, and when it boyles one houre or two the rind or skinne comes off wth ease, wch we take and drie it in the smoake and then reduce it into powder betwixt two graine-stoans, and putting the kettle wth the same watter upon the fire, we make it a kind of broath, wch nourished us . . . ."

* * * * * *

A number of trees and wild plants provided Chippewa Indians with the makings for hot beverages. Packets of fresh or dried leaves of Labrador tea, creeping snowberry, wintergreen, hemlock, and spruce were steeped in water, sweetened with maple sugar, and drunk while hot. The twigs of red raspberry, chokecherry, and wild cherry were also used. The twigs were wrapped into bundles about four inches long and about an inch in diameter.

* * * * * *

Keeping food in the days before refrigeration (and those days varied considerably from family to family and region to region) was a problem solved with more or less success in a number of ways. Springs were an asset in food storage. In fact, in the days when land was plentiful, the presence of a spring often determined the location of a farmhouse or a tavern. Over or beside the bubbling water, the owner would build a spring house, piping the water through a trough fitted with stone jars or crocks in which to keep the food. Lacking a spring, a settler might dig a root cellar below ground or into a hillside.

Some kept food on the stone protrusions inside a well. Putting or fetching the food was often the job of the children of the family. As one Czech immigrant recalled of the days around World War I: "When we wanted food like butter and milk and eggs to keep cool, it was my job to go down in the well on the ladder and put it there. And lots a time I could see eyes looking at me, and they were frogs."

The earthen floor of the basement was another keeping spot. A pile of sand on the basement floor made a good storage spot for root vegetables, and crocks placed in tubs of cold water could keep butter for long periods.

A method of preserving eggs was included in an early twentieth-century Wisconsin cookbook: "Slake one and one-half pints of lime and add one and one-half gallons of water. Render out five cents worth of suet and combine with lime mixture. Let all boil a minute. With a wire ladle, dip a few eggs at a time into the hot solution for a second. Lay the eggs on something to dry. Then pack them away in new oats or bran. Be sure the eggs are fresh at first."

* * * * * *

The culinary plight of female teachers in the late 1870's was well illustrated by the remembrances of Melissa Brown, who grew up near Ironton and was later a co-owner of Brown's Book Store in Madison: " . . . I taught about four miles from my home and boarded with Uncle Jimmy and Aunt Jemina. They charged me $1.25 a week for board, and as I went home Friday evening and came back Sunday afternoon, they deducted for the time I was away, so that my board amounted to 98 cents per week. And the good things I had to eat! Fried chicken, baking powder biscuit—and such biscuit—with honey, and smoked ham and bacon, stand out prominently in my memory. As I was a picture of health and had an appetite to match, you can imagine how much they made 'off of me.'

"In comparison to this, I remember another boarding place. I think I paid $2.00 a week for board. This family 'always boarded the teacher,' so there was no place else to go. They had a farm near the schoolhouse, and were considered quite well to do. Our food for breakfast was always fat salt pork (fried), bread and butter, and coffee. They made the coffee by putting two tablespoons of coffee in a coffee pot, holding at least two gallons, then they would fill it up with water. Consequently the coffee was faint amber in color and tasted like anything but coffee. They kept cows and all kinds of stock, but we never had any cream for coffee, but only very blue milk. All the cream was sold. In the same way the strawberries which they raised were sold. I do not remember that we ever had any to eat."

* * * * * *

Of all the types of cheese made in the state over the years, only one could be called a native Wisconsin variety: Colby. This moist, mild, yellow cheese was developed in 1885 by Joseph Steinwand, whose father, Ambrose, had opened a cheese factory west of the Clark County town of Colby three years before.

Steinwand's cheese differed from Cheddar, its closest relative, in the handling of the curds after the whey was drained off. The Colby curd is cooled in cold water and then pressed into forms and aged. The drier Cheddar, on the other hand, is immediately molded and then repeatedly rotated until all excess whey is expelled.

* * * * * *

Wisconsin's ethnic mix, and resulting gustatory manifestations, are lightly recounted in a bit of verse that emerged from Sheboygan's large German and Irish populations. It seems that St. Patrick, returning to Ireland to gather shamrocks, found that most of his friends had emigrated to the New World. He went in search of them and found familiar faces in Sheboygan.

'Tis a wonderful town, Sheboygan;
My people must be here;
Then he noticed Mrs. Whealan,
And his heart was filled with cheer.

She was whipping up a frosting,
As lovely and white as starch,
For a cake to honor St. Patrick
On the seventeenth of March.

St. Patrick wept for gladness;
And he said, "They are so kind,
I'll leave the shamrock here;
The Father will not mind."

And, faith, we can be certain
'Twill flourish every year,
For St. Patrick loved Sheboygan
And left the shamrock here.

But I haven't quite finished my story;
When Patrick left the bouquet,
He took some bratwurst and kuchen
To eat along the way.

And he said, "Next time, I'll visit
The Whealans and Kennedys too.
And have corned beef and cabbage,
As well as Irish stew."

* * * * * *

Manifestations of Wisconsin's culinary cross-fertilization still abound. In legendary Hurley, to cite one example, a neon sign over a main-street cafe proclaims GUIDO'S PASTIES. In Madison, the eclectic diner may be drawn towards TONY'S CHOP SUEY RESTAURANT. And the pride of Medford, TOMBSTONE PIZZA, was considered worthy of mention in a foot-of-the-page item in the *New Yorker*.

* * * * * *

In the latter part of the nineteenth century, the idea of oleomargarine was about as popular in Wisconsin as bovine tuberculosis.

Robert M. La Follette wanted the federal government to tax it so heavily it would melt away: "Ingenuity, striking hands with cunning trickery, compounds a substance to counterfeit an article of food," he once declared. "It is made to look like something it is not; to taste and smell like something it is not; to sell for something it is not, and so deceive the purchaser. It follows faithfully two rules: 'Miss no opportunity to deceive'; 'At all times put money in thy purse.' "

Oleomargarine, La Follette concluded, was "a monstrous product of greed and hypocrisy."

In 1895, the Wisconsin legislature adopted strict labelling laws, so that grocers and restaurant operators could not palm off the substitute for the genuine article. If they were caught, they were liable to fines of $50 to $500, and, for repeated, offenses, to jail terms.

But it was not until 1931 that the legislature took stronger steps to curb the "monstrous product." Then it passed a law requiring a license—ranging from $1,000 a year for manufacturers down to $5 for bakers, confectioners, and some boardinghouse keepers—to make, sell, or serve margarine. (It actually passed two sets of laws the same year, refining the license categories in a special session convened late in 1931.) In addition, it tacked on a tax of six cents a pound and required detailed quarterly reports of manufacturing, sales, and use to be sent to the state agricultural department.

The tax was hiked to fifteen cents a pound in 1935. Furthermore, margarine sold in Wisconsin for many years had to be "free of coloration or ingredients that cause it to look like butter."

In 1967, after a long fight between dairy interests and consumer groups, Wisconsin became the last state in the union to permit the unlicensed sale of colored oleomargarine. In 1979, the law still prohibited the serving of margarine "to student, patients, or inmates of any state institution as a substitute for table butter unless ordered by a doctor."

* * * * * *

As the *Waukesha Freeman* put it in a flight of nineteenth-century prose, "there has gurgled forth a fount of God's elixir of life, and the afflicted of every country shall look here for a revival of lost hopes."

What the paper was reporting on in its issue of March 4, 1869, was the beneficial effects that resulted when New Yorker Colonel Richard Dunbar, who suffered from diabetes, drank from a spring on pasture land owned by his sister-in-law in Waukesha. Two other people similarly claimed cures from their afflictions after drinking the water.

Dunbar acquired ownership of the marvelous spring, named it Bethesda after the Biblical pool in Jerusalem, and began promoting the curative water nationwide, even though analysis by Columbia University scientists showed nothing unusual about it. Soon, other springs were discovered, and Waukesha began calling itself the "Saratoga of the West."

Elegant hotels were built that attracted both the afflicted seeking cures for a wide range of diseases—diabetes, kidney and loin pain, dropsy, gout, dyspepsia, Bright's disease—and the well-to-do from all over the country, particularly Southerners escaping the summer heat. In the 1880's and 1890's, its heyday, Waukesha had a dozen hotels and two dozen boardinghouses accommodating altogether about 1,600 people. And those who could not make the trip to the source could buy Waukesha waters in bottles most places in the country and points abroad.

Probably the best known of the Waukesha-bottled spring water was White Rock, whose fame was no doubt due as much to the company's symbol (a "topless" Psyche admiring herself in a pool of water) as the contents of the bottle. Tradition has it that Edward VII of England diluted his wine with sparkling White Rock at the banquet marking his coronation. And in 1927, Charles A. Lindbergh broke a bottle of White Rock over the nose of a silver monoplane he christened the "Spirit of St. Louis."

After the turn of the century, Waukesha's popularity as a spa went into decline. Now, a few of the springs have dried up or disappeared, some have become polluted, and still others have been capped. One company, Bon-Ton Beverages, Inc., was still bottling water in the late 1970's, using Bethesda spring itself for a supply.

Waukesha was not without competitors as contenders for the title of "Saratoga of the West." One aspirant was Osceola, on the St. Croix River, which pinned its hopes on the Bethania Mineral Springs after dreams of flourishing hotels evaporated in the 1880's and 1890's. Widely distributed in the early decades of this century was not only the mineral water alone, but also a variety of soda pops, fruit drinks, and mixes made with the water. Included in the Bethania line were Orange, Blackberry, and Chocolate Sodas, Lime Juice Champagne, Raspberry and Lime Frappes, Sarsaparilla, Dole's Pineapple Nectarade, and an astonishing drink called Alfa-lusa, which was made from alfalfa. The Celebrated Bethania Mineral Spring Co. Bottle Works ceased operations in the late 1950's.

Another, more recent, mineral water, operation in Wisconsin is still bubbling gently. The mildly alkaline Rocky Dell Springs in Grant County relieved Mrs. Fond Culver's rheumatism within one year after her husband bought the eighty acre farm with the spring in 1926. Soon Culver and his brother-in-law, Harold Steinbach of Chicago, were involved in bottling and selling the water, which tested high in calcium and contained a number of other valuable minerals.

Rocky Dell has always been a modest operation, and in the late 1970's, the couple operating the bottling plant put up around 500 cases of half-gallon bottles a month. Gallon and five-gallon jugs, and some seven-ounce bottles, were also filled and shipped regularly by truck to Madison, Milwaukee, Boscobel, Davenport, Iowa, Chicago, and other points; and seven-ounce bottles of Rocky Dell could be had in a number of fine restaurants and taverns in Milwaukee and Chicago.

* * * * * *

CITY HOTEL
At Richland City, Wisconsin.
By W. J. Frame.

No gambling or card playing allowed in the house or at the barn.
No profane or vulgar language allowed.
No sky-larking allowed.

RATES OF FARE.

Meals, each,	.25
Lodging, one night	.10
Board by the week, with lodging,	$2.50
Board by the week, without lodging,	$2.00
Board by the day, with lodging,	.75

STABLE RATES.

Horse to grain hay and care	.37½

—Ad in the *Richland County Observer,* June 3, 1856.

* * * * * *

For a brief period, from June 1, 1935, to March 1, 1937, it was the law that any hotel or restaurant had to serve, with each meal costing twenty-five cents or more, at least two-thirds of an ounce each of Wisconsin butter and Wisconsin cheese. This legislation was the work of Democratic Assemblyman William J. Sweeney, a De Pere farmer, who got the idea on a trip to California when he "noticed that we received a California orange with each meal. When I got back, I kept on buying them. The same principle should work out for Wisconsin cheese."

Needless to say, the law was not popular with restaurateurs and hotel keepers. It carried no penalties and was probably not complied with most of the time, particularly with those twenty-five cent meals. The law was written to include the 1937 expiration date, but was formally repealed in 1943.

* * * * * *

For a number of years in the early part of this century, one of the culinary and social highlights of the summer in the southwestern corner of the state was the annual barbeque and bowery dance at Pleasant Ridge, an early black farming community in Grant County.

Pleasant Ridge was founded in 1848 by freed slaves from the South, and the little settlement grew and thrived for a while. By the end of the century, however, it had begun to decline. In 1906, the Autumn Leaf Club was organized as a forum for discussion and for social gatherings, and its members also tried to relieve "sickness and sorrow" in their community. Later they undertook maintenance of their cemetery's combination chapel and utility building. The necessary funds were raised during annual get-togethers, which served as homecomings and as a social excursion for blacks from all over the Midwest. The event was always held around August 4, the date the slaves of the British West Indies had been emancipated in 1833.

For years, the food preparation was in the hands of Joe Grimes, whose family had settled in the area in 1861, and Samuel C. Craig, who had come to Wisconsin in 1895. Cap'n Craig, as he was popularly known, was in later years the head chef, and he and Grimes would start early in the morning roasting whole pigs and frying chickens, whose distinctive taste, Grimes claimed facetiously, came from the use of essence of squid oil.

The annual affair was attended by white residents of the area as well, both for the food and the dance that followed. Cap'n Craig died in 1935, but Grimes with the help of others kept the tradition going for a few years after that, until World War II and gas shortages intervened. A picnic or two held after the war never achieved the earlier success.

* * * * * *

The Rolla B. Schufelts in proud, intimate contact with their dairy herd,
near Oconto, about 1900. [WHi(X3)23303]

THE FLAVOR OF WISCONSIN

*A Portfolio of Photographs from the
Collections of the State Historical
Society of Wisconsin*

Cupcakes, frosting, and utensils to be lick-
ed. Milwaukee, 1950's. [*Milwaukee
Journal photo.* WHi(M56)3610]

*The numbers following picture captions signify
negative numbers in the Iconographic Collections
of the State Historical Society of Wisconsin.*

Ten acres of seed onions near Hudson, St. Croix County, photographed by Harvey J. Perkins as part of a campaign to encourage agricultural settlement in the Wisconsin cutover. [WHi(H44)35]

Churning butter on freshly mopped steps.
[WHi(W6)16281]

Knee-deep in cranberries.
[WHi(X3)7903]

When Mrs. Martin was not baking or putting food by, she could feed the chickens. Green Bay vicinity, about 1895. [*Frederick L. G. Straubel, photographer.* WHi(S85)62]

It takes a lot of sap and a lot of boiling to produce maple syrup. Northern Wisconsin, 1927. [*Melvin E. Diemer, photographer.* WHi(D483)4317]

Melvin E. Diemer recorded the stark realities of turning hogs into bacon in a sequence of photographs he entitled "Killing a Pig," 1921.   [WHi(D487)5300]

Unidentified growers proudly posing with the fruits of a season's labors, about 1910. [*From the James G. Milward Collection.* WHi(X21)18921]

Angler with trout. [*Charles J. Van Schaick, photographer.* WHi(V2)735]

Young men with rabbits.[*Matthew Witt, photographer.*WHi(X3)28609]

Hunters with ruffed grouse. [*Wisconsin Rapids Daily Tribune.* WHi(X3)28562]

Whatever it was you produced, it had to be gotten to market and processed. Unidentified creamery, southern Wisconsin, 1870's. [*Andrew L. Dahl, photographer.* WHi(D31)625]

Pea-canning line, Columbus, about 1939.
[*Melvin E. Diemer, photographer.*
WHi(D479)12198]

Creamery workers, Madison, 1922.
[*Melvin E. Diemer, photographer.*
WHi(D483)7910]

Candling and grading eggs, Manawa, about 1939. [*Melvin E. Diemer, photographer.* WHi(D479)12473]

Sorting dill, Baraboo, 1950's. [*John Newhouse, photographer.* WHi(N48)21000]

This exhibit of the Wisconsin Potato Growers' Association, c. 1910, was no doubt intended to inspire as well as inform.   [*From the James G. Milward Collection.* WHi(X21)15594]

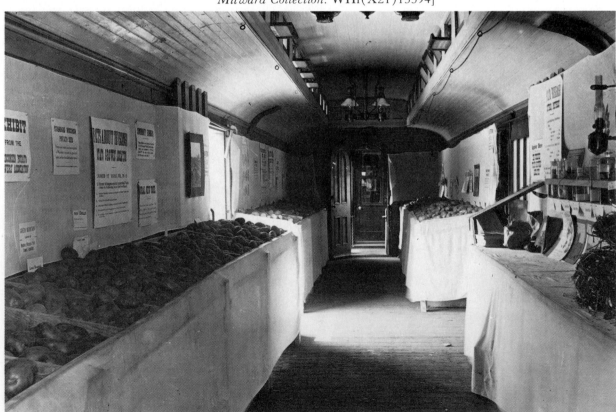

Sorting apples in the Kickapoo valley, late 1940's.
[*John Newhouse, photographer,* WHi(N48)13049]

Alfred Klumb in a tree full of Cortland
apples, near Cedarburg, 1968. [*Milwaukee Sentinel photo by Ernest Anheuser.*
WHi(X3)28596]

End of the line: a Black
River Falls store front,
about 1895. [*Charles J.
Van Schaick,
photographer.*
WHi(V2)120]

Lutefisk dinner, Norway Grove and De-Forest, 1950's. [*John Newhouse, photographer.* WHi(N48)9028]

Hispanic migratory farm workers, picking cherries in a Door County orchard, 1950's. [*Hagedorn Studio.* WHi(X3)28571]

Even in the machine age, human hands and eyes play their roles in food processing. Cedarburg vicinity, 1968. [*Milwaukee Sentinel photo by Ernest Anheuser.* WHi(X3)28599]

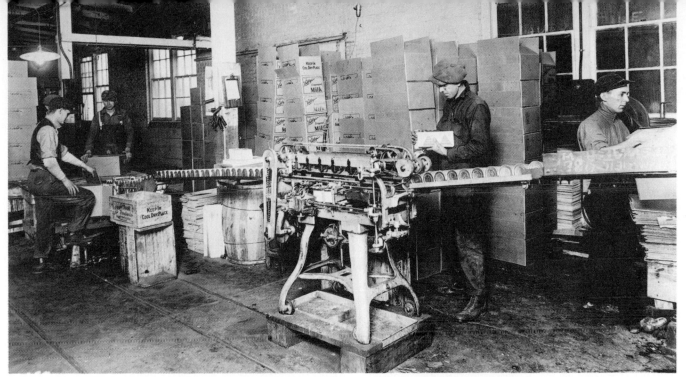

Libby canned milk processing plant, 1920's. [WHi(D485)6559]

Governor Walter S. Goodland and his wife, Madge, pickling pears in the mid-1940's. [*Richard Cass, photographer.* WHi(X91)3972]

When local pride cross-pollinates with giant vegetables, silliness results. [*Alfred Stanley Johnson, Jr., photographer.* WHi(X3)27920]

University of Wisconsin boxing team, 1939. [*Melvin E. Diemer, photographer.* WHi(D479)11608]

Wisconsin exhibit in Agriculture Hall, Louisiana Purchase Exposition, St. Louis, 1904. [WHi(X3)28558]

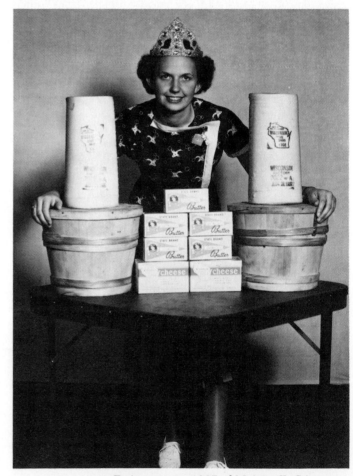

Dairy queen, 1937. [*Melvin E. Diemer, photographer.* WHi(D487)10742]

America's Dairyland on display in a store window in Washington, D.C., 1939. [*Buckingham Studio, Inc.* WHi(X3)28564]

Place unknown, about 1940. [*John New-house, photographer.* WHi(N48)13007]

Display window, Milwaukee, 1967. [*Milwaukee Journal photo by Niels Lau-ritzen.* WHi(X3)28598]

If you had enough faith in your product, you didn't have to put up a sign or even wear a smile. Merrill, 1924. [WHi(X3)28585]

These dairymen had just completed a short course in corn farming and animal husbandry offered by the University of Wisconsin. North Lake, Waukesha County, 1915. [*E. F. Chapman, photographer.* WHi(W6)6405]

The livestock, like the farmer and his sons, always showed up at meal time. [*Melvin E. Diemer, photographer.* WHi(X21)19599]

Farmers' market, Milwaukee, about 1948. [*Milwaukee Journal photo by Bob Boyd*. WHi(M56)5618]

Place and date unknown. [*From the Melvin E. Diemer Collection.* WHi(D48)720]

It took time to pick and choose, but at least you knew that the produce was fresh and home-grown. Farmers' market, Stevens Point, 1930's. [WHi(W61)30171]

The Broadway Farmer's Store was organized with Teutonic thorough-
ness and precision. Menomonie, about 1925. [WHi(X3)29669]

Margraff's store in New London, about
1895, was a bit more casual. [*Grace Gil-
bert Viel, photographer.* WHi(X3)4401]

Madison, 1921. [*Melvin E. Diemer, photographer.* WHi(D483)6967]

Giving good weight at Kieswalter's grocery and delicatessen, Madison, about 1950. [*John Newhouse, photographer.* WHi(N48)21179]

Absalom Erickson & Co. grocery, Black River Falls, about 1895. [*Charles J. Van Schaick, photographer.* WHi(V24)1685]

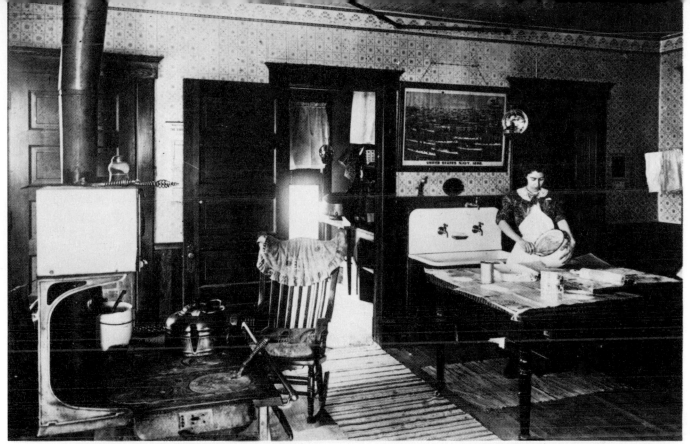

Wherever and whatever you were cooking, you put something of yourself into it. Place and date unknown. [WHi(X3)31044]

Tomah, early 1950's. [*John Newhouse, photographer.* WHi(N48)30180]

Milwaukee, 1968. [*Milwaukee Journal photo by Robert Nandell.* WHi(X3)28565]

Sun Prairie, 1956. [Cap-
ital Times photo by
Herb Jacobs.]

[Milwaukee Journal photo.
WHi(M56)5803]

[Milwaukee Sentinel photo by
Sherman A. Gessert, Jr.
WHi(X3)28561]

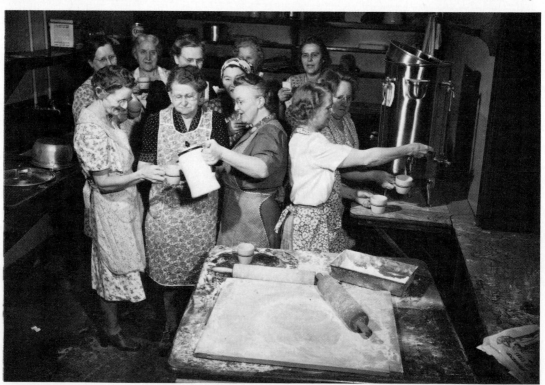

Before the women of Trinity Lutheran Church got down to the business
of rolling out lefse for the annual Norwegian church supper, they naturally had to have a cup of coffee. [John Newhouse, photographer.
WHi(N48)9153]

Part of the pleasure of home-made pasties resided in watching the as-
semblage of meat, vegetables, herbs, and freshly rolled pastry. Linden,
1953. [*John Newhouse, photographer.* WHi(N48)32120]

Farmers' meeting, Lancaster, late 1940's.
[*John Newhouse, photographer.*
WHi(N48)9054]

Block party, Milwaukee, 1967. [*Milwaukee Journal photo.* WHi(X3)28563]

Governor Philip F. La Follette presided at the silver anniversary celebration of the 1912 University of Wisconsin championship football team, in the reception room of the Executive Chambers in the Capitol, Madison, 1937. [*Melvin E. Diemer, photographer.* WHi(D487)10824]

The food was often rather plain—pork chops, vegetables, plenty of
bread and milk—but everybody got enough, and nobody complained.
[*John Newhouse, photographer.* WHi(N48)13085]

Golden wedding anniversary, late
1940's. [*John Newhouse, photographer.* WHi(N48)49]

Mrs. Scofield, little Lloyd, and brother Stanley. Sturgeon Bay, about
1895. [*Herbert C. Scofield, photographer.* WHi(X3)37050]

Every March there was a wonderful Italian buffet to mark
the feast day of St. Joseph. Madison, 1950's. [*John Newhouse, photographer.* WHi(N48)9161]

Learning Proper Behavior, Milwaukee,
1950's. [*Milwaukee Journal photo.*
WHi(M56)8017]

Tailgate party prior to the Packer game,
County Stadium, Milwaukee, 1962.
[*Milwaukee Sentinel photo.*
WHi(X3)28570]

Some women in Black River Falls—presumably the ones who did not belong to the inner circle—called them the DMC, or Damn Mean Crowd. [*Charles J. Van Schaick, photographer.* WHi(V24)1923]

Dining hall in a northwoods camp—probably lumberjacks or conservation workers, 1930's. [*Wisconsin Conservation Department photo.* WHi(X3)32673]

Farm workers near Cross Plains, about 1920. [*Matthew Witt, photographer.* WHi(X3)28553]

They were big, rough-looking men, and they surely could pack away the groceries. Henry Vinette's logging camp dining hall, near Chippewa Falls, about 1900. [*A. A. Bish, photographer.* WHi(B5)265]

Andrew (originally Andreas) Dahl took many such pictures among his
Norwegian-born countrymen in southern Wisconsin during the 1870's.
It seems fair to assume that the general glumness evaporated once the
photographer was finished and the eating had commenced.
[WHi(D31)688]

The cheerful girl behind the counter was earning her way through college. Madison, 1934, when Kresge's was truly a five-and-ten-cent store. [*Melvin E. Diemer, photographer.* WHi(D487)12800]

Somewhere in Goral's Uneeda Restaurant there must have been that coy little sign saying "In God We Trust—All Others Pay Cash." Antigo, about 1950. [WHi(X3)33179]

Madison, about 1955. [*Richard Vesey, photographer.* WHi(V4)145]

In not too many years, the Eighteenth Amendment was to put a temporary stop to beer drinking and lakeside revelry. Oconomowoc, about 1905. [*Henry F. Bergmann, photographer.* WHi(B61)92]

Calvin Hawksworth (left) keeping an eye on things in his ice cream parlor on Main Street, Winneconne, about 1910. [WHi(W353)71]

There was always a place like this, called Tiny's or Tony's or some such. Unidentified diner, c. 1910. [WHi(X3)28574]

Street scene with young sports, Black River Falls, about 1895. [*Charles J. Van Schaick, photographer.* WHi(V2)127]

Detroit and Jefferson streets, Milwaukee, late 1930's. [*J. Robert Taylor, photographer.* WHi(T35)14]

Postcard picture of the Sunflower Cottage Resort dining room, Tomahawk Lake, c. 1915. [WHi(X3)28587]

Every city in America worth its salt had its converted streetcar or railroad car diner. This classic was on Williamson Street in Madison, about 1952. [*John Newhouse, photographer.* WHi(N48)21174]

Cooking and serving staff of a church-operated dining hall at the Wisconsin State Fair, Milwaukee, about 1920. [WHi(X22)298]

This young woman toiled in a well-equipped, almost idyllic kitchen—in fact, the "practice cottage" of the University of Wisconsin's department of home economics, about 1913. [*Melvin E. Diemer, photographer.* WHi(D482)935]

Cafeteria-style service, Milwaukee, 1950's. [*Milwaukee Journal photo.* WHi(M56)8400]

Holiday dinners bring out the best in people, and the more so when strangers in uniform share the family table. Thanksgiving dinner, Milwaukee, 1956. [*Milwaukee Journal photo.* WHi(X3)28575]

The Joseph Smith family, Wausau, c. 1914. [*Joseph Smith, photographer.* WHi(S65)19]

Christmas dinner for the staff at the Marshfield Steam Laundry, c. 1918. [WHi(X3)18371]

Moment of grace: Thanksgiving Day dinner at the Volunteers of America, Madison, 1952. [*Wisconsin State Journal photo by Arthur M. Vinje*. WHi(V5)15]

The Recipes

BREADS

Yeast Breads

UNTIL RELATIVELY RECENT TIMES, BREAD WAS the mainstay of the American diet. It was filling, exceedingly nutritious (particularly before highly refined flour became so readily available), and, especially in rural areas, the ingredients to make it were usually right at hand. Making bread was part of the housekeeping routine for most Wisconsin women in years past. Joyce Bauer, in her *History of Kohlsville*, a town settled mostly by Germans, described how it was done in the early days:

"Every pioneer had a hearth (an oven built of brick). These hearths were about six feet long, four feet high and four feet wide. A roaring fire was made in the oven, then the wood and ashes were removed and the bread was put in by means of a pole with a board attached to the end. The breadmaker would jerk the pole, enabling the bread to slip off the board and into the oven. Even the mixing of the bread differed from our modern methods. Since there were no pans or dishes such as we use, the pioneer women made bread baskets of straw. My great grandmother mixed her bread in a bread trough carved out of a log. Enough bread was baked at one time to last two weeks. Fresh bread was never eaten as it was considered harmful to the stomach."

Bread fresh from the oven was not regarded with suspicion by all people; but fresh or not, it was eaten at every meal and as a snack in between.

Before stirring up the dough, many housewives had to make their own yeast ahead of time. A hop vine was a fixture in many a garden around the state. Cecelia B. Nieman of Muskego remembers the vine at the rear of the family's old frame home, which had been built in Muskego in 1847 by her Yankee grandfather. The hop vine itself had been brought from "Down East," and "furnished an abundance of hops which were picked when ripe and were dried and stored in bags hung up in the large pantry." This is how the yeast was made.

OLD-FASHIONED LIQUID YEAST

1 ounce hops
2 quarts water
4 tablespoons salt
4 tablespoons brown sugar
2 cups flour
1 cup boiled potatoes, mashed smooth

Boil the hops in the water for 30 minutes.

Strain the liquid into an earthenware crock or bowl and cool to lukewarm. Add salt and sugar and stir to dissolve. In a separate bowl, combine flour and 3 or 4 cups of the liquid and beat well; return to the crock and mix well. Set in a warm place three days.

Add mashed potatoes and stir well. Keep in a warm place, stirring frequently, until mixture is well fermented.

Place in sterilized glass jars and seal tightly; store in a cool place. This should keep for two months and improves with age.

To use, shake jar well and pour out amount needed. Use same quantity as any other yeast.

Submitted by Mrs. Elmer Hare, Dalton.

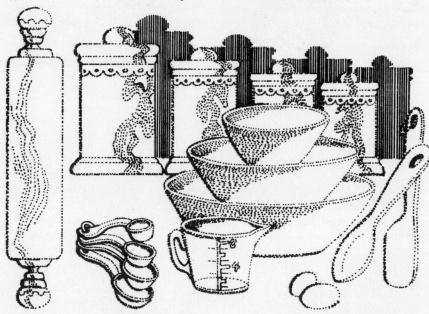

Yeast was also made from mashed potatoes or potato water, sugar, salt, and warm water allowed to ferment for several days. This was called Witch or Spook Yeast.

Yeast from beer was called barm, and was used often in breads made in the British Isles. All ethnic groups had one form or another of sourdough starters, made by combining flour, salt, sugar, and potato water and allowing it to stand until fermented several days. Most starters could be renewed by adding fresh ingredients after some was taken out for use. In this way these starters could—and did—last for years.

Most ethnic groups had a bread or breads that could call up memories of the Old World like no other single food. What follows is a sampling of the great variety of loaves baked in Wisconsin.

OATMEAL BREAD

2 cups oatmeal (regular or quick-cooking)
5 tablespoons butter
1 cup brown sugar
2 ½ teaspoons salt
2 cups boiling water
1 cup cold water
2 packages active dry yeast dissolved in ½ cup
lukewarm water
2 tablespoons white sugar
About 9 cups flour
Melted butter

In a bowl, combine oatmeal, 5 tablespoons butter, brown sugar, and salt. Add boiling water and mix until blended. Mix in cold water, blending thoroughly. Add dissolved yeast and white sugar. Beat in enough flour to make a stiff dough.

Turn dough out onto a lightly floured board and knead until smooth and elastic. Place in a greased pan, cover, and let rise in a warm place until double in bulk. Punch down and let rise until double again. Form into 2 or 3 loaves, brush tops with melted butter, and let rise until double in bulk.

Bake on greased baking sheet at 375 degrees for 45 to 50 minutes. When done, and while still hot, brush top with additional butter.

Mrs. Spencer W. Turner of Rice Lake submitted this recipe for a typical British Isles oatmeal bread.

SAFFRON ROLLS (Cornish)

1 teaspoon Spanish saffron
½ cup boiling water
2 packages active dry yeast softened in ¼ cup
lukewarm water
½ cup scalded milk
½ cup sugar
2 teaspoons salt
¼ cup shortening
About 5 cups sifted, enriched flour
2 eggs

Pour boiling water over saffron; steep 5 minutes and cool.

To scalded milk add saffron mixture, sugar, salt, and shortening. Cool to lukewarm. Add enough flour to make a thick batter, mixing well. Add softened yeast and eggs and beat well. Add enough more flour to make a soft dough.

Turn out onto lightly floured board and knead until smooth and satiny. Place in a greased bowl, cover, and let rise in a warm place until doubled in bulk. Punch down and let rest 10 minutes. Shape into rolls and let rise until doubled again.

Bake on a greased baking sheet at 350 degrees for 20 minutes.

Makes about 3 ½ dozen rolls.

Submitted by a former Wisconsinite, Miss Margaret I. Gibson, White Plains, New York.

BORREEN BRACK (Irish)

1 cup scalded milk
½ cup freshly churned butter, salted
3 large eggs
⅔ cup sugar
1 large spoon of barm (beer yeast)
5 cups flour
1 small spoon salt
1 small spoon allspice
1 ½ cups currants

Pour scalded milk over butter to melt; cool.

Mix well eggs, sugar, and barm and add to cooled milk mixture. Mix in flour, salt, allspice, and currants.

Knead the dough thoroughly and then place in a buttered bowl and cover. Let rise to double in bulk. Turn out and punch down. Divide dough and put into 2 buttered pans. Cover and let rise again until doubled in bulk. Bake at 350 degrees for 30 to 45 minutes. By this time it should be browned and done. Brush the loaves with melted butter and sprinkle with sugar.

This handed-down recipe was submitted by Dr. Lois Byrns, Dane. The size of loaves for Borreen Brack, which means Speckled Loaf, she adds, were measured by the fist size of a woman. A loaf was generally two fists long and two wide (ten inches), and one fist thick (five inches).

CHALLAH (Jewish Egg Bread)

2 ¼ cups lukewarm water
1 package active dry yeast
2 tablespoons sugar
1 tablespoon salt
¼ cup oil
2 eggs, beaten
About 8 cups unsifted flour
1 egg yolk mixed with 1 tablespoon water

Measure warm water into a large bowl. Sprinkle in yeast and stir until dissolved. Stir in sugar, salt, oil, eggs and 4 cups flour; beat until smooth. Add enough additional flour to make a soft dough.

Turn out onto lightly floured board and knead until smooth and elastic, about 10 minutes. Place dough in an oiled bowl, turning to grease top. Cover and let rise in a warm place until doubled in bulk, about 1 hour. Punch down.

Turn out onto lightly floured board and divide into 8 pieces. Shape each piece into a 14-inch roll. Braid 3 of these rolls together. Make a "dent" down the center of the braid and place a fourth strip of dough in the dent, stretching strip underneath the braid. Repeat with remaining 4 strips of dough.

Place on oiled baking sheets, cover, and let rise in a warm place until doubled in bulk, about 45 minutes. Brush tops with egg yolk mixture. Bake in a 350 degree oven about 30 minutes or until wooden toothpicks inserted in center comes out clean and dry.

Makes two loaves.

Submitted by Mrs. Manfred Swarsensky, Madison.

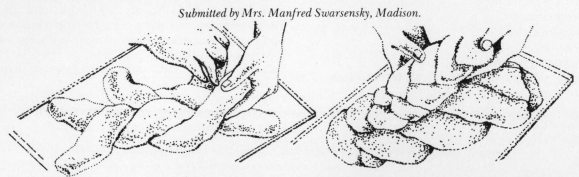

CARAWAY SEED BISCUITS (Cornish)

2 ½ cups milk
1 cake compressed yeast
About 3 or 4 cups flour
1 cup sugar
1 teaspoon salt
4 tablespoons caraway seeds
⅔ cup melted shortening

Scald milk and then cool to lukewarm. Dissolve yeast in milk and beat in 3 cups of flour thoroughly. Cover and put in a warm place until light (about double in bulk). Add sugar, salt, caraway seeds, melted shortening, and enough additional flour so the dough can be kneaded.

Pinch off small amounts of dough and knead each into a flat biscuit. Place on greased baking sheets and let stand until double in bulk. Bake at 400 degrees about 20 minutes.

Submitted by Mrs. William Lindauer, Dodgeville, who warned not to use any more flour than necessary as a soft dough makes a lighter biscuit.

SALT RISING BREAD

1 cup milk
3 tablespoons sugar
7 tablespoons white or water-ground corn meal
1 teaspoon salt
2 cups lukewarm water
3 tablespoons shortening
10½ cups soft wheat flour

Scald milk and stir in 1 tablespoon sugar, corn meal, and salt. Place in a clean, covered jar and place jar in water as hot as the hand can bear. Allow to stand 6 to 7 hours in a warm place or until gas can be heard to escape, indicating fermentation is sufficient.

Add water, shortening, remaining sugar, and 2 cups flour. Beat thoroughly. Place jar in warm water to maintain an even temperature and let rise in a warm place until sponge is very light and full of bubbles, about double in bulk.

Turn into bowl and add remaining flour which will give a stiff dough. Knead on a floured board 10 to 15 minutes. Cut, form into loaves, and place in greased pans. Let rise in a warm place until 2½ times original bulk. Bake at 375 degrees 35 to 45 minutes.

Makes 3¼ pounds of bread.

Submitted by Mrs. Elmer Hare, Dalton.

CRACKLING BISCUITS (Czech)

1 cup milk
¼ cup sugar
1 ½ teaspoons salt
1 cake compressed yeast dissolved in ½ cup
   lukewarm water
1 egg, beaten
4 cups flour
2 cups cracklings (leftovers from lard rendering)

Scald milk. Add sugar and salt and stir. Cool until lukewarm. Combine egg, flour, milk mixture, yeast, and cracklings. Knead until smooth. Cover and let rise in a warm place until double in bulk.

Turn out onto floured board and roll out to ¼ inch thickness. Cut with a large glass or biscuit cutter. Place on greased baking sheet, brush with additional beaten egg, and let rise until doubled. Bake at 375 degrees for 20 minutes, or until brown.

Submitted by Mrs. John Desris, Kenosha.

Middle and Northern Europeans, particularly, brought with them the taste for rye breads. They came in all shadings from sepia to black pumpernickel; some were sour dough; often they were flavored with caraway seeds.

HEIDELBERG RYE BREAD

1 cup lukewarm water
2 tablespoons salt
¼ cup cocoa
⅓ cup molasses
2 tablespoons caraway seed
2 cups rye flour
2 packages active dry yeast softened in ½ cup lukewarm water
About 3 cups white flour
1 tablespoon soft shortening

Mix together lukewarm water, salt, cocoa, molasses, and caraway seed. Beat in rye flour. Add yeast and mix well. Mix in 1 cup white flour and soft shortening. Add 1 ½ to 2 cups more of white flour until dough is no longer sticky.

Turn out onto lightly floured board and knead until smooth and elastic. Grease the top, cover, and let rise until double in bulk, about 2 hours. Punch down and shape into 2 round or long loaves. Let rise again until double, about 1 hour. Bake on greased baking sheet at 375 degrees for 45 minutes.

Submitted by Mrs. Edith Gotz, Pittsville.

FINNISH RYE BREAD

3 packages active dry yeast dissolved in 1 cup lukewarm water
6 cups rye or pumpernickel flour
6 tablespoons brown sugar
½ cup molasses
4 cups lukewarm milk
3 tablespoons salt
About 8 or 9 cups white flour

Add rye or pumpernickel flour to yeast mixture 1 cup at a time, blending well. Add sugar, molasses, milk, and salt and blend. Add 2 cups white flour and beat well. Add remaining flour until dough is no longer sticky.

Knead on a floured board until dough is smooth and elastic. Divide into 5 loaves and bake on greased baking sheets at 300 degrees for 1 hour. Brush tops with butter.

Submitted by Eva Koopikka, Calumet, Michigan.

RUSSIAN SOUR DOUGH RYE BREAD

1 ¾ cups medium rye flour
1 ½ cups warm water
1 teaspoon vinegar
1 cup cooled potato water
1 tablespoon salt (figure in salt used in cooking
    potatoes)
2 packages active dry yeast, softened in ½ cup
    lukewarm water
About 3 or 4 cups white flour

Twenty-four hours before making bread, mix rye flour, warm water, and vinegar. Cover and let stand in a warm place.

Mix this starter with potato water, salt, yeast, and enough white flour to handle. Beat well with a wooden spoon. Add more flour if dough is sticky. Cover and let rise in a warm place until double in bulk.

Punch down and mix well with a wooden spoon or knead on a floured board to press out bubbles. Shape into 2 loaves and let rise until double in bulk. Bake on greased baking sheets at 375 degrees for 1 hour.

Submitted by Mrs. Edward Kisser, East Troy.

WAR BREAD

⅛ cup sugar
1 ounce active dry yeast
¼ cup lukewarm water
3 cups oatmeal
4 cups hot water
3 tablespoons vegetable shortening
2 ½ teaspoons salt
6 cups flour

Combine sugar, yeast, and lukewarm water. Combine oatmeal, hot water, shortening, and salt. Mix both mixtures together. Add flour and mix well. Let rise in a warm place until double in bulk.

Punch down and shape into 2 loaves and let rise until double, about 30 to 60 minutes. Bake at 350 degrees for 1 hour.

Submitted by Celia M. (Mrs. Clarence) Thorson, Cedarburg. It dates, she noted, from World War I when her mother-in-law had to buy a certain amount of oatmeal to get white flour

---

Yeast Sweet Breads

LARDIE CAKE (English)

Enough white bread dough for 1 loaf
Lard or pork drippings
½ cup sugar
½ teaspoon cinnamon
⅔ cup currants
Sugar

When making bread, take enough dough for 1 loaf and roll out about 1 inch thick. Spread generously with lard or drippings. Sprinkle with sugar, cinnamon, and currants. Roll up, seal ends and seam. Put seams side down in a greased loaf pan. Let rise to double in bulk. Bake in a 350 degree oven for 1 hour.

Remove from pan and spread top with lard or drippings and sprinkle well with granulated sugar.

Submitted by Mrs. Walter H. Waite, Clinton.

KOLACHE (Bohemian)

½ cup milk
¾ cup butter
½ cup sugar
1 teaspoon salt
4 egg yolks
2 packages active dry yeast dissolved in ½ cup
  lukewarm water
4 ½ cups sifted flour
Prune Filling (see below)

Scald milk in a small saucepan; cool to luke-warm. Beat butter with sugar, salt, and egg yolks until light. Stir in dissolved yeast, cooled milk, and 2 cups flour. Beat 5 minutes at medium speed of electric mixer. Stir in remaining flour to make a very soft dough. Cover with a towel and let rise in a warm place until double in bulk, about 1 hour.

Stir dough down. Turn out on a lightly floured board, flour hands, and knead several minutes.

Divide dough in half. Cut into about 24 pieces, shaping each into a small ball. Place 2 inches apart on a greased baking sheet. Cover and let rise 45 minutes or until double in bulk.

Press large hollows in centers of balls with fingertips. Place 1 tablespoon prune filling in each.

Bake in a 350 degree oven for 15 minutes.

Prune Filling

12 ounces pitted prunes
2 cups water
2 tablespoons sugar
2 teaspoons grated orange rind

Chop prunes and combine with water and sugar in a saucepan. Cook over low heat, stirring constantly, until thick, about 15 minutes. Cool. Stir in orange rind. Makes 1 ¾ cups.

Submitted by Mrs. Wencel F. Dufek, Manitowoc, who notes that the prune filling may be varied with poppy seed or cottage cheese filling.

Poppyseed Filling

6 eggs, separated
1 cup ground poppyseed
¾ cup sugar
Rind of 1 lemon, grated
¼ cup blanched almonds, finely chopped
6 bitter almonds, finely chopped

Mix well egg yolks, poppyseed, sugar, lemon rind, and almonds. Beat egg whites until stiff and fold in.

Submitted by Mrs. Bess Mantuefel, Green Bay.

Cottage Cheese Filling

2 eggs
½ cup sugar
Pinch salt
1 pound cottage cheese, sieved
Dash vanilla
Grated lemon rind to taste
½ cup light raisins, optional

Mix all ingredients well.

Submitted by Mrs. John Desris, Kenosha.

BARA BRITH (Welsh)

½ cake compressed yeast dissolved in ¼ cup
   lukewarm water
2 cups hot milk
1 cup lukewarm water
1 cup sugar
½ cup butter, melted
½ cup lard, melted
Scant ½ tablespoon salt
½ pound small white raisins, floured
¼ pound candied citron
¼ cup chopped lemon or orange peel
½ pound currants
½ cup grated carrot
About 10 cups flour

Combine dissolved yeast, milk, water, sugar, butter, lard, and salt. Mix well. Add raisins, citron, peel, currants, and carrot. Sift in flour until dough can be easily kneaded. Cover and set in a warm place until double in bulk.

Shape into several small loaves and let rise again until double. Bake on greased baking sheets at 350 degrees for 35 to 50 minutes. Cool thoroughly. Serve in thin slices.

For a Quick Bread version of Bara Brith, see next section. * * * * *

Ruth and Margaret Keizer, Platteville, who submitted this recipe, added that Bara Brith (speckled bread) is served with tea. "It is an old custom in Wales to show hospitality to visitors by serving it. No well-ordered Welsh home is ever without this delicious bread. Welsh people are very secretive about some things, especially their household recipes. These are usually passed from mother to daughter by practice in the making."

WALNUT POTICA (Yugoslavian)

Dough:
2 cakes compressed yeast dissolved in ¼ cup
   lukewarm water
¾ cup plus 1 tablespoon sugar
2 cups milk, scalded
¼ pound butter
1 tablespoon salt
3 large eggs, beaten
6 to 7 cups flour

Filling:
1 pound butter, melted
1 pound honey
2 pounds walnuts, finely ground
1 cup cream
3 cups sugar
Pinch salt
½ pound dates, chopped
2 eggs

Combine dissolved yeast with 1 tablespoon sugar. Add ¾ cup sugar to scalded milk with butter and salt. Cool, then add yeast mixture. Add beaten eggs. Beat in flour until stiff.

Knead on a floured board until smooth and elastic, about 20 to 25 minutes. Place dough in greased bowl, cover with a cloth and let rise in a warm place for 1 ½ hours.

Make filling by adding honey and walnuts to melted butter. Stir in cream. Add sugar, salt, and dates. Cook until mixture starts bubbling, being careful not to scorch. Cool slightly. Add one egg at a time, beating quickly after each addition. Set aside.

Cover a large table with a cloth and sprinkle with flour. Roll out dough with a rolling pin, then pull with fingers until paper thin, being careful not to tear. (Patch any tears with dough.) Spread filling over entire area and roll up like a jelly roll. Place on greased baking sheet or cut in 5 portions and place in greased bread pans. Let rise about 30 minutes. Bake at 300 degrees for 70 minutes. May be glazed.

Submitted by Jeanne Cragin (Mrs. Lawrence) Atkinson, Superior.

A sweet bread embellished with nuts, raisins, and dried or candied fruit was a standard part of Christmas eating for many Europeans. In Germany, this bread was called Stollen; in Switzerland, Pear Bread; in Czechoslovakia, Vanocka; and in Norway—where that favored spice, cardamon, was added—it was Julekaka.

The Czech and German versions were usually flavored with mace instead of cardamon. Blanche Mendl, Deerbrook, contributed her family traditions concerning Vanocka. "It would not be Christmas without a Vanocka, a braided holiday bread," she wrote. "My mother told us that her father always made the Vanocka, as he had experience as a baker while serving in the Austrian army as a youth. The Vanocka was made of raised sweet dough to which almonds, dark and light raisins, candied citron, vanilla, and mace were added. Grandpa started with a five-strand braid of dough for the bottom layer; then, a four; then three, and a two on top. Being artistic, he made two doves for the top. Most of the Vanocka were not as large or elaborate, but, heavens, he needed it for his twelve kids. The breads were taken to a baker to have them baked in large outdoor ovens."

JULEKAKA

2 cups milk, scalded
1 cup sugar
2 teaspoons salt
1 cup butter, melted
2 cakes compressed yeast dissolved in ½ cup
    lukewarm water
8 cups flour
1 teaspoon ground cardamon
1 cup raisins
½ cup citron, chopped
½ cup candied cherries
½ cup almonds, chopped

Combine milk, sugar, salt, and melted butter. Cool to lukewarm. Add yeast and 4 cups flour. Beat well. Set in a warm place until double in bulk. Add cardamon, raisins, citron, candied cherries, almonds, and remaining flour. Mix well.

Turn out onto floured board and knead well. Set in a warm place until doubled in bulk. Cut into thirds and form loaves. Place in buttered pans and let rise until almost doubled in bulk. Bake at 400 degrees for 50 minutes.

Submitted by Mrs. August Sommerfield, Chippewa Falls.

PEAR BREAD

3 large potatoes, peeled and cut up
½ cup water
2 tablespoons sugar
2 tablespoons salt
2 cakes compressed yeast dissolved in ½ cup lukewarm water
2 pounds dried pears
1 pound currants
1 pound raisins
½ pound figs
¼ pound walnuts
2 quarts water
2 cups brown sugar
1 cup shortening
1½ teaspoons cinnamon
Flour to make a medium stiff dough

The night before baking, combine potatoes, water, sugar, and salt in a saucepan and boil until potatoes are done. Mash mixture and cool to lukewarm. Add dissolved yeast. Keep warm overnight. In a separate bowl, combine pears, currants, raisins, figs, and walnuts. Cover with 2 quarts water and let stand overnight.

The next morning, heat fruit mixture just to boiling, then cool to lukewarm. Add fruit and juice to yeast mixture. Mix in brown sugar, shortening, cinnamon, and enough flour to make a medium stiff dough.

Knead on a floured board. Let rise 3 hours. Divide into small loaves and let rise about 1 hour or until top springs back when touched. Bake at 425 degrees for 30 minutes; reduce heat to 375 degrees and continue baking about 1 hour. Brush top of loaves with butter.

When cool, store in a cool place. These will stay moist 2 months or more. Makes 10 loaves.

Submitted by Mrs. Leon Grimm, Arpin, who notes that Pear Bread "has a better flavor when it is made ahead as the fruit mellows up. I find it freezes well."

Quick Breads and Tea Breads

BLOOD BREAD (Swedish)

1 quart cow's blood mixed with ½ quart water
1 teaspoon salt
1 heaping tablespoon baking powder
4 cups white flour
2 cups graham flour

Sift together salt, baking powder, and 2 cups white flour. Add gradually with the graham flour to the blood and water mixture, using a wooden spoon. Keep adding remaining white flour until the dough can be worked by hand. Knead lightly; dough should be loose.

On a floured board, shape dough into flat rounds and place in greased, round cake pans, flattening dough out to the edges of the pan. Bake at 375 degrees about 1 hour. Serve with butter while hot.

Submitted by Hilda Hillman (Mrs. Sulo) Sukanen, Marengo. The bread, she says, will be about 1 inch high. Blood Bread was also used for a soup by cutting the bread into cubes and cooking in hot milk seasoned with salt and butter; it was served at breakfast.

RYE AND INDIAN BREAD

For a good, thick loaf, take one pint rye flour to three pints of corn meal, one-half tea-cup molasses, or brown sugar, scald with boiling water—be sure to stir in water enough to thoroughly scald it—cover it up and let stand until cool, then reduce with cold, sweet milk until thin enough to pour into your pan; bake all day, let it stand in the oven all night, and in the morning you will have the best loaf of bread you ever tasted. If your crust is too hard to eat, remove it, soak in water, and add to your next loaf. If will be richer than the first.

From A Helping Hand for Town and Country: An American Home Book of Practical and Scientific Information, *by Lyman C. Draper and W. A. Croffut, 1870.*

Norwegian Flat Bread bakes up thin and crisp like a cracker.

FLAT BREAD (Norwegian)

1 quart buttermilk
½ cup sugar
2 teaspoons baking soda
½ cup butter, melted
Whole wheat flour

Combine buttermilk, sugar, baking soda, and melted butter. Mix well. Add enough wheat flour to make a stiff dough. Roll out on a board dusted with white flour; roll as thinly as possible. Cut into squares and bake on baking sheets at 300 degrees. Watch closely, as it browns quickly.

Submitted by Mary L. Albrecht, Auburndale.

Other recipes for flat breads call for cornmeal and white flour. Flat Bread squares may be baked in a fry pan on top of the stove and then placed in the oven to brown.

It was the Indians who introduced the first settlers to cornmeal, which became a mainstay in one form or another for all who followed. The most basic cornbread was widely known as Johnnycake. It was made of cornmeal and water and baked on a griddle. (These were also called Bannocks.) Such a simple dish could be made under the most primitive of conditions. Later, as the country became more settled, other ingredients, like milk, shortening, and eggs, were added to the batter.

This Spider Johnnycake is an example of a more elaborate recipe. A spider is a cast-iron skillet with legs so it could be placed right over hot coals. Originally, this Johnnycake would have been made over an open fire or on top of the stove.

SPIDER JOHNNYCAKE

1 cup cornmeal
⅓ cup flour
¼ cup sugar
1 cup milk
2 teaspoons baking powder
1 teaspoon salt
3 eggs
2 tablespoons butter or lard
1 cup half and half

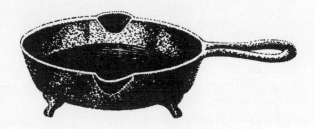

Mix together cornmeal, flour, sugar, milk, baking powder, salt, and two of the eggs well beaten.

Heat a spider and grease with butter or lard. Pour batter into hot spider. Beat remaining egg and combine with half and half. With the Johnnycake already in the oven, spoon egg mixture over the top evenly. Bake at 375 degrees for 30 minutes.

Submitted by Mrs. Leslie N. Jones, Holcombe. "The added milk and egg settles in the middle of the cake and makes it moist and good," she noted. "With a salad and vegetable that Spider Johnnycake makes a delicious meal."

Cornbread contains a higher proportion of white flour and is baked in pans, muffin tins, or the old-fashioned ear-of-corn shaped tins.

GOLDEN CORN BREAD (French-Canadian)

1 cup yellow cornmeal
1 cup sifted flour
¼ cup sugar
½ teaspoon salt
4 teaspoons baking powder
1 egg
1 cup milk
¼ cup shortening

Sift together dry ingredients into a bowl. Add egg, milk, and shortening. Beat with an egg beater for about 1 minute; do not overbeat.

Pour batter into greased 8-inch square pan or into muffin tins. Bake at 425 degrees for 20 to 25 minutes.

Serve warm with butter, syrup, creamed chicken, fish, or gravy.

Submitted by Georgya Tatreau, Platteville.

Cornbread recipes also came in verse:

MOTHER'S CORNBREAD

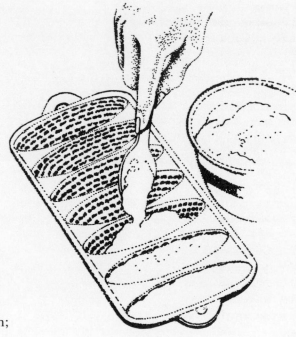

> Two cups Indian, one cup wheat,
> One cup sour milk, one cup sweet;
> One good egg that you will beat,
> Half a cup molasses, too.
> Half a cup sugar add thereto;
> With one spoon of butter new.
> Salt and soda each a spoon,
> Mix it quickly, bake it soon.
> Then you'll have corn bread complete
> Best of all corn bread you meet.
> It will make your boy's eyes shine,
> If he's like that boy of mine;
> If you have a dozen boys
> To increase your household joys,
> Double, then, this rule, I should,
> And you'll have two corn cakes good.
> When you've nothing nice for tea,
> This the very thing will be.
> All the men that I have seen
> Say it is, of all cakes, queen,
> Good enough for any King
> That a husband home may bring:
> Warming up the human stone,
> Cheering up the hearts you love;
> And only Tyndale can explain
> The links between corn bread and brain;
> Get a husband what he likes
> And save a hundred household strikes.

Submitted by Mrs. Elmer Hare, Dalton.

STEAMED BROWN BREAD (English)

2 cups graham flour
½ cup white flour
1 teaspoon baking soda
1 teaspoon salt
2 tablespoons sugar
1 egg, beaten
1½ cups buttermilk
½ cup molasses
1 cup currants

Combine flours, baking soda, salt, and sugar. Beat in egg, then buttermilk and molasses. Mix in currants.

Pour batter into 3 greased 1-pound cans or a large bowl. Place cloth over pudding and under the steamer cover. Steam 1 hour and 20 minutes or until done.

Ruth Weber (Mrs. Harland) Huebner, Oconomowoc, submitted this recipe and still has the old family steamer used to make this bread.

TIP TOP GINGERBREAD (English)

½ cup butter
½ cup sugar
2 eggs, unbeaten
½ cup molasses
1 teaspoon baking soda
1½ cups flour
1 teaspoon ginger
1 cup sour milk or cold water

Cream butter and sugar together. Blend in eggs. Combine molasses and baking soda and beat together thoroughly; add to butter mixture. Blend in flour combined with ginger alternately with sour milk.

Pour into a greased 9-inch square pan and bake at 350 degrees about 40 minutes.

Submitted by Elinore L. Loveland, Platteville. "The secret of having it light and tender," she reports, "is in beating the soda and molasses together thoroughly and in not beating the eggs."

Gingerbread was a popular quickbread in nineteenth century America and was usually spicier than the English recipe.

OLD-FASHIONED GINGERBREAD

½ cup butter
1 cup sugar
2 eggs, beaten
1 cup molasses
3 cups flour
2 teaspoons baking soda
2 teaspoons ginger
2 teaspoons cinnamon
1 teaspoon nutmeg
1 teaspoon allspice
½ teaspoon cloves
¾ teaspoon salt
1 cup buttermilk

Cream butter and sugar; add beaten eggs and molasses. Sift flour, soda, spices, and salt together 3 times. Add to butter-eggs mixture alternately with the buttermilk, beating well after each addition.

Bake in a greased loaf pan at 350 degrees about 1 hour or until a toothpick inserted in the center comes out clean.

Submitted by Mrs. Claire Rood, Shawano. She points out that raisins and nuts can be added if desired. This 150-year-old recipe may be served plain or with an icing or whipped cream, ice cream, or a sauce.

ORANGE BREAD

Yellow peel of 3 oranges, cut very fine
1 cup sugar
About 4 tablespoons water
1 cup milk
2½ cups flour
3 teaspoons baking powder
Pinch salt

Combine thinly cut orange peel, sugar, and water in a saucepan and bring to a boil. Cook until mixture is a syrup and sugar is dissolved. Cool.

Add milk and flour which has been combined with baking powder and salt alternately a little at a time. Mix well after each addition.

Bake in a greased 9-inch bread pan at 350 degrees about 40 minutes.

Norma J. Kolthoff, Madison, submitted this recipe for a specialty of the Seven Gables Inn in Lake Geneva. The Inn, which operated from 1915 to 1925, was owned by her great uncle, Josiah Barfield, and his wife Genieveve. To fill the requests made for the recipe, the Barfields kept a supply typed on 3 by 5-inch cards on hand to pass out. Ms. Kolthoff's mother appended a note that she would add an egg to the batter.

ALL BRAN PRUNE BREAD

2 cups all bran
²⁄₃ cup prune juice
²⁄₃ cup milk
1 tablespoon shortening
½ cup sugar
1 egg
1¼ cups flour
¼ teaspoon salt
1½ teaspoons baking soda
²⁄₃ cup chopped cooked prunes
⅓ cup chopped nuts

Combine all bran, prune juice, and milk. Let stand.

Cream shortening and sugar. Add egg and beat well. Add all bran mixture and mix well. Blend in flour, salt, baking soda, prunes, and nuts. Mix only until flour is incorporated.

Bake in well-greased loaf pan at 325 degrees for 1 hour and 20 minutes.

Submitted by Gladys Gauthier, Oconto Falls.

APRICOT NUT BREAD

1½ cups (½ pound) dried apricots
1 cup water
2¼ cups flour
¾ cups sugar
4 teaspoons baking powder
1 teaspoon baking soda
1 teaspoon salt
¾ cup coarsely chopped nuts
1 egg, well beaten
1 cup buttermilk
3 tablespoons melted butter

Wash, drain, and coarsely chop apricots. Combine with water in a heavy saucepan. Bring to a boil, reduce heat, and simmer uncovered 10 minutes or until water is absorbed. Set aside to cool.

Blend flour, sugar, baking powder, baking soda, and salt in a bowl. Mix in nuts. Combine egg, buttermilk, and butter with the apricots; blend well. Make a well in center of dry ingredients and add the apricot mixture all at once. Stir only enough to moisten the dry ingredients.

Turn into a 9½-inch loaf pan that has been greased on the bottom only; spread batter evenly to corners. Bake at 350 degrees about 1 hour or until wooden pick inserted in center comes out clean.

Cool in pan on a rack 10 minutes, then turn out and cool completely.

Submitted by Mrs. R. J. Burgoyne, Plymouth.

FRUIT KUCHEN (German)

1 ¼ cups plus 1 tablespoon flour
½ teaspoon baking powder
1 cup plus 1 tablespoon sugar
1 teaspoon salt
½ teaspoon baking soda
½ cup lard
3 eggs
1 cup sour cream
1 quart berries or apples, sliced

Mix together 1 ¼ cups flour, baking powder, 1 tablespoon sugar, salt, and baking soda. With pastry cutter, blend in lard until like coarse crumbs. Add 1 egg, beaten, and ¼ cup sour cream. Mix until dough holds together. Pat into the bottom and sides of a greased 9 by 13-inch pan.

Mix remaining sugar, flour, sour cream, and eggs, beaten. Add berries or apples. Pour into prepared pan. Bake at 450 degrees for 10 minutes, then reduce heat to 350 degrees and continue baking until custard is set.

Submitted by Marion Philippi (Mrs. John A.) Urich, Madison.

BARA BRITH (Welsh)

1 pound candied fruit
½ pound brown sugar
1 ½ teaspoon salt
1 cup brewed tea
4 cups flour
1 teaspoon baking soda
½ teaspoon baking powder

Combine candied fruit, sugar, salt, and tea. Let stand overnight.

Combine flour, baking soda, and baking powder. Add to candied fruit mixture. Mix well.

Bake in two large, greased loaf pans at 350 degrees for about 1 hour. Serve thinly sliced and buttered.

Submitted by Mrs. Stanley Holland, Mineral Point.

TEA BISCUITS OR SCONES (English)

2 cups flour
1 teaspoon salt
4 teaspoons baking powder
¼ cup sugar
¼ pound butter
1 egg, beaten
½ cup milk
1 cup dried currants
Sugar

Sift together flour, salt, baking powder, and sugar. Cut in butter as for pie crust. Add egg, milk, and currants. Knead about 12 strokes and roll out about ½-inch thick. Sprinkle with sugar and cut with a cookie cutter. Place on greased baking sheet and let stand about 10 minutes.

Bake at 425 degrees for 12 to 15 minutes. Serve warm with butter and honey or marmalade.

Submitted by Hope C. (Mrs. R. H.) Loveland, Cassville.

Pancakes and Waffles

Whether they were called griddle cakes, lefse, latkes, crepes, flapjacks, or pfannkuchen, pancakes appeared with regularity on Wisconsin tables at all meals, not only at breakfast.

They were filling and easy to cook on a stove or over an open fire. "We had a griddle that covered the first two front lids of the old cookstove," Cecelia E. Nieman of Muskego remembers. "We had a good wood fire underneath and pancakes were golden brown and plate size." Not least, pancakes frequently were a means of using leftovers such as mashed potatoes or sour milk.

The basic pancake, of course, consists of flour, milk or water, and eggs beaten into a batter— thick or thin according to taste—and baked on a griddle or frying pan. The proportions and ingredients (more eggs, milk for water, or cream for milk) and the embellishments (spices, fruit, toppings) were determined by seasonal supplies, the state of the family's finances, and the family's Old World traditions.

A thin pancake was the favorite of many European groups—French, German, Slovak, Norwegian, Swedish. They were served flat or spread with a variety of things—jelly, syrup, butter, fruit—and rolled up.

NORWEGIAN PANCAKES

1 cup melted butter
1 cup sugar
3 eggs, beaten until lemon colored
1 cup cream or half and half
1 cup flour
Grated rind of 1 lemon

Beat all ingredients together. Batter will be very thin.

Heat a heavy iron skillet and grease lightly with a piece of lard wrapped in cloth; just barely rub the bottom and sides of the skillet. Pour in ⅓ cup batter, tipping skillet so batter runs up the sides. When pancake loses its gloss, turn by gently loosening the sides. It will brown quickly. Fold into fourths and place in a heated casserole in a 250 degree oven until all the batter is used up.

Serve with syrup or thickened fruit juice as a dessert.

SWEDISH PANCAKES

1½ cups flour
1 teaspoon salt
1¼ teaspoons cinnamon
2 tablespoons sugar
4 eggs, beaten
2 tablespoons melted butter
2 cups milk

Sift dry ingredients together. Beat into beaten eggs. Add butter and milk. Bake on a hot griddle. Serve with lingonberries.

Submitted by Betty Hanson and Mrs. Sanford Hanson, Sturgeon Bay. These pancakes have been served for many years at the family's summer resort in Door County. The Norwegian pancakes recipe belonged to Susanna Beskow Hanson, who began cooking for the city folks who had summer houses on Sturgeon Bay after her husband's death in 1895. "Susanna had become a Norwegian," Betty Hanson wrote, "when a sailor named Lalland rescued her from a shipwreck in which her Russian parents were lost." Susanna's son, John, married a Swedish girl, Matilda Peterson, who helped Susanna occasionally. Eventually, John and Matilda converted their fruit farm into their summer resort, which is still operating.

Thicker pancakes required more flour and in some recipes, a leavening agent.

MOTHER'S FLAPJACKS (Scottish)

1 egg, beaten until light
1 tablespoon melted butter or bacon grease
2 teaspoons cream of tartar
2 cups flour
Pinch salt
Milk

Combine egg, butter, cream of tartar, flour, salt, and enough milk to make a batter that can be poured from a pitcher. Pour batter onto a hot, oiled griddle and bake until bubbles appear. Turn and brown on other side.

Spread hot flapjacks generously with butter and thick maple syrup and stack on a platter. Cut like a pie and serve with additional maple syrup, thick cream, and nutmeg.

Submitted by Mrs. Ora P. Taylor, Drummond.

CORNMEAL MOUNTAIN CAKES

1 egg
1¼ cups buttermilk
1 tablespoon molasses
¼ cup melted shortening
1 cup sifted flour
1 teaspoon salt
½ teaspoon baking soda
2 teaspoons baking powder
½ cup yellow cornmeal

In a large bowl, combine eggs, buttermilk, molasses, and shortening. Add flour sifted with salt, baking soda, and baking powder. Add cornmeal and stir until batter is slightly lumpy. Bake on a hot griddle, turning once. Serve with butter and honey.

Submitted by Mrs. Hugh Severson, Greenwood.

IZLENSKUR PONNUKOKUR (Icelandic Pancakes)

2 eggs, beaten
½ cup sour milk or buttermilk
2 cups milk
⅓ cup sugar
½ teaspoon baking powder
1 teaspoon baking soda
1½ cups flour
½ teaspoon vanilla

¼ teaspoon salt
½ teaspoon cinnamon

Blend all ingredients thoroughly in a blender. Pour batter into lightly greased electric skillet at 325 to 350 degrees. Bake until bubbles appear; turn and continue baking until done. Sprinkle with sugar or jam.
Serves six.

Submitted by Roger W. Gunnerson, Washington Island, who uses modern appliances to make this recipe brought from Iceland to Washington Island in 1882 by his grandmother. Mr. Gunnerson sometimes adds shortening to the batter and then bakes the cakes on a dry skillet. "I have been told by my grandmother," he added, "that cinnamon was one of the most highly prized of the spices they used."

Sourdough pancakes were a fixture in logging camps. The batter was mixed the night before and only needed to be stirred down and baked the next morning to stoke up the lumberjacks for a good morning's work.

SOURDOUGH PANCAKES

1 cup Sourdough Starter (see below)
2 tablespoons sugar, or to taste
Salt to taste
2 cups warm milk or water
½ to ¾ cup buckwheat flour
¼ cup cornmeal
White flour
½ teaspoon baking soda
½ teaspoon baking powder
4 tablespoons melted shortening

The night before, combine starter, sugar, salt, milk, buckwheat flour, and cornmeal. Add enough white flour to make a "runny" batter. Place batter in a deep bowl (so it won't run over) and let stand at room temperature overnight.

The next morning, stir down the batter. Add baking soda, baking powder, and enough more white flour to make a medium batter. Stir in melted shortening. Bake on a hot griddle. Stir batter frequently while making the pancakes.
Serves about 6.

Sourdough Starter:

1⅓ cups flour
1 tablespoon sugar
1 tablespoon salt
1 package active dry yeast
2½ cups lukewarm water

Combine flour, sugar, salt, and undissolved yeast in a large bowl. Gradually add lukewarm water and beat 2 minutes at medium speed, scraping bowl occasionally. Cover and let stand at room temperature 4 days. Stir down daily.

To replenish after taking out the starter for the pancakes or bread, add 1½ cups lukewarm water, ¾ cup flour, and 1½ teaspoons sugar to remaining starter. Beat for 1 minute at medium speed. Cover and let stand, stirring down daily, until needed.

Submitted by Leona (Mrs. Raymond) Shirek, Junction City, whose uncles, Frank and John Huser, were cooks in lumber camps near Vesper and Arpin.

MELLOW APPLE PANCAKES (German)

2 or 3 apples
1½ cups sifted flour
½ teaspoon baking soda
⅔ teaspoon salt
2 eggs, separated
1⅓ cups buttermilk
2 tablespoons melted, cooled butter

Peel, core, and thinly slice the apples. Sift together flour, baking soda, and salt. Beat egg whites until stiff but not dry. In another bowl, beat egg yolks with unwashed beater and add buttermilk. Stir in sifted dry ingredients and cooled butter. Fold in egg whites.

Spoon batter onto moderately hot, well greased griddle and arrange apple slices on each pancake. When underside is lightly browned, turn and bake until apples are cooked thoroughly.

Makes 16 small to medium pancakes.

Alexa Young of Madison submitted this recipe that her mother, whose parents came from Pomerania, perfected. Her parents' farm in Dodge County included a bearing orchard: "For these pancakes, Mother preferred either Wealthy apples or an un-named old, flat variety, which she had named 'those big pie apples.' Both were of a soft variety, which, when moderately ripe, cooked up mellow and juicy on top of these pancakes."

Potato pancakes can be made in many ways. Probably every cook who makes them has his or her special recipe that makes them just a bit different than the neighbor's. Some recipes call for mashed potatoes, the best known of that variety being Lefse. Some recipes submitted noted that the secret of making Lefse was the same as for pie crusts: handling the dough as little as possible. Others call for kneading the thick batter until it is no longer sticky.

The ingredients are minimal: mashed potatoes, salt, cream or condensed milk, and shortening.

LEFSE (Norwegian)

5 large potatoes
½ cup cream
3 tablespoons melted butter
1 teaspoon salt
Flour

Boil potatoes, peel, and put through a ricer. Add cream, butter, and salt. Cool. Add ½ cup flour for each cup of mashed potatoes and mix until smooth.

For each lefse, form about ¼ cup of dough into a small ball. Roll out as thinly as possible on a floured board.

Bake on an ungreased lefse griddle over moderate heat (about 400 degrees) until light brown. Turn and brown other side. Place on a cloth until cold.

For serving, cut each Lefse into four pieces. May be spread with butter or cinnamon and sugar.

Submitted by Mrs. Albert Larson, Manitowoc.

Mashed potatoes mixed with meat was a supper dish for some.

SAUSAGE POTATO CAKES (Swedish)

¼ pound pork sausage meat
1½ cups mashed potatoes
1 egg, beaten
Salt to taste

Crumble and brown sausage in a frying pan; drain off and reserve drippings. Add sausage and some of the drippings to potatoes. Mix in salt and beaten egg. Form into patties and fry, browning both sides nicely.

Submitted by Dagmar P. Noel, Waukesha.

Raw potatoes pancakes are typically German and were served in many ways. They were a main dish with applesauce with or without bratwurst or other sausage; they accompanied other meats; with syrup or jam, or just with sugar, they were a breakfast dish or a sweet.

POTATO PANCAKES (German)

2 cups raw potatoes, peeled and grated
2 eggs, beaten
1 tablespoon flour

½ teaspoon salt
½ teaspoon baking powder

Mix all ingredients well. Bake on a greased, hot griddle like pancakes.

Submitted by Mrs. Freida Hirsch, Wisconsin Dells, who added that these Potato Pancakes were always served the day the family completed the potato harvest: "Several hundred bushels were always picked up by hand as we followed the plow down the row."

Jewish cooks favor the addition of onion when making Potato Latkes.

POTATO LATKES (Jewish)

4 large potatoes, grated
1 small onion, grated
3 eggs, beaten
½ teaspoon salt
2 tablespoons flour
¼ teaspoon baking powder
Cooking oil for frying

Combine potatoes and onion and mix well. Beat in eggs, salt, flour, and baking powder.

Heat about ¼ inch cooking oil in a heavy pan over moderately hot fire. Drop batter by spoonsful into oil and fry on both sides until brown. A large mixing spoon full makes thin pancakes; more batter makes thicker ones.

Serve, drained, with sour cream or applesauce.

These may also be baked in muffin tins or a baking pan. For muffins, heat greased tins and fill ¾ full; bake at 400 degrees 1 hour or until brown. Or heat in a 375 degree oven a 9 by 13-inch baking pan containing ¼-inch cooking oil; add batter spread thinly and bake until well browned, 20 to 40 minutes.

Submitted by Mrs. Herman Tuchman, Milwaukee, who notes that these pancakes are traditional for Chanukah, the Feast of Lights.

Boiled rice was sometimes an ingredient of pancakes or waffles, too. This is the way a recipe for German Rice Waffles appeared in an old recipe file:

GERMAN RICE WAFFLES

Boil ½ pound of rice in milk until it becomes thoroughly soft. Then remove it from the fire, stirring it constantly, and adding a little at a time 1 quart of sifted flour, 5 beaten eggs, 2 spoonfuls of yeast, ½ pound of melted butter, a little salt and a teacupful of warm milk. Set the batter in a warm place, and when risen, bake in the ordinary way.

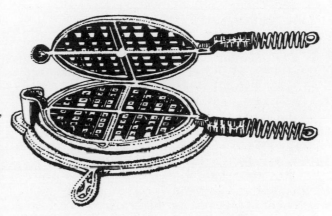

Submitted by Mrs. Betty E. Harnack, Janesville, who found it in the recipe collection of her ancestors who settled in Rock County in the 1870's.

French crepes are well-known as a dessert, but other groups have recipes for ending a meal with thin pancakes. These are close to an omelet.

CSUSZTATOTT PALACSINTA (Hungarian)

¼ cup butter
¼ cup sugar
¼ teaspoon salt
5 eggs, separated
¼ cup sifted flour
½ cup milk
¼ teaspoon vanilla
Sugar and cinnamon

Cream together the butter, sugar, and salt. Add egg yolks and beat well. Stir in flour and then the milk. Beat egg whites until stiff but not dry; add vanilla. Fold into the batter.

Using unsalted butter, grease a moderately hot iron skillet. Pour in a scant ¼ cup of batter. Do not tip pan or spread; these pancakes will be 5 to 6 inches across and about ¼-inch thick when baked.

Brown lightly on one side only. Lift gently and place cooked side down on a flat baking dish. Set in a 300 degree oven while making second pancake. Sprinkle uncooked side of first pancake with sugar and cinnamon and top with second pancake. Continue until there are five layers, then start another stack. Bake stacks an additional 15 to 20 minutes or until top is delicately brown. Serve at once.

Submitted by Darlene Kronschnabel, Greenleaf.

Doughnuts and Fry Cakes

The memoirs of many early Wisconsin residents contain references to a crock in the kitchen always filled with doughnuts or fry cakes. And a platter of them was standard fare at most meals in the logging camps. Usually, dough prepared by frying was —and still is—a sweet dish. But not always. Pieces of bread dough were fried on occasion, usually as a snack on baking day.

Mrs. Ruszella Christensen, who was eighty years old and living in Freeport, Illinois, when she sent in material for this book, reported that fried bread dough was called "Pigs Ears" in her family. "First take a piece of white bread dough," she wrote, "a little bigger than a good-sized egg, but first have a frying pan with melted hot lard a couple inches deep, and pull this piece of dough long and thin about the size of a pig ear. Drop in the hot lard and turn when light brown. You will be surprised how light and fluffy this will get as it bakes or cooks. . . .

"When I was short of bread I often baked them long before this bread was ready for pans. I would make a couple dozen; half of them I served plain with the main meal and the other half I would roll in sugar and they would take the place of dessert. By the time they had their potatoes, vegetables, and meat and the pigs ears, they would be filled up."

Fry Bread is a favorite in Native American households, too, served frequently for family meals and always at feasts.

FRY BREAD (Indian)

12 cups flour
3 cups lukewarm water
¼ to ½ teaspoon salt
3 teaspoons baking powder
Shortening for frying

Put flour into a 6 quart bowl and push up high along the sides so there is a deep well in the center. Add water combined with salt and baking powder, pouring it into the prepared well. Mix with a spoon until the dough will not absorb any more flour. Remove spoon and knead well in the bowl. Let stand 1 hour.

Heat shortening in a large frying pan until very hot, but not smoking. With a knife, cut a piece of dough about the size of a small fist, and with floured hands, stretch it out flat. Drop into hot shortening. Brown both sides, turning once.

Submitted by Mrs. Rosella Mallory, Milwaukee, a Winnebago, who warned if the shortening gets too hot, the bread won't get done on the inside. These are also called Dough Gods.

FRIED CAKES (Yankee)

2 tablespoons melted butter
2 eggs, beaten
1 cup sugar
1 cup milk
About 3 cups flour
3 teaspoons baking powder
Lard for frying
Whole cloves and stick cinnamon

Pour melted butter over beaten eggs, then stir in sugar and milk. Sift together flour and baking powder and stir in, mixing well.

Roll dough into strips about little-finger thick; don't handle the dough too much but get it smooth, adding more flour, a little at a time on top to avoid sticky spots. Form rolls into circles and pinch together.

Deep fry in very hot lard into which a few whole cloves and pieces of stick cinnamon have been added. Turn cakes over as soon as they rise and turn once again. Drain on paper towels.

Submitted by Marion Tubbs Lawson, now of New York City. Mrs. Lawson added that besides the usual shape, her mother, a resident of Elkhorn, wound the strips of dough into figure eights. "The use of spices in the lard gave an indescribably subtle flavor as well as kept the lard sweet," she wrote. "My mother had two large blown-glass candy jars on a curly maple chest of drawers in the dining room, this chest originally made for her aunt in Winooski, Sheboygan County, in 1846. The jars were kept full of fried cakes and available to the hand of husband, children, and guests. When she made them for Congregational church sales they were always spoken for before they ever got to the sales table."

Raised doughnuts have many names. In Polish they are known as Paczski and may be made plain or filled with jam.

PACZSKI (Polish)

¼ cup active dry yeast
2 cups milk, scalded and cooled to lukewarm
About 7 cups flour
4 egg yolks
1 egg
½ cup sugar
½ teaspoon vanilla
Grated rind of ½ lemon
1 teaspoon salt
1 teaspoon nutmeg
½ teaspoon cinnamon
¼ pound butter, melted
About 2 cups very thick prune jam (optional)
Shortening for frying

Dissolve yeast in lukewarm milk. Add 2 cups flour. Let stand about 30 minutes.

Beat egg yolks, egg, sugar, vanilla, lemon rind, salt, nutmeg, and cinnamon until light. Add to yeast-flour sponge. Add melted butter and about 5 cups flour. Blend well. Cover with a cloth and let stand in a warm place until double in bulk.

Turn out on a floured board and pat out with hands until about ½-inch thick. Cut with doughnut cutter, cover and let rise until double. Drop into deep, hot fat (365 degrees) and fry 3 minutes. Roll in granulated or powdered sugar and serve warm.

For filled Paczski, pat out half the dough into a round about ¼-inch thick. Place ½ to ¾ teaspoon jam in dollops over the dough, leaving space to cut a circle with a cutter. (You could lightly mark the circles with the cutter to be sure you get the jam in the center.) Roll out remaining dough ¼-inch thick and place over jam spotted round. Cut, centering the cutter over the jam. (The two layers will be sealed in the cutting process.) Let rise until double and fry as for unfilled doughnuts.

Hedwig A. (Mrs. Victor) Semran, Milwaukee, submitted this recipe that has been handed down in her family which came from Poland in 1919. "These doughnuts are made on Shrove Tuesday which is the day before Ash Wednesday," she wrote. "So this is the last big feed before the long six-week fast."

Danes and Germans make a raised doughnut that are round and made in a special pan that looks like a cross between a frying pan and a muffin tin. These may be leavened with yeast or baking powder.

ÆBELSKIVER (Danish)

3 eggs, separated
2 teaspoons sugar
½ teaspoon salt
2 cups buttermilk
2 cups flour
1 teaspoon baking soda
1 teaspoon baking powder
Shortening

Beat egg yolks. Add sugar, salt, and buttermilk. Sift together flour, baking soda, and baking powder and stir in. Fold in egg whites that have been beaten stiff but not dry.

Heat an *æbelskiver* pan and put in a small amount of shortening in each of the 7 cups. Fill the cups ⅔ full with dough. Cook until bubbly. Turn with a fork and brown other side. Serve hot with sugar or syrup.

Chopped apples may be added to the dough before cooking.

Submitted by Mrs. Frieda Hirsch, Wisconsin Dells.

Other recipes call for currants instead of apples if you wish to add fruit. The Germans call these *Fuetjens* and sometimes add cardamon to the batter.

Potatoes also found their way into doughnuts.

MASHED POTATO DROP DOUGHNUTS (German)

1 cup freshly mashed potatoes
1 cup sugar
1 cup milk
2 eggs, beaten
3 tablespoons melted butter
3½ cups flour
2 teaspoons baking powder
½ teaspoon salt
Lard for frying
Cinnamon and sugar

Combine potatoes, sugar, milk, eggs, and butter. Sift together flour, baking powder, and salt. Add to potato mixture and blend well.

Drop by teaspoonsful into very hot, deep lard. Fry until brown. When done, drain and roll in a mixture of cinnamon and sugar.

Submitted by Mrs. Doris Reichert, West Allis.

Edible blossoms and leaves, dipped into a batter and fried into a fritter, was once a common dish in the days before pesticides and other chemical sprays. If you want to try this, be sure the blooms have not been sprayed. Elderberry blossoms take well to this, as do squash blossoms.

ELDERBERRY BLOSSOM FRITTERS

2 eggs, separated
1½ cups milk
About 2 cups flour
Pinch of salt
**Elderberry blossoms picked with the dew on
  and patted dry**

Beat egg yolks and beat in milk. Add enough flour to make a medium-thick pancake batter. (A spoonful of batter held above the mixing bowl should run in a 1½-inch length, then drop in triangular plops.) Beat until smooth. Cover and refrigerate 2 hours if possible. Just before using, beat egg whites until stiff but not dry and fold in.

Dip well-dried blossoms into batter and deep-fry at about 350 degrees. Delicious served with hot cherry sauce. These may also be dusted with powdered sugar.

Submitted by Mrs. Floyd Myron, Milwaukee.

A CHILD'S SCHOOL LESSON

One cup of sugar,
One of milk,
  Two eggs beaten
  Fine as silk.
Salt and nutmeg,
Lemon will do,
  Of baking powder
  Teaspoons two.

Lightly stir
The flour in;
  Roll on pie board,
  Not too thin.
Cut in diamonds,
Twists or rings;
  Drop with care
  The doughy things
Into fat that
Briskly swells
  Evenly the
  Spongy cells.

Watch with care
The time for turning;
  Get them brown,
  Just short of burning.
Roll in sugar;
Serve when cool.
  This for donuts
  Is the rule.

Taught by Notre Dame nuns at Holy Cross School, Blue Mound Road, Milwaukee, in the 1890's.
Submitted by Carlyne M. (Mrs. Otto) Klein, Burlington.

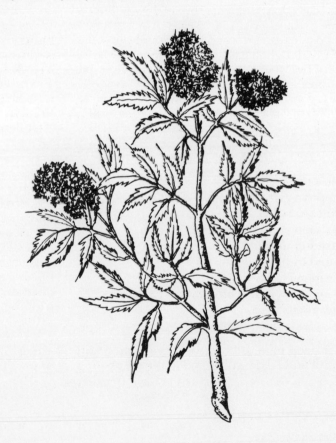

Bread Dishes and Toasts

Breads of various kinds were not only a mainstay of many diets, they were the basis for snacks, too. And none was wasted; stale bread was used up in one way or another.

Many Wisconsinites have fond memories of treats associated with bread. David J. Borth, Bayfield, remembers that when his mother "wanted a special treat for her children, she took one third of a batch of white bread dough. Mixed in some extra sugar and two eggs. After this mixture had risen, she worked it down and put some rolled out dough in cake pans, pushing down the center. Then she would put in applesauce or pitted prunes. When this rose, she baked it. By golly that was good on a cold winter's night."

For Mrs. Robert Sanford, River Falls, when she was growing up, "the main snack at our home was bread, milk, and onions. A bowl of bread and milk eaten with raw onions was almost a must after farm chores in the evening."

And Rebecca Trumpy Gillings, Redgranite, whose family was Pennsylvania-Dutch, remembers "there was always a pot of coffee on the back of the stove. Sometimes when we got home from school we would put a slice of homemade bread on a plate, pour hot coffee over it, scoop thick cream from the top of the bowl of milk in the pantry onto that, sprinkle sugar over the cream—and umm-mmm was that good at four o'clock on a cold winter day!"

The classic way to use stale bread was to fry it in some manner. The best-known is what we call French Toast and the French-Canadians call Pain Perdu, which means lost bread.

PAIN PERDU (French Canadian)

2 large eggs, separated
⅛ teaspoon salt
½ cup cold milk
¼ teaspoon vanilla or brandy or rum
⅛ teaspoon nutmeg
¼ pound butter
2 tablespoons vegetable oil
6 to 8 slices of stale white or French bread
4 tablespoons sugar
Jelly

In a deep mixing bowl, beat egg whites with salt until stiff. Add yolks and continue beating while pouring in milk, vanilla or brandy, and nutmeg. Mix well.

Place butter and oil in large iron skillet on medium heat. When the shortening is hot enough to brown a cube of bread in 60 seconds, slowly dip each slice of bread into egg mixture to coat on both sides and place in skillet. Fry on both sides, turning once, until browned.

Drain on absorbent paper. Sprinkle one side with sugar and spread the other with jam. Serve at once to 6 or 8.

Fry several slices at a time depending on size of skillet. May also be served with cinnamon-sugar or maple syrup.

Submitted by Mrs. Florence M. Vint, Springfield, Virginia, formerly of Milwaukee.

GERMAN FRITTERS

Stalebread or cake
Lard for frying
Boiling milk
Powdered sugar or preserves

Cut bread or cake slices into rounds. Deep fry in hot lard to a light brown. Dip each slice in boiling milk to remove the grease; drain quickly and dust with powdered sugar or spread with preserves. Sweet wine sauce poured over them is very nice.

Submitted by Lynora Jean Harnack, Janesville. It is from an 1892 cookbook.

Stale bread could be made into pancakes, also.

GRANDMA'S PANCAKES FOR TWO

2 slices of salt bread
1 cup buttermilk
1 egg, beaten
⅓ cup flour
½ teaspoon baking soda
1 teaspoon baking powder
½ teaspoon salt

Soak bread in buttermilk for several hours. Break up bread with a spoon and beat until smooth. Add flour, baking soda, baking powder, and salt. Beat smooth.

Fry on a hot griddle as for pancakes. The recipe may be doubled or tripled.

Submitted by Kathryn Parkinson, Madison.

Stale bread combined with poppy seeds provided a special dish for Eastern Europeans

MAKÓWKA (Polish)

Milk
Homemade bread at least a day old, sliced
Ground poppy seeds mixed with sugar to taste

Scald milk and let cool to lukewarm. Dip slices of bread into warm milk and let excess drip off. As each piece is dipped and drained, sprinkle with poppy seed mixture and layer in a heavy earthenware or ironstone bowl. Continue until ingredients are used up.

Cover top with a plate and press down lightly until the milk oozes up to the top. If necessary, add more milk just to cover bread. Let stand 3 to 4 hours.

This tastes best when served slightly warm. However, leftovers may be refrigerated and served cold. Warm Makówka may be garnished with cooked prunes.

Mrs. Joseph Meinholz, Eau Claire, submitted this recipe, which was traditionally served at her house on both Christmas and New Years Eve.

SOUP

A GOOD HEARTY SOUP KEPT MANY A NINE-teenth-century Wisconsinite stoked up for his or her strenuous labors. Not only were soups nutritious, they were budget-stretchers as well. They could be expanded to feed a large number of people; they could be made with whatever ingredients were on hand or plentiful; they provided a fine use for leftovers. Indeed, the line between a stew and a soup is drawn with water.

There were meat-based clear soups, chowders, cream soups, soups of legumes, and wine and fruit soups. The vegetable and spice combinations varied from ethnic group to ethnic group, and certain soup dishes are firmly identified with Old World origins, as borscht is with Russia.

The produce from the kitchen garden was one source for soup fixings, including seasonings. Marie T. St. Louis of Shorewood still has her French-Canadian great-aunt's recipe for Soup Seasoning:

"When the first onions come out I start salting them. I cut up onions and stems in small pieces and cover them with salt . . . and the day after just add more onions and salt. Then come the carrots. I pick out some of the green leaves and cut them small with a pair of scissors. Then I use the large knife of my meat grinder and I pass through the meat grinder as many as I want or as many as I have that day, and some more another day, always adding salt. Then I cut in parsley and a lot more celery and salt again. (I put in a lot of salt.) All of this you put in a crock with a cover and weight and it will keep the year around. Then when you want to use it, take as much as you want and pour hot water on it, and it will get green and look fresh. Put it in your soup when you put in your meat so it will all be well cooked."

BORSCHT (Russian)

1 to 2 pounds beef neck or soup bones
10 cups water
Salt
5 large beets, cut in thin strips
1 bay leaf
1 large onion, coarsely chopped
2 carrots, cut in thin strips
1 turnip, cut in strips
2 to 3 cups shredded cabbage
3 or 4 tomatoes, peeled and quartered
½ cup sliced celery
Beet greens (if fresh and tender), chopped
  (optional)
1 medium potato, peeled and diced (optional)
About 3 tablespoons lemon juice or vinegar
Sour cream
Dill weed, fresh or dried

Combine bones, water, and salt to taste. Bring to a boil and skim. Cover and simmer 1½ hours.

Remove meat and bones; cut meat into pieces and reserve. In a saucepan, combine 1 cup of beets and one cup of the stock. Bring to a boil and simmer until beets are tender. Reserve.

To the stock pot, add bay leaf, onions, carrots, remaining beets, and turnip and cook 20 minutes. Add cabbage, tomatoes, celery, and greens and potato if desired, and simmer about 30 minutes or until the vegetables are cooked.

Strain stock in which the beets were cooked separately and add to soup. (Beets may be used for soup garnish or salads.) Add lemon juice or vinegar to taste. Add meat and adjust seasoning. Serve with a dollop of sour cream and a sprinkle of fresh or dried dill weed.

Submitted by Mari Taniguchi, Appleton.

A SWISS SOUP

Boil three pounds potatoes; wash them well; add slowly some beef broth; sprinkle parsley, thyme, lemon, mint, sage, all chopped fine; boil five minutes; pepper and salt to taste. Just before taking off the fire, add two well-beaten eggs.

From Mrs. Winslow's Domestic Recipe Book *(1864), submitted by Mrs. Jean Beyer, Appleton.*

KIELBASA SOUP (Polish)

2 tablespoons butter
1 pound kielbasa (Polish sausage)
1 cup chopped onion
2 cups chopped celery and leaves
4 cups shredded cabbage
2 cups sliced, pared carrots
1 bay leaf
½ teaspoon dried leaf thyme
2 tablespoons vinegar
1 tablespoon salt

1½ cups beef bouillon
5 cups water
3 cups cubed, peeled potatoes

In a soup kettle, melt butter; add kielbasa, onion, and celery. Cook until onion and celery are tender. Add cabbage, carrots, bay leaf, thyme, vinegar, salt, bouillon, and water. Cover and simmer for 1½ hours. Add potatoes, cover and cook 20 minutes or until potatoes are done. Makes 8 cups.

Submitted by Charles Shetler, Madison.

CHICKEN CORN SOUP (Pennsylvania-Dutch)

1 chicken, cut up
3 quarts water
Salt and pepper to taste
Corn from 12 ears
1 large onion, chopped
3 stalks celery
1 teaspoon chopped parsley
4 hard boiled eggs, sliced
1 egg, beaten
About ¼ cup flour

Stew chicken in seasoned water; remove meat from bones and cut up.

To the broth, add corn, onion, celery, and parsley; adjust seasoning. Simmer about 30 minutes. Return chicken to broth and simmer another 15 minutes. Add hard-boiled eggs. Add enough flour to beaten egg to make a mixture that crumbles between the fingers. Crumble into soup and continue simmering until thickened. (This egg-flour thickening is called Rivels and will be lumpy, like rice.)

Submitted by Mrs. Martie Steele, Fond du Lac.

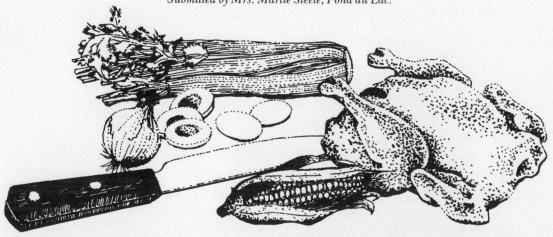

Dried mushrooms were an important ingredient in the kitchens of those from Eastern Europe. Their strong flavor added a special taste to soup.

ZUPA GRZYBOWA (Polish)

¼ pound dried mushrooms
Warm water
Salt
1 small onion, chopped
2 tablespoons butter
2 tablespoons flour
⅛ teaspoon pepper
Cooked thin noodles
Sour cream

Soak mushrooms in warm water to cover. Drain. Cover with fresh water, add ¼ teaspoon salt, and simmer covered until mushrooms are soft. Remove mushrooms, slice into juliene strips.

Let the broth settle, then carefully transfer to another pot so dregs may be discarded.

Saute onion until cooked and add to broth. Make a roux of the butter and flour and blend into the soup. Return mushrooms to soup and add pepper and salt to taste.

Serve over a large spoonful of noodles and garnish with sour cream.

Submitted by Eleanor (Mrs. Anthony) Yankowski, Neenah, who noted that mushrooms need quite a bit of salt, which should be added when the soup is almost done and with frequent tasting.

Dried mushrooms were also used in this unusual soup from Czechoslovakia.

SLOVAK CHRISTMAS SOUP

1 pint sauerkraut juice
1 cup dried mushrooms, washed, or 2 cups
    canned mushrooms, drained
Salt and pepper
1 tablespoon plus ½ cup flour
1 tablespoon butter
1 small onion, chopped (optional)
2 eggs, well beaten

Combine sauerkraut juice and 1½ to 2 quarts water and bring to a boil. Add mushrooms and simmer 1 hour if using dried mushrooms or 30 minutes for canned. Season with salt and pepper.

Combine 1 tablespoon flour, butter, and onion in a moderately hot skillet and stir until nicely browned. Remove from heat and add ¼ cup cold water, stirring constantly to prevent lumps. Add mixture to soup and mix well.

Mix eggs with a pinch of salt, 1 tablespoon water, and remaining flour. Pour slowly from the end of a spoon or fork into boiling soup and boil 2 or 3 minutes. The shape of these egg drops will improve if batter is poured from considerable height. Makes 4 to 5 servings.

Submitted by Mrs. John Desris, Kenosha. The proportion of sauerkraut juice and water, she noted, can be adjusted according to taste for more or less sour soup: "This is an unusual speciality for which some may have to acquire a taste."

The secret of the unusual color and taste of this soup is in toasting some of the vegetables before they go into the pot.

SOUP AND MEAT BISCUITS

2½ to 3 pounds beef chuck meat and bone
1 medium onion, sliced
3 carrots, peeled
3 stalks celery with leaves
3 whole allspice
Salt to taste
4 sprigs parsley
3 quarts water
Meat Biscuits (see below)

Place in a soup pot meat and bone, ½ the onions, 1½ of the carrots (leave whole), celery, allspice, salt to taste, parsley, and water. Bring to a boil.

Meanwhile, slice remaining carrots lengthwise in flat strips. Combine carrots and remaining sliced onion in an old pan or pie plate and place over a high heat. Toast vegetables until they are slightly black on both sides.

Skim soup, then add toasted vegetables and air the room. Simmer soup about 3 hours until meat is tender.

Remove meat and whole carrots; reserve. Strain stock and discard remaining vegetables. Cut up carrots.

Serve soup with garnish of reserved carrots and fresh chopped parsley. Biscuits are served warm and can be dunked into the soup like doughnuts.

Meat Biscuits:

1 package active dry yeast or 1 cake
  compressed yeast
¼ cup lukewarm water
Dash sugar
1¾ cups milk, scalded
½ cup butter, melted
½ cup sugar
1 teaspoon salt
About 6 cups flour
2 eggs
Reserved soup meat
½ onion, finely chopped
Fat for frying

While soup is simmering, dissolve yeast in lukewarm water and add dash sugar. Mix milk, butter, sugar, and salt; cool slightly, then add 1 egg and mix well. Add yeast and stir. Add enough flour to make dough workable. Knead until smooth and elastic. Cover and let rise in a warm place until doubled in bulk.

Grind or blend soup meat until shredded finely. Saute chopped onion in a little fat until translucent. Add meat and brown. Season to taste with salt and pepper.

Roll out dough in 2 batches to ⅛ to ¼-inch thick; cut in rounds. Place a little meat on a round of dough, bring up edges into a half-moon and pinch to seal. Beat remaining egg and brush over biscuits. Place on greased baking sheet and bake at 375 degrees about 20 minutes or until golden brown.

Mrs. Mary Anderson submitted this unusual recipe, which was handed down from her Swedish grandmother who worked as a cook for a wealthy family in Russia before emigrating to Milwaukee at the turn of the century.

The bounty of Wisconsin's lakes frequently ended up in the soup pot.

FISH CHOWDER (German)

2 to 4 slices bacon
⅓ cup diced onion
½ teaspoon salt
1½ cups diced peeled potatoes
⅛ teaspoon pepper
½ cup water
1 pound walleyed pike, diced
3 cups milk
1 tablespoon chopped parsley

In a Dutch oven, fry bacon until golden brown. Add potatoes, onion, salt, pepper, and water. Cover and cook at moderate heat until half done, 5 to 10 minutes. Add fish, cover and continue cooking until potatoes are done, from 10 to 12 minutes. Add milk and heat thoroughly but do not boil. Add parsley and serve.

Submitted by Mrs. Janice Runge, Merrill.

Considering the nature of Wisconsin's agriculture, it is not surprising that milk formed the basis for many soup combinations. The simplest, called just Milk Soup and described by Mrs. J. Gericke of Appleton, was to "heat milk with one bay leaf. Make noodles by beating one egg and adding ½ of an egg shell of water and enough flour to make a stiff dough. Drop into hot milk and cook. Don't leave the stove as the milk may boil over. Serve with large soda crackers."

Cream of Chicken Soup was a particular favorite, since it was a way to use up old hens. This recipe is from a copy of *Marine Cooks and Stewards Guide* published in 1915 and given to John Weinert of Manitowoc because he advertised his wholesale steam bakery (the town's first bakery) in the book. Weinert or his wife marked this recipe, among others, with an X.

CHICKEN CREAM SOUP

An old chicken for soup is much the best. Cut it up into quarters, put it into a soup kettle with half a pound of corned ham, and an onion; add four quarts of cold water. Bring slowly to a gentle boil, and keep this up until the liquid has diminished one-third, and the meat drops from the bones; then add half a cup of rice. Season with salt, pepper, and a bunch of chopped parsley.

Cook slowly until the rice is tender, then the meat should be taken out. Now, stir in two cups of rich milk thickened with a little flour. The chicken could be fried in a spoonful of butter and a gravy made, reserving some of the white part of the meat, chopping it and adding it to the soup.

Submitted by Ruth (Mrs. C.E.) Nelson, Manitowoc, Weinert's granddaughter.

POTATO SOUP

6 medium sized potatoes
2 cups milk
2 cups cold water
2 slices onions
1 teaspoon salt
½ teaspoon pepper
Speck cayenne pepper
1 tablespoon flour
2 tablespoons butter
1 teaspoon chopped parsley

Wash and pare potatoes and let them soak in cold water until ready to cook. Put them in boiling water & cook until very soft.

Cook onion with milk in double boiler. Melt butter in large saucepan and add gradually the flour, salt & pepper and pour into it gradually the scalding milk. Cook thoroughly.

Mash potatoes & add to them the thickened soup, rub through a strainer, taste and add more seasoning if necessary and serve in hot soup plates. Into soup tureen put 1 teaspoon parsley (chopped) and pour on the soup.

From Lizzie Black Kander's notebook for Lesson I of the first cooking class at The Settlement in Milwaukee in 1898. These classes led to the publication of The Settlement Cookbook.

An uncooked, cold soup with poppy seeds was cooling on a hot summer day.

MOHN-SUPPE (German)

1 cup white poppy seeds
4 cups cold water
2½ quarts cold milk
½ teaspoon salt
½ to 1 teaspoon ground cinnamon
½ cup sugar
Bread

Soak poppy seeds in water overnight. Drain and grind or crush with a wooden pestle very thoroughly until not one whole seed remains.

Place seeds in a large serving bowl and keep cool. About 1 hour before serving, add milk, salt, cinnamon, and sugar. Stir well. Keep in a cool place and stir several times during the hour. Cube 1 slice of bread into each bowl to be served and add the cold soup.

Submitted by Alexa Young, Madison, who remembers that her mother's garden always had a patch of poppies which "produced the dried pods, from which she got her year's supply of white poppy seed. We children were allowed to pop one or two pods open, and pour the fresh, dry seeds into our up-turned mouths. It was understood that over-indulgence was frowned upon, because it was important to leave an ample supply for the Christmas Stollen and for Mohn-Suppe (poppy-seed soup)."

PUMPKIN SOUP (German)

1 medium sized pumpkin, seeded, peeled and
** cut into 1-inch pieces**
2 quarts milk
2½ teaspoons salt
6 eggs
2 tablespoons water
About 1 to 1½ cups flour
Butter

Place pumpkin in a kettle and add water to cover. Add 1 teaspoon salt, bring to a boil, and simmer until soft. Drain and mash into a fine pulp.

In an aluminum kettle, combine milk and 1 teaspoon salt and slowly heat to just below boiling, stirring frequently.

While milk is heating, beat eggs and add remaining salt and 2 tablespoons water. Add enough flour to make a very firm dough. Drop by spoonfuls into heated milk and simmer 20 to 30 minutes until dumplings are firm throughout. Stir in mashed pumpkin and continue to simmer a few minutes to blend flavors.

Serve hot with a lump of butter on each serving.

Submitted by Mrs. Zane Pautz, Milton, who noted that her mother always served this soup on Saturday nights in pumpkin season.

Beans or lentils combined with dried fruit was a favorite and nourishing mixture enjoyed by Germans, Czechs, and other eastern Europeans. It could be made with a bit of pork or ham or without any meat at all. Sometimes meatless versions were flavored with a bit of bacon fat.

FRUITED BEAN SOUP (Czech)

1 cup dried pinto beans
1 cup dried prunes, rinsed
½ to 1 cup dried apples or pears (optional)
1 cup potato, peeled and cut in 1-inch cubes
1 teaspoon salt or to taste
2 tablespoons butter
2 tablespoons flour
¾ cup cold water

Wash and pick over beans. Rinse; cover with water and soak overnight. Rinse beans and put into soup pot with water to cover, about 6 cups.

Simmer until almost tender, about 2½ hours. Add prunes and other fruits as desired. Simmer 20 minutes until prunes are soft but not mushy. Add potato and salt to taste. Simmer until potatoes are done.

Melt butter in a skillet and add flour. Cook, stirring constantly, until flour is lightly browned. Remove from heat and add cold water, stirring to prevent lumps. Return to heat and cook until thickened. Stir into soup, simmer a few minutes, then serve.

Mrs. John Desris, Kenosha, submitted this recipe, adding that this soup made "a very satisfying meal accompanied by a thick slice of homemade bread with fresh churned butter." Her mother grew her own pinto beans, and this was one of the family's favorite winter soups.

Soup made of dried fruits and thickened with tapioca or barley is a standard Scandinavian dish. Germans made a version, too, usually adding dumplings. Prunes were always included and other dried fruits—raisins, apricots, apples, currants, lemon, cherries, oranges—could be added according to taste and availability. Called Fruit Soup or Sweet Soup, it was regarded as easy to digest and was usually brought as a gift to new mothers. This is an elaborate version.

FRUGT SUPPE (Norwegian)

½ pound prunes
¼ pound dried apricots
1 cup raisins
Cold water
1 orange, sliced
1 lemon, sliced
1 cup sugar
1 tablespoon vinegar
1 stick cinnamon
4 tablespoons pearl tapioca
1 can cherries
½ cup grape juice (optional)

Combine prunes, apricots, and raisins. Cover with cold water, bring to a boil, and simmer until soft. Add orange, lemon, sugar, vinegar, cinnamon, tapioca, and cherries. Simmer until clear and thick, about 20 minutes. (If too thick, add more water.) If desired, add grape juice before serving hot or cold.

Submitted by Mrs. Alex Meunier, Sturgeon Bay.

A simple fruit soup can be made of sour cherries. Germans served it with dumplings.

CHERRY SOUP (German)

3 cups sour cherries, pitted
2 or 3 quarts water
½ to 1 cup sugar
1 piece stick cinnamon
Flour
1 tablespoon butter
Egg Dumplings or Spaetzl

Combine cherries, water, sugar to taste, and cinnamon. Bring to a boil and simmer until cherries are cooked. Drop small Egg Dumplings or Spaetzl into soup and cook until done. In the bowl used to mix the dumplings, combine a little flour with butter and stir into the soup to thicken slightly.

This is a summer soup that is served cold.

Submitted by Mrs. Bernice Forrer, West Allis.

A soup made of chicken stock and wine was highly regarded as a restorative for invalids by some ethnic groups. It is a form of chicken soup, still considered highly endowed with medicinal properties.

WEINSUPPE (Alsace-Lorraine)

2 eggs
2 tablespoons wheat or potato flour
½ cup cold water
4 cups boiling chicken stock, well seasoned
  with parsley, thyme, or bay leaf
2 cups white wine

In the top of a double boiler, beat eggs, flour, and water together to make a smooth paste. Pour boiling stock and wine over the flour mixture, stirring to keep smooth. Place over simmering water for 5 minutes.

Mrs. Ronald Daggett, Madison, submitted this recipe which was handed down from her grandmother, Catharina Hatch, who came from Alsace-Lorraine as a child. She married about 1858 and she and her husband, Henry Loerch, lived in Milwaukee until 1868. Family tradition has it that Catharina made this wine soup, as well as squab broth, for the wife of a mayor of Milwaukee, who then rallied and recovered from her serious illness.

EGGS AND CHEESE

A S THEY ARE TODAY, EGGS WERE AN IMPORTANT staple in Wisconsin households no matter what the occupants' ethnic background. They not only were needed as an ingredient in numer- ous types of dishes, but could also be the main offering of any meal of the day.

A simple, pioneer favorite combined eggs with one of Wisconsin's native products.

EGGS POACHED IN MAPLE SYRUP (French-Canadian)

Eggs
Maple Syrup

Heat the maple syrup to boiling and poach eggs as you would in water. Serve with some of the syrup spooned over.

Submitted by Mrs. Henry R. Bowers, Marion. "This was, of course," she noted, "a spring treat to be had when the maple sap was running."

OMELETTES SOUFFLEES (French)

Take 8 eggs of which you separate the white and yolks. Mix the yolks with 5 tablespoons pow- dered sugar; stir in finely grated rind of ½ a le- mon. Beat the white just until snowy; fold into yolks. Melt in a frying pan, ¼ pound butter; when the butter is just a little more than luke- warm, add the eggs and stir just until they have soaked up the butter, then turn out onto a but- tered plate; place this plate on hot ashes, sprinkle sugar over the omelette, and place covered in a very hot portable bread oven. Serve hot as soon as it is cooked.

Translated from La Cuisinière Bourgeoise, *the 1838 edition of a cookbook used by the Dousman family at the Villa Louis in Prairie du Chien.*

[181]

BAKED EGGS IN MORNAY SAUCE (French)

4 tablespoons butter
4 tablespoons flour
1 teaspoon salt
½ teaspoon white pepper
1 bay leaf
1 teaspoon minced parsley
1 tablespoon minced onion
2 cups milk
4 tablespoons grated Parmesan cheese
4 tablespoons grated Swiss cheese
6 eggs

Melt butter in a saucepan. Add flour, salt, pepper, bay leaf, parsley, and onion. Blend. Cook over low heat 2 minutes. Add milk and cook until thickened, stirring constantly. Remove bay leaf; add cheeses and stir until melted.

Place half of sauce in a 1½-quart shallow baking dish. Break eggs evenly over the top and cover with remaining sauce. Bake at 350 degrees until eggs are set, about 25 minutes.

Submitted by Jean Schoch (Mrs. Donald) Magarian, Milwaukee.

SWEET SOUR EGGS

¼ pound bacon, cut in small squares
½ cup flour
2 cups water
¾ cup vinegar
1 cup sugar
1 teaspoon salt
Eggs as needed
Mashed potatoes

Fry bacon in a frying pan until browned. Stir in flour, water, vinegar, sugar, and salt. Cook, stirring, until thickened. Break eggs into mixture about 3 at a time and poach until whites are set but yolks are still soft, turning over once gently with a spoon. Keep cooked eggs in a separate bowl until all are cooked, then return all eggs to the sauce.

To serve, place eggs on mashed potatoes and spoon sauce over.

Submitted by Viola (Mrs. Felix) Schuster, Menomonee Falls.

Variations of the omelet showed up on the table when eggs were plentiful.

OLD FASHIONED EGG CAKES

12 eggs
1½ cups milk
1½ cups flour
1 tablespoon salt

Beat eggs well. Add milk, flour, and salt and mix smooth. Fry on a buttered griddle like pancakes.

Submitted by Mrs. Ervin Zahn, Shawano. "Sometimes they were served at breakfast and sometimes at supper; sometimes we ate them plain and sometimes with butter and/or jam," she wrote. "Egg cakes taste something like an omelet—crisp and buttery—and we loved them."

SHMORN (Slovenian)

2 cups milk
¼ cup sugar
4 eggs, separated
1 cup plus 3 tablespoons flour
1 teaspoon baking powder
½ teaspoon salt
1 teaspoon vanilla
½ teaspoon lemon juice
1 cup raisins, washed and drained (optional)
4 tablespoons butter

Place milk, sugar, and egg yolks into a bowl. Beat well with a rotary beater. Add flour, baking powder, salt, vanilla, and lemon juice, beating constantly until batter is smooth. Fold in raisins (if desired) and stiffly beaten egg whites.

Melt butter in a broad, heavy skillet and pour in batter. Cook over high heat for a few minutes until a crust forms on the bottom. Cover and cook over low heat about 20 minutes or until mixture doubles in height. Remove cover and with a pancake turner, chop into a crumbly texture, turning over frequently. Continue chopping and turning over low heat about 15 or 20 minutes.

Submitted by Mrs. Anne Shoberg, Milwaukee. Mrs. Shoberg serves this "crumble omelette" as a luncheon dish "with a salad such as fruit salad, lettuce, or cole slaw and a beverage. In spring, it is very good served with dandelion greens. During the Depression, when we lived on the farm, we had this for dinner many times with the various salads."

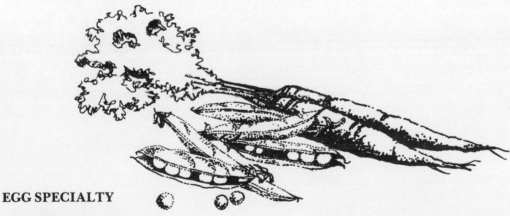

EGG SPECIALTY

12 hard-boiled eggs
¾ cup mayonnaise
1 pint sour cream
Salt and pepper
Minced onion
Minced garlic
Sugar
1-pound can peas and carrots, drained
Paprika

Cut eggs in half; remove yolks and mash. Combine mayonnaise and sour cream, and salt, pepper, minced onion, garlic, and sugar to taste. Moisten yolks with a little of the mixture and stuff into whites. Add peas and carrots to remaining sour cream mixture. Spread in an 8 by 10-inch dish and arrange eggs, yolks down, in mixture. Sprinkle with paprika, cover, and refrigerate overnight.

Submitted by Mrs. Rosalie Franckowiak, Cudahy, who got it from a Polish friend. With rye bread and butter, it makes a fine supper dish.

PICKLED EGGS

6 hard-boiled eggs, peeled
24 whole cloves
½ teaspoon salt
½ teaspoon pepper
½ teaspoon dry mustard
2 cups vinegar
1 stick cinnamon
¼ bay leaf
1 small cooked beet with cooking liquid
    or ½ cup pickled beet juice

Stud each egg with 4 cloves. Mix salt, pepper, and mustard and moisten with enough cold vinegar so mixture pours. Heat remaining vinegar to boiling. Add cinnamon, bay leaf, and beet and liquid or beet juice. Slowly pour in mixed seasonings. Boil for 1 minute.

Place eggs in sterilized glass jar. Pour in boiling liquid and seal. Eggs will be ready to eat in two weeks.

Mrs. Byron Dolgner, Pardeeville, submitted this recipe from a 1924 cookbook.

Eggs have always received special attention at Easter time.

KÜMMEL EIER (German)

4 dozen eggs
2 quarts water
¾ cup caraway seed
1 teaspoon salt

Hard boil the eggs. While still hot, crack and roll the eggs between your hands so the entire shell has little cracks; but do not peel. Place in a bowl.

Bring water, caraway seed, and salt to a boil and boil 1 or 2 minutes. Pour over eggs. Make enough liquid to cover the eggs and let stand at least overnight. To keep longer, put eggs in refrigerator. The caraway taste penetrates the shells.

Submitted by Mrs. Theodore Toepel, Howards Grove. These were made at Easter time to be eaten as a snack.

Mrs. Toepel's family, like many other Wisconsinites, colored their Easter eggs with red onions in the days before store-bought dyes. Coffee grounds were sometimes added for a deeper brown color.

COLORED EASTER EGGS

Fill any size saucepan or kettle half full of [red] onion peels. Add 1 cup of coffee grounds (from boiled coffee) and as many eggs as needed. Cover with water and let slowly come to a good boil. Cook until eggs are hard boiled.

Submitted by Mrs. Theodore Toepel, Howards Grove. "I still color some eggs this way," she noted. "It seems a certain flavor even penetrates into these onion-peel-colored eggs."

In many places in Wisconsin, the woman of the house routinely made cheese of various kinds when milk was plentiful. Gladys M. Randall of Hustisford, for instance, remembers that her "great grandmother used to make American cheese for all her family using a large copper kettle. They had a small shed she called the cheese house, where she kept her utensils and made the cheese." Cottage cheese was the simplest to make.

SCHMEIR KASE (Pennsylvania-Dutch)

1 gallon whole raw milk

Sour the milk by placing in a large pan or bowl at the back of the stove over a very low heat for several hours or until the curd has separated from the whey, and it is cooked through. Do not let it boil or get to the boiling point.

Spread a clean dish towel over a large pan and pour the soured milk into the towel. Bring the four corners together and hold up to drain. Hang and let curd drain for at least a day.

Serve with salt and pepper or sugar or syrup.

Mrs. Rebecca Trumpy Gillings, Redgranite, submitted this recipe for cottage cheese. Her aunt, Mrs. Francis Riemer Burt, formerly of Albany and Brodhead, remembers that there was always a bowl of sour milk at the back of the stove and a bag of cottage cheese on the clothes line. Sometimes, instead of letting the whey drip on the ground, the Pennsylvania Dutch would put a dish pan under the bag so the ducks could feed on it.

BAKED FLAT CHEESE (Finnish)

2 gallons new (raw) whole milk
½ rennet tablet
1 tablespoon water
1 teaspoon salt

Heat milk to lukewarm. Crush and dissolve rennet tablet in water and add to warmed milk. Add salt. Let stand a few seconds, then stir with a ladle so the whey separates from the curd. Pour off whey. Press curds with hands until remaining whey is eliminated. Continue pressing into a ¾-inch flat cake. Place on a wooden slat and place in a slanting position on top of a frying or baking pan (to catch any additional whey) into a 450 degree oven and bake until golden brown on both sides.

Submitted by Mrs. Edward Pudas, Iron River, who added that her mother curdled the milk with the inner membrane of the stomach of a very young calf in the days before rennet tablets were on the market.

CHEDDAR CHEESE

2 yellow coloring tablets (optional)
1 rennet tablet
10 gallons fresh raw whole milk
⅔ cup salt
Paraffin

Dissolve coloring tablets, if used, in cold water. Dissolve rennet tablet in cold water.

Heat milk to 80 degrees and add color solution. Remove from stove and add rennet solution. Allow milk to stand 10 to 20 minutes or until a firm curd has formed.

Using a long knife, cut curd into 2-inch strips; cut strips crosswise. With hands, dip down at edge of kettle and bring curd up toward the center, wiggling fingers to break curd into smaller pieces. Do this slowly and continue for about 10 minutes.

Return to heat and bring temperature to 102 degrees very slowly, stirring constantly. It should take 20 to 25 minutes to bring the temperature from 80 degrees to 102. Keep at 102 degrees until the curd is firm and springs back when pressed.

Pour off whey and add salt to curd.

Line a 7-quart press with muslin that has been wrung out of very hot water. Place a "bandage" of cheese cloth around the sides of the press. Put curd into lined press and top with another round of muslin; weight down. After 20 or 30 minutes, remove and straighten bandage and smooth out all wrinkles in the muslin. Replace and continue pressing 36 to 48 hours.

Remove from press and store in a cool, well-ventilated room. After 3 days, dip cheese round in hot paraffin. The cheese should be turned end over end daily for 10 days or longer if moisture shows on the board where the cheese is kept.

Miss Louise Keiner, Greenwood, contributed this recipe that her family brought over from Switzerland.

A number of cuisines, including Russian and Polish, have a dish that calls for a cottage cheese mixture folded into an eggy pancake. This version is Jewish.

CHEESE BLINTZES (Jewish)

1 cup sifted flour
3 eggs, beaten with a little salt
About ¾ cup water
Butter
Cottage Cheese Filling (see below)
Sour cream or fruit sauce

Add flour little by little into beaten eggs, mixing with a whip. Add enough water to make a runny consistency.

Heat a heavy 6-inch skillet over medium heat. Keep heat at medium during the making of the pancakes and do not let the skillet get too hot. Grease skillet lightly with butter and pour about ⅛ cup of batter into pan, tilting to distribute evenly. Fry until pancake blisters. Turn out, fried side up, on a cutting board covered with a clean dish cloth (not terrycloth). Repeat until all batter is used up, stirring batter frequently so flour does not settle at the bottom.

When all pancakes have been made and cooled, place a rounded tablespoon of Cottage Cheese Filling in the middle of each pancake, fold over from both sides, then fold ends into envelope shape. (Or place mixture at top of circle, fold over both sides, then roll into sausage shape.)

Just before serving, fry blintzes in butter until golden brown.

Serve hot with sour cream or blueberry (or any fruit) sauce. Makes 25 blintzes.

Cottage Cheese Filling:

1½ cups dry cottage cheese
Salt
2 egg yolks, beaten
1 tablespoon melted butter
1 tablespoon sugar

Press cheese through a colander or sieve. Salt lightly and add egg yolks, butter, and sugar.

Submitted by Mrs. Herman Tuchman, Milwaukee.

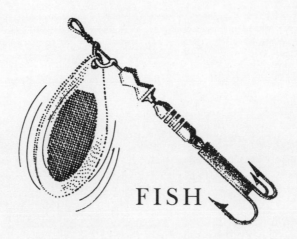

FISH

WISCONSIN'S BOUNTY OF FISH WAS WELL USED and much enjoyed from the time the first people settled this region. Since it was free for the taking, fish from lakes and streams kept many a pioneer family from starving in the first, hard years. Though pollution and growing population have taken their toll, a lot of delicious eating can still be hauled from the state's waters today.

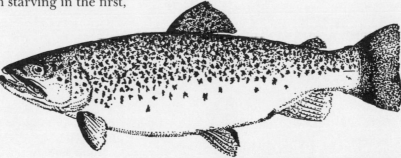

BOILED TROUT

1½ pounds trout
Salt
1 large onion
1 teaspoon peppercorns
1 bay leaf
1 tablespoon melted butter
1 tablespoon flour
2 or 3 slices lemon

Scale, clean, and wash fish; cut into 3-inch pieces and salt. Let stand at least 1 hour.

Into a stew pot, put enough water to barely cover the fish when it is added. Place onion, peppercorns, and bay leaf into water, bring to a boil and boil 2 minutes. Add fish and simmer until it is cooked. Skim foam frequently. Take care not to overcook fish. Remove from pot; strain and reserve stock. Keep fish warm.

In a frying pan, mix melted butter and flour; cook until flour is brown. Add fish stock, a little at a time, stirring constantly, until slightly thickened; then add all stock. Add lemon slices and simmer for a few minutes. Add fish, let come to a good boil, and remove from heat immediately.

Submitted by Elva G. Hart, Milwaukee.

[187]

FIRELESS COOKER BOILED FISH

Roll fish in cheese cloth and tie the ends. Lower into kettle of boiling water. Boil on stove 5 to 10 minutes. Remove [kettle] to cabinet [fireless cooker] for 3 or 4 hours.

From the 1924 Calumet Baking Powder Cook Book, *submitted by Mrs. Byron Dolgner, Pardeeville.*

The Fish Boil has become as closely identified with Door County as cool summer breezes. This legacy of the feeding of pioneer Scandinavian loggers has long provided gustatory enjoyment to the area's many summer vacationers. And those who want to duplicate this specialty in their own back yards can buy the special fish-boil kettle that has evolved from its popularity. This 3-part, 12½-quart kettle has a metal basket that fits into the large, outer container and a lid with vents that can be opened. (You can get the same results using a large steamer or any soup pot plus a basket or collander that will fit inside; when boiling, place the cover so that steam can escape.)

This recipe calls for a great deal of salt. The cooked product, however, is not salty.

DOOR COUNTY FISH BOIL

**Large fresh-water fish such as whitefish, lake
  trout, steelhead, coho salmon, pike**
New potatoes of uniform size
Onions
Salt
Melted butter
Chopped parsley
Sliced lemon

Figure about ½ pound of fish per person. For each pound of fish, you will need 2 potatoes and 1 onion. A campfire is the ideal place to cook a fish boil.

Clean fish. One type of fish may be used or a combination of varieties can go into the pot, depending on the catch. Cut fish crosswise into 1½-inch steaks.

Scrub but do not peel potatoes. Peel onions and leave whole.

Into the container of the fish boiler, place potatoes and 8 quarts of water. Cover with vents open and bring to a boil over high heat. Add onions and salt and return to a boil. Boil 20 minutes covered (and vents open).

Place fish in basket and lower into boiling water. Replace lid with vents open and cook at a rolling boil for 12 minutes or until potatoes and fish are cooked.

Drain and serve with melted butter, chopped parsley, and lemon slices.

Submitted by Rosalie (Mrs. Oscar) Mayer, Madison.

CHRISTMAS FRUITED FISH IN GINGER SAUCE (Czech)

½ pound prunes
⅔ cup raisins
¼ cup candied citron, cut fine
Juice and rind of 1 lemon
2½ to 3 pounds fish—pike, whitefish, carp, etc.
1 tablespoon salt
1 bay leaf
1 tablespoon mixed pickling spices
1 small onion
1 clove garlic
1 cup celery in ½-inch slices
¼ cup slivered almonds
⅔ cup vinegar
⅔ cup dark corn syrup
8 or 10 ginger snaps

Combine prunes, raisins, citron, lemon juice, and lemon rind cut fine, and simmer in water to barely cover until cooked. Set aside.

Cut the fish in half down the back and then into serving-size pieces. In a 4-quart kettle, place 2 quarts water, salt, bay leaf and pickling spices tied in a cheesecloth bag, onion, and garlic. Bring to a boil. Add fish and simmer 8 to 10 minutes or until fish is done. Remove fish carefully, to a flat pan. When cool enough to handle, pull out the bones without breaking up the fish. Set fish aside.

To the cooking liquid, add celery and almonds and cook until tender but still crisp. Remove spice bag and discard. Add vinegar and corn syrup and return to a boil. Add fruit mixture and ginger snaps and simmer, stirring until the ginger snaps are dissolved. Return fish to sauce, remove from heat, and cool. Store in refrigerator overnight to blend flavors.

May be served cold or hot after reheating slowly.

Submitted by Mrs. Mae A. Krueger, Kaukauna. This sauce, Mrs. Krueger noted, can be used for beef or lamb as well as fish. As a fish dish, it "was a must for Christmas eve and all through the holidays until Three Kings Day."

ESCALOPED OYSTERS

Butter the dish (common earthen pie-plates are the best), put in a layer of oysters, seasoned well with butter, salt, and pepper; alternate with bread crumbs and oysters until you have three layers, finish with crumbs; add a tea-cup of cream or milk; bake half an hour.

From the Capital City Cook Book, by the Women's Guild of Grace Church, Madison, 1906.

Not all fish dished out in Wisconsin came from local waters. Canned salmon showed up frequently on logging camp menus.

SALMON BALLS

1 can (16-ounces) salmon
1 cup dry bread crumbs
1 tablespoon flour
3 tablespoons milk
1 egg, beaten

Salt and pepper
Lard for frying

Combine salmon, bread crumbs, flour, milk, egg, salt, and pepper. Form into patties or balls and fry in lard until light brown on both sides.

Mrs. Daniel E. Taylor, Oconomowoc, submitted this recipe. It is a scaled-down, family-sized version of the one her father used when he worked as a cook for the Hines Lumber Company at Cousins, near Iron River, in the early years of the twentieth century.

BAKED LAKE TROUT

1 3-to-4 pound lake trout
Salt
1 tablespoon lemon juice
1 egg, slightly beaten
Bread crumbs
2 teaspoons butter
Lemon slices

Scale and wash fish; wipe dry. Remove head, tail, and backbone. Sprinkle fish with salt and refrigerate about 6 hours or overnight. Make a broth with the head, tail, and backbone. Reserve.

To use, wash fish quickly in cold water and wipe dry. Sprinkle with lemon juice, dip in egg and then in bread crumbs. Melt butter in a baking pan and arrange fish, opened and skin side down. Bake at 400 degrees 15 minutes; reduce heat to 375 degrees and continue baking 20 minutes or until done, basting lightly with fish broth.

Serve with lemon slices.

Mary L. Monisen, Wauwatosa, submitted this recipe that, she reported, was "invented" by her mother, who was of Swedish background.

Another "foreign" fish imported in considerable quantity to satisfy Scandinavians and other northern Europeans was—and is—dried and salt cod. It was the basis for the well-known and still widely eaten Norwegian specialty, Lutefisk. In other times, long strips of dried cod were a common sight in grocery stores; now, lutefisk makers can buy the cod ready to use. Lutefisk and Lefse (see section on pancakes) are a traditional part of Norwegian Christmas meals.

This is a "from-scratch" recipe.

LUTEFISK (Norwegian)
9 pounds dried salt cod
2 pounds slaked lime
1⅓ pounds washing soda
Melted butter
Salt and pepper to taste

Saw the fish into convenient pieces. Place in a wooden receptacle and cover with cold water. Change water every day for a week.

Make a solution of slaked lime, soda, and 15 quarts of water. Place fish in this solution, weighting it to keep pieces submerged. Let soak until fish is properly softened, about a week. Remove and rinse thoroughly. Place fish in cold water to cover and soak for 8 days, changing water twice daily for the first few days.

Cut pieces into serving-sized portions, skin, and wash. Tie fish in cheesecloth and place in boiling water, simmering for 10 or 15 minutes until tender. Serve with melted butter and salt and pepper to taste.

Submitted by Ethel J. Odegard, Whitewater, whose job when growing up in Merrill was to change the water as necessary. This required hauling both fresh and used water up and down stairs as the fish was kept soaking in the basement.

CREAMED CODFISH (Norwegian)

1 pound boned, salt cod
3 tablespoons butter
3 tablespoons flour
2½ cups milk
1 egg, beaten
Pepper
Hot, boiled new potatoes
Paprika

Soak cod overnight in cold water. Drain. During the day, continue to soak, changing the water several times.

In fresh water, bring codfish to a boil and simmer 3 minutes. Drain into a colander. When cool enough to handle, tear or cut fish into medium-sized pieces.

In a saucepan, melt butter and blend in flour; cook over low heat a few minutes, but do not brown. Stir in milk slowly, and bring almost to boiling. Add some of milk mixture to egg and stir them into the sauce. Add cod pieces and pepper to taste; simmer for about 3 minutes, stirring constantly.

Serve over potatoes and garnish with paprika.

Submitted by Gwendolyn Kaltenbach, Potosi. "I still fix this dish whenever I can find the little wooden boxes with mortised corners which contain one pound of boned salt codfish," she reported.

BAKED WHITEFISH

2 fillets of whitefish
Lemon juice
½ teaspoon salt
Dash of pepper
½ teaspoon paprika
1½ teaspoons chopped parsley
½ teaspoon dried tarragon or 1 tablespoon fresh
1 onion, sliced thinly
Lemon slices
½ cup white wine
½ cup melted butter

Place fillets in well-buttered, shallow baking pan. Sprinkle with lemon juice, salt and pepper, paprika, parsley, and tarragon. Arrange 2 or 3 onion slices and several lemon slices on fish. Pour over wine and melted butter. Bake at 400 degrees for 20 minutes or until fish is done. Serve with pan juices and more lemon slices.

Submitted by Florence Buckner, Antigo, who was the head cook at the Executive Residence during Governor Warren P. Knowles' administration. It was one of his favorite dishes, she reported, and was served many times.

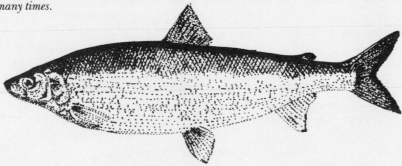

There are probably as many recipes for the Jewish specialty, Gefilte Fish, as there are cooks who make it. Infinite variety of taste and texture can be achieved by the number of kinds of fish used and the proportion of onions, eggs, meal, and seasonings. The preferred flavoring depends on Old World traditions. Eastern and Middle European Jews favor salt and pepper, while some Polish, Hungarian, and Galician Jews like it sweet, cooked with honey, ginger, and sugar. Traditionally, carp was always one of the fish used for this dish; it produced a coarser, grayer-colored product and nowadays is not always used.

GEFILTE FISH (Jewish)

3 pounds filleted fish: whitefish, trout, sheephead, carp (reserve bones, heads, and tails)
6 large onions
2 large carrots
3 eggs, well-beaten
2 teaspoons matzo meal
Salt and pepper to taste
½ to 1 cup water
1 stalk celery, cut into pieces

Grind fish with 3 of the onions and 1 carrot, grated. Add eggs, matzo meal, salt and pepper and water. The finer the fish is ground, the fluffier the gefilte fish will be.

Cook bones, heads, and tails of fish, one onion, and salt to taste with water in a large kettle for 1 hour. Add remaining onions and carrot both sliced, and celery. Bring to a boil. Make fish balls with hands moistened in cold water and lower gently into the boiling fish stock. Cover and simmer 1½ to 2 hours, shaking the pot from time to time to keep the fish balls from sticking to the pan.

Submitted by Meyer Katz, La Crosse, who noted that this should be accompanied by red horseradish. Gefilte Fish is served with some of the broth over it; the broth will jell when chilled. Gefilte Fish, he reported, is usually on the menu at festive and holiday occasions and Sabbath dinners.

Pickled fish was enjoyed by persons from many ethnic groups. Pickled herring was available from kegs in markets in the latter half of the nineteenth century and many cooks pickled Wisconsin fish. Some was put up in jars for later eating; some was served warm or with sauce right after preparation.

PICKLED FISH (German)

2 to 4 pounds fish
1 teaspoon salt
1 cup vinegar
½ cup sugar
⅓ cup pickling spices tied in a cheesecloth bag
3 or 4 bay leaves

Clean fish and cut into serving-sized pieces. Place in kettle with salt, vinegar, sugar, spice bag, bay leaves, and enough water to cover. Bring to a boil and simmer 10 minutes. Put fish into sterilized jars, cover with pickling liquid, and seal.
Serve with rye bread and beer.

Submitted by Mrs. J. Gericke, Appleton.

A more delicately seasoned version was used in a creamed dish.

COOKED FISH (German)

3 large onions, sliced
1 medium-sized pike, cleaned, skinned, and
   cut into serving-sized pieces
1 teaspoon salt
¼ teaspoon pepper
2 bay leaves
10 whole allspice
½ teaspoon ginger
¼ cup vinegar
1 teaspoon sugar
1 tablespoon butter
1 cup rich milk or cream
Carmelized sugar
Mashed potatoes

Place onions in the bottom of a large kettle. Arrange fish on top of onions. Add salt, pepper, bay leaves, allspice, ginger, vinegar, sugar, and enough water to barely cover the fish. Bring to a boil and simmer until fish is done, about 12 to 15 minutes. Remove kettle from heat and allow fish to marinate at room temperature for 4 to 6 hours.

When ready to serve, reheat and add butter, milk or cream, and a small amount of carmelized sugar to color the sauce golden. Serve from a tureen over mashed potatoes.

Mrs. B. E. Wrensch, Brookfield, submitted this recipe, reporting that it "was enjoyed by German immigrants who arrived in Dodge County in 1844." They had come from Brandenburg and "established themselves in the area of Lebanon on the Rock River, the source of their fish."

POULTRY

CHICKEN DUCKS AND GEESE WERE FIXTURES OF most Wisconsin farms in earlier times. Even on the poorest of land, barnyard fowl were able to scratch up enough feed to provide the family with makings of a fine meal on special occasions. In these days of mass production and frozen foods, it is hard to remember that there was a time when the ability to serve "chicken every Sunday" was a mark of affluence and the good life. (And a goose at Christmas was almost as important as providing gifts for the children!)

Then as now, chicken was served in many ways, but unlike today, the determination was made according to the age of the bird rather than personal preference: older ones for fricassee, stew, or soup; younger ones roasted, broiled, fried, or baked. It was possible, though, to fry stewing chickens.

FRIED CHICKEN
1 5-or-6-pound stewing chicken
1 onion
5 peppercorns
2 stalks celery
Salt and pepper to taste
Flour
Shortening and butter for frying

Cut up chicken. Combine with onion, peppercorns, celery, salt, pepper, and water to cover. Bring to a boil, reduce heat, and simmer until chicken is done. Drain.

Dredge chicken pieces in flour and brown in equal parts of shortening and butter until golden brown. Serve at once.

Submitted by Mrs. F. Knurr, Mukwonago.

ROAST CHICKEN (Greek)

1 3-to-4-pound roasting chicken
1 clove garlic, crushed
¼ cup lemon juice
⅓ cup olive oil
Scant teaspoon oregano

Clean and wash chicken thoroughly. Wipe dry and put into roaster. Combine garlic, lemon juice, olive oil, and oregano in a bowl and beat with a fork. Pour over chicken and roast at 375 degrees until chicken is tender. Add water as needed. Baste frequently.

From the cookbook of the Annunciation Greek Orthodox Church, Milwaukee.

CHICKEN AND CHICK PEAS (Italian)

1 onion, chopped fine
2 stalks celery with leaves, chopped
2 frying or broiling chickens, quartered
3 tablespoons olive oil
2 cans (1 pound 4 ounces each) chick peas, drained
1 teaspoon salt
Pepper to taste
1 15-ounce and 1 8-ounce can tomato sauce
1 teaspoon orgeano

Place a large sheet of foil in a shallow pan. Add onion and celery. Add chicken, cut side up. Brush with oil and brown lightly under broiler, turning chicken once and brushing underside with oil. Brown only enough to take off the raw look. Add chick peas, salt, pepper, tomato sauce, and oregano, spreading all evenly over chicken. Bring foil up over chicken and close tightly with a double fold. Bake at 350 degrees 1½ hours.
Serves 6.

From the Milwaukee League of Women Voters Cookbook, *submitted by Mrs. Rosemary Thielke, Milwaukee.*

CHICKEN TURNOVERS

Chop cold roast chicken very fine. Put it into a sauce-pan, place it over the fire, moisten it with a little water and gravy, or a piece of butter. Season with salt and pepper; add a small tablespoonful of sifted flour, dissolved in a little water; heat all through, and remove from the fire to become cool. When cooled, roll out some plain pie-crust quite thin, cut out in rounds as large as a saucer; wet the edge with cold water, and put a large spoonful of the minced meat on one-half of the round; fold the other half over, and pinch the edges well together, then fry them in hot drippings or fat to a nice brown. They may also be cooked in a moderate oven.

A marked recipe in the White House Cook Book *of 1891, used at the Old Wade House in Greenbush during the time of Althea Stannard Wade, wife of the second Wade House proprietor.*

CANARD EN HOCHEPOT (French)

Singe, draw, and quarter the duck; scald for a quarter hour, then cook in a small cooking pot with turnips, a quarter of a cabbage, parsnip, carrots, onions all cut uniformly, and rich bouillon; a piece of lard, sliced, rendered to crackling, and tied; a bouquet garni, a little salt. When all is cooked, place the duck in a serving dish and arrange the vegetables around it. Defat the cooking liquid and reduce; strain and serve small amounts of the sauce on the vegetables and the duck, taking care beforehand to taste if the sauce has good flavor.

Translated from the 1838 edition of La Cuisinière Bourgeoise *used by the Dousman family at Villa Louis, Prairie du Chien.*

Goose was the most ceremonial of all poultry, prized particularly in German and Jewish cuisine and traditional for many at Christmas including those from the British Isles. The bird's heavy layer of fat was one of its appeals, providing as it did shortening for cooking, spreads for bread, and the makings of medicinal rubs and concoctions.

Watertown's famous "noodled"—or force-fed—geese were rarely eaten by the farmers who produced them, according to Mrs. Fred Rumler of Watertown, who with her husband was one of the last to produce this delicacy commercially in Wisconsin. The heavy birds were simply too valuable for home consumption. And since so much of the weight was in the liver and the excess fat, Mrs. Rumler reported, there was not that much meat to be had. She remembered as a child occasionally having smoked goose breast and legs.

The liver of the force-fed geese—called foie gras—was a gourmet delicacy. It was most often made into a pate but was sometimes served sauteed.

Helen Ratzsch, who for years worked beside her husband in Karl Ratzsch's Restaurant in Milwaukee, served roast goose with an apple dressing and frequently offered the livers sauteed.

RATZSCH'S GOOSE LIVER

Goose liver, sliced into service-sized pieces, or if small left whole
Salt and pepper
Flour
Vegetable shortening (Crisco)
Butter
Sliced apples and sliced onions, braised until soft
Water cress
Parsley

Season liver with salt and pepper and dip in flour; shake off excess. Brown liver quickly in hot shortening (do not use butter for sauteeing, as it will burn). Drain livers and glaze with butter. Serve with braised apple and onion slices and garnish all with water cress and parsley.

Contributed by Helen (Mrs. Karl) Ratzsch, Milwaukee.

Poultry Dressings

The mixtures used to stuff chicken, duck, and goose for roasting usually reflected the cook's ethnic background. Bread stuffings were quite standard and most were flavored at least with sage.

TURKEY OR CHICKEN DRESSING

½ package bread cubes
4 medium potatoes, boiled and chopped
Diced celery (optional)
1 large onion, chopped
½ to 1 pound giblets, cooked and chopped
   (reserve broth)
About ¼ pound sausage
Salt and pepper to taste
Sage to taste

Combine bread cubes, potatoes, celery, onion, giblets, and sausage. Season to taste with salt, pepper, and sage. Add giblet broth until dressing is as moist as desired. Mix well and stuff bird.

Submitted by Patricia (Mrs. Ronald J.) Kelly, La Crosse, who added that this recipe can also be baked alone and served with fried chicken. "When I make it, I double the amounts," she wrote, "and make a side dish, baking less than an hour."

Many Irish favored a peppery potato stuffing.

TRADITIONAL IRISH POTATO STUFFING

2 pounds potatoes
2 large onions, chopped
Butter
½ teaspoon thyme *or* 1 leaf sage, crumbled
Pepper

Boil potatoes in salted water, peel, and mash while warm. Saute onions in butter until limp. Mix with potatoes and add thyme or sage (or broth). Add generous amount of pepper as stuffing should be slightly "hot." Stuff bird.

Variations: Cook giblets and chop or mash. Add to potato stuffing along with about 4 cups cubed, dried, homemade bread moistened with giblet broth.

Add to potato stuffing a stalk of celery chopped fine and sauteed until limp in butter and a pound of mushrooms, sliced and sauteed in butter.

Submitted by Ms. Marion I. Kraemer, Merrimac.

Soda crackers form the base for this unusual dressing.

GRANDMOTHER'S DRESSING (German)

3 or 4 medium sized onions, chopped
Butter or margarine
2 eggs
About 1 pint milk
8 to 10 soda crackers
Sage to taste

Saute onions in butter until tender in a large frying pan. In a bowl, beat eggs and add milk. Break, crumble, or roll soda crackers and add to egg mixture. This will be quite moist. Add to onions in frying pan and season well with sage. Cook slowly, tossing lightly to keep dressing from sticking to the pan. The dressing will puff up but remain a bit moist. Cool in a bowl before adding to fowl. The dressing may be prepared the night before, covered, and refrigerated.

The dressing can be used with pork chops or pork roast. With pork, it need not be cooled before using.

Submitted by Mary Anna White (Mrs. Peter) Mowat, Waukesha. This dressing, she reported, is delicious with both domestic and wild fowl.

Dried or fresh fruit often appeared in dressings, particularly for the richer fowl like duck and goose.

FOWL DRESSING (German)

12 cups cubed bread, preferably day-old and home-made
Giblets, cooked and diced small
4 cups diced apples
2 cups raisins
1 to 1½ cups diced onions
3 eggs
2 teaspoons salt
About ¼ teaspoon pepper
½ to ¾ cup sugar
¼ cup milk

Combine bread cubes, giblets, apples, raisins, and onions. (This may be done the night before, but reserve giblets and add just before completing.

In a bowl, beat eggs and add salt, pepper, and sugar to taste. Add to bread mixture. Rinse out egg bowl with milk and add. Stuff fowl. May also be baked separately

Submitted by Pat Grottschal (Mrs. B.A.) Schukenecht, Lodi.

MEAT

Beef

THE PLANNING OF MEALS AROUND A LARGE serving of meat is a comparatively recent development in America. In earlier times, a family that could afford meat two or three times a week was fortunate, indeed. When meat did appear on the table, it was usually in dishes with other things so that it would stretch as far as possible. Furthermore, growing methods being what they were, meat usually required long cooking to overcome toughness. The broiled T-bone steak was not a nineteenth-century delight.

The meat pies baked by the Cornish miners' wives in the lead region of southwestern Wisconsin are a good example of long cooking and meat stretching. Today's recipes for Cornish Pasty call for round or sirloin steak, cuts those 1830 and 1840 settlers never heard of. And today's recipes usually call for just meat, potatoes, and onions, though there is no reason to believe the transplanted Cornish housewife abandoned the old-country habit of including other vegetables she might have had on hand.

CORNISH PASTY

¾ cup shortening
2 cups flour
Water
4 medium potatoes, peeled and sliced thinly
3 onions, peeled and sliced thinly
1½ pounds sirloin steak, cut in small cubes
Salt and pepper to taste
Butter

Work shortening into flour and add enough cold water to make a pie crust. Roll out to the size of a thick dinner plate.

Combine potatoes, onions, and steak and season well with salt and pepper. On one-half of the pastry, arrange vegetables and meat. Dot with butter. Wet edge of crust and fold over, pinching edges together tightly. All steam must be retained inside the pastry. Bake at 350 degrees for 1 to 1½ hours.

The dough may be rolled out into smaller portions to make individual pasties.

Submitted by Ruth H. (Mrs. Thomas A.) Roberts, Brown Deer.

Other pasty recipes called for seasonings of herbs like marjoram or sage, or ground beef, or a combination of beef and pork. After Wisconsin's lead mines gave out, many of the Cornish moved on to the copper mines in Upper Michigan. It was there and in Wisconsin's north woods that the Finnish immigrant acquired a taste for pasties. This version was carried by a Finnish miner in his lunch box.

"FINNISH" PASTIES

5 cups flour
2 cups shortening
1 cup water
1 tablespoon salt
3 pounds pork and beef, diced small
2 medium onions, diced
6 carrots, diced
½ rutabaga, diced
10 medium potatoes, peeled and diced
Salt and pepper

Mix flour and shortening to cornmeal stage with a fork and add water until pasty holds together.

Combine pork and beef, onions, carrots, rutabaga, and potatoes and season well with salt and pepper.

Roll out pasty into a circle, using a 9-inch pan turned upside down for a template. Place meat filling on half the pastry, fold over and press dough firmly together and crimp to seal. Bake in pie pan at 350 degrees 1 to 1½ hours.

Makes 10 servings.

Submitted by Marian Sheko, Loyal, who noted that her grandfather carried his pasties, made in individual servings, wrapped in newspaper to keep them warm.

The Cornish put other fillings into a pastry crust. Green onions combined with ham or bacon was another favored combination, sometimes called Herby Pie.

LETTUCE AND ONION PIE (Cornish)

About 6 or 8 green onions, cut up tops and all
5 cups leaf lettuce, cut up
1 egg, beaten
4 or 5 slices cooked bacon, crumbled
1 teaspoon salt
Pastry dough

Mix onions, lettuce, egg, bacon, and salt. Roll out pastry into a round of about ¼ inch thickness. Place mixture on one-half of the round and fold over, crimping edges well to seal. Bake in a 350 degree oven for 1 hour.

Submitted by Mrs. Mary Symanek, Beloit.

The Cornish were not the only peoples who made their meat supply go farther by baking it into a pie of some kind.

PIIRAKKAA (Finnish)

½ pound butter or margarine
1 cup hot water
4 cups white flour or 2 cups each white and rye
10 to 12 hard-boiled eggs, chopped
Salt and pepper
4 to 6 tablespoons milk
3 pounds ground chuck
1 onion, chopped, or to taste
2 cups cooked rice (do not use instant)

Season eggs with salt and pepper and mix in milk.

Combine chuck and onion and season with salt and pepper; saute until meat is lightly browned.

Melt butter in hot water. Add flour and mix. Divide dough into 4 or 5 portions and roll into 8-inch circles.

Place a layer of rice on one-half of each dough circle. Top with layer of meat, then one of egg mixture. Fold over other half of dough, seal, and crimp edges. Bake at 375 degrees for 45 minutes.

Submitted by Eva Koopikka, Calumet, Michigan.

BEEFSTEAK AND KIDNEY PIE (English)

1 pound beefsteak, cut in ½-inch slices
¾ pound veal kidneys, cut in ½-inch pieces
1 tablespoon chopped onion
Pinch chopped parsley
Salt and pepper
Tarragon vinegar
Beef stock or water
Puff pastry
1 egg yolk beaten with 2 tablespoons milk

Line a deep, 9-inch pie pan with beef slices and place kidney pieces in the center. Sprinkle with onion and parsley. Season with salt and pepper and a few drops of tarragon vinegar. Add enough stock or water to cover the meat. Seal the pie pan with a round of puff pastry; gild top with egg yolk mixture and make a slit in the center. Bake at 350 degrees about 2½ hours.

This was the recipe used by the University Club of Milwaukee. It appeared in the New Milwaukee Cookbook *(1938) compiled by the Visiting Nurses' Association and was submitted by Patricia (Mrs. William) Taylor, Whitefish Bay.*

Other recipes call for baking the meat mixture, covered, for about 1½ or 2 hours before topping the pie with crust and baking at 400 degrees for about 15 minutes.

Many Eastern Europeans meat pie recipes call for a bread dough instead of pastry. This version is Estonian and was as often filled with cabbage, mushroom, vegetable, or berry mixtures as with the meat and carrot fillings given here.

PIRUKAD (Estonian)

1 cake compressed yeast
¼ cup lukewarm water
1½ cups milk, scalded and cooled
1 tablespoon sugar
¼ pound butter or margarine, melted
Salt
1 egg
About 8 cups flour
1 pound ground beef
¼ pound butter or margarine
1 small onion, diced
Pepper
2 tablespoons water
2 hard-boiled eggs, chopped
3 tablespoons cooked rice
1 egg, beaten, or sweetened black coffee

Dissolve yeast in lukewarm water. Add milk, sugar, melted butter, ¼ teaspoon salt, and egg. Mix well. Add enough flour to make a dough that is easy to handle. Turn out on floured board and knead until smooth. Let rise in a covered, greased bowl until double in bulk; punch down and let rise again.

While dough is rising, cook beef slowly in butter, covered, about ½ hour. Add onion, salt and pepper to taste, and water and saute uncovered until browned. Add hard-boiled eggs and rice. Mix well. Let cool.

Divide dough into three or four pieces. Roll out, one piece at a time, on a floured surface until very thin. With a medium-sized glass, cut out circles. Place some meat mixture on half of the circle, fold over other half and seal with fingers dipped in water or a fork, pressing edges together. Do not fill circles too full of meat mixture or they will break apart during baking. Place on greased baking sheet, 2 inches apart, and let rise until doubled. Brush tops with beaten egg or black coffee. Bake at 375 degrees for 20 minutes or until nicely browned.

Or use a carrot filling.

Carrot Filling:

2 pounds carrots, cooked and finely diced
Butter or margarine
½ tablespoon sugar
Salt and pepper
½ cup cooked rice

Cool carrots before dicing. Add remaining ingredients and mix well.

Submitted by Mrs. Koidula Maeste, Milwaukee, on behalf of the Estonian House. Mrs. Maeste noted that Pirukad are served with clear broth, coffee, or tea. They may also be fried in deep, hot fat.

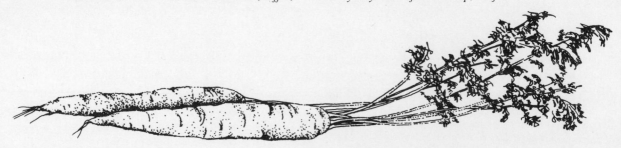

Cabbage stuffed with a meat and rice mixture is another recipe found in many ethnic cuisines.

TOLTOTT KAPOSZTA (Hungarian)

1 cabbage, about 3 or 4 pounds
2½ pounds ground beef
2 eggs, beaten slightly
2 cups cooked rice
1 medium onion, finely chopped
1 teaspoon salt
1½ tablespoons Hungarian paprika
1 clove garlic, finely chopped
¼ teaspoon pepper
3 cups sauerkraut
4 cups tomato juice
1 cup water
2 tablespoons shortening
2 tablespoons flour

Wash and core cabbage. Drop the whole head into a large kettle of boiling water and simmer 5 minutes. Remove, drain, and cool. Carefully peel off outer leaves until you reach the tough, inner white leaves. You will need about 15 to 18 cabbage leaves.

Mix beef, eggs, rice, onion, salt, paprika, garlic, and pepper; blend well. Place a portion of meat mixture on the large core end of the cabbage leaf. Fold sides over the mixture and roll up carefully; tuck end in. Repeat to use up all cabbage leaves.

Spread one half of sauerkraut on the bottom of a large kettle. Carefully place cabbage rolls on sauerkraut. Top with remaining sauerkraut and the rest of the head of cabbage, chopped, as desired. Carefully pour in tomato juice and water. Simmer for 1 to 2 hours or until the meat is done.

Melt shortening in a small pan and stir in flour; brown slightly over medium heat. Slowly blend in about ½ cup of the cooking liquid from the cabbage rolls and cook several minutes. Pour over the cabbage rolls and simmer for 5 minutes.

If possible, let stand, refrigerated, for 24 hours, as this improves with age.

Submitted by Darlene Kronschnabel, Greenleaf. Toltott Kaposzta always had "a place of honor with the roast turkey at Christmas dinner," she reported; and it was also part of the Easter repast along with boiled ham and about six dozen eggs.

Ground beef appeared in many other forms in times past as it does today. Often the taste was enhanced with the addition of a small portion of pork.

KJOD KAGER (Norwegian)

1 pound beef
¼ pound pork
1 egg, beaten slightly
½ cup milk, scalded
1 tablespoon cornstarch
1 medium onion, minced
Salt and pepper to taste
⅛ teaspoon nutmeg
⅛ teaspoon allspice
⅛ teaspoon ginger
Butter
2 tablespoons flour

Grind meat very fine. Add egg, milk, and cornstarch and mix well. Add onion and seasonings; beat thoroughly until very light. Form into small balls. Brown meatballs in a small amount of butter and simmer slowly, adding a little water if necessary, until done.

Remove meat balls and add 2 tablespoons butter to the drippings. Stir in flour and cook until brown. Add enough water, stirring constantly, to make a medium-thick gravy. Season with salt and pepper and return meatballs to gravy and heat.

These may be prepared several hours before serving as they are delicious reheated.

Submitted by Leone Nelson, Cobb.

EGG NOODLES AND BEEF

2 or 3 beef shanks
Salt and pepper
1 onion, cut up
1 small carrot, diced
1 stalk celery, cut in pieces
1 2-egg batch of homemade noodles

Cover beef shanks with water in a Dutch oven. Season with salt and pepper and add onion, carrot, and celery. Simmer until meat falls from bone. Remove meat.

Bring cooking liquid to a boil; drop in noodles. Bring to a boil again, reduce heat, and cover tightly. Simmer about 30 minutes or until noodles have absorbed the broth and are cooked.

Cut meat into bite-sized pieces, discarding fat and gristle; add to noodles toward end of the cooking period.

Submitted by Ade (Mrs. Stanley) Garvin, Janesville, who suggests serving this with a green vegetable or salad.

Long, slow cooking of meat, either in stews or braised and baked dishes, was necessary in earlier days. Most farm families only slaughtered a cow when it was too old to produce milk so the meat was sure to be tough, even the better cuts. And the beef that was raised for slaughter was usually only grass-fed. Every cuisine has its distinctively flavored stew specialty that evolved out of this culinary fact of life. Today they are often considered gourmet dishes.

The best-known German version is based on the favored sweet-sour taste.

SAUERBRATEN (German)

4 pounds pot roast or beef
1 pint red wine vinegar
¼ cup plus 1 tablespoon sugar
1 onion, sliced
2 teaspoons salt
10 peppercorns
5 whole cloves
2 bay leaves
Shortening for frying
¼ cup butter
¼ flour
10 ginger snaps, crushed

Place meat in a bowl. Combine vinegar, ¼ cup sugar, onion, salt, peppercorns, cloves, and bay leaves; heat but do not boil. Pour over meat and allow to cool. Cover and marinate in refrigerator 4 days, turning meat once each day. On the fifth day, remove meat from marinade and dry with paper towel.

In a stew pot, brown meat on all sides in hot shortening. Add enough marinade to barely cover; cover pot tightly and simmer slowly about 3 hours, adding more marinade as needed. When tender, place meat on platter and slice. Keep warm.

Strain cooking liquid and reserve. Melt butter and add flour, stirring constantly until golden brown. Add strained liquid, 1 tablespoon sugar, and ginger snaps. Simmer gently until ginger snaps are melted. Pour gravy over meat and serve with potato dumplings.

Submitted by Mrs. Carl T. Barth, Coleman.

A Czech version of marinated beef produces a different, but equally delicious result.

SVÍČKOVÁ (Czech)

3 or 4 pounds beef roast
Bacon
Salt
1 onion, sliced
1-inch piece ginger root
Peppercorns, allspice, and whole cloves to
  taste
Pinch thyme
1 bay leaf
1 clove garlic or to taste
2 cups vinegar
2 cups water
2 tablespoons sugar
3 or 4 slices lemon
Gravy (see below)

Make slits in roast and insert pieces of bacon. Rub meat with salt and place in a deep dish or crock.

In a saucepan, combine onion, ginger, whole spices, thyme, bay leave, garlic, vinegar, water, sugar, and lemon slices. Bring to a boil and simmer 30 minutes. Cool. Pour over the meat and let it marinate in the refrigerator at least 2 days, turning each day.

Place meat in a roasting pan and roast at 325 degrees until done, basting frequently with the marinade.

Slice and serve with preferred gravy.

Gravy:

In a frying pan, melt 2 tablespoons butter or lard and stir in 2 tablespoons flour and brown. Add pan drippings and enough water to make a gravy of desired consistency.

Or pour over meat in the roasting pan, about 1 cup sour cream to which a little flour or corn starch has been added. Heat until pan juices are thickened, but do not boil.

Submitted by Blanche Mendl, Deerbrook, who added that when she is short of time, she cooks the meat in the marinade instead of letting it marinate for two days. She also reports that hare, venison, and horse meat are prepared in this way, too, in Czechoslovakia.

Many stews included various vegetables both for nutrition and to make the dish go farther.

OX TAIL STEW

3 pounds ox tails, disjointed
Fat for frying
2 onions, sliced
1 clove garlic, minced
3 quarts water
4 carrots, diced
2 turnips, diced
2 large potatoes, diced
2 tablespoons chopped celery
½ teaspoon paprika
Salt and pepper to taste
1 teaspoon Worcestershire Sauce
1 6-ounce can tomato paste
Flour

Wash and wipe dry the ox tail pieces. Brown in a very small amount of fat; the fat in the tails will be rendered. Remove meat and cook onions and garlic in drippings until soft. Return meat, add water, and simmer about 3 hours or until meat is almost done. Add carrots, turnips, and potatoes and cook until vegetables are almost tender. Add celery, paprika, salt, pepper, Worcestershire sauce, and tomato paste and continue simmering until all is cooked. Combine a small amount of flour and about ¼ cup cold water and add to stew, stirring; cook until thickened.

Submitted by Mrs. Cecil A. Fisher, Milwaukee, who remembers her mother making this dish in an iron pot on a coal stove in the early 1900's. She now sometimes uses a pressure cooker and serves it with egg corn bread or rolls.

Two traditional Jewish dishes are stews that can be varied with different combinations of ingredients. Tzimmes is a sweet stew mixture of fruit, vegetables, and meat. Carrots are often used as the basic vegetable but combinations of prunes and potatoes, carrots and sweet potatoes, prunes and rice, and fruit alone are equally favored. There is also a meatless version (see under Potatoes).

PRUNE AND POTATO TZIMMES (Jewish)

2 or 3 pounds chuck roast or flank steak
1 pound pitted prunes
5 or 6 medium potatoes, peeled and quartered
1 tablespoon lemon juice
½ cup sugar or honey or to taste
½ teaspoon salt
½ teaspoon cinnamon (optional)
1 small onion, sliced (optional)

In a stew pot or Dutch oven, cover meat with water and simmer 1 to 1½ hours until nearly tender. Add prunes, potatoes, lemon juice, sugar, salt, and cinnamon and onions if desired. Cover and cook at a simmer for another hour. Uncover and place in a 350 degree oven for about 30 minutes or until meat is tender and potatoes are a golden brown.

Submitted by Meyer Katz, La Crosse, who noted that the name of this dish has become a Yiddish slang expression, meaning to make a fuss or a big deal of something. "Don't make a tzimmes about it" means "don't make a big production of it."

The other Jewish stew is Cholent or Sholent and is similar to the Russian Shalet. Cholent is the traditional Saturday night main dish; orthodox observance of the Sabbath, which for Jews is Saturday, prohibits cooking, so the dish is prepared the night before and placed in a slow oven until the Sabbath is ended. The starch for this dish can be varied—potatoes, dumplings, or beans as in this version.

LIMA BEAN CHOLENT (Jewish)

1 pound dried lima beans
3 pounds boneless beef brisket
Salt and pepper
Paprika
Ginger
¼ cup chicken fat or shortening
3 onions, sliced
1 clove garlic, minced
6 potatoes, peeled *or* 1 cup barley
1 bay leaf

Soak lima beans in water to cover overnight. Drain.

Rub brisket with salt, pepper, paprika, and ginger; brown in chicken fat; remove meat. In some pan, brown onions and garlic. Place meat and onions in a bean crock or deep casserole. Add beans, potatoes or barley, and bay leaf. Cover with boiling water. Cover tightly and bake at 400 degrees for 30 minutes. Reduce heat to 250 degrees and cook overnight.*

Submitted by Meyer Katz, La Crosse. He added that Great Northern or navy beans may be substituted and a cup or so of dried chick-peas may be included. However, pinto or red beans or green or yellow dried peas should not be used.

---

*Home economists do not approve of such slow cooking for meat. They recommend 300 or 325 degrees minimum until meat and beans are tender.

Round steak rolled around a stuffing of some sort goes by many names—Beef Birds, Rouladen, Labskaus, etc.—depending on the nationality of the cook. Lithuanians call it Zrazai.

ZRAZAI (Lithuanian)

2 pounds round steak, thinly sliced
2 tablespoons parsley, chopped
1 cup onion, finely chopped
3 tablespoons butter or margarine
1 cup dry bread crumbs
1 4½-ounce can mushroom pieces with liquid
1 egg, well beaten
Salt and pepper to taste
Fat for browning
2 cups hot beef broth
2 onions, sliced

Cut steak into 4-by-2-inch strips. Pound flat. Saute chopped onion and parsley in butter. Reduce heat to low and stir in bread crumbs. Stir in mushrooms, reserving liquid. Add egg slowly, stirring rapidly. Season with salt and pepper and mix well.

Place a spoonful of mixture on each strip of meat; roll up and fasten with toothpicks. Season with salt and pepper. Brown gently in hot fat in a large skillet. Reduce heat and pour in hot broth. Scatter onion slices across top. Cover and simmer over low heat for 1½ hours.

From Jubilee Gems, *compiled by the Sisters of St. Casimir Auxiliary, Chicago, and submitted by Ann Short, Madison.*

Leftovers were used up in many tasty ways. Since meat and potatoes were a basic menu combination, many recipes call for them as well as the gravy used the first time around.

LABERJAL (Welsh)

Onions, sliced or diced
Shortening
Cold cooked potatoes, diced
Leftover beef, diced
Gravy

In an iron frying pan, saute onions until transparent, but not brown. Add potatoes, beef, and gravy. Cook until the consistency of potato salad.

Submitted by Elizabeth J. Rojahn, Oshkosh who notes that since leftover gravy is "not found in abundance in most kitchens today," a prepared gravy mix may be used but would probably require the addition of seasonings to taste.

RED FLANNEL HASH

2 tablespoons shortening
1 cup ground roast beef
1 cup finely diced, cooked potatoes
2 tablespoons chopped onion
1 teaspoon salt
2 tablespoons catsup
Poached eggs

Heat shortening in a heavy frying pan. Combine beef, potatoes, and onion and season with salt. Heat slowly in hot shortening, without stirring, for about 15 minutes. Spread catsup over top.

To serve, lift out portion with pancake turner and top with a poached egg.

Submitted by Mrs. Florence Paczkowski, Milwaukee.

ROAST BEEF PIE WITH POTATO CRUST

When you have a cold roast of beef, cut off as much as will half fill a baking-dish suited to the size of your family; put this sliced beef into a stew-pan with any gravy that you may have saved, a lump of butter, a bit of sliced onion, and a seasoning of pepper and salt, with enough water to make plenty of gravy; thicken it, too, by dredging in a teaspoonful of flour; cover it up on the fire, where it may stew gently, but not be in danger of burning. Meanwhile there must be boiled a sufficient quantity of potatoes to fill up your baking-dish, after the stewed meat has been transferred to it. The potatoes must be boiled done, mashed smooth, and beaten up with milk and butter, as if they were to be served along, and placed in a thick layer over top of the meat. Brush it over with egg, place the dish in an oven, and let it remain there long enough to be brown. There should be a goodly quantity of gravy left with the beef, that the dish be not dry and tasteless. Serve it with tomato sauce, Worcestershire sauce, or any other kind that you prefer. A good, plain dish.

A marked recipe in the White House Cook Book *(1891) used at Old Wade House, Greenbush.*

Veal

Around the turn of the century, the La Crosse area had a sizable Syrian population. The cinnamon gave this version of stuffed cabbage its distinctive Middle Eastern flavor.

CIGARETTE CABBAGE (Syrian)

1 large cabbage, quartered
2 pounds veal, finely ground
1 cup uncooked rice
Cinnamon
Salt and pepper
1 pound canned tomatoes
1 large onion, sliced
2 tablespoons butter

Place cabbage in boiling water until soaked through and leaves are pliable. Reserve water.

Combine veal and rice and season to taste with cinnamon (use generously), salt, and pepper. (Test for taste by frying up a small amount of the mixture.) Cut out large vein of cabbage leaves, put some meat mixture in the leaf and roll. Repeat until cabbage and meat is used up. Pack rolls in bottom of a stew kettle; add tomatoes, onions, and additional salt and pepper. Add butter and cover with the water the cabbage was soaked in. Cover and simmer 1 hour.

Mrs. Jack Boone, Appleton, contributed this recipe, which was given to her grandparents by Father Salamone, who served the Syrian community in the La Crosse area about 1905.

PAPRIKA VEAL (Hungarian)

2 large onions, chopped
4 tablespoons shortening
2 tablespoons Hungarian paprika
3 pounds neck of veal, cubed
1 teaspoon salt
1 cup sour cream

Brown the onions in shortening. Add paprika, veal, and salt. Saute until meat is browned, then cover and simmer about 1 hour or until meat is tender. Add a few tablespoons water as needed to prevent meat from over-browning. Stir in the sour cream 5 minutes before serving.
Serve with potatoes or noodles.

Submitted by Darlene Kronschnabel, Greenleaf.

A jellied veal dish was made in many countries bordering on the Baltic Sea. In some places it is called Sulze and is often served with hot boiled potatoes.

KALV SYLTA (Swedish)

3 or 4 pounds veal shank or shoulder with
   bones
1½ pounds lean pork steak
1 stalk celery with leaves
2 medium onions
1 tablespoon salt
1 teaspoon peppercorns
½ teaspoon whole allspice
3 bay leaves

Cover veal and pork with cold water. Add celery, onions, and salt. Tie in a cheesecloth bag peppercorns, allspice, and bay leaves and add to veal. Bring to a boil and simmer 2½ hours or until meat falls off the bones. Remove spice bag and meat and strain and reserve stock. Remove meat from bones and grind or chop medium coarse. Combine reserved stock and ground meat and boil 2 minutes. Pour into oiled molds until set.

Submitted by Mrs. E. R. Hasselkus, Madison. "Sylta," she noted, "was traditionally served on Christmas Eve along with lutefisk, flatbrod, and rice pudding."

Lamb

Lamb is a particular favorite of Mediterranean and Middle Eastern groups.

TAVA (Armenian)

4 shoulder lamb chops, 1-inch thick
1 teaspoon dried mint
1 teaspoon dried rosemary
½ teaspoon garlic powder
1 teaspoon salt
½ teaspoon pepper
3 medium baking potatoes, peeled and cut in
   ¾-inch strips
2 green peppers, cut in ¾-inch strips
2 large onions, cut in ½-inch wedges
4 carrots, cut in ½-inch strips
1 8-ounce can tomatoes

Place lamb chops in a 12 by 7 by 2-inch casserole. Combine mint, rosemary, garlic powder, salt, and pepper. Sprinkle chops with ½ of the spice mixture. Arrange potatoes, peppers, onions, and carrots on top of chops. Cut up tomatoes and place on top with juice. Sprinkle with ½ of remaining spice mixture. Cover with aluminum foil and bake at 350 degrees for 45 minutes. Remove foil, lift chops to top and continue baking, uncovered, for 15 minutes. Turn chops and sprinkle with remaining spice mixture. Bake, uncovered, 15 minutes longer.

Submitted by Jean Schoch (Mrs. Donald) Magarian, Milwaukee.

Greek cooks know many ways of preparing lamb. These two examples are from the cookbook compiled by the women of Annunciation Greek Orthodox Church in Milwaukee.

VRASTO ARNI ME FAVA (Greek)

2 cups dried fava beans (large lima beans may be substituted)
6 cups water
1 large onion, chopped
1 clove garlic, minced
¼ cup olive oil
2 pounds lean lamb stew meat
1 32-ounce can solid pack tomatoes
1 teaspoon dried mint, crushed
Salt and pepper
Chopped parsley

Soak beans overnight in water. In the morning, simmer beans 1 hour; drain.

Saute onion and garlic in olive oil until golden. Remove onion and garlic and brown meat well. In a saucepan, combine beans, meat, onion, garlic, tomatoes, mint, and salt and pepper to taste. Cover and simmer 2 hours or until meat and beans are tender (add water as needed). Sprinkle with parsley and serve in bowls.

ROAST LEG OF LAMB (Greek)

5 pounds leg of lamb
Salt and pepper to taste
2 cloves garlic, minced
4 tablespoons butter
Juice of 1 lemon (about 3 tablespoons)
1 cup water
Small peeled potatoes (optional)

Wash and dry meat and place in roasting pan. In a small bowl, mix salt, pepper, and minced garlic. Make incisions in the leg of lamb with a sharp knife and fill with garlic-seasoning mixture and a little butter. Spread remaining softened butter over leg and rub in remaining garlic mixture. Pour lemon juice over meat, cover, and bake at 350 degrees. After about 1 hour, add water to drippings in pan and baste often until meat is well browned and tender.

If desired, place potatoes in pan around meat about ½ hour before done. When meat is almost tender, uncover pan if crisp skin roast is desired, and continue roasting until meat and potatoes are cooked.

From the Collection of Secret Greek Recipes *by the women of the Annunciation Greek Orthodox Church, Milwaukee.*

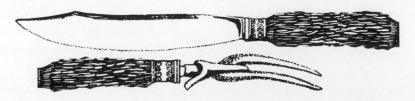

Pork

From the earliest times of settlement in the state, hogs were a welcome critter in the barnyard. At butchering time, the meat provided the fixings for meals in great variety—fresh, smoked, salted, in sausages—not to mention the lard so necessary for baking and frying.

The importance of salt pork and its versatility on the frontier has been well documented. Often it was the only meat available and could be further stretched when used only as a flavoring. Even in later, more affluent times, salt pork remained as a seasoning staple and the basis for breakfast or a light meal.

The French-Canadians baked fresh pork into a pie that has become a hallmark of that cuisine in the years since. In the old days, the pie was baked in a pottery casserole, called a *tourte*, hence the name Tourtière.

As is true with many dishes, there are as many recipes as there are cooks. Some include a bit of beef; some cook the meat mixture as long as 5 hours, others just 25 minutes before it is baked into the pie; some include mashed or diced potatoes; all have favorite and differing spice combinations. This is a typical, basic version.

TOURTIÈRE (French-Canadian)
1½ pounds ground, lean, raw pork
1 small onion, chopped
½ teaspoon sage
¼ cup water
1 teaspoon salt
Lard pastry for a 2-crust, 9-inch pie (see Pastry section)

Combine pork, onion, sage, water, and salt. Cook over low heat for 25 minutes. Cool and skim off fat. Pour into a pastry-lined pie pan; cover with top crust, seal or crimp edges, and cut slits in the top to vent. Bake at 450 for 15 minutes then reduce to 350 degrees and bake until crust is nicely browned, about 15 minutes.

Submitted by Mrs. Florence M. Vint, Springfield, Virginia, who added that "a frequent variation is the addition of garlic, mashed potatoes, or spices." Instead of sage, ⅛ teaspoon each of cloves and cinnamon may be used. Tourtière was the traditional dish served at Christmas. "After going to midnight mass," Mrs. Vint wrote, "we returned home and were served generous portions of pork pie from a table laden with breads, cakes, and fruit plus grandfather's home made wine and plenty of hot chocolate. There was also a choice of cheese."

PORK ROAST (Danish)

1 pork roast
Flour
Pepper
Rubbed sage

Rub the roast with flour combined with small amount of pepper and sage. Place in roaster or Dutch oven, fat side up; add about ½-inch of water to bottom of pan. Cover and roast at 325 degrees at least 3 hours for a 3-pound roast and ½ hour longer for each additional pound.

Alice (Mrs. H. E.) Johnson, Racine, contributed this method of roasting pork. "The roast will become brown while kept covered," she noted, "and it will not be necessary to baste it at any time. To test when pork is done, the grain of the meat can easily be separated. Never salt the pork until after it is cooked as salt dries out the meat and is apt to make it tough."

PORK ROAST WITH WINE SAUCE (Italian)

2 pounds lean pork roast
1 clove garlic
1 large onion, sliced (optional)
1 teaspoon salt
½ teaspoon freshly ground pepper
½ teaspoon crushed rosemary
½ teaspoon sweet basil
1 to 2 cups dry red wine
Polenta (see Cornmeal section)

Rub roast with garlic or add the garlic, crushed, along with sliced onion during the first hour of roasting. Combine salt, pepper, rosemary, basil, and 1 cup red wine. Pour over meat in roaster and roast at 350 degrees until done. Baste with pan juices and add more wine as needed. There should be two cups of pan juices to serve with the meat and Polenta.

Submitted by Mrs. Julia M. Vanderschaegen, Iron Belt. It was a dish served by her mother, who was born in Italy.

Spareribs appeared in many combinations and were a particular favorite of Germans and other Middle and Eastern European cooks.

GERMAN SPARERIBS

3 pounds spareribs
4 cups bread crumbs
4 cups sliced apples
Salt and pepper
Baked potatoes

Place a layer of ribs in a roasting pan and season with salt and pepper; top with a layer of sliced apples then one of bread crumbs. Repeat, ending with a layer of ribs on top. Bake at 350 degrees for 2 hours. Serve with baked potatoes.

Submitted by Priscilla Kay Harnack, Janesville.

SPARERIBS WITH SAUERKRAUT (Czech)

4 pounds spareribs
3 tablespoons fat
1½ quarts sauerkraut
2 medium carrots, grated
1½ teaspoons caraway seeds
Salt and pepper to taste
3 medium onions, sliced
2 large apples, cored and cut into rings
1½ cups water

Cut the ribs into serving-size pieces and brown quickly in a skillet in fat. Drain the sauerkraut and combine with grated carrot, caraway seeds, salt, and pepper. Place half of sauerkraut mixture in a buttered roasting pan. Cover with half of the sliced onions and apple rings. Top with browned ribs. Layer over remaining sauerkraut, onions, and apple rings. Pour water over all, cover, and bake at 350 degrees about 2 hours. Add more water if needed to keep the sauerkraut moist.

Submitted by Helen F. Andruskevicz, Green Bay. This dish, she added, was always served with boiled potatoes.

SAUERKRAUT AND SCHUPNOODLES (German)

5 pounds spareribs
1½ quarts sauerkraut with liquid
Caraway seeds
2 tablespoons lard
1 teaspoon salt
White bread dough
1 teaspoon salt

Boil spareribs in water to cover until done. Drain and keep warm in oven.

Simmer sauerkraut in enough water from spareribs to which a pinch of caraway seeds has been added until flavors are well blended. Drain sauerkraut and saute over low heat in 1 tablespoon lard until golden brown, stirring often to keep from burning.

Bring a kettle of water to a boil; add salt. Knead down ¾ of a loaf of bread dough on a floured board. Nip off small pieces of dough, flour palms, and roll dough from wrist to finger tips. When all dough is used, drop several at a time into boiling water until they rise to the top; remove. When all are cooked, fry in remaining lard until golden brown. Combine noodles and sauerkraut and toss gently. Arrange on a large platter with the spareribs to serve.

Submitted by Lillian A. Marsh, Chilton, who added that the dish was usually made "on bread baking day so as to have access to the yeast-raised bread dough."

POT ESSEN (German)

2 pounds very lean pork
½ cup pearl barley
Diced sweet apples, cored but not peeled
8 potatoes, peeled and sliced
Corn syrup
Butter (optional)

Simmer pork and barley in water to barely cover for about 2½ hours. Add apples and potatoes and simmer until cooked. Serve warm with a little syrup and melted butter if desired.

Submitted by Betty Westra, Waupun.

SCHWEINE BRAUTE MIT KARTOFFEL (German)

6 cups water
4 pounds pork loin
1 large bay leaf
1 to 1½ tablespoons salt
1 teaspoon pepper
1 tablespoon whole allspice
2 medium onions, thickly sliced
6 potatoes
Chopped parsley

Heat water to boiling. Add meat and reduce heat to medium. After 15 minutes, remove scum from top. Add bay leaf, salt, pepper, allspice, and onions. Simmer 3 hours. Add potatoes and continue simmering 30 minutes.

Transfer potatoes and remaining cooking liquid into a 13 by 9 by 2½-inch baking pan. Place under preheated broiler for 5 minutes or until browned and crusty. Slice meat and arrange down center of potatoes. Garnish potatoes with parsley.

Submitted by Elsia V. Ruselink, Milwaukee. "In this day of cholesterol conscious meal planners," she wrote, "I cook the shanks to vver half done, remove them from the liquid and place liquid in the refrigerator. When cold, remove all fat from the top and discard it. Then proceed with the recipe."

CARROTS AND POTATOES (Dutch)

6 pork shanks
6 to 8 medium carrots
6 to 8 medium potatoes
1 medium onion, peeled and sliced
1 medium apple, peeled, cored, and sliced
Salt to taste

Cover pork shanks with water and simmer until more than half done. Remove shanks and add to the pot all other ingredients. Place pork shanks on top and simmer until meat and vegetables are cooked. Total cooking time is about 1½ hours.

Remove pork shanks to a platter. Drain and reserve half of the liquid and mash all vegetables in the remaining liquid. Add reserved liquid until vegetables are consistency of mashed potatoes.

Submitted by Elsia V. Ruselink, Milwaukee. "In this day of cholesterol conscious meal planners," she wrote "I cook the shanks to over half done, remove them from the liquid and place liquid in the refrigerator. When cold, remove all fat from the top and discard it. Then proceed with the recipe."

Meat from pigs feet and hocks was made into a jellied dish and served cold. Many cuisines have one or two versions, sometimes requiring a soaking in a pickling liquid.

KOCSONYA (Hungarian)

3 to 4 pigs feet, cut up
3 large pork hocks, cut up
2 teaspoons salt
¾ teaspoon pepper
3 cloves garlic
2 tablespoons Hungarian paprika

Clean and wash all pieces of meat and place in a large, heavy kettle. Cover with cold water and slowly bring to a simmer. Cook, partially covered, skimming off scum as it forms. After 1 hour, add salt, pepper, garlic, and paprika. Continue simmering, partially covered, removing the fat and froth from time to time, about 1 hour or until meat is tender. Strain and reserve broth. Let the broth cool and then skim off fat. Add more salt if necessary. Discard skin and bones and cut meat into bite-size pieces. Distribute meat in individual bowls or spread evenly in a large, shallow serving dish. Pour the broth over the meat. Let stand until it begins to jell, then cover loosely and refrigerate. Serve cold.

Submitted by Darlene Kronschnabel, Greenleaf.

PORK TREAT (Pennsylvania-Dutch)

"When we had fresh pork fried, mother did as her mother. She'd put a bit of milk in the skillet— not too much, and after the grease had been poured off. That milk seemed to rinse out the pan, and is it ever delicious on bread!"

Submitted by Rebecca Trumpy Gillings, Redgranite.

Variety Meats

What have come to be called "variety meats"—liver, kidney, heart, etc.—were standard fare in Wisconsin's past. No edible part of an animal was discarded. And because these cuts were available only at butchering time, they were usually looked upon as delicacies. Often they required long cooking. Spices were generously used; sometimes the dish was pickled.

KIDNEY AND BRAINS (Austrian)

1 pound pork kidneys
1 pound brains
1 onion, chopped
1 green pepper, chopped
2 tablespoons butter or shortening
Salt, pepper, and paprika to taste

Simmer kidneys in water to cover about 1 hour. Rinse, drain, and cut in pieces.

Saute brains, onion, and green pepper in butter in a large skillet until tender, stirring frequently. Add kidneys, salt, pepper, and paprika and simmer over low heat 30 minutes, covered.

Serve with mashed potatoes and pickled beets, or applesauce.

Mary K. Koestler, Cudahy, contributed her Austrian-born mother's recipe, which she now calls "Brains plus Imagination." "With present day meat markets as they are, all packaged foods, and so many items like kidneys discarded and not for sale, I have added 'plus imagination' to clear out leftovers in the refrigerator and add seasonings to suit everyone's taste." When kidneys are not available, she uses chicken gizzards, diced leftover meat, hamburger, sausage and any cut vegetables, tomato sauce, and spices.

The "plug" of a meat animal is the lungs and heart, which used to be left connected when butchering and for sale.

ASHAY (German)

1 veal plug
1 extra heart
1 large onion
1½ tablespoons lard or drippings
1 bay leaf
¼ cup vinegar
1 teaspoon flour

Cut off and discard windpipes. Wash heart and lungs and simmer in salted water to cover until lungs and hearts are tender. Remove meat and reserve cooking liquid. Discard all tissue and fat, retaining only heart and lung meat. Chop meat with onion until very fine.

Melt lard in a frying pan and saute meat mixture, but do not brown. Add bay leaf, and vinegar; sprinkle flour over all and blend well. Add enough of reserved cooking liquid until of a nice stew consistency. Simmer until flavors are well blended.

Submitted by Elva G. Hart, Milwaukee, who added that the leftover broth can be used for soup.

Dried or fresh fruit was sometimes added to scrap cuts for a sweet-sour taste. Fowl heart, gizzard, wings, and other leftovers were often used instead of the pork leavings of this recipe.

SWATZUE (German)

Pigs feet, ears, shanks, heart, or tongue—or
  some of each
Salt
1 cup vinegar
Cloves, cinnamon, and allspice to taste
1 pound prunes
1 pound dried peaches
1 pound dried apples
Sugar to taste
½ cup flour

In a kettle, cover meat or meats with salted water and simmer until almost tender. Add vinegar, cloves, cinnamon, and allspice, and simmer until done.

Meanwhile, combine prunes, peaches, and apples. Sweeten to taste and simmer in water until tender.

Stir flour into about 1 cup of water and add to meat mixture; stir until thickened. Add stewed fruit to meat and simmer to mix flavors.

Submitted by Mrs. Daisy Frase, Eau Claire.

PICKLED SOUSE (German)

1 beef tongue or 2 or 3 pork or veal tongues
1 onion, sliced
1 teaspoon salt
3 or 4 pork hocks
Salt and freshly ground pepper to taste
½ cup vinegar

Wash tongue well. Cover with water, add onion and 1 teaspoon salt, and simmer until tender. Cool; skim tongue and trim fat.

In a separate pan, barely cover with water the pork hocks and cook until tender. Remove meat from bones. Reserve liquid.

Chop both tongue and hocks coarsely. Add salt and pepper and vinegar, and mix thoroughly. Place in a loaf pan and fill to top with liquid from the pork hocks. Stir briefly to mix. Chill in refrigerator at least 24 hours. Slice and serve cold.

Submitted by Mrs. C.W. Loomer, Madison.

HOT SPICED TONGUE

Boil a fresh tongue for 3½ hours. Skin and trim it and rub the surface well with ½ teaspoon ginger and 1 teaspoon allspice. Slice a small onion and fry in butter. Place (tongue) in a casserole and make a sauce by blending 1 tablespoon flour with the fat in the pan and add 1 cup soup stock, juice of 1 lemon, and 1 cup seeded raisins. Pour sauce over tongue in casserole and bake for 1 hour at 375 to 400 degrees.

From the New Milwaukee Cookbook *(1938) compiled by the Visiting Nurses Association and sent in by Patricia (Mrs. William) Taylor, Whitefish Bay.*

BAKED LIVER

1 cup fine dry bread crumbs
½ teaspoon poultry seasoning
¼ cup minced parsley
¾ pound liver, thinly sliced
Juice of 1 lemon
1 cup minced onions
⅔ cup minced celery with leaves
1 tablespoon fat
1 teaspoon salt
Dash pepper
1 bouillon cube
¼ cup boiling water
1 tablespoon butter or margarine

Mix crumbs, poultry seasoning, and parsley. Put half of mixture in bottom of well-greased, shallow baking pan. Arrange slices of liver on top and sprinkle with lemon juice.

Cook onions and celery in fat in a skillet for 5 minutes; spread on liver. Add salt, pepper, and bouillon cube to water and mix well. Pour over liver. Top with remaining crumb mixture and dot with butter or margarine. Bake at 350 degrees for 1 hour.

Submitted by Chris Kuehl, Milwaukee.

SUOMALAINEN MAKSA KAKKU (Finnish)

1 cup raw rice
2 pound beef or calf liver
3 cups milk
1 medium onion, chopped
¼ cup sugar
¼ cup raisins
1 teaspoon salt
¼ teaspoon pepper
1 egg, beaten
3 tablespoons butter, melted

Cook rice until half done; rinse under cold water and drain.

Boil liver slightly in a pan of water. Drain and grind fine in a food chopper.

Combine rice and liver in a large bowl. Add milk, onion, sugar, raisins, salt, pepper, egg, and butter and mix well. Place in a greased 12-inch bread pan. Bake at 400 degrees for 45 minutes.

Submitted by Mrs. Linda Rajala Sereno, Montreal, Wisconsin.

PENNEY DUCKS (English)

4 cups ground pork liver
Dry bread
2 cups ground lean pork
¾ cup ground onions
2 teaspoons salt
½ teaspoon rubbed sage
Dash pepper
Pork skirting (lining of stomach) or thin bacon
  slices

Liver should be ground with about ½ cup dry bread cup up into small pieces.

Mix liver, pork, onions, salt, sage, and pepper. Place about 2 tablespoons of liver mixture on pieces of pork skirting and fold over and around the mixture. Place Penney Ducks in a pan and bake at 350 degrees about ½ hour. If pork skirting is not available and bacon is used, pour off excess grease while baking or bake on a rack.

Submitted by Mrs. Jerome L. Riedy, Fort Atkinson. "Whenever a pig was butchered on the farm, the liver was ground and Penney Ducks were made," she reported. They were frequently served for breakfast.

Sausage and Preserved Meat

Sausage making is the traditional way dating from ancient times of both preserving meat and making use of all edible portions of meat animals. The mixtures of bits and pieces from butchering, fat, organ meats, and offal, usually well spiced, were—and are—cured, dried, or smoked. Most sausages were put into casings made of the cleaned intestines of the butchered animals, but some were formed into loaves, generally to be used up quickly.

Meat was the primary ingredient in most sausages, though delicious mixtures also called for inclusion of some sort of starch: rice, potatoes, bread, grain.

Head Cheese is one of the loaf varieties of sausage, deriving its name, of course, from the meat used—that of a pig's head. Just about every ethnic group made head cheese that differed only in the spices used. It was served cold or warmed in a bit of vinegar, or thickly sliced and fried.

HEAD CHEESE (German)

1 pig's head
³/₈ teaspoon marjoram
³/₈ teaspoon black pepper
1 teaspoon salt
³/₈ teaspoon thyme
¹/₂ teaspoon poultry seasoning (optional)

Remove eyes, brains, and nosetip from pig's head. Cut head in half or quarters and place in a large kettle. Cover with water and simmer over medium to medium low heat for several hours or until meat is cooked. Remove meat from bones and place in a colander. Set colander in a baking pan and place in a 250 degree oven to allow as much fat as possible to drip out.

Mix drained meat with the spices. Place in a loaf pan and place in a cool place or refrigerator to set.

Submitted by Susanne Marie Williams-Brown, Clintonville.

In this recipe, the meat from the head was combined with other cuts and further stretched with bread.

BOHEMIAN SAUSAGE

1 pig's head
Liver, heart, and tongue of the pig
2 large loaves homemade bread, dried and in
** pieces as for dressing**
3 peppercorns, crushed
3 tablespoons ground pepper
1 heaping tablespoon marjoram
Salt to taste

Clean and cut apart pig head; boil in salted water to cover until tender. Cool; remove meat from bones.

Cook liver, heart, and tongue in salted water until tender. Skin tongue.

Put all meats through a meat grinder using coarse blade. Combine ground meat, bread, and spices. Add enough cooled cooking liquid to get a soft consistency. Heat to boiling, stirring often.

Cool and package in serving-size portions for freezer. May also be canned and processed in a pressure canner.

Submitted by Mrs. Albert Rokus, Vesper.

Blood Sausage was another loaf product. It had to be made the same day as the animal was butchered as the blood could not be stored.

BLOD POLSE (Norwegian)

½ cup raw rice
2 quarts pork or beef blood
½ cup sugar
½ teaspoon ginger
½ teaspoon allspice
1 tablespoon salt
Flour
Fresh pork, diced

Cook rice in boiling salted water until nearly done. Drain and cool.

Combine rice with blood, sugar, ginger, allspice, and salt. Add enough flour to make a thin batter and stir until smooth. Pour batter into clean, wet cloth bags about 4 by 10 inches. Add diced pork at intervals while filling bags so it is distributed evenly throughout. Do not fill bags completely as sausage expands during cooking. Sew ends of bags together and place into slightly salted boiling water. Simmer 1½ to 2 hours or until well done.

When ready to serve, remove from bags and slice. Serve hot with butter or fry in pork drippings and top with butter and syrup.

Submitted by Mrs. Alice Knutson, Iola.

KIELBASA (Polish)

10 pounds pork
2 onions
1 pint water
Salt
Pepper
Marjoram
Casings

Cut up pork and onions and grind together well. Add water and salt, pepper and marjoram to taste. Work together, mixing well. Fill casings and tie up. Hang by an open window in the basement; if possible, keep in a continual breeze. Keep cool.

The sausage can be eaten almost immediately. Simmer in water about 20 minutes to serve.

Submitted by Mrs. Catherine Ellingboe, Milwaukee, whose Polish-born grandmother always included this Kielbasa on the Easter dinner menu.

KRANSKŸA (Slovenian)

12 pounds pork shoulder and rib trimmings
6 ounces salt
2 ounces sodium nitrate
2 ounces ground pepper
1 cup water
1 clove garlic, crushed
Hog casings

Put meat through coarse blade of a meat chopper. Add salt, sodium nitrate, pepper, water, and garlic. Knead for about 30 minutes. Must be well mixed. Stuff mixture into small hog casings and tie in pairs. Hang on rods and dry 1 to 3 days in a smokehouse with a well-banked, even fire.

To cook, simmer slowly about 45 minutes. Sausages may be smoked for a longer period until well dried; cut thinly and serve like salami.

Submitted by Mrs. Anne Shoberg, Milwaukee, who added that cooked Kranskya were delicious served with sauerkraut or turnip kraut and mashed potatoes.

BRAUNSCHWEIGER (German)

Equal parts of pork meat and pork liver
Onions
Salt
Cloves
Nutmeg
Allspice
Casings

Boil the pork until done. Blanch the liver in boiling water. Boil as many onions as desired.

Grind pork, liver, and onions as finely as possible. If an even finer texture is desired, put the mixture through a sieve. Add salt, cloves, nutmeg, and allspice sparingly to taste. Stuff into casings, leaving 2 inches for expansion before tying at the desired length.

Place sausages into simmering water for 45 minutes, keeping the sausages down with a wooden spoon and turning them occasionally to prevent bursting. Dip into cold water immediatley to keep the fat from settling on one side. Place on a clean cloth; after a few days, they may be smoked slightly. The flavor improves after a day or two.

Submitted by Agnes A. (Mrs. Oscar) Hoyer, Milwaukee. The recipe was used by her father, who learned the art of sausage making as a young man in German before studying for the ministry and emigrating to Door County. "I have fond memories of winter days when my parents made all kinds of sausages," she wrote. "There was much sampling and tasting. Braunschweiger was a favorite. We children each had our very own sausage. My brother's was made the longest since he was the oldest. Mine was a bit shorter, and little sister's was still shorter. What a thrill it was for us when our special sausage was served!" Her father's reputation for sausage making was well-known and his parishioners often had him add the spices to their prepared meats for sausage.

SUMMER SAUSAGE

33 pounds beef
66 pounds pork
3 pounds salt
12 pounds black pepper
1 cup mustard seed

1 piece garlic as big as a walnut
Large casings

Grind meats. Grind or finely mince garlic. Combine meats, garlic, and seasonings and mix well. Stuff into large casings and tie. Smoke with hickory wood.

Makes 100 pounds of sausage.

Mrs. Henry Weddig, Kewaskum, submitted this recipe, which is over a hundred years old. "I can remember mother putting it in large casings and tying them with butcher string," she added. "Some were ten and twenty pounds in weight and more."

BOLOGNA SAUSAGE

2 pounds lean pork
2 pounds lean veal
2 pounds lean beef
1 pound salt pork
1 pound beef suet
10 tablespoons powdered sage
1 ounce each parsley, savory, marjoram, and
    thyme
2 teaspoons pepper
2 teaspoons cayenne pepper
1 nutmeg, grated

1 teaspoon cloves
1 onion, chopped
Salt to taste
Beef casings
Ginger or pepper

Grind meats and suet. Mix with sage, parsley, savory, marjoram, thyme, pepper, cayene pepper, nutmeg, cloves, onion, and salt to taste. Put into beef casings, tie, and prick each one. Put into hot water, then slowly bring to a boil. Simmer for 1 hour. When cooked, lay in sun or dry or on a clean, dry stove. Rub outside with ginger or pepper. Eat at once or smoke like ham.

Submitted by William E. Kostka, Algoma.

KARTOFFEL WURST (German)

Leaf lard, back fat, and fat scraps from 1 pig
Salt
1 pork liver
1½ gallons grated raw potatoes
2 cups meat stock
1 tablespoon ground allspice
About ¾ cup dried thyme
Pork casings

Cut lard, back fat, and fat scraps into pieces and render in a kettle on the stove or a roaster in the oven. Salt lightly. Strain off fat and reserve cracklings for the wurst.

Cook pork liver in water until very firm. Cool; grate.

Scald grated potatoes with boiling hot meat stock. Add cracklings and grated liver and mix in allspice, thyme, and salt to taste. Mix well. Cut pork casings into desired lengths, tie one end with string and stuff, not too tightly, tying the opening with the same string. Prick each sausage several times to prevent bursting in cooking. Cook, a few at a time, in salted, simmering water, turning often until when pricked with a darning needle, the oozing juice looks cooked. Cool on a board and store in a cold cellar or freeze.

To serve, bake at 350 or 375 degrees for 1 hour or until browned.

The meat mixture can also be frozen without stuffing. Divide into meal-sized portions in containers and freeze. To serve, thaw, slice, and bake as above.

Submitted by Magdalena W. Tank, New London.

Meats were preserved in other ways besides in sausages. Drying over an open fire is the most ancient. Mrs. Rosella Mallory, Milwaukee, contributed a description of the Indian way she observed growing up: "Raw meat was cut into long strips about a half inch or so thick and either wound around sticks or hung over supported sticks near the fire, but not too close. In this way the meat was cooked slowly and also dried and made it easy to keep. It actually was like a barbecue."

DRIED BEEF (Norwegian)

Lean, boneless beef cut in 3 pound pieces
Salt
Brown sugar
Saltpeter
Red wine

Rub each piece of beef with plenty of salt until beef appears white. Sprinkle each piece with ¼ cup brown sugar and 1 tablespoon saltpeter. Place in a stone jar and pour over all ⅓ cup of wine for each piece. Change pieces from top to bottom of the jar about 2 times a day for 10 days. The meat will form its own brine.

Thread a large darning needle with heavy cotton cord and push through a corner of the meat to make a loop for stringing on a pole. Hang the meat in a cool dry place for about a month. When ready, meat will be a deep red-brown color— moist on the inside and white, dry and salty on the outside. Remove from drying poles and keep in a cool, damp place to maintain proper moisture content.

Madelyn Lee (Mrs. Arne V.) Larson, Clintonville, submitted this method of drying beef that was given her by her grandmother. "I can still see so clearly, in my mind's eye, the pieces of dried beef hanging along a pole in her attic to 'finish,' " she wrote. "This recipe makes a quality dried beef I have never been able to purchase in a store."

PRESERVED MEAT

5 pounds beef steak
5 teaspoons salt
5 teaspoons sugar
1 teaspoon saltpeter
1 scant teaspoon black pepper

Slice meat. Mix together salt, sugar, saltpeter, and pepper. Put a layer of meat in the bottom of an earthenware jar and sprinkle with seasoning mixture. Repeat until all is used up. Cover with a large plate close to the size of the inside of the jar and weight down with a large, heavy stone. Store in a cool place. This will keep for quite a long time.

Submitted by Mrs. Ann Strathman, Waterloo, who reported that she used this recipe for many years on the farm before it was electrified.

Game

A GOOD—OR LUCKY—HUNTER COULD MAKE A significant contribution to the family's larder, as is true today. Most early settlers were wise in the ways of preparing game, but many gratefully received instruction from their Indian neighbors. Over the years, game dishes evolved into gourmet specialties, aided by age-old recipes brought by European immigrants; on the frontier the tough meat of game was generally merely boiled or stewed.

The fat of most game animals is pungent and was almost always removed and used for other purposes—medicinally for chest rubs or hand lotions or soap or softening leather, greasing axles, and the like. The meat was then larded with salt pork or bacon for cooking.

BEAR MEAT

Bear meat is not suitable for a dry roast, but it will make a tender pot roast if it is first put in a marinade liquid for a few days before cooking. Wine seasoned with grated onion and a little lemon juice works very nicely; or into about 3 cups of cold water and ½ cup of vinegar, place 1 minced clove of garlic, 3 slices of onion, 10 peppercorns, 1 crushed bay leaf, and a large teaspoon of salt. When marinated, remove the meat, rinse in cold water and discard the marinade liquid. Place pieces of parboiled salt pork in the cavities, roll tightly, and tie with a strong cord. Dredge in flour and brown in hot beef fat on all sides. Place in a Dutch oven or roasting pan with a tight cover, adding about 3 cups of water and some

dried vegetables for gravy flavor. Replace cover and bake slowly at about 300 degrees, turning and basting it occasionally until tender. Remove the meat, strain the broth, adding water to make 3 cups. Mix together with ½ cup each of salt pork and flour, stirring briskly while it thickens. Add seasoning, wine and lemon juice to taste.

Submitted by Mrs. Beatrice Durand Derrick, Webster, who found it in an old cook book belonging to her mother, an 1890's settler of Scott Township in Burnett County, and included it in her book about the area, "Great Scott."

VENISON

In the past, many Wisconsin housewives had venison to make into sausages or preserve in other ways.

Pamela Schalk, Milwaukee, described the ingenious method her great-grandmother, who was of Irish extraction, used in the 1890's:

"She'd cut the meat into slices against the grain, then melt a little bacon grease in a large skillet and fry up the slices. After the first batch of slices were well done, they were arranged in a layer at the bottom of an iron kettle and the fat poured over them. The next batch was fried in the remaining tallow and the layering process was repeated until all the meat was cooked. She allowed the kettle to cool until the tallow covering the top layer was solidified. Then the kettle was covered with a tight lid and stored in a cool, dark place such as a root cellar.

"To use a portion of her store, she would break the top layer of tallow and remove the desired quantity of venison, melt the broken tallow and pour it back over the store to reseal it. Venison prepared this way will keep for two to four months."

VENISON STEAK

Venison round steak cut
  into 6 serving-size pieces
Monosodium glutamate
⅔ cup flour
1 teaspoon salt
½ teaspoon pepper
¼ teaspoon paprika
½ cup lard
½ cup melted butter
1 onion, sliced
Tarragon
Parsley flakes
Oregano
2 small bay leaves
1 1-pound 13-ounce can tomatoes
1 green pepper, sliced or cut in chunks

Pound and tenderize steak pieces. Sprinkle with monosodium glutamate. Combine flour, salt, pepper, and paprika; dredge steaks in flour mixture. Brown in hot lard and transfer to a baking pan. Cover with melted butter and add sliced onion. Sprinkle with tarragon, parsley flakes, and oregano to taste. Add bay leaves and tomatoes, cover, and bake at 350 degrees from 2 to 3 hours, depending on age of meat. When meat is almost tender, add green pepper and pour over 1 cup boiling water. Continue baking until done. Serve with each slice topped with green pepper and pieces of tomato and use pan drippings as gravy.

Submitted by Florence Buckner, Antigo, who served this dish frequently when she was cook at the Executive Residence in Governor Warren P. Knowles's administration.

RACCOON

"Coon" is good only in cold, freezing weather. Skin and be very careful to remove scent glands along either side of the back bone, in the small of the back. Also remove all visible fat. Soak in cold water overnight. Parboil in fresh water. Remove, wipe dry, and stuff with a sage dressing to which an apple or two has been added. Place a number of strips of salt pork on top of the meat. Roast at 350 degrees until brown and tender. Serve with applesauce.

Submitted by the Reverend Cormac Dwyer, Milwaukee.

SQUIRREL PIE

Skin squirrel by hanging up by the head, cutting off feet and tail. Slit from throat downward to remove entrails, cut off head. Soak in cold salted water overnight. Cut into pieces—the legs and upper and lower back, and boil until tender.

Fry floured pieces in butter until brown, then cover with dough made of 2 cups flour, 1 teaspoon salt, 3 teaspoons baking powder, 5 tablespoons butter, and ¾ cup milk. Bake until top is brown.

Submitted by Coral (Mrs. John) Brahm, West Allis.

PAN BAKED PHEASANT

1 pheasant
1½ teaspoons salt
½ teaspoon pepper
½ teaspoon monosodium glutamate
About ½ pound butter
1 cup cooking sherry
1 tablespoon honey
2 cans cream of chicken soup

Dress and clean pheasant. Cut into serving sized pieces and wash well. Season with salt, pepper, and monosodium glutamate. Brown pheasant in a skillet with plenty of butter. Place in a roasting pan. Combine sherry, honey, and soup and mix well. Pour over pheasant pieces. Bake at 350 degrees until tender, about 2 hours.

Another dish served by Florence Buckner, Antigo, when a cook for Governor Warren P. Knowles. This is a recipe she adapted from one she found in the files of the Executive Residence kitchen library.

Rabbit, both wild and domestic, was a favorite of Middle and Eastern Europeans. The well-known Hasenpfeffer was usually made with wild hare.

HASENPFEFFER (German)
1 rabbit, cut in pieces
Vinegar
1 large onion, sliced
Salt
Pepper
Cloves
1 or 2 bay leaves
Raisins
Brown sugar

The day before, place rabbit meat in a stone jar and cover with equal parts of vinegar and water. Add sliced onion and salt, pepper, cloves, and bay leaves to taste.

The next day, remove meat and simmer in water to barely cover until meat is almost done. Add raisins and sugar to taste; gradually stir in some of the pickling liquid. Let simmer until meat is tender.

Submitted by Mrs. Wilfred Posbrig, Muskego, who added that she serves the dish with raw onion.

Other recipes submitted called for browning the meat before stewing or including red wine in the cooking liquid or using many more onions.

The following is an unexpected rabbit in fish stew.

LAPIN EN MATELOTE (French)

Disjoint rabbit. Make a roux with one spoonful of flour and a piece of butter; put in the rabbit pieces with the liver; roll pieces in the roux to coat evenly; add a glass of red wine, two cups water and bouillon, a bunch of parsley, leek, one clove garlic, two cloves, thyme, bay leaf, basil, salt, coarsely ground pepper. Cook over a low fire; after one-half hour, add one dozen small white onions; if desired, add one eel, cut in bite-sized pieces when the rabbit is almost cooked. Before serving, discard parsley, defat the sauce, and add a generous pinch of capers, and one chopped anchovy. Serve with croutons tossed in butter; and cover overall with sauce.

Translated from the 1838 edition of La Cuisinière Bourgeoise, *used by the Dousman family in Villa Louis.*

RABBIT WITH CREAM SAUCE (Czech)

1 skinned rabbit, about 3 pounds
3 tablespoons butter
About 2 cups water
¼ cup vinegar or lemon juice
1 carrot, cut up
1 medium onion, sliced
1 rib celery
Parsley
10 peppercorns
1 bay leaf
2 tablespoons flour
1 cup cream
Potato Dumplings (see Dumpling section)

Cut up rabbit and place in a roaster. Add butter and brown on top of the stove, adding a little water at times as needed, until meat is evenly browned. Add remaining water, vinegar, carrot, onion, celery, parsley, peppercorns, and bay leaf. Roast at 350 degrees about 1 hour, basting occasionally. Remove meat when tender. Add flour and cream to pan drippings and simmer 15 minutes. Season to taste. Spoon sauce over rabbit and potato dumplings.

Submitted by Mrs. Wencil Weber, Whitelaw.

MEATLESS MAIN DISHES

Euuropean immigrants were usually much struck by the amount of meat Americans ate compared with the accustomed fare they had left behind. However, it was only a relative few who could afford unlimited amounts of meat; in most nineteenth-century households, meatless or almost meatless meals at least once a day if not more were standard. These dishes, of course, were heavy on starches, especially potatoes.

POTATO STEW

¼ to ½ pound salt pork, sliced or cubed
3 medium potatoes, sliced
1 medium onion, sliced
2 tablespoons flour
Pepper to taste (optional)
3 or 4 slices bread, halved or quartered

In a stew pan, heat salt pork to sizzling. Add potatoes and then onion. Sprinkle with flour and cover with hot water. Season with pepper if desired. Simmer slowly until potatoes are slightly tender. Add bread and continue simmering about 10 minutes.

Submitted by Vivian M. Jenkins, Marshfield, who often adds a few drops of hot pepper sauce "to give it a little zip." The bread, she notes, serves as dumplings.

MULGIPUDER (Estonian)

1 cup pearl barley
2 pounds potatoes, peeled and quartered
1 quart water
Salt to taste
2 small onions, diced
Butter
Sour cream
Crumbled cooked bacon

Wash barley and let stand in cold water to cover for 2 hours. Drain.

Cook potatoes in 1 quart water for 10 minutes, then add barley, salt, and onion and simmer until barley is tender and water is absorbed. Add 2 tablespoons butter and mix well.

Place mixture into individual serving bowls; with the back of a spoon, press a hole in the center. Fill each with 1 teaspoon butter, some sour cream, and garnish with bacon.

To eat, dip a spoonful of potato-barley mash into butter and sour cream.

Submitted by Mrs. Koidula Maeste, Milwaukee, on behalf of The Estonian House. Mrs. Maeste explained that buttermilk was the usual beverage served with this dish, which was often the main offering, along with a vegetable, as the evening meal.

MALUNZ or REEBLE (Swiss)

4 or 5 small potatoes
Flour
2 or 3 tablespoons hot bacon drippings or oil
Warm milk or berry sauce

Cook potatoes; peel and cool.

Cover with flour in a skillet. Place skillet over low heat and, with a chopping blade or cutting knife, blend potatoes and flour until the consistency of coarse cornmeal, as if for pie crust. Continue blending until thoroughly warmed but not sticky; be careful not to scorch. When well blended and dry, pour over hot bacon drippings or oil. Serve with warm milk or berry sauce.

Submitted by Ada (Mrs. Gust) Federman, Sauk City, who said that "this is a substantial dish for a cold day for a hard working man."

PRUNE-POTATO TZIMMES (Jewish)

½ pound prunes
1 quart water
8 medium whole potatoes plus 3 potatoes grated and undrained
⅓ cup sugar
1½ teaspoons salt
1½ tablespoons lemon juice
⅓ cup flour
2 tablespoons butter
Dash pepper

Cover prunes with water, bring to a boil and remove from heat. Place whole potatoes in a 3-quart greased casserole. Add prunes and water in which they were heated. Add sugar, 1 teaspoon salt, and lemon juice. Cover and bake at 350 degrees 1½ hours. Mix together grated potatoes, flour, butter, dash pepper, and remaining salt. Pour mixture over casserole, cover, and continue baking for 1 hour. Remove cover and bake about 30 or 45 minutes or until top is golden brown.

Submitted by Meyer Katz, La Crosse.

HUNGARIAN SPAGHETTI

1 pound spaghetti
½ pound bacon, diced
½ diced green pepper
1 pound cheddar cheese, shredded

Cook and drain spaghetti. Fry bacon until crisp; drain off half of the fat. Remove some bacon and reserve for topping.

Butter a casserole dish and put in a layer of spaghetti; sprinkle with some bacon and fat, green pepper, and cheese. Repeat layers until all is used up, ending with cheese. Top with reserved bacon. Bake at 350 degrees 30 minutes.

Submitted by Mrs. Lewis G. Fedyn, Wauwatosa. Her grandmother got it from a friend and it has been passed down for four generations.

ABENKATER (German)

4 eggs, beaten
1 cup milk
1 cup flour
1 teaspoon salt
Bacon strips
Cherry sauce or canned cherry pie filling,
  warmed

Combine eggs and ½ cup milk. Beat in flour and salt. Beat in remaining milk. Grease a baking pan generously with bacon fat and pour in batter. Place strips of uncooked bacon across the top. Bake at 375 degrees for 40 to 60 minutes. Serve immediately with cherry sauce or pie filling.

Place the whole Abenkater on the table and cut into large pieces to serve.

Submitted by Ruth Jochimsen (Mrs. John) Mattke, Sheboygan. This dish, a sort of German Yorkshire Pudding, puffs up like a popover.

ZWIEBELKUCHEN (German)

6 large onions, slivered
1 tablespoon butter
Salt and pepper to taste
1 egg, beaten
Bread dough
Cooked bacon cubes

Steam onions in butter seasoned with salt and pepper until onions are half cooked. (Do not use water.) Cool. Add egg.

Line a square cake pan with bread dough. Fill with onion mixture and sprinkle bacon cubes over the top. Bake at 400 degrees 30 minutes. Serve warm.

Submitted by Trudie Meixner, Milwaukee.

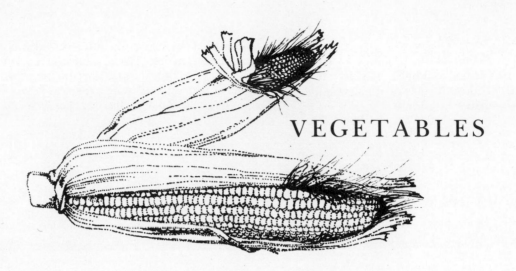

VEGETABLES

IN THE DAYS BEFORE FROZEN FOODS, REFRIG erated trucks, and nation-wide foodmarketing, the fresh products of the kitchen garden were a much anticipated culinary treat. "Gardens were a must for everyone," recounted Mrs. Robert Sanford, River Falls, who grew up in Pierce County, "and the produce was enjoyed to the fullest. As a child, I remember looking forward to many delicacies from the garden. The first meal of fresh peas and new potatoes was always an event of the season. The potatoes, about the size of golf balls, were scrubbed and boiled with freshly shelled peas. When done, the water was drained off and milk poured over the peas and potatoes. Salt and pepper and butter were added just before serving.

"Tomatoes were eaten, in the garden, like apples. We liked scalloped tomatoes, too, but the favorite dish of tomatoes was, and still is, freshly picked tomatoes, pared and cut into chunks in a cereal bowl. Sprinkle the tomatoes with sugar and pour cream over them and eat as cereal, for dessert or for a snack . . .

"In the spring, when the red stalks of rhubarb were big enough to eat, mother would give each child a cup with sugar in it and we'd head for the rhubarb patch, pull up the fresh rhubarb, dip it in the sugar and eat it raw."

The Indians, of course, introduced the early European settlers to native American produce like corn, Jerusalem artichokes, most varieties of beans, peanuts, white and sweet potatoes, sunflowers, and the like. Succotash—the combination of corn and beans, not as popular as it once was—was an Indian combination eaten all over America, since the two ingredients could be grown everywhere. According to food historians Waverly Root and Richard de Rochemont, succotash was originally a stew made of whatever vegetables and meats, fish, or fowl were at hand. Corn was always one of the ingredients, and beans usually. Later succotash came to be corn and beans sweetened in this part of the country with maple syrup.

For winter use, corn was dried or made into hominy.

DRIED CORN

Cook sweet corn on the cob in salted water for about 20 minutes. Cut the corn from the cob, spread it out in a shallow pan, and dry very slowly in a rather cool oven (about 150 degrees). Put the dried corn in sacks and store in a warm, dry place. If in ten days the corn shows no sign of moisture, it will keep well. However, if any moisture remains in the corn, it will mildew.

To prepare the corn for dinner, begin soaking one pint of corn in cold water the night before. At 10 o'clock the next morning, the corn should be put over the fire with a small piece of lean fresh pork or salted pork. Also add one dozen potatoes, peeled and cut into small pieces. Add enough water to cook.

Alice Thorpe, Stanley, contributed this recipe her grandmother often used. She in turn received it from her mother-in-law who, the family believes, originally got it from her Indian neighbors in Chippewa County in the 1870's.

One Indian method of parching corn into hominy is described in this recipe:

HOMINY WITH MEAT (Indian)

2 cups wood ashes from an open fire
5 quarts water
4 cups shelled Indian corn
3 pounds venison ribs
1 cup navy beans (optional)

Combine ashes with 3 quarts water in a cast iron or enamel kettle. Mix and stir with a stick or wooden spoon and bring to a boil. Strain; all that remains is lye.

To the lye add 2 quarts water and corn. Bring to a boil and keep boiling for about 1 hour. Add more water if necessary when kernels start to expand and pop open. When the skins on the kernels begin to open and the hearts come out, remove from fire. Drain and place corn in a large dishpan; fill with fresh water and drain again. Repeat 3 times, taking care not to put your hands into the corn until the washing is completed.

After the fourth washing, rub the corn between fingers and change the water 4 times more. Put the corn back in the kettle with water to cover and boil 30 minutes. Drain and wash 4 times again. By this time, the skins of the kernels will float on top of the water; pour them out. The water will then be clear.

Add meat to hominy, and uncooked beans if desired. Add water to cover and simmer 2 hours or more until meat, corn, and beans are cooked.

Submitted by Mrs. Rosella Mallory, Milwaukee, who noted that beef short ribs may be substituted for venison. This recipe serves 6 or 8 people and is also called Corn Soup. "This soup was traditionally served at feasts and continues to be served as a festive food," she added.

The shelled corn could also be soaked in a lye solution instead of boiled.

WOOD LYE HOMINY (Pioneer)

During the winter months, add wood ash from stoves to a large wood-stave barrel until ¼ filled. Let snow and rain keep barrel filled with water. ,

In late fall, pick and shell from cob kernels of white corn. (This was a variety grown just for hominy-making.) Fill gunny sack with about a half bushel measure of shelled corn. Tie sack and drop in barrel. Test occasionally, and when kernel shell loosens from heart, remove sack from lye barrel and place in a tub of boiling water; work vigorously to loosen shells. Empty corn into hot water and wash well in several changes of hot water; hand pick kernels clean.

Hominy can be dried, packed in jars, and "cold packed" in a canner, or eaten at once with butter, cream, and salt and pepper.

Submitted by Loretta Holmes, Beloit. "Lye water remaining in the barrel was used to make soft soap from collected grease and meat drippings in the spring," she added. "On visits to grandfather's home, we children were warned not to get near the lye barrel which always stood by the woodshed door. A relative who did not heed the warning lost an eye to the splashed liquid."

Hominy has passed into standard American regional cooking, but other Indian dishes have not—for example the following recipe for Milkweed:

MA-HEECH (Indian)

Pick the milkweeds in May or early June. Pick only the buds. A quart will serve 4 or 6 people.

Let the buds stand in cold water about 1 hour. Add six small slices of salt pork or any flavoring meat. Place on the fire and simmer no more than 45 minutes as the vegetable is very tender. Mix 2 tablespoons of flour in a little water and add, stirring occasionally, until thickened as desired. Serve hot.

Submitted by Mrs. Rosella Mallory, Milwaukee.

Yankee settlers arrived with many ways to use dried beans. Here are two.

BEAN PORRIDGE (Yankee)
3 cups dry navy beans
3 pounds beef soup bones with marrow
2 tablespoons salt
¼ teaspoon black pepper
¼ cup yellow cornmeal

Soak beans in water to cover overnight. In the morning, parboil until skins crack; drain.

Cook soup bones until meat and marrow falls away; cut meat in pieces. Add enough water to meat cooking liquid to make 4 quarts; add the beans, salt, and pepper and cook until beans are tender but not mushy. Add cornmeal that has been wetted with water and cook 30 minutes, stirring often to avoid sticking. Allow to set, and keep cold or freeze.

To serve, cut small amounts as needed and heat in boiling water.

Submitted by Mrs. W. Paul Sawyer, Racine. Bean Porridge, she reported, was traditional on Christmas Eve in her husband's family which came to Wisconsin from Vermont in 1850. "A large bowl was served to each person and crisp soda crackers were crumbled over it," she wrote. "Milk was generally poured over. The porridge is very filling and usually the meal was completed with dessert. Bean Porridge was always made in large quantities and kept in a crock in the back hall, which was very cold. It was served often until spring."

BAKED BEANS (Yankee)

3 pounds dried navy beans
1 teaspoon baking soda
1 small onion, sliced
1 cup homemade catsup
2 tablespoons dry mustard
2 tablespoons salt
½ teaspoon pepper
2 cups brown sugar
1½ pounds fresh side pork, cubed

Pick over and wash beans. Soak overnight in cold water to cover. In the morning, drain beans and cover with hot water. Add baking soda and parboil until skins burst when blown upon.

Place onion and catsup in the bottom of a heavy earthenware jar. Add half the beans. Combine mustard, salt, pepper, and brown sugar. Sprinkle beans with half this mixture. Repeat with remainder of beans and sugar mixture. Top with pork cubes and cover with boiling water. Bake, covered, in a 200 degree oven about 24 hours. (See note on temperature and baking time, below.) Uncover during last hour of baking.

Virginia M. Derridinger, Appleton, submitted this recipe which was given to her mother by the woman with whom she boarded while teaching school in the Greenville area. Ms. Derridinger reported that she still uses this recipe but bakes it 2 or 3 hours at 350 degrees. Today, experts recommend cooking anything with pork at no less than 325 degrees.

HARICOTS Á LA PROVENÇALE (French)

Put in a saucepan 1 liter lima beans, 2 ladles of bouillon, 2 onions sliced, a bouquet garni, a leg of goose or of pickled pork, 4 spoons oil, a little butter, pepper and nutmeg, and salt if necessary. Simmer just until perfectly cooked, adding bouillon if it is necessary, but not too much, for the sauce should be properly thick. Peas and lentils accommodate themselves to the same manner of cooking.

Translated from the 1838 edition of La Cuisinière Bourgeoise, *used by the Dousman family at Villa Louis.*

STRING BEANS AND BACON (Pennsylvania-Dutch)

1 pound fresh beans
¼ pound bacon, diced
2 potatoes, peeled and cut in ½-inch cubes
¼ teaspoon salt
1 small onion, diced
About 1½ cup water

Wash, trim, and cut beans in desired lengths. Brown bacon and pour off fat. Combine beans, potatoes, salt, onion, and water with bacon and simmer until potatoes are soft, about 30 minutes.

Submitted by Victoria (Mrs. Ralph C.) Pierce, Racine. Green beans—called string beans in earlier days—were found in most gardens.

CREAMED BEETS (Polish)

2 cans beets
2 medium onions, chopped
4 tablespoons butter
2 tablespoons flour
2 tablespoons vinegar
1 teaspoon sugar
Salt and pepper to taste
Sour cream

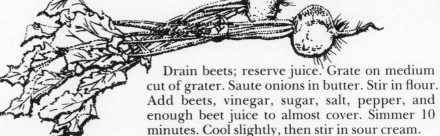

Drain beets; reserve juice. Grate on medium cut of grater. Saute onions in butter. Stir in flour. Add beets, vinegar, sugar, salt, pepper, and enough beet juice to almost cover. Simmer 10 minutes. Cool slightly, then stir in sour cream.

Submitted by Mary Staj, Neenah.

Wisconsin's soil proved very hospitable to cabbage, which was cooked with infinite variety.

RED CABBAGE WITH APPLES

1 medium red cabbage
1 or 2 tart apples
2 tablespoons butter
1 onion, sliced
2 cups water
½ cup vinegar
½ cup sugar
½ teaspoon salt
¼ teaspoon pepper
2 to 3 tablespoons flour

Wash cabbage; drain and shred as for slaw. Wash, core, and peel apples; chop or cut coarsely. Melt butter and saute onions and apples a few minutes. Add water, vinegar, sugar, and salt and pepper. Stir well, bring to a boil, and add cabbage. Simmer, covered, until tender, about 30 or 40 minutes. Just before serving, sprinkle flour on top and stir and cook briefly to thicken.

Submitted by Mrs. R. J. Burgoyne, Plymouth. Similar recipes submitted called for the addition of 4 or 5 whole cloves to the cooking water.

JUTTE (Belgian)

1 medium head cabbage, preferrably Savoy
Salt
4 slices bacon or salt pork
1 medium onion, chopped

Strip off as many leaves as possible from cabbage. Drop into lightly salted boiling water; simmer about 5 minutes or until leaves are pliable and limp, but not mushy. Drain, and cool enough to handle.

Fry bacon in a large skillet until medium crisp; remove and set aside but reserve fat. Saute onions in bacon grease until yellow. Cut cabbage leaves in strips crosswise, removing hard veins if necessary. Cut bacon in strips crosswise. Add cabbage and bacon to skillet and saute until cabbage is tender, stirring often. To hasten cooking, cover skillet the first 5 minutes.

Serve with ham or pork.

Submitted by Mrs. Florence M. Vint, Springfield, Virginia. This is a Walloon dish, she added.

BROWNED FLOUR SAUERKRAUT (Bohemian)

6 strips bacon
4 tablespoons flour
1 medium onion, chopped
1 quart sauerkraut

Fry bacon until crisp and drain on absorbent paper. Add flour to bacon drippings, and stir and cook until browned. Add onion and sauerkraut and cook until both are tender, about 20 minutes. Crumble bacon and add to kraut mixture before serving.

Submitted by Emma Marshall, Gillingham, who remembered that this "was especially good when cooked on the old-fashioned wood stove. When it was cooked, it could be covered and pulled back on the back lids of the range where it would stay hot until meal time. This is delicious served over hot dumplings split in half."

SAUERKRAUT WITH RAISINS (German)

2 pounds sauerkraut
4 tablespoons sugar
½ cup raisins
4 tablespoons unsalted fat rendered from
   chicken, goose, duck, turkey, or roast pork
½ cup water
1 tablespoon flour if necessary

Drain sauerkraut well. Add sugar, raisins, and fat and mix well. Add water, cover and simmer 2 hours. If sauerkraut has too much liquid, stir in flour and cook a little longer before serving.

Submitted by Mrs. Ronald Daggett, Madison. This dish, she added, gains flavor when reheated. It may be frozen.

TURNIP KRAUT (Yugoslavian)

Wash turnips; cut away tops and stems. If turnips are young, do not peel. Shred as for shoestring potatoes and layer with salt in the same proportion as sauerkraut (1 to 2 teaspoons per pound of turnips) in a stone crock. Press down on each layer until some juice appears. Fill crock about ¾ full. Cover with a clean wooden lid or dinner plate that fits into crock. Weight with a large clean stone and cover all with a clean white dish towel. Place in a cool place. In due time it will start to ferment and brine will form. When brine foams over the top, wash lid, stone, dish towel, and crock top at least once a week. Kraut is ready when foaming stops after about 5 or 6 weeks. May be sealed in quart jars or left in the crock in a cool place.

To serve, remove turnip kraut from crock with a little of the brine. Add water to barely cover and simmer until tender. Drain, reserving cooking water. Make a medium white sauce with fat drippings, flour, and reserved water as needed. Combine turnips and sauce and heat through.

Submitted by Mrs. Anne Shoberg, Milwaukee. "This is especially good if homemade cracklings are used."

BAKED CABBAGE (Polish)

4 cups shredded cabbage
1 tablespoon salt
½ teaspoon pepper
1 quart milk
1 egg, beaten
½ cup flour

Season cabbage with salt and pepper. Combine milk, egg, and flour and pour over cabbage, mixing well. Pour into a well-greased 13-by-9-inch baking pan and bake at 350 degrees until brown on bottom. May be flipped over and browned on other side. Takes about 1 hour, depending on thickness of cabbage mixture.

Submitted by Mrs. Frank M. Suess, Luxemburg.

CHOUX Á LA FLAMANDE (French)

Take a cabbage that you have cut into fourths; blanch in boiling water one quarter of an hour and refresh in cold water, then drain and press out water. Cut away core, re-form cabbage and tie with string. Cook in a bit of butter, rich bouillon, seven or eight onions, a bouquet garni, a bit of salt and coarsely ground pepper; when it is almost done, put in some fresh sausage; while the ragout is cooking, take a bread crust larger than the hand and fry with butter. Put it in the bottom of the serving dish, add cabbage then sausages which have been well drained of fat. Degrease sauce. If you have a little tomato paste, add to sauce; when it is well reduced and of good taste, pour over all.

Translated from the 1838 edition of La Cuisiniére Bourgeoise, *used by the Dousman family at Villa Louis.*

Much of Wisconsin's cabbage was made into sauerkraut, which is merely shredded cabbage pickled at least a month in salt. The proportions, according to Edith (Mrs. Francis) McConnell, Wisconsin Rapids, were 2 tablespoons salt to every 5 pounds of cabbage. Mature heads were chosen for sauerkraut and ideally were fermented at 60 degrees or below for the best-tasting results. Sometimes the sauerkraut was combined with fresh cabbage.

KAPUSTA (Polish)

1 onion, sliced or chopped
2 tablespoons bacon fat
1½ to 2 pounds sauerkraut, rinsed
1 small head cabbage, finely shredded
2 cups water
2 tablespoons brown sugar
Salt and pepper to taste

Saute onion in bacon fat. Add sauerkraut and top with fresh cabbage. Add water, sugar, salt, and pepper. Simmer 2 hours.

Submitted by Mrs. F.J. Gall, Eagle River, who added that this is "so good you can't stop eating."

BAVARIAN SAUERKRAUT (German)

4 tablespoons bacon fat
1 onion, sliced
2 pounds sauerkraut
3 apples, peeled, cored, and quartered
¼ teaspoon salt
1 teaspoon caraway seeds
2 potatoes, finely grated

Soup stock or beef broth
Brown sugar

Heat bacon fat; add onion and saute until brown. Add sauerkraut and simmer 5 minutes. Mix in salt, apples, caraway seeds, and grated potatoes. Add enough hot soup stock or beef broth to just cover; simmer 30 minutes. Sweeten with brown sugar.

Submitted by Lydia Catherine Phillips Kleinschmidt, Milwaukee.

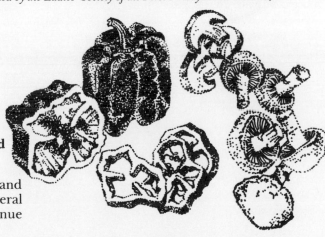

GLAZED CARROTS AND MINT FOR LAMB

Cut into slices ¼-inch thick, six carrots, add a little salt, parboil, and drain. Add ½ cup butter, ½ cup sugar, and 1 tablespoon finely chopped mint leaves. Cook until dry and glazed.

From The La Crosse Cook Book, *published by the Ladies' Society of the First Presbyterian Church, La Crosse, 1923.*

FRIED GREEN PEPPERS (Bohemian)

About 6 large green peppers, seeded and washed
Butter and salad oil for frying
1 or 2 large onions, cut up
½ to 1 pound fresh mushrooms, washed and cut up

Cut peppers into large squares or strips and saute slowly; watch carefully and turn several times. Add onions and mushrooms and continue to saute until all are as tender as desired.

Mrs. John Gehler, Ladysmith, contributed this family recipe. She recommended it as a wonderful accompaniment for any meat.

COUNTRY SPINACH

About 2 pounds fresh spinach
4 large potatoes

Cut out the tough green stalks of the spinach. Boil spinach with potatoes until done. Drain and mash potatoes and spinach together.

Submitted by Elizabeth D. Fischer, Stockbridge, who serves this with boiled fresh pork cut in large chunks and decorated with hard-boiled eggs.

GREEN PUMPKIN (Pioneer)

1 green pumpkin
Salt
Flour
1 egg, slightly beaten
Butter and lard

Select a green pumpkin with seeds that are formed but not hard. Peel and cut in ½-inch thick slices. Sprinkle generously with salt. Let stand about 1 hour; drain. Dip pumpkin pieces in flour, then in egg, and fry in equal parts butter and lard until tender and somewhat transparent.

Submitted by Mrs. Verna Jensen Barnes, Darlington, who calls this dish Mother-in-Law's Green Pumpkin because it has been handed down from mother-in-law to daughter-in-law for generations back to the days before Wisconsin was a state. The dish, she noted, tastes much like fried eggplant and is usually served with a bit of butter and honey.

RUTABAGAS (Canadian)

2 medium rutabagas, peeled, quartered, and
   sliced ¼-inch thick
Salt
2 tablespoons brown sugar
⅛ teaspoon pepper
2 tablespoons butter

Cook rutabagas in boiling salted water until tender. Drain. Combine brown sugar, ½ teaspoon salt, and pepper and mix thoroughly with rutabagas. Add butter and stir gently over low heat until sugar melts, about 2 to 3 minutes. Serves 6.

Mrs. Charles Mowbray, Janesville, submitted this dish which was served frequently by her grandparents who settled in Rusk County in the early 1900's. In 1919, her grandfather's displays of rutabagas and other root vegetables won top prizes at the Mid-West Horticultural Exposition and, according to a letter from the Wisconsin Department of Agriculture, caused more comment than any other single entry.

LANTTULAATIKKO (Finnish)

2 medium rutabagas
¼ cup fine dry bread crumbs
¼ cup cream
½ teaspoon nutmeg
1 teaspoon salt
2 eggs, beaten
3 tablespoons butter

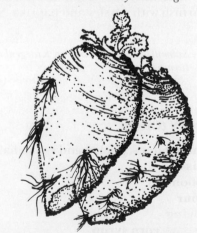

Peel and dice rutabagas. (There will be about 6 cups.) Cook in salted water to cover about 20 minutes or until soft. Drain and mash. Soak bread crumbs in cream and stir in nutmeg, salt, and beaten eggs. Combine with mashed rutabagas. Turn into a buttered 2½-quart casserole, dot with butter, and bake at 350 degrees for 1 hour or until lightly browned on top. Serves 6 to 8.

Submitted by Mrs. Milton M. Mandelin, Greenfield, who added that turnips may also be used in this way. Her Finnish-born mother always included Lanttulaatikko on the Christmas dinner menu.

FRIED PARSNIPS

6 large parsnips
1 cup flour
Salt and pepper
2 tablespoons butter

Peel parsnips and slice lengthwise. Parboil for about 10 minutes. In a bowl, mix flour and salt and pepper to taste. Roll parsnip slices in flour and fry in butter until nicely browned.

Submitted by Mrs. Robert Sanford, River Falls, who noted that these were a springtime treat, for parsnips were left in the garden through the winter and dug in the spring.

TURNIP AND POTATO WHIP (German)

3 cups peeled and cubed turnips
3 cups peeled and cubed potatoes
2 tablespoons chopped onion
2 tablespoons butter
Salt and pepper to taste
Hot milk or cream
Parsley and paprika for garnish

Cook turnips, potatoes, and onion in boiling salted water until tender. Drain and dry. Mash quickly together with butter and seasoning; add hot milk or cream a little at a time until light and fluffy. Garnish with parsley and paprika. Serves 4 to 6.

Submitted by Mrs. Virginia Kraegenbrink, Menomonee Falls. Rutabaga may be substituted for the turnips.

ŠKUBANKY (Czech)

6 medium potatoes, peeled and cut in half
  crosswise
1 tablespoon salt
2 cups flour
Fat for frying
Maple or dark corn syrup
Poppy seeds

Place potatoes in a 6-quart pot. Add salt and water to cover. When potatoes begin to boil, sift flour carefully and evenly over the entire top. Reduce heat to simmer. *Do not stir.* Make a few holes through the flour so water can bubble over the flour and the steam escape. When potatoes are tender, drain water and mash and mix in flour until no lumps remain. Form into rolls 3 or 4 inches long and 1 inch in diameter. Fry in deep fat until brown. Serve with syrup and a sprinkle of poppy seeds.

Submitted by Mrs. Mae A. Krueger, Kaukauna. The syrup and poppy seeds may be omitted, she added.

NEW YEAR'S EVE PANCAKES (German)

10 large potatoes, peeled and grated
2 carrots, grated
2 eggs
½ teaspoon salt
1 cup milk
2 teaspoons baking powder
Flour
About ½ pound bacon, cut in small squares
1 or 2 apples, sliced
Maple syrup

Combine potatoes, carrots, eggs, salt, milk, baking powder, and enough flour to thicken. Place bacon pieces in bottom of a 13-by-9-inch baking pan and brown slightly. Cover over with potato mixture. Place more bacon squares over the top and poke in apple slices. Bake at 350 degrees for about 1 hour. Cut in squares and serve with maple syrup.

Submitted by Mrs. Harvey Neuman, Appleton. This was a dish her grandmother always served on New Year's Eve.

KUGELIS (Lithuanian)

4 slices bacon, cut in narrow strips
½ cup butter or margarine
1 medium onion, chopped
10 large potatoes, peeled and grated
¼ cup hot milk
2 eggs, beaten
2 teaspoons salt
½ teaspoon pepper
Sour cream

Fry bacon until crisp; remove from pan and drain. To pan, add butter and melt. Add half the chopped onion and saute until translucent. Return bacon to pan and pour over potatoes. Add hot milk and mix well. Mix in eggs, salt, pepper, and remaining onions. Pour into a greased baking dish and bake at 400 degrees for 15 minutes; reduce heat to 350 and continue baking for 45 minutes. Cut in squares and serve with sour cream.

Submitted by Stefanija Pelanis, Kenosha.

POTATO PUFF

To 3 teacups of finely mashed potatoes, add 2 tablespoons of soft butter and beat to a white creamy mass. Beat the yolks of 2 eggs very light and stir thoroughly into the potato, and then add ½ or ⅔ of a cupful of warm milk. When smooth add the well beaten whites of 2 eggs, pile on a buttered hot dish, and lightly brown in the oven.

Mrs. Spencer W. Turner, Rice Lake, contributed this recipe which she copied from her grandmother's hand-written recipe book.

BAZOUKLA (Swiss)

5 or 6 medium potatoes, peeled and quartered
1½ cups flour
⅔ cup milk
1 egg, beaten
¼ teaspoon salt
2 or 3 tablespoons shortening
Grated cheddar cheese

Cover potatoes with water and bring to a rolling boil.

Meanwhile combine flour, milk, egg, and salt into a smooth batter. When potatoes boil, drip batter slowly over edge of pan into potatoes and water. Cover a few minutes and simmer until potatoes are cooked. Drain (save liquid for making bread).

Melt shortening slowly in a skillet and add potatoes and dumplings. When nicely browned, turn into a serving bowl and sprinkle with cheese.

Submitted by Ada (Mrs. Gust) Federman, Sauk City.

APFEL BREI (German)

3 pounds apples, peeled and cored
Sugar to taste
1 pound white potatoes, peeled
Salt to taste
Browned butter

Cook apples, covered, in almost no water until soft. Sweeten to taste. In another pot, cook potatoes until soft; drain. Season with salt and mash. Mix apples and potatoes. Heat well and serve in a large bowl with enough browned butter to cover top amply.

Submitted by Irene I. Luethge, Kiel, who noted that her mother had a special ironstone bowl for Apfel Brei, which was served with hamburger patties, pork sausage, or pork chops.

POTATO NOODLES (Swiss)

6 potatoes, peeled
½ teaspoon salt
2 cups flour
1 tablespoon lard
½ pint cream
Butter

Boil potatoes, drain, and mash. Add salt and flour and mix into a ball. Roll out on a well-floured board to ¼-inch thick. Cut into ½-inch strips, pile them up, and cut into little noodles. Melt lard in a baking pan and add noodles. Bake at 350 degrees until brown. Pour cream over all and dot with generous chunks of butter. Continue baking until butter is melted. Stir well and serve.

Submitted by Mrs. Edith H. Gotz, Pittsville.

FRIED TOMATOES (Bohemian)

8 to 10 large, firm, partially ripe tomatoes
Flour
Salt and pepper to taste
Butter and salad oil for frying

Peel and quarter tomatoes. Combine flour, salt, and pepper. Dip tomatoes in flour mixture, coating well. Heat equal amounts of butter and oil and slowly fry tomatoes until browned; turn and brown other side.

Submitted by Mrs. John Gehler, Ladysmith, who warned that the tomatoes may blend together in the frying. "The only addition to the meal of fried tomatoes," she added, "would be bread and butter and a glass of milk."

Wisconsin, with its many wooded areas, has always been a delight for mushroom fanciers. Numerous varieties are to be found by those who know exactly what they are doing, starting with morels in May.

The Potosi area in the southwestern corner of the state is one place that attracts hoards of people seeking the elusive fungi each spring. According to Pamela Pier of Potosi, some people believe that morels pop up overnight; actually they grow, like most everything else. Potosi's reputation for morels has inspired the many local artists to use them as subjects for paintings and drawings, Mrs. Pier reported; those who are unsuccessful after a day of searching in the cool, verdant woodlands can always buy a painting or drawing to remind them of what they have missed. Morels, like all mushrooms, can be dried or frozen, and can be served in many ways.

CREAMED MORELS

Morels
Milk
Butter
Cornstarch
Salt and pepper to taste

Soak morels overnight in salted water (to kill insects). Drain and slice in half lengthwise. Parboil in salted water until tender. Drain, reserving 2 tablespoons cooking water. Add milk (about ½ cup per person to be served), 2 tablespoons butter and cornstarch to thicken. Season with salt and pepper. Serve in a bowl like soup.

Mrs. Veva Thill, Potosi, contributed this recipe that her grandmother used in morel season when she ran a hotel in Potosi about sixty years ago. This dish makes a meal in itself when served with crackers.

Eastern Europeans were—and are—mushroom connoisseurs, and most had some version of this mushroom with barley recipe:

KUBA (Polish)

1 pound pearl barley (not instant)
2 eggs, slightly beaten
2 quarts mushrooms, coarsely chopped
Salt and pepper to taste
Butter

Cook barley according to package directions; drain. Add eggs, mushrooms, salt, and pepper. Mix well and dot with butter. Bake at 350 degrees for about 30 minutes.

Submitted by Mrs. Frank M. Suess, Luxemburg.

Salsify (also known as vegetable oyster or oyster plant) was a more popular kitchen-garden crop in times past than it is now.

SALSIFY PATTIES (German)

1 pint ground salsify
1 egg, beaten
Salt and pepper to taste
About 1½ tablespoons flour
Shortening

Combine salsify, egg, salt, and pepper. Add enough flour to bind. Melt shortening in a skillet. Form salsify mixture into patties, using about a tablespoonful for each and flattening slightly in the pan with the back of the spoon. Saute over low heat until golden brown on each side.

Submitted by Carlyne (Mrs. Otto A.) Klein, Burlington. To prepare salsify, she directed, wash roots thoroughly; place in a kettle with water to cover, and simmer until tender. Then remove skins and let cool thoroughly. Grind. If not used immediately, pack into freezer cartons and freeze.

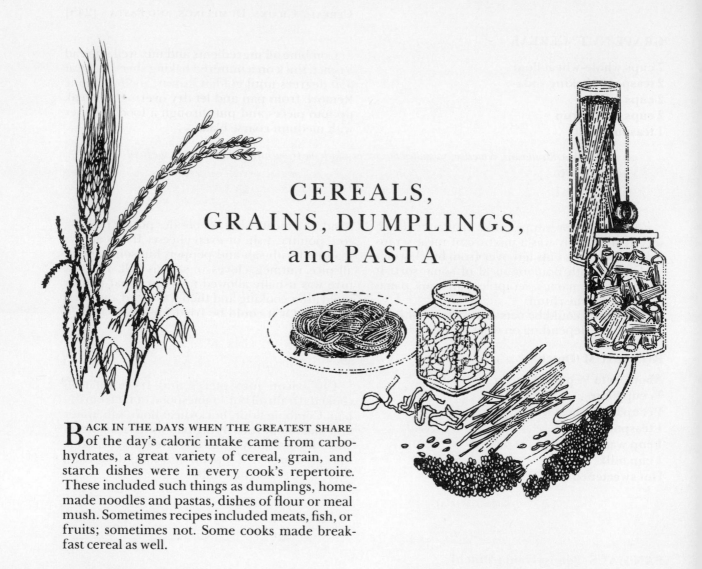

CEREALS,
GRAINS, DUMPLINGS,
and PASTA

BACK IN THE DAYS WHEN THE GREATEST SHARE of the day's caloric intake came from carbohydrates, a great variety of cereal, grain, and starch dishes were in every cook's repertoire. These included such things as dumplings, homemade noodles and pastas, dishes of flour or meal mush. Sometimes recipes included meats, fish, or fruits; sometimes not. Some cooks made breakfast cereal as well.

HOMEMADE CEREAL

1 cup leftover cornbread
1 tablespoon shortening
1 tablespoon sugar
¼ teaspoon cinnamon
Milk

Crumble leftover cornbread into small crumbs. Place skillet over medium heat for 1 minute; add shortening and melt completely. Add bread and stir until evenly brown. Combine sugar and cinnamon in a brown paper bag; add bread crumbs; shake well to season evenly. Serve in a bowl with milk. Makes one serving.

Submitted by Carolyn C. Brown, Milwaukee, who reported that there was always leftover cornbread from supper to make this delicious cereal.

"GRAPE-NUT" CEREAL

7 cups whole-wheat flour
2 teaspoons baking soda
2 cups milk
2 cups corn syrup
1 teaspoon salt

Combine all ingredients and mix well. Spread ¼-inch thick on a buttered baking sheet. Bake at 350 degrees until golden brown, about ½ hour. Remove from pan and let dry overnight. Break up into pieces and put through a food chopper with medium-coarse blade.

Mrs. Ann Strathman, Waterloo, submitted this recipe which she frequently made in the days she lived on a farm.

A breakfast or supper dish that used to be served frequently was a mixture of meat scraps (most often pork cuts left over from butchering) cooked up with flour or meal of some sort. It went by many names: scrapple, pan haus, panas, bolleka brei, rhe rhum.

The starch could be oats or cornmeal or buckwheat flour, depending on what was raised or on hand; the meat could be, besides pork scraps, bacon, poultry, fish, or even cheese. It was always seasoned with salt and pepper, but some added allspice, nutmeg, cloves, or sage as well. The mixture was usually allowed to set in a loaf pan or mold after cooking and then was sliced and fried to serve. Or it could be fried up like scrambled eggs.

RHE RHUM (Dutch)

About ¼ to ½ pound bacon
¾ cup flour
¾ cup buckwheat flour
1 teaspoon salt
1 cup water
1 cup milk
Hot sweetened milk

Cut bacon into pieces and fry until well cooked. Drain all but 1 tablespoon of fat from the pan. Combine flour, buckwheat flour, salt, water, and milk. Pour into frying pan with bacon pieces and stir constantly while mixture thickens. Cook until well browned. Spoon into soup dishes and serve with sweetened milk.

Submitted by Mrs. Eleanor Van Putten Oelstrom, Waukesha.

PAN HAUS (Pennsylvania-Dutch)

Hog's head
Salt
Pepper
Sage
Onion, chopped
Cornmeal

Cook hog's head in water to cover until meat falls from the bones. Remove head and boil cooking water rapidly until reduced by half. Season broth with salt, pepper, sage, and onion to taste. Pick cooked meat apart, discarding skin, fat, eyes, and bone. Chop meat and return to broth. Bring to a rapid boil and stir in enough cornmeal to form a thick pudding; simmer until cornmeal is cooked. Pour into a wide-mouthed crock and place in a cool spot until set.

Slice thickly and fry in a hot skillet. Serve with watermelon jam, sorghum molasses, or pan drippings and sugar.

Submitted by Loretta Holmes, Beloit.

KNIPP (German)

4 pounds scrap meat from pig when
butchering, for example cheeks, jowls, and
neck (see italicized note, below)
1 tablespoon salt
3 medium onions, cut up
1¼ cups steel cut oats
1 teaspoon pepper
2 teaspoons allspice
2 teaspoons nutmeg
½ to 1 teaspoon cloves

In a kettle combine meat, salt, and onions; add water to cover. Simmer, covered, until meat is tender, about 2 or 2½ hours. Remove meat from broth.

To the broth add oats and cook until done. Meanwhile, chop or pick apart meat. Add meat to oats with pepper, allspice, nutmeg, and cloves. Simmer for about 30 minutes to blend flavors. If mixture is extremely stiff, add water or broth; consistency should be like cooked oatmeal.

Pour into pans or molds and store in a very cold place. May be frozen.

To serve, put desired amount in a small amount of fat in an iron skillet, stirring occasionally until brown.

Submitted by Delta (Mrs. Herbert) Woinowsky, Madison, who still uses her grandmother's recipe but in a modern version that her mother developed since she did not live on a farm. This calls for substituting for the pork scraps 3 pounds of pork shoulder roast and 1 or 1½ pounds of beef chuck roast. All other ingredients and method remain the same. Knipp, incidentally, means "snips" in German.

CORN PONE PUDDING

1 egg, beaten
1½ cups sour milk
1 teaspoon baking soda
2 tablespoons melted butter
1 cup flour
2 cups cornmeal
½ cup sugar
Sauce (see below)

Combine egg, sour milk, baking soda, and melted butter and mix well. Combine flour, cornmeal, and sugar and mix into egg-milk mixture. Pour into a steamer or into a pan set in hot water and steam for 40 minutes. Serve warm with sauce.

Sauce:

1 cup water
⅓ cup vinegar
1 tablespoon butter
½ cup sugar
2 tablespoons flour
2 teaspoons lemon extract

Combine all ingredients and bring to a boil. Simmer 5 minutes.

Submitted by Coral (Mrs. John) Brahm, West Allis.

POLENTA (Italian)

1½ cups cornmeal
1 teaspoon salt
½ cup cold water
4 cups hot water

Using a heavy kettle, mix cornmeal, salt, and cold water. Slowly add 2 cups of hot water, stirring constantly. Continue cooking on medium heat for 20 minutes while adding remaining boiling water. Complete cooking for 10 minutes on high heat until polenta leaves the side of the kettle and is very firm. Shake the kettle and turn polenta out onto a wooden plate or board.

Serve with a tomato sauce or wine sauce as an accompaniment to chicken, veal, pork, or beef.

Submitted by Mrs. Julia M. Vanderschaegen, Iron Belt, who remembered it was her job as a child to clean the polenta-caked kettle. "How I hated it," she noted, "but how I enjoyed mother's polenta!"

Many housewives, particularly those of Middle and Eastern European backgrounds, made noodles as routinely as they made bread. As Helen F. Andruskevicz of Green Bay remembered the event: "When my mother [who was born in Czechoslovakia] got out the 'oversized' bread board from the pantry, she was going to make noodles for chicken soup. She sifted 4 cups of flour on the board and made a well in the middle so that she could break 5 eggs into it. A little salt was added and it was kneaded into a smooth dough. She divided this dough into 4 pieces and let them stand for about 10 minutes before rolling out into a rather thin sheet. These sheets were hung to dry over clean dish towels placed on the backs of the kitchen chairs. When these leathery-looking sheets were dried to just the right leather stage, they were cut into long strips. Then the strips were cut into 'noodle size.' (Today we find that these noodles freeze very well.)"

Generally each cup of flour and each egg used in the dough makes a half pound of dry noodles.

GOOD FRIDAY NOODLES (French)

2 quarts stewed tomatoes
¼ cup sugar
¼ teaspoon salt
½ teaspoon cinnamon
Pepper to taste
⅛ teaspoon cayenne pepper (optional)
Homemade noodles
½ pound Swiss cheese, grated

Combine tomatoes, sugar, salt, cinnamon, pepper, and cayenne. Simmer while making the noodles (about 1 or 1½ hours).

Make a 4-egg batch of noodles. Cook until almost tender; drain and rinse in cold running water.

Butter several casserole dishes. Layer noodles, tomato sauce, and Swiss cheese. Bake at 350 degrees 1 hour.

Submitted by Mrs. L. P. Baerwolf, Madison, who added that any leftovers of this traditional Good Friday dish are delicious fried in butter on Easter morning for breakfast.

NOODLES WITH POPPY SEED (Polish)

1 cup poppy seeds
1 to 1½ pounds homemade noodles
3½ tablespoons butter, melted
Honey to taste

Cover poppy seeds with boiling water; cover and let stand until seeds can be crushed between the fingers. Drain well in a fine sieve. Grind through a food grinder 3 times.

Make noodles and cook until done. Drain and place in a bowl. Mix with poppy seeds and butter and drizzle with honey to taste.

Submitted by Mrs. Waclaw Soroka, Stevens Point. This is often served as a Christmas Eve dessert. With just a little honey, others use it as a main dish served with salad and a bit of sliced meat or cold cuts.

Noodle dough is the casing used for meat-stuffed dumplings like ravioli, won ton, and kreplach.

KREPLACH (Jewish)

1 egg
¼ teaspoon salt
1½ cups flour
Water
1 pound cooked (or leftover) chuck roast, ground
Small piece of cooked chicken or a chicken liver (if available)
1 small onion, chopped and sauteed in chicken fat
1 hard-boiled egg
Salt, pepper, and garlic salt to taste

Combine egg, salt, and flour and add enough water to make a dough that can be handled. Knead; let stand 30 minutes. Roll out on a floured board to ¼-inch thickness. Cut in 2-inch squares.

In a food grinder, grind together chuck roast, chicken or liver, sauteed onion, egg, and seasonings. Mix into a paste. Place a rounded teaspoon of meat mixture on a square of noodle dough; fold into a triangle, pressing edges together well. Triangles must be well sealed. Drop triangles into just boiling salted water (water should not be boiling too hard or kreplach will disintegrate). When kreplach rise to top, increase heat and cook 15 minutes. Lift out, one at a time, with a slotted spoon into a collander. Drain well.

Kreplach may be served in chicken soup, covered with gravy, or fried crisp in fat. Makes 12 to 16 kreplach.

Mrs. Herman Tuchman, Milwaukee, submitted this family recipe. Kreplach are traditionally included in the meal preceeding the fast day of Yom Kippur, the day of atonement.

A thin batter made with eggs and flour and then cooked in boiling liquid was another way to fill out a meal. Called spatzen, spaetzle, egg dumplings, knofli, etc., they could be cooked and eaten in soup, or as a side dish with meat, or embellished with cheese, or with sugar and vanilla as a pudding for dessert. The batter could be dropped from a spoon or pushed through a colander.

KNOFLI (German)

2 eggs
¼ cup milk
1 cup flour
1 teaspoon salt
Grated cheese

Beat eggs slightly and add milk. Stir in flour and salt. Place a colander over a kettle of boiling

water. Place ⅓ the mixture into colander and force through with a potato masher. As soon as dumplings rise to top, remove with a skimmer into a hot vegetable dish. Sprinkle with salt and grated cheese. Repeat until all batter is used up. Place in a 300 degree oven for 5 minutes.

Submitted by Mrs. Margaret Weber, St. Nazianz.

Dumplings appeared in many guises. They could be made of flour, raw or cooked potatoes, farina, bread, cracker crumbs, matzo meal, marrow, meat, or blood. Sometimes dumplings were stuffed—with fruit, or cheese, bacon, or meat mixtures. And they could be eaten from soup to dessert. Here is a sampling of the many dumpling recipes that were submitted.

CLAYS (Swiss)

2 cups sifted flour
3 teaspoons baking powder
1 teaspoon salt
1 teaspoon sugar
2 eggs, beaten
1 cup milk
Onions sauteed in butter or bread crumbs
   sauteed in butter

Sift together flour, baking powder, salt, and sugar. Combine eggs and milk and add to dry ingredients. Mix just until moistened. Form into balls and place in a kettle of boiling salted water. Simmer, covered, for 20 minutes. Do not lift the lid during cooking. Drain and place in a covered dish.

Top with onions and serve with gravy, or top with bread crumbs and serve with applesauce.

Submitted by Mrs. Edith H. Gotz, Pittsville.

BREAD DUMPLINGS

1 loaf white bread (day old)
1 tablespoon chopped onion
1 tablespoon chopped parsley
½ cup butter
1½ cups milk
2 eggs, beaten
1 tablespoon salt
About 1 cup flour

Dice bread. Saute onion and parsley in butter; add bread and fry until crisp. Place in a bowl. Mix milk, eggs, and salt and pour over the bread. Blend in enough flour to make a firm dough. Form into dumplings and simmer gently in salted water for 10 minutes.

Submitted by Mrs. Joe Kucera, Cudahy.

GRANDMOTHER OSTHOFF'S SOUP DUMPLINGS

1 cup milk
2 tablespoons butter
½ to ¾ cup flour
½ teaspoon salt
1 egg, beaten
¼ cup chopped parsley
¼ teaspoon nutmeg or mace, or to taste

Scald milk; add butter. Bring to a boil and sift in flour and salt. Stir constantly over heat until flour is cooked and forms a stiff, smooth dough. Cool. Add egg, parsley, and nutmeg or mace.

Bring beef broth or chicken soup to a simmer. Dip a teaspoon into soup then form a dumpling by rolling spoonful of dough along edge of bowl. Drop dumpling into broth. Wet spoon again for next dumpling and repeat until all dough is used. Keep soup at a simmer; do not let it boil. Finished dumplings will rise to top so use a pot large enough to keep dumplings from crowding, but deep enough to cook covered in soup.

These may be made in salted water to serve with a meat course.

Florence (Mrs. Charles) Weckerle, Milwaukee, submitted this recipe which her grandmother served at the Osthoff Hotel at Elkhart Lake, a resort known for good food. Mrs. Weckerle's grandparents ran Schlitz Park in Milwaukee before starting the hotel.

KARTOFFEL KLOSS (German)

3 cups cold mashed potatoes, preferably
  cooked the day before
1¾ to 2 cups flour
Salt to taste
Bread cubes browned in fat

Combine potatoes with enough flour to make a firm dough. Salt to taste. Form into balls and insert 3 or 4 bread cubes into each. Drop into gently boiling water and cook for 30 minutes. Remove with slotted spoon.

Makes about 8 dumplings. Serve with poultry or roast pork. Leftover dumplings may be sliced and browned in fat.

Submitted by Mrs. Francis Palma, Greenfield.

Other serving suggestions for mashed potato dumplings included:

Cut into pieces and fry until golden brown with sauerkraut and season with salt and pepper. Or eat unfried and topped with a milk gravy along with sauerkraut. *Submitted by Marian Sheko, Loyal.*

Add egg to dough mixture and browned chopped onions to bread crumbs. After dumplings are cooked, they may be deep-fried. Or pour sour cream over boiled dumplings and top with additional filling mixture. Serve with roast beef. *Submitted by Mrs. Marcia Smith Kolar, Westminster, California.*

RAW POTATO DUMPLINGS (German)

6 large baking potatoes
¾ cup milk
¼ cup flour
8 slices white bread
2 to 3 tablespoons butter
2 eggs, beaten
2 teaspoons salt
¼ teaspoon freshly ground nutmeg

Peel potatoes and soak in cold water 1 hour.

Scald milk and mix with flour to form a paste. Cut bread into cubes and saute in butter. Grate potatoes, place in a cloth, and squeeze dry, reserving liquid. Let potato liquid stand 15 minutes until all starch settles. Slowly pour liquid off, reserving starch. Add potatoes to starch; add flour paste and mix well. Mix in eggs, bread cubes, salt, and nutmeg. Shape into tennis-ball-sized dumplings. Drop into boiling salted water and cook 20 minutes. Serve immediately with sauerbraten gravy.

Leftover dumplings may be served the next day, sliced and warmed in a pan with gravy.

Submitted by Mrs. Robert A. Burmeister, East Troy.

Another suggestion for serving Raw Potato Dumplings:

Serve hot with a meat gravy that has been thickened with grated horseradish instead of with flour. *Submitted by Mrs. Theodore Toepel, Howards Grove.*

WICKEL KLOSSIG (German)

36 soda crackers
4 tablespoons butter
5 cups mashed potatoes, salted to taste and
   cooled
4 eggs, beaten
3 cups flour
Melted butter

Roll out soda crackers into very fine crumbs. Brown in a heavy frying pan; watch closely, as they burn easily. Add butter and mix well. Set aside.

Add eggs and flour to cooled potatoes. Mix and knead thoroughly. (If dough is sticky, add more flour.) Roll out on a well-floured board to about ¼-inch thickness. Cut into 5-inch squares. Spread each square with 1 teaspoon melted butter and about 1 tablespoon cracker crumbs; roll as for jelly roll, pressing firmly to seal. Drop into gently boiling water 7 to 10 minutes. Serve with melted butter or rich gravy.

Submitted by Mrs. Warren H. Stevens, Kenosha. In her family, these are called "wiggle clasers," which is how her Yankee husband pronounced the German name when he first heard it.

MATZO BALLS (Jewish)

2 eggs
½ cup matzo meal
2 tablespoons chicken fat
About 1 teaspoon salt

Beat eggs thoroughly. Add matzo meal, fat, and salt to taste. Mix and refrigerate several hours. Mixture will be solid.

Shape into balls and drop into water at a medium-hard boil. Cover and cook for 20 to 25 minutes. Makes 8 large, if measured out with a tablespoon, or 16 small, if measured out with a teaspoon.
Serve in chicken soup.

Submitted by Mrs. Herman Tuchman, Milwaukee.

VERIKÄKID (Estonian)

2 pounds slab bacon, cut into cubes
1 onion, diced
2 cups pork or beef blood
1 cup beef broth
1 tablespoon marjoram leaves
1 teaspoon salt
¼ teaspoon pepper
2 pounds rye flour
Butter, margarine, or bacon fat for frying
Sour cream or sour cream sauce

Lightly brown bacon cubes with diced onion. Put blood through a sieve and add to broth along with bacon, onion, marjoram, salt, and pepper. Gradually add flour until dough is stiff and can be worked with the hands. Form into ovals about size of average potato. Drop into 4 quarts boiling salted water and cook for 15 to 20 minutes. Cool in a colander. Cut in half lengthwise and fry on both sides in butter, margarine, or bacon fat. Serve with sour cream or sour cream sauce.

Submitted by Mrs. Koidula Maeste, Milwaukee, on behalf of The Estonian House.

MARK KLOSSCHEN (German)

Marrow from 2 soup bones
2 cups dry bread, grated
1 medium onion, grated
1 large egg, beaten
½ teaspoon salt
⅛ teaspoon nutmeg
Soup

Render marrow in a small pan; strain. Keep marrow in liquid form.

Combine bread, onion, egg, salt, and nutmeg. Mix well. Add melted marrow and enough soup broth to moisten. Form into a walnut-sized ball and drop into soup and cook. If ball is too firm, add a bit more marrow to the mixture; if it is too soft and falls apart, add more bread crumbs. Form remaining mixture into balls and cook until they rise to the surface.

These are especially for vegetable soup but can be used for meat-based soups.

Submitted by Maya Presber Custer, Marshfield.

LEBER KNOEDEL (Austrian)

Rich beef broth
1 pound beef liver
1 large onion
1 stalk celery
2 or 3 eggs
1 teaspoon poultry seasoning
About 1 teaspoon salt
Dash pepper
2 to 3 cups dry bread crumbs
About ½ cup flour

Cook liver slightly in a little of the beef broth; cut in small pieces and grind in food chopper or in a blender. Grind onion and celery. Combine liver, onion, celery, eggs, poultry seasoning, salt, and pepper. Pour over bread crumbs in a large mixing bowl. Add enough flour to form a soft dough. Moisten hands and roll into balls a little larger than walnuts. Put on moistened waxed paper until all are rolled. Drop into boiling beef broth 6 or 8 at a time and boil until dumplings come to the top. Remove with a slotted spoon to a large bowl.

Submitted by Viola (Mrs. Felix) Schuster, Menomonee Falls.

ZWETCHEN KNOEDEL (Austrian)

Mashed potato dumpling dough
24 ripe Italian plums
¼ pound butter
About 2 cups bread crumbs
1 cup brown sugar

With moistened hands, form dough around each plum about ¼ to ⅓-inch thick. Drop 6 dumplings at a time into boiling salted water. Remove with a slotted spoon when they rise to the surface. Drain.

Melt butter in frying pan and add crumbs and sugar. Heat until crumbs start to brown. Place some of the crumb mixture into a large bowl; as each batch of dumplings is cooked, place in bowl and roll in crumbs. Repeat.

Submitted by Viola (Mrs. Felix) Schuster, Menomonee Falls, who added that these plum dumplings go very well with baked ham or pork sausages.

Flour, meal, and raw and cooked potato dumplings can also be stuffed with various meat or vegetable mixtures:

USZKA (Polish)

½ pound cooked meat (can use meat from soup stock)
1 onion, chopped
2 tablespoons butter
Salt and pepper to taste
Soup stock
Flour dumpling dough

Grind meat. Saute onion in butter until cooked; add meat, season well, and saute together. Moisten as needed with soup stock.

Roll out dumpling on well-floured board until it is very thin. Cut in 2-inch squares. Place 1 teaspoon of meat mixture in center and bring up corners and pinch together, to make "ears." Drop into boiling water and cook about 15 minutes or until dumplings float to top.

Finely chopped mushrooms may be substituted for the meat.

Submitted by Mrs. Catherine Ellingboe, Milwaukee. Uszka means "ears" in Polish.

LENIWE PIEROGI (Polish)

1 pound dry cottage cheese
3 tablespoons melted butter
3 eggs, separated
Salt to taste
1 cup flour
Browned butter

Grind cheese, add melted butter, egg yolks, and salt to taste. Mix well. Beat egg whites and add to mixture together with flour; mix well until smooth. On a floured board, form into a ½-inch thick roll and cut diagonally into small pieces. Drop into boiling water; remove with a strainer as soon as they rise to the surface. To serve, place on a plate and pour slightly browned butter over dumplings.

Submitted by Maria Kulawik, Stevens Point.

PIEROGI (Polish)

4 cups flour
1 teaspoon salt
4 eggs
1 cup cold water
Filling (see below)

Combine flour and salt in a large bowl. Cut in eggs with pastry blender, one at a time. Add water, ¼ cup at a time. Blend well. Knead on a floured board until dough is elastic. Let rest under a bowl for 30 minutes.

Divide into 3 or 4 portions and roll out as needed on a floured board as for pie crust. Cut 3-inch circles (using a glass with rim dipped in

flour) and place 1 tablespoon (or more) of filling on one side. Fold over to form half-circle; moisten edges with water and seal well.

Drop pierogi, a few at a time, into large kettle of salted boiling water; when they rise to the surface, remove with slotted spoon and drain well on a cake rack set over a large roasting pan; remove to buttered waxed paper; do not stack.

To serve, fry until crisp in half shortening, and half butter. Or saute onions, in butter, then add pierogi and cover.

Submitted by Eleanor (Mrs. Anthony) Yankowski, Neenah

Cabbage Filling:

1 large cabbage
1 medium onion, chopped
Butter
Salt and pepper to taste

Quarter cabbage and remove core. Boil until tender and drain well; chop as for cole slaw. Press out as much liquid as possible. Saute onion in butter until well browned. Add cabbage and stir and fry until almost dry. Season to taste.

Potato and Cream Cheese Filling:

1 8-ounce package cream cheese
3 potatoes, peeled and boiled
2 onions, chopped fine
¼ pound butter

Soften cream cheese. Mash cheese and potatoes together. Saute onions in butter and add to potatoes while hot.

Submitted by Eleanor (Mrs. Anthony) Yankowski, Neenah.

Prune Filling:

1 cup prunes
1 teaspoon lemon juice
1 teaspoon sugar
Bread crumbs browned in butter

Soak prunes overnight. Cook in water with lemon juice and sugar. Cool and drain. Remove pits. Fill pierogi with a prune and serve after boiling topped with bread crumbs.

Submitted by Mrs. Rosalie Franckowiak, Cudahy.

Cottage Cheese Filling:

2 egg yolks
1 tablespoon butter
1 pound cottage cheese, mashed
1 tablespoon sugar
¼ cup raisins

Cream yolks and butter together. Combine with cheese and salt and mix thoroughly. Add sugar and raisins. Serve with drawn butter after boiling.

Fruit Filling:

Fill dough pockets with a spoonful of blackberries or blueberries or 3 or 4 pitted cherries. Serve after boiling and draining with sour cream or melted butter and sugar.

Submitted by Mrs. Eugene Bukowski, Wisconsin Rapids.

Blueberry Filling:

5 cups blueberries
2 tablespoons bread crumbs
3 tablespoons butter, browned
Confectioners' sugar
Sour cream

Rinse and drain blueberries. Mix with bread crumbs. Fill pierogi with 1 tablespoon mixture. After boiling, rinse with warm water. Place on a plate and top with browned butter. Cover and heat over boiling water. Serve with confectioners' sugar and sour cream.

Raspberries or blackberries may be substituted for blueberries.

May be served cold.

Submitted by Mrs. Waclaw Soroka, Stevens Point.

CHIPPEWA WILD RICE

1 cup wild rice, washed in cold water
2½ cups water
1½ teaspoons salt
4 slices bacon, cut into strips
6 eggs
¼ teaspoon pepper
2 tablespoons minced chives
Butter or margarine

Place wild rice, water, and 1 teaspoon salt in a saucepan and bring slowly to a boil. Reduce heat and simmer, uncovered, until all water is absorbed.

Fry bacon in a large, heavy skillet until cooked; drain bacon on absorbent paper. Pour off and reserve drippings.

Beat eggs with remaining salt and pepper until light. Pour into the skillet in which bacon was fried and brown eggs slightly. Turn, pancake-style, and brown other side. Cut into julienne strips.

Lightly toss bacon, egg strips, chives, and bacon drippings, to which enough melted butter or margarine to make ½ cup has been added, with cooked rice. Serve hot. Makes four servings.

From Native & Latin American Cooking *by Rosa Diaz de Culver, published by Winnebago United Church of Christ, 1974, Black River Falls.*

RICE PILAF (Armenian)

4 tablespoons butter
½ cup fine egg noodles, uncooked
1 cup long grain rice
2 cups boiling chicken broth
Salt to taste

Melt butter in a pan; add noodles and saute until slightly browned, stirring constantly. Wash and drain the rice well, then add to noodles and saute a few minutes, stirring constantly. Add boiling broth and salt; cover and simmer for 20 minutes or until water is absorbed and rice is cooked. Stir with a fork and remove from stove. Let set 15 or 20 minutes. Stir once more with a fork. Keep warm and serve hot.

From the files of the International Institute of Milwaukee County.

SAUCES and SPREADS

A TASTY SAUCE HAS COME, IN RECENT YEARS, TO be equated with gourmet cooking. But sauces have always been a part of everyday home cooking, a means of attaining variety with limited choices of meats or vegetables.

BLUE CHEESE SAUCE

8 ounces cream cheese
¾ cup evaporated milk
½ teaspoon salt
2 ounces blue cheese

Bring cream cheese to room temperature. Cream in a saucepan until soft and smooth. Gradually beat in evaporated milk until blended. Add salt and mix. Crumble in blue cheese. Place over very low heat until hot and bubbly, about 5 minutes, stirring frequently.

Serve over asparagus, broccoli, green beans, or baked potato.

Submitted by Mathilda Jadin, Green Bay.

SOS CHRZANOWY (Polish)

½ tablespoon flour
½ tablespoon butter, melted
2 tablespoons grated horseradish
Soup broth
1 pint sour cream
Salt and sugar to taste
3 or 4 drops lemon juice
2 egg yolks, well-beaten (optional)

Combine flour and butter and saute briefly. Add horseradish and saute until well blended. Add broth to moisten well; stir in sour cream, salt, sugar, and lemon juice. Heat just to boiling. If a rich sauce is desired, mix several tablespoons of hot mixture into egg yolks, then stir into sauce.

Serve with boiled beef or fish.

Submitted by Mrs. Catherine Ellingboe, Milwaukee.

COLD HORSERADISH SAUCE (Czech)

1 horseradish root
1 apple
Sugar, salt, and vinegar to taste

Grate horseradish and apple. Combine and season with sugar, salt, and vinegar. Serve with boiled beef.

Submitted by Blanche Mendl, Deerbrook.

BOHEMIAN SAUCE

1 tablespoon butter, melted
1 tablespoon flour
1 teaspoon sugar
1 tablespoon prepared mustard *or*
   1 tablespoon vinegar mixed with
   1 teaspoon dry mustard
Salt and nutmeg to taste
Boiling water

Combine butter, flour, sugar, mustard, salt, and nutmeg. Stir in boiling water until sauce is desired consistency.

Serve with beef heart or tongue or on other meats as desired.

Submitted by Mrs. Ronald Daggett, Madison.

ONION SAUCE (Yugoslavian)

Onions
Butter
Flour
Stock or water
Salt and pepper to taste

Dice onions and saute in butter until tender. Add several tablespoons flour and saute until mixture is a golden brown. Add stock and simmer 20 minutes. Season with salt and pepper. Sauce should be thick.

Serve warm with meat, or as a vegetable.

WINE SAUCE (Yugoslavian)

Bread crumbs
Fat
Flour
Homemade sour red wine
Water
Sugar

Brown crumbs in fat very slowly. Add a little flour and continue sauteeing until mixture is golden brown, stirring constantly. Add wine diluted with a little water and sugar to sweeten. Simmer slowly until like a thick applesauce. Very good with poultry or smoked meats.

Mrs. Anne Shoberg, Milwaukee, contributed both these sauces that she learned to make by watching her mother, who had no written recipes. For the wine sauce, "I would guess the proportions to be 1 cup bread crumbs, 3 tablespoons flour, 3 to 4 tablespoons fat, 3 cups wine (possibly more), water, and sugar to taste."

GRAVY COLORING (Swedish)

About 2 tablespoons sugar
Water

Put 2 or more tablespoons sugar in a frying pan and brown until it smokes. Add water *gradually* until mixture is thin.

Add to gravy for coloring and flavor. In larger amounts, may be added to cold packed beef or venison to give flavor and color.

Submitted by Dagmar P. Noel, Waukesha, who noted that "before gravy coloring was on the market, my mother made her own."

TOMATO SAUCE (Italian)

1 medium onion, finely chopped
1 clove garlic, crushed
2 tablespoons butter
1 1-pound 12-ounce can tomatoes
1 6-ounce can tomato paste
½ cup water or stock
½ teaspoon salt
Pepper to taste
1 teaspoon sugar
½ teaspoon crushed rosemary
½ teaspoon crushed sweet basil

Saute onion and garlic in butter until limp. Add tomatoes, tomato paste, water, salt, pepper, sugar, rosemary, and basil. Simmer 1 hour.

Pour over fried chicken and bake at 350 degrees for 30 minutes.

Submitted by Mrs. Julia Vanderschaegen, Iron Belt.

Some of the lard obtained at butchering time was used to make a spread.

SPREAD FOR BREAD (German)

Pork lard
4 large or 6 medium apples
1 cup water
1 bay leaf, crumbled
3 whole allspice
3 tablespoons sugar
½ teaspoon salt
1 tablespoon chopped onion (optional)

Fry out lard, but not too dry. Measure out 4 cups including the cracklings.

Peel and cut up apples. Combine with water, bay leaf, allspice, sugar, salt, and onion if desired. Simmer until apples are cooked. Stir in rendered lard and cracklings and continue cooking, stirring until very thick. Cool and spread on bread.

Submitted by Mrs. Darwin Kamke, Seymour.

SALADS and SALAD DRESSINGS

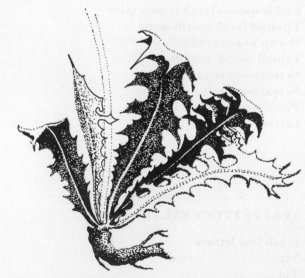

THE URGE FOR CRISP GREENS COMES FROM MAN'S primal past. And in a climate like Wisconsin's, the appearance of edible leaves and stalks heralded the arrival of spring and the promise of fresh foods after the preserves and canned ingredients of the long, hard winter.

Numerous salad fixings still grow wild, and many more are cultivated in home garden plots. These provide variety from frequently pallid and limp store-bought greens that are available year round. Dandelions, water cress, and mushrooms are among the wild edibles that can be tossed into a salad bowl.

DANDELION GREENS SALAD

Pick dandelion greens that are white or light-colored towards the root section; all green ones may also be used, if they are not too old and tough. Wash greens and discard all but the leaves. If small, leave whole or tear into 2-inch lengths. Place in a salad bowl and season with salt. Add a dressing of vinegar and oil diluted to taste with water. Toss well. Garnish with hard-boiled egg slices.

Submitted by Mrs. Anne Shoberg, Milwaukee, who added that "we always knew spring had come when mother served a salad of dandelion greens and hard-boiled eggs for lunch."

WATER CRESS SALAD

Water cress
3 slices bacon
3 tablespoons sugar
½ cup water
½ cup vinegar

Wash water cress and shake dry. Discard tough stem portion. Place in a bowl.

Chop and fry bacon until crisp. Add sugar, water, and vinegar and bring to a boil. Pour over the water cress.

Submitted by Mrs. Charles Spitzbarth, Fennimore. This is the way her mother prepared the water cress the family gathered at their spring. "When we were kids," Mrs. Spitzbarth wrote, "spring was always signaled when Father would say, 'Let's go after water cress.' He would get two milk pails and with us kids following would take off for the spring. The water would be so clear and cold, and the water cress so green! It seemed to be the only thing green at the time. Coming back the trip always seemed longer because the pails were heavy and we would have to stop and rest. I still can't resist the urge of fresh water cress in the spring, and my children delight in the walk to the spring with the warm sun of spring on our backs."

SIENISLAATTI (Finnish)

2 cups water
2 tablespoons fresh lemon juice
1 pound fresh mushrooms
½ cup heavy cream
1 small onion, grated
¼ teaspoon sugar
¾ teaspoon salt
Pinch white pepper
Lettuce

Place water and lemon juice in an enamel or stainless steel sauce pan; bring to a boil.

Meantime wash mushrooms and cut into tiny slices. Add mushrooms to sauce pan, cover, and simmer 3 to 4 minutes. Drain in a colander, then gently pat dry with absorbent paper.

In a 2-quart bowl, combine cream, onion, sugar, salt, and pepper. Add mushrooms and toss lightly until coated. Serve on lettuce leaves. Serves 8.

Submitted by Mrs. Irving W. Zirbel, Elm Grove.

LEAF LETTUCE SALAD

Fresh leaf lettuce
3 tablespoons vinegar
3 tablespoons sugar
Salt and pepper to taste
About ½ cup sweet or sour cream

Wash lettuce 3 or 4 times, leaf by leaf, to remove all sand and dirt. Drain well.

In a salad bowl, mix vinegar, sugar, salt, and pepper. Add cream and stir. Just before serving, roll lettuce in the dressing so every leaf is covered.

Variation: Use a hot bacon dressing.

Submitted by Edith (Mrs. Francis) McConnell, Wisconsin Rapids, who reported that she had this salad daily while growing up as long as the lettuce in the garden was tender.

CELERY ROOT SALAD (German)

3 or 4 medium celery roots (celeriac)
1 to 2 cups pared, quartered, and sliced firm
  apples
1 teaspoon salt
2 slices onion
½ to ¾ cup blanched, sliced almonds
Dressing (see below)

Wash, pare, and quarter celery roots. Simmer in water until tender. Cool and slice.

In a frying pan in a little water, simmer sliced apples, salt, and onion until cooked but still firm. Drain apples; discard onion. Cool.

Combine celery root, apples, and almonds. Toss with dressing. When serving, garnish top with additional almonds. This salad is excellent prepared a day or two ahead and refrigerated.

Dressing:

2 eggs, beaten well
½ cup vinegar (dilute with water if strong)
4 teaspoons sugar
1 teaspoon salt
1 teaspoon dry mustard
1 scant cup cream

Beat eggs in a round-bottomed stainless steel bowl. In a saucepan, bring vinegar, sugar, salt, and mustard to a boil. Slowly pour mixture into eggs, beating constantly with a rotary beater. On the stove over very low heat, continue beating until mixture is fluffy. Just before using, add cream.

Submitted by Carlyne M. (Mrs. Otto A.) Klein, Burlington, who suggests saving the cooking liquid from the celery root, cooling, and freezing in ice-cube trays to use as seasoning in stews and soups.

Another version of Celery Root Salad calls for potatoes instead of apples.

CELERY ROOT SALAD II (German)

3 celery roots (celeriac)
2 large potatoes
1 large onion
5 large eggs, hard-boiled and cooled
4 stalks celery, sliced
4 stems parsley, chopped
½ cup vinegar
1 teaspoon dry mustard
½ teaspoon pepper
1 teaspoon salt
1 pint cream

Wash and pare celery root. Simmer until cooked but firm. Cook potatoes; pare. Chill celery root and potatoes overnight.

Finely chop celery root, potatoes, and onions.

Remove yolks of 4 of the eggs; chop whites and combine with celery root, potatoes, onion, celery slices, and parsley.

Mash yolks fine; add vinegar, mustard, salt, and pepper and blend well. Mix thoroughly with cream. Add to salad and toss. Refrigerate 24 hours, stirring occasionally. At serving time, garnish with remaining egg, sliced, and parsley.

Submitted by Mrs. Gordon Austin, St. Francis. This dish was traditional at holidays; it is delicious, she reported, with any kind of meat, and keeps well.

LETTUCE AND POTATO SLAW (Dutch)

1 large bunch leaf lettuce or ½ head iceberg
   lettuce
8 slices bacon, diced
3 or 4 medium potatoes
½ teaspoon salt
3 hard boiled eggs, cut up fine
⅓ cup vinegar
½ cup water
½ teaspoon sugar
Salt and pepper to taste

Shred lettuce, wash, and drain well. Fry bacon, drain on absorbent paper, reserve fat. Peel, quarter, and boil potatoes in water with salt; drain. Mash potatoes lightly in a large mixing bowl; add bacon and eggs.

To bacon grease in fry pan, add vinegar, water, sugar, salt, and pepper and heat slowly. Carefully mix lettuce with potatoes and add dressing.

Serve immediately to 3 or 4.

Submitted by Genevieve (Mrs. John E.) Butenhoff, Milwaukee, who noted that her grandmother's salad is especially good in warm weather "because it is an easy-to-prepare one-dish meal."

CREAMED POTATO SALAD (English)

4 or 5 potatoes
2 onions
½ cup vinegar
1 tablespoon butter
3 tablespoons sugar
1 teaspoon salt
Pepper to taste
2 eggs
1 cup sour cream

Boil potatoes; drain and slice. Slice onions very finely and mix with potatoes.

Combine vinegar, butter, sugar, salt, and pepper and bring to a boil. Beat eggs into sour cream, then beat in boiling vinegar mixture, a little at a time. Return to heat and simmer until thick. Pour over potatoes.

Serve warm or cold.

Submitted by Mrs. Bernice Forrer, West Allis.

SILLSALAD (Norwegian)

1½ pounds salt herring
1½ cups leftover roast meat, diced
2 cups cooked beets, diced
2½ cups cold boiled potatoes, diced
1 dill pickle, diced
2 raw apples, diced
5 tablespoons vinegar
3 tablespoons sugar
Pinch white pepper

½ cup heavy cream
Juice from beets
Hard-boiled eggs

Soak herring in water 12 hours; skin, bone, and dice. Combine with meat, beets, potatoes, pickle, and apple.

Combine vinegar, sugar, pepper, cream, and a little beet juice for color. Pour over salad and toss gently. Garnish with sliced hard-boiled eggs.

Submitted by Violet Fendry Schumacher, Franklin.

FRUIT SALAD DRESSING (German)

1¼ cups sugar
½ teaspoon salt
½ cup plus 2 tablespoons sifted flour
2 teaspoons dry mustard
1¼ cups vinegar
1¾ cups plus 2 tablespoons hot water
2 eggs, well beaten
¼ teaspoon paprika
Evaporated milk or cream

Mix sugar, salt, and flour. Dissolve mustard in a small amount of the vinegar; add with remaining vinegar slowly to dry ingredients. Add water, paprika, and beaten egg. Stir to mix well. Cook in a double boiler over simmering water for 30 minutes, stirring constantly until thick and occasionally during remainder of cooking period.

Makes about 1 quart. Keep in refrigerator and dilute with evaporated milk or cream to use.

Submitted by Carlyne M. (Mrs. Otto A.) Klein, Burlington, who noted that this is excellent for all fruit salads, especially Waldorf salad. This dressing, she added, was originally part of a sweetbread salad recipe which called for mixing 2 pounds cooked sweetbreads, 2 bunches celery, 2 small bottles capers, 1 small bottle olive meats, and 12 hard-boiled eggs.

FRUIT JUICE DRESSING

¼ cup pineapple juice
¼ cup orange juice
¼ cup lemon juice
½ cup sugar
1 tablespoon flour
2 eggs
½ cup heavy cream

Put pineapple, orange, and lemon juices in the top of a double boiler. Combine flour and sugar and gradually add to juices. Beat eggs well and add to the juices which have been set over simmering water. Stir until mixture coats a spoon. After dressing cools, whip cream and add.

Mrs. Byron Dolgner, Pardeeville, contributed her favorite dressing for fruit salad.

GOURMET SALAD DRESSING

2 cups buttermilk
1 cup mayonnaise
½ cup sour cream
1 tablespoon white vinegar
1 tablespoon tarragon vinegar
½ cup chopped chives or shallots
¼ cup chopped parsley
½ teaspoon salt
Pepper to taste

Combine all ingredients, mix well, and refrigerate.

Excellent on most salads and with meats, poultry, etc.

Variations: Add a mashed avocado or 4 anchovies mashed with 1 clove garlic.

Submitted by Mrs. Marion I. Kraemer, Merrimac.

MUSTARD SALAD DRESSING (Yankee)

5 egg yolks
⅓ cup sugar
1 tablespoon flour
1 tablespoon dry mustard
½ teaspoon salt
¾ cup vinegar
6 tablespoons cream
Whipped or sour cream

Beat egg yolks slightly. Add sugar, flour, mustard, and salt. Mix in vinegar and cream, stirring to make a smooth mixture. Cook in a double boiler over simmering water until thick, stirring constantly. Keep refrigerated and dilute with whipped or sour cream when using.

Submitted by Vera (Mrs. Meredith) Richter, Janesville. "It is unexcelled as a dressing for a good old-fashioned potato salad," she added.

PIES
and PASTRIES

IN ALL COUNTRIES, SKILL IN MAKING TENDER, tasty pies, tarts, strudel, or any other kind of pastry was the crowning testament to a good cook. For many, no meal was complete without a sweet ending of this kind.

Wisconsin's astonishing winters, even in the days before electric freezers, enabled many a housewife to make pies in large numbers. Mrs. Verne Cluppert, Markesan, for instance, recalled that her great grandmother "made stacks of pies at one time and kept them frozen all winter long in a shed or attic. Then when she wanted a pie for dessert, she'd take a frozen pie and put it in the oven to thaw and bake."

A good pie or pastry starts, of course, with a good crust. Here is Mrs. Cluppert's.

PASTRY MIX

3½ pounds (14 cups) flour
2 tablespoons salt
4 cups vegetable shortening

Sift flour and salt into a large bowl. Add 2 cups of the shortening and cut in until mixture is as fine as meal. Add remaining shortening and continue cutting, using as few strokes as possible, until particles are the size of large peas. Store in a covered container.

Makes enough for six 2-crust pies.

To use for a 2-crust pie, mix 3 cups of the pastry mix with 5 tablespoons cold water. For a 1-crust pie, use 1 ¾ cups mix and 3 tablespoons water.

For a rich dough, blend 1 ¾ cups mix with 1 well-beaten egg.

Submitted by Mrs. Verne Cluppert, Markesan.

NEVER FAIL PIE CRUST

1 egg
Water
5 cups flour
2 teaspoons salt
2 tablespoons sugar
2 cups lard

Put egg into a measuring cup; beat slightly with a fork and add enough cold water to measure 1 cup. Combine flour, salt, and sugar and mix in lard and egg-water mixture, using hands. Chill in the refrigerator; dough will be soft. May use plenty of flour when rolling out.

Variation: Use juice of a lemon and grated rind as part of the liquid.

Submitted by Mrs. Isabel Mertens, Withee.

FLAKY PIE CRUST

2½ cups sifted flour
1 teaspoon salt
¾ cup lard
¾ cup water

Remove ⅓ cup flour and reserve. Combine remaining flour and salt; work in lard until it is all absorbed. Make a paste with reserved flour and water. Mix into dough. Roll out into 2 crusts.

Submitted by Mrs. Joe Kucera, Cudahy.

CREAM PUFFS

1 cup water
½ cup butter
1 cup flour
4 eggs, at room temperature

Bring water and butter to a boil. Add flour all at once, stirring quickly with a wooden spoon. Cook, stirring constantly, until thick and mixture does not cling to sides of pan.

Remove from heat and after 2 minutes, beat in eggs, one at a time, beating thoroughly after each addition. Drop by tablespoon on a greased cookie sheet 2 inches apart. Bake at 450 degrees for 10 minutes; reduce heat to 350 degrees and bake 25 minutes more.

When cool, cut and fill with freshly whipped cream or any filling desired.

Submitted by Marlyne Schantz (Mrs. William) Seymour, ELkhorn.

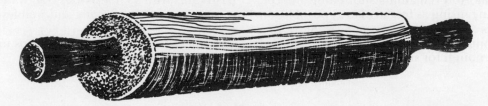

STRUDEL DOUGH (Slovenian)

1 tablespoon vinegar
Warm water
4 cups sifted flour
Melted butter
1 egg, slightly beaten

Place vinegar in measuring cup and add enough water to make 1 cup. In a large bowl, make a well in center of flour. Add 1 tablespoon melted butter and egg. Add liquid mixture gradually, mixing until flour is moistened. Turn out onto a lightly floured pastry board and knead. Hold dough high above board and hit it hard against the board about 100 or 125 times or until dough is smooth and elastic and small bubbles appear on the surface. Knead dough occasionally during the hitting process. Shape the dough into a smooth ball and place on lightly floured board. Brush top with melted butter and cover with an inverted bowl. Allow to rest 30 minutes.

Cover a large table with a clean white cloth and sprinkle entire surface lightly with flour. Place dough on center of cloth and sprinkle very lightly with flour. Working with half the dough at a time, roll dough into a rectangle ⅛ to ¼-inch thick. Butter fingers and stretch dough until it is paper thin. Allow to dry 5 minutes or until no longer sticky before filling and baking. Makes enough for two strudels.

APPLE STRUDEL

4 or 5 medium cooking apples, peeled and
  cored
Strudel dough
½ cup melted butter
¼ cup dry bread crumbs
½ cup raisins
½ to ¾ cup sugar
1 teaspoon cinnamon
1 egg white, beaten

Cut apples into ⅛-inch slices and set aside. Sprinkle evenly over strudel dough, cooled melted butter and bread crumbs. Cover with apple slices and raisins. Combine sugar (amount depends on tartness of the apples) and cinnamon and sprinkle over fruit. Fold outside edge of dough over about 3 inches wide and keep rolling, brushing off flour. Brush top slightly with egg white. Bake at 350 degrees for 35 to 45 minutes or until brown.

CHEESE STRUDEL

2 egg yolks
¼ cup sugar
1 teaspoon salt
2 cups firmly packed dry cottage cheese
¼ cup raisins
½ teaspoon vanilla
½ teaspoon lemon peel

In a large bowl, beat egg yolks, sugar, and salt until thick and lemon-colored. Gradually add cottage cheese, blending after each addition. Mix in raisins, vanilla, and lemon peel.

After strudel dough has been spread with melted butter and bread crumbs as above, cover with cheese filling, and roll and bake as directed.

These strudel recipes were submitted by Jeanne Cragin (Mrs. Lawrence) Atkinson, Superior.

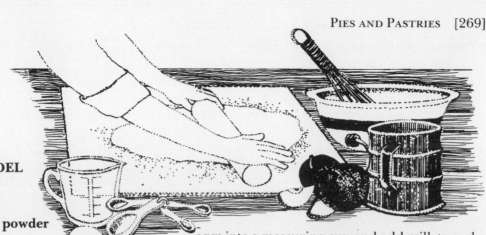

SURPRISE STRUDEL

2 cups flour
1 tablespoon sugar
3 teaspoons baking powder
½ teaspoon salt
⅓ cup shortening or butter
2 large or 3 small eggs
About ½ cup milk
Brown sugar
2 tablespoons cinnamon
Butter or margarine
Confectioners' sugar or frosting, as desired

Combine flour, sugar, baking powder, and salt. Cut in shortening until mixture is crumbly. Make a well in the middle of this mixture. Break eggs into a measuring cup and add milk to make 1 cup. Beat with a fork. Slowly pour into well, then mix as for pie dough.

Toss dough onto a floured bread board and roll out as large as possible. Sprinkle generously with brown sugar and cinnamon and dot with butter. Roll up like a jelly roll and bake at 350 degrees for 20 minutes or until golden brown.

Sprinkle with confectioners' sugar while hot or frost when cool if desired.

Variations: Fill with dried or fresh fruit or jam instead of brown sugar.

Submitted by Mrs. Norma Gedamske, Milwaukee, who wished she had a penny for each strudel she has made in her seventy-plus years: "I think I would be almost a rich lady."

The ingredients for pies and pastries are as limitless as a cook's imagination and traditions. What follows is a mere sampling of the pies enjoyed in Wisconsin over the years.

SALT PORK APPLE PIE (Yankee)

2 ¼-inch slices very fat salt pork, diced
Pastry for 2-crust, 9-inch pie, rolled out
About 2 pounds cooking apples, peeled, cored, and sliced
1 cup sugar
¼ teaspoon cinnamon
¼ teaspoon nutmeg
2 teaspoons lemon juice

Fry salt pork slowly until golden brown.

Line a 9-inch pie pan with pastry and cover with apple slices. Mix sugar, cinnamon, and nutmeg and sprinkle over apples. Drip lemon juice over, then pour salt pork with fat over the apples. Cover with top crust, seal edges, and make several slits in top. Bake at 425 degrees for 10 minutes; reduce heat to 350 degrees and continue baking 30 minutes.

Submitted by Mrs. Clarence Schwebke, Beloit. She found it in an old, almost illegible cookbook which came from New England before the Civil War.

TESSIE'S APPLE SLICES

2½ cups plus 6 or 7 tablespoons flour
⅔ cup plus 1 tablespoon sugar
½ teaspoon salt
½ pound butter
½ cup milk
½ cake compressed yeast
2 egg yolks, beaten
8 to 10 apples, peeled, cored, and sliced
1 teaspoon vanilla
Butter
Confectioners' sugar

Combine 2½ cups flour, 1 tablespoon sugar, and salt. Cut in butter. Dissolve yeast in milk and add egg yolks. Mix into flour mixture and blend. Roll out two-thirds of the dough to fit the bottom and sides of a 13-by-9-inch pan. Cover with apple slices. Combine remaining sugar and flour and vanilla, and sprinkle over apples. Dot with butter. Cover with remaining dough, overlapping bottom dough with the top; cut slits in top. Bake at 350 degrees for 1 hour. Frost with a thin frosting made of confectioners' sugar and water. Cut into squares when cold.

Submitted by Mr. and Mrs. Bay. Sprengel, New Berlin, who run the Sprengel Apple Orchard.

FRESH CHERRY PIE

1 quart fresh cherries
Dough for an 8-or-9-inch lattice pie
Melted shortening
2 or 3 tablespoons flour
¼ teaspoon salt
1 cup sugar
½ teaspoon almond flavoring

Wash and pit cherries. Line pie pan with bottom crust and brush lightly with melted shortening.

Combine flour, salt, and sugar and mix with cherries. Pour into pie shell and sprinkle on almond flavoring. Top with a lattice crust. Bake at 450 degrees for 10 minutes; reduce heat to 350 degrees and continue baking about 30 minutes or until done.

Submitted by Mrs. Ann Strathman, Waterloo.

CARROT PIE

1½ cups cooked, mashed carrots
1 cup brown sugar
1 teaspoon cinnamon
½ teaspoon ginger
½ teaspoon salt
2 eggs, slightly beaten
1½ cups evaporated milk
Uncooked 9-inch pastry shell

Combine carrots, sugar, cinnamon, ginger, salt, eggs, and evaporated milk. Mix well. Pour into pie shell and bake at 400 degrees for 45 minutes.

Submitted by Roscella Berdal, Montello.

RHUBARB CUSTARD PIE (Danish)

3 eggs, separated
2 cups sliced rhubarb
1½ cups plus 2 tablespoons flour
1½ cups plus 2 teaspoons sugar
½ cup plus 1 tablespoon butter or margarine
1 teaspoon salt
1 teaspoon baking powder
1 egg yolk
2 tablespoons milk
¼ teaspoon cream of tartar

Beat 3 egg yolks and add rhubarb, 2 tablespoons flour, 1 cup sugar, and 1 tablespoon butter or margarine. Mix well and set aside.

Sift together remaining flour, 2 teaspoons sugar, salt, and baking powder. Cut in remaining butter or margarine. Mix egg yolk and milk together and add to dry ingredients. Press into greased 8 or 9-inch pie pan. Pour in rhubarb mixture. Bake at 375 degrees for 45 minutes.

Top with a meringue made of 3 egg whites, remaining sugar, and cream of tartar. Return to oven until top is brown.

Submitted by Mrs. Ruth V. Calvin, Elkhorn, who remembered that her mother served this pie every Sunday during rhubarb season.

SWEET POTATO PIE (Afro-American)

3 pounds sweet potatoes, peeled, cooked, and
  mashed
1½ cups butter, softened
1½ cups sugar
½ teaspoon salt
1 teaspoon nutmeg
3 eggs
1 cup milk
2 unbaked 8-inch pie shells

Add softened butter to mashed sweet potato. Blend in sugar, salt, and nutmeg and mash until consistency of mush. Beat in eggs and milk. Pour into prepared pie shells. Bake at 425 degrees for 10 minutes; reduce heat to 350 and continue baking 30 minutes or until a knife inserted in the center comes out clean.

This recipe of Mrs. John Blathers, Milwaukee, was sent in by Mrs. L. Tornowske, Patch Grove.

RAW PUMPKIN PIE

Dough for a 2-crust 8-or-9-inch pie
Raw pumpkin, peeled and sliced paper thin
1 teaspoon cinnamon
1 cup sugar

Fill prepared pie pan with pumpkin mixed with cinnamon and sugar. Cover with top crust, seal, and bake at 375 degrees for 45 minutes or until done.

Submitted by Pastor Lloyd C. Denzer, Wild Rose.

SHOOFLY PIE (Pennsylvania-Dutch)

2 cups water
1 teaspoon baking soda
½ dark molasses
2 cups plus 3 tablespoons flour
1 egg, beaten
2 unbaked 8 or 9-inch pie shells
1 cup brown sugar
½ cup butter
½ teaspoon cinnamon
½ teaspoon salt
⅛ teaspoon nutmeg
⅛ teaspoon ginger
⅛ teaspoon ground cloves

Bring water to a boil. Remove from heat and add baking soda, molasses, and 3 tablespoons flour and stir well. Add egg and mix well. Pour evenly into pie shells.

Combine brown sugar, remaining flour, butter, cinnamon, salt, nutmeg, ginger, and cloves, mixing well with hands. Gently sprinkle over top of filling in pie shells. Bake at 400 degrees for 15 minutes; reduce heat to 325 degrees and bake 20 minutes more, or until curst is done.

Submitted by Mrs. Martie Steele, Fond du Lac.

GREEN TOMATO PIE

Rich pastry for 2-crust 8-or-9-inch pie
Green tomatoes
¼ cup sugar
½ teaspoon nutmeg
½ teaspoon cinnamon
Butter

Line pie pan with bottom crust. Peel and slice enough green tomatoes to fill the pie pan very full (filling shrinks in cooking). Mix sugar, nutmeg, and cinnamon. Alternate layers of tomatoes with a sprinkling of sugar mixture and dots of butter. Top with upper crust, seal, and bake at 450 degrees for 10 minutes. Reduce temperature to 350 degrees and continue baking 30 or 35 minutes.

Contributed by Mrs. C. W. Loomer, Madison. This tastes, she reported, like apple pie.

MAPLE SYRUP PIE

Pastry for 2-crust 8-or-9-inch pie
1 cup maple syrup
½ cup boiling water
3 tablespoons cold water
3 tablespoons cornstarch
1 tablespoons butter
Chopped hickory or other nuts

Line pie pan with bottom crust. Boil maple syrup and water together for 5 minutes. Mix cold water with cornstarch. Pour slowly into boiling syrup to thicken. Add butter and pour into pie pan. Sprinkle chopped nuts evenly over top. Cover with top crust, seal, and vent. Bake at 400 degrees for 30 minutes.

Submitted by Mrs. Florence M. Vint, Springfield, Virginia, who noted that hickory nuts were always used in her family because they were plentiful in northern Wisconsin. "If you like the taste of maple," she added, "you will love this pie."

BOUILLE PIE (French-Canadian)

Baked pie shell
2 cups milk
¼ cup flour
½ teaspoon salt
Brown sugar

Combine milk, flour, and salt and cook over a low heat until medium thick. Pour into crust and sprinkle generously with brown sugar. Serve hot.

Submitted by Mrs. Henry R. Bowers, Marion. Bouille, she wrote, means "boiled" in French. This simple pie was frequently served by her grandmother, who raised 10 children on a very limited budget.

LEMON TARTS (English)

3 eggs
2 cups sugar
Grated rinds of 3 lemons
½ cup lemon juice
Baked tartlet shells or baked pie crust
Whipped cream or meringue (optional)

Combine eggs, sugar, lemon rind, and lemon juice. Cook over low heat until thickened. Put in a jar and store in refrigerator until needed.

To use, spoon into tartlet shells or pie crust and cover with whipped cream or meringue if desired.

Submitted by Mrs. L. P. Baerwolf, Madison.

VIENNA TARTS (Austrian)

½ cup cottage cheese or cream cheese
½ cup butter or margarine
1 cup flour
Jelly or preserves

Combine cheese, butter, and flour into a smooth paste. Chill for 30 minutes.

Cut into small pieces and roll out into squares. Place a spoonful of jelly or preserves in the center of each square, pick up corners, and pinch together. Bake at 450 degrees until delicately brown.

Submitted by Viola (Mrs. Felix) Schuster, Menomonee Falls.

SWEDISH TEA TARTS

½ cup butter or margarine
1 cup sugar
3 eggs, separated
1 whole egg
1½ cups flour
1 teaspoon baking powder
1 teaspoon vanilla
½ chopped walnuts
2 cups brown sugar

Cream butter. Gradually add sugar and beat well. Add 3 egg yolks and whole egg and beat well. Stir in flour which has been sifted with baking powder. Add vanilla. Spread mixture, which will be quite heavy, in a 10-by-15-inch jelly roll pan. Sprinkle with chopped walnuts.

Beat egg whites until very stiff. Gradually add brown sugar. Beat until very heavy. Spread over dough and walnuts. Bake at 350 degrees for 30 minutes. Cool and cut into squares.

Submitted by Patricia (Mrs. Ronald R.) Kolwitz, Menomonee Falls.

RICE CAKES (Cornish)

Pastry dough
¼ cup butter
1 cup sugar
2 eggs, beaten
¼ cup milk
¾ cup rice flour (or farina)
1 cup currants
1 teaspoon cinnamon

Pinch allspice
Pinch cloves

Line muffin tins with pastry dough.

Cream butter and sugar together. Beat in eggs and milk. Mix in rice flour, currants, cinnamon, allspice, and cloves. Fill pastry shells about ⅔ full. Bake at 350 degrees until filling is firm.

Submitted by Mrs. R. W. Peterman, Wauwatosa.

BACKPFLAUME TORTE MIT MUERBE TEIG (Austrian)

1 cup flour
2 tablespoons sugar
½ cup butter
1 egg yolk
Small pinch salt
1 pound prunes, cooked
2 egg whites
½ cup sugar
Grated rind of 1 lemon
Chopped nuts

Mix flour and sugar. Cut in butter; add egg yolk and salt. Mix and place in a 7½-by-11-inch pan, patting crust evenly over bottom and along sides.

Pit prunes and arrange over crust. Beat egg whites until very stiff; add sugar and grated lemon rind. Spread over prunes. Sprinkle evenly with chopped nuts. Bake at 375 degrees for 40 minutes or until crust is well baked.

Submitted by Mrs. Ruth L. Jaeger, Brown Deer.

MAZUREK RODZYNKOWY (Polish)

2 cups flour
1 cup sugar
¼ teaspoon salt
½ cup butter
1 egg, beaten
3 tablespoons cream
Raisin Topping (see below)

Sift together flour, sugar, and salt. Cut in butter until crumbly. Mix egg and cream and add to flour mixture. Mix lightly by hand and spread evenly on a greased baking sheet. Bake at 350 degrees for 20 minutes. Immediately cover evenly with Raisin Topping, using a heated knife dipped in hot water. Return to oven and bake for 15 minutes more. When cool, slice into squares or bars.

Raisin Topping:

½ pound golden seedless raisins
1⅛ cups sugar
1½ or 2 cups chopped nuts or sliced almonds
Grated peel of 1 lemon
1 egg plus 1 yolk

Combine all ingredients.

Submitted by Mrs. Waclaw Soroka, Stevens Point. These traditional Polish Easter pastries can be made with other toppings.

One of the traditions the Belgian settlers of Door County transplanted to their new home was the Kermiss celebration. Kermiss, or *Kirk-Messe* (Church-Mass), is an observance of Thanksgiving starting the last Sunday in August and continuing for seven consecutive Sundays. Following a mass of thanksgiving for the bounty of the land, the churchgoers would adjourn to the church yard to partake of the food piled high on tables set up in the open air. Games and dancing came after the feast, which always concluded with Belgian Pie.

These pies are made with a yeast crust filled with a variety of mixtures and crowned with a cottage-cheese topping.

BELGIAN PIE

6 eggs, separated
½ cup sugar
2 tablespoons butter
2 packages active dry yeast
½ cup lukewarm water
3½ cups flour
½ teaspoon salt
Filling (see below)
Topping (see below)

Beat egg whites until stiff; add yolks and beat. Add sugar and butter. Dissolve yeast in lukewarm water and mix in. Sift flour and salt together; mix and work into egg mixture, a little at a time, until dough is no longer sticky. Let rise 1 hour.

Knead down and roll into three circles to fit into 8 or 9-inch pie pans. Place in pans and prick pastry. Add filling and cover with topping. Bake at 325 degrees for 30 minutes.

Prune Filling (enough for 1 pie):

2 cups cooked prunes, pitted and mashed
½ cup light brown sugar
½ teaspoon nutmeg
Juice of ½ lemon

Mix well and spread over dough.

Topping (enough for 3 pies):

1 pound small-curd cottage cheese
2 tablespoons flour
½ teaspoon salt
½ cup heavy cream
Juice of ½ lemon

Combine all ingredients in order given. Spread over filling.

Submitted by Virginia Nelson, Middleton, who explained that the recipe for the prune filling may be multiplied for the other two pies; prepared or other fillings may also be used.

Other filling recipes submitted included:

Raisin Filling (enough for 1 pie):

¾ cup seedless raisins
2 tablespoons cream
2 tablespoons sugar
1 teaspoon flour

Cook raisins in water until soft; drain. Add cream, sugar, and flour. Mix and cook until mixture begins to thicken. Spread on crust.

Rice Filling (enough for 1 pie):

¾ cup cooked rice
6 tablespoons milk
1 tablespoon cream
1 small egg yolk
2½ tablespoons sugar
¼ teaspoon vanilla

To the rice in a heavy pot, add milk and cream. Bring to a boil and stir in egg yolk well beaten with sugar. Cook until slightly thick. Add vanilla. Spread on crust.

Submitted by Mrs. Emma Heesakker, Appleton.

CAKES, FILLINGS, and FROSTINGS

No LESS THAN PIES (PERHAPS EVEN MORE SO), cakes have been the pride of good cooks everywhere. Special occasions, holidays, and religious observances of any kind rarely pass without a culminating cake.

As they are today, recipes were passed among friends and relations; and cake recipes usually make up the bulk of the hand-written collections handed down from generation to generation. Chances are, if you ask someone for his or her personal favorite or most special recipe, you will be given one for a cake. Spice, fruit, ginger, chocolate, oatmeal, honey, date, angel food, orange, potato, nut, cheese, apple, kirsch, poppy seed—the variety is mouth-wateringly endless.

CORNISH SAFFRON CAKE

15 grains saffron (1 big pinch)
1 cup boiling water
½ cup butter
1½ cups sugar
2 eggs
1 teaspoon lemon flavoring
2½ cups flour
2 teaspoons baking powder
¼ teaspoon salt
1½ cups raisins

¼ cup currants
¼ cup candied fruit

Steep saffron in the boiling water for 1 hour.

Cream together butter, sugar, eggs, and lemon flavoring. Sift together flour, baking powder, and salt. Dredge raisins, currants, and candied fruit in flour mixture. Add to butter mixture alternately with steeped saffron. Pour into 2 medium, well-greased and floured loaf pans. Bake at 325 or 350 degrees for 1 hour.

This is the recipe for the Cornish Saffron Cake served visitors at Pendarvis, the Cornish restoration at Mineral Point operated by the State Historical Society of Wisconsin.

PANU-KAKU (Swede-Finnish)

¾ quart new milk (the milk from the second
   milking after a cow has freshened)
¾ quart whole or skim milk
1 teaspoon salt
2 teaspoons baking powder
1½ cups flour
Cinnamon
Sugar

Combine two milks. Sift together salt, baking powder, and flour and add to milk. Beat well with an egg beater or spoon. Mixture will be the consistency of thick pancake batter. Pour into a greased 9-by-13-inch cake pan. Bake at 400 degrees for about 1 hour or until golden brown. After 40 minutes, sprinkle with cinnamon and then with sugar and finish baking.

Cake will have two custard-like layers.

Submitted by Hilda Hillman (Mrs. Sulo) Sukanen, Marengo. "Panu-Kaku was a real treat for children coming in hungry after playing hard outdoors in the fresh air" she recalled. "Panu-Kaku is especially delicious warm, but it can also be eaten cold."

OATMEAL CAKE

1½ cups boiling water
1 cup quick-cooking oatmeal
½ cup butter
1 cup brown sugar
¾ cup sugar
2 eggs
1½ cups sifted flour
1 teaspoon baking soda
1 teaspoon cinnamon
½ teaspoon salt
Topping (see below)

cinnamon, and salt and add. Pour into a well-greased 9-by-13-inch pan and bake at 350 degrees for 30 to 35 minutes. Cool and frost with Topping.

Topping:
¼ cup brown sugar
½ cup light cream
3 tablespoons butter
½ teaspoon vanilla
1 cup flaked coconut
1 cup chopped nuts

Pour boiling water over oatmeal. Mix well. Let stand until cool.

Cream butter and sugars; beat in eggs. Stir in cooled oatmeal. Sift together flour, baking soda,

Combine sugar and cream and boil until bubbly. Add butter, vanilla, coconut, and nuts. Spread on cooled cake. Place under broiler to brown.

Submitted by Mrs. Leo Wesolowski, Oconto Falls.

DATE-NUT CAKE

1 teaspoon baking soda
½ cup shortening
1 cup hot water
1 cup dates, pitted
1 egg, lightly beaten
1 cup sugar
1 cup sifted flour
1 cup nuts, chopped

1 teaspoon salt
1 teaspoon vanilla
Whipped cream or ice cream

Combine baking soda and shortening with hot water; pour over dates. Add egg, sugar, flour, nuts, salt, and vanilla. Mix well. Bake in an 8 or 9-inch square pan at 375 degrees for 35 minutes. Serve with whipped cream or ice cream.

Submitted by Charles Hendricksen, Milwaukee.

RIBBON CAKE

1 cup butter
2 cups sugar
Lemon flavoring to taste
4 eggs
1 cup milk
4 cups (scant) sifted flour
½ teaspoon baking soda
1 teaspoon cream of tartar
4 teaspoons cinnamon
1 cup currants
⅓ cup citron
Currant jelly

Cream butter thoroughly; add sugar gradually, beating continuously. Beat in lemon flavoring. Beat eggs until very light; add to butter mixture with milk. Sift together sifted flour, baking soda, and cream of tartar and sift into batter. Beat quickly and thoroughly.

Grease and flour three square pans of the same size, 8 or 9 inches. Pour ⅓ of batter into each of two pans. Into the remaining ⅓ of batter, stir cinnamon, currants, and citron; pour into remaining pan. Bake at 350 degrees until done, about 30 minutes.

Cool slightly and remove from pans. Put layers together with thin spreadings of currant jelly, placing thinly spread cinnamon-currant layer in the center. While still warm, firmly weight the layers down; a pair of iron flatirons works nicely.

Submitted by Mrs. Forrest Wilms, Neenah.

MARZIPAN CAKE (Bohemian)

1 teaspoon cinnamon
¼ teaspoon cloves
¼ teaspoon nutmeg
1 cup, sugar
4 eggs, *very well beaten*
1 teaspoon light corn syrup
2 teaspoons cream
½ cup light rye flour
½ cup flour
2 teaspoons baking powder
Sliced almonds
Confectioners' sugar

Mix spices with sugar; add gradually to well beaten eggs and continue beating until light and fluffy. Beat in corn syrup and cream. Mix flours with baking powder and gradually add to the batter, beating thoroughly. Pour into an oiled and floured 9-by-13-inch cake pan. Top with sliced almonds. Bake at 350 degrees for about 25 minutes. Sift confectioners' sugar over the cake while still warm. Cut in squares while still warm.

Submitted by Helen F. Andruskevicz, Green Bay, who "had the foresight to copy this delicious recipe" when she was 14 years old in the 1920's. Every year, Bohemian women from Menominee, Michigan, and Marinette would make a pilgrimage to Robinsonville, near Green Bay, on August 15 for the feast of the Assumption. After mass and the procession through the fields, the women and their families would eat the lunch they brought with them, which always included this Marzipan Cake. "When they returned to our home on one of these occasions, one of the women baked a marzipan for us and I 'caught' all of the ingredients into measuring cups and spoons, for these were cooks without recipes. My mother was the interpreter, because none of these women spoke English."

ORANGE CAKE

½ cup shortening
1½ cups sugar
2 eggs
1 cup sour milk
2¼ cups flour
1 teaspoon baking soda
Pinch salt
½ cup finely chopped raisins
½ cup chopped nuts
2 oranges, juice and grated rinds

Cream shortening and 1 cup sugar. Mix in eggs, milk, flour, baking soda, salt, raisins, and nuts. Bake in a square or rectangular pan at 350 degrees until done, about 30 minutes.

Mix orange juice, grated rind, and remaining sugar; let stand while cake is baking. While cake is still warm, pour orange mixture over cake evenly.

Orange juice mixture forms a glaze and the juice soaks into the cake. No icing is needed.

Submitted by Mrs. Harold Clumpner, Ogdensburg.

RHUBARB CAKE

1 cup shortening
1½ cups brown sugar
1 egg
1 cup sour milk or buttermilk
1 teaspoon baking soda
2 cups flour
1 teaspoon vanilla
1½ cups finely cut raw rhubarb
¼ cup sugar
1½ teaspoons cinnamon
Whipped cream

Cream shortening and brown sugar; beat in egg. Stir into milk or buttermilk ½ teaspoon baking soda and add. Combine flour and remaining baking soda and mix into batter with vanilla. Fold in rhubarb. Pour into a buttered 9-by-13-inch pan. Sprinkle with sugar and cinnamon. Bake at 350 degrees for 40 minutes.

Serve topped with whipped cream and sprinkled with additional cinnamon and sugar.

Submitted by La Verne (Mrs. Walter) Turnquist, Eagle River.

POOR MAN'S CAKE

2¼ cups water
1 cup sugar
⅓ cup lard
½ cup chopped raisins
1 teaspoon nutmeg
1 teaspoon cinnamon
⅓ teaspoon cloves
⅓ teaspoon allspice
1 teaspoon baking soda
¾ cup chopped walnuts

Pinch salt
2 cups sifted flour
½ teaspoon baking powder

Combine water, sugar, lard, raisins, nutmeg, cinnamon, cloves, and allspice, and bring to a boil. Remove from stove and add baking soda. Let cool. Add nuts, salt, flour, and baking powder and mix well. Bake at 350 degrees for about 30 minutes.

Submitted by Jane Steinhorst Lyons, Greenfield. This eggless, milkless, butterless recipe came from her husband's grandmother who baked the cake as a girl. In those days, walnuts were comparatively cheap!

REDOWAK (Bohemian)

1 pound butter
2 pounds sugar
1 pound flour
1 pound blanched almonds, finely ground
1 pound eggs, weighed in shells
2 dozen sour apples, peeled, cored, and cut in small pieces
1 teaspoon grated lemon grind

Cream butter. Mix in 1 pound sugar, flour, and almonds. Beat in eggs. Roll out into a thin cake. Bake at 350 degrees until golden, 10 to 15 minutes.

Meanwhile, make a heavy syrup of remaining sugar and water and bring to a rolling boil. Add apples and cook over low heat into a very thick, transparent marmalade. Add lemon rind and continue cooking until mixture starts to stick to the pan, then spread thickly over cake. Store in a cool place.

Submitted by Edna Meudt, Dodgeville.

MISS SABIN'S PUDDING

½ cup butter, at room temperature
½ cup sugar
2 eggs
½ cup molasses
½ cup buttermilk
1 teaspoon baking soda
1¾ cups flour
1 teaspoon ginger
½ teaspoon cinammon
¼ teaspoon salt
Lemon Sauce (see below)
Cream Topping (see below)

Cream butter and sugar until light with an electric beater. Add eggs and continue to beat. Stir in molasses. Add baking soda to buttermilk and stir in dissolve. Add it to creamed mixture alternately with flour, ginger, cinnamon, and salt which have been sifted together. Beat well to blend. Spoon into a well-buttered and floured 8 or 9-inch square cake pan and bake at 350 degrees for 25 minutes or until cake shrinks from side of pan.

Split serving-size pieces of cake while warm and spoon on Lemon Sauce. Replace top piece and spoon more sauce over it. Top with Cream Topping and serve at once.

Lemon Sauce:

2 eggs
1 cup sugar
1 lemon, juice and grated rind
¼ teaspoon salt
1 tablespoon butter

Beat eggs and sugar together; add lemon juice and rind, salt, and butter. Cook in a double boiler over simmering water until thick, stirring constantly. Makes about a cup of sauce for 2 or 3 servings.

Cream Topping:

1 cup heavy cream
2 tablespoons confectioners' sugar
1 tablespoon rum or rum flavoring to taste

Whip cream until stiff. Sweeten with sugar and flavor with rum.

Submitted by Marjorie V. O. (Mrs. Alfred) Miley, Sheboygan Falls, who explained that this ginger cake was the favorite dessert of Ellen Sabin, the formidable and distinguished president of Milwaukee-Downer College from 1890 to 1921. It was served to the students on special occasions and was known as Miss Sabin's Pudding. "It has since been a favorite in my family for three generations," Mrs. Miley added.

APPLE SAUCE CAKE

1 cup butter
1 cup sugar
1 egg, beaten
1 cup chopped dates
1 cup raisins
1½ cups apple sauce
½ teaspoon cinnamon
¼ teaspoon cloves
1 teaspoon vanilla
2 cups flour
2 teaspoons baking soda

Using a wooden spoon, cream butter and sugar. Mix in egg, dates, raisins, apple sauce, cinnamon, cloves, and vanilla and mix well. Mix in flour and baking soda. Batter will be very thick. Bake in large cake pan or in two or three loaf pans at 325 or 350 until done, about 30 to 60 minutes, depending on size of pan.

Submitted by Mrs. Ruth Bunker Christiansen, Frederic, who noted "This is not a fussy cake and seems to turn out well no matter what size tins it is baked in. For a Christmas cake, I found that by adding candied fruits and nuts, and/or orange peel, this makes a delicious fruit cake. I bake it in loaves, set aside for two days, and wrap in waxed paper; it will keep for as long as two years, not frozen but in the refrigerator. If no dates are at hand, add another cup of raisins. If your apple sauce is thick, add a tablespoon of water or cider, but don't let the batter get thin." Mrs. Christiansen's older sister, a schoolteacher who boarded out during the week, brought the recipe home to their mother about 60 years ago.

BUTTERMILK POUND CAKE

1 cup butter
2 cups sugar
1 teaspoon vanilla
1 teaspoon lemon extract
4 eggs
3 cups flour
½ teaspoon baking soda
½ teaspoon baking powder
¾ teaspoon salt
1 cup buttermilk

Butter and flour a 10-inch tube pan. Line bottom with brown paper.

Cream butter and sugar with vanilla and lemon extract until light. Add eggs, one at a time, beating well after each addition. Sift together flour, baking soda, baking powder, and salt. Add to creamed mixture alternately with buttermilk. Beat until smooth. Pour into prepared pan and bake at 350 degrees for about 1 hour and 10 minutes or until done.

Submitted by Mrs. Rosalie Franckowiak, Cudahy.

KARTOFFEL TORTE (German)

1 cup butter
2 cups confectioners' sugar
4 eggs, separated
¾ cup milk
1 cup mashed potatoes
4 ounces bitter chocolate, melted
2 cups flour
2 teaspoons baking powder
½ teaspoon cloves
½ teaspoon cinnamon
½ teaspoon nutmeg

Cream butter and sugar. Add egg yolks. Add milk, mashed potatoes, chocolate, flour, and spices. Beat egg whites until stiff and fold in. Bake in an ungreased 9-inch spring-form pan at 350 degrees for 1 hour.

Submitted by Mrs. Edward Hoffman, Pewaukee.

Other Potato Torte recipes contributed included raisins and called for sour cream instead of milk.

KAESE TORTE (German)

1 package zwieback, grated (about 1 or 1½ cups)
2 cups sugar
½ teaspoon cinnamon
¼ cup melted butter
4 to 6 eggs (depending on how dry you like the filling)
2 pounds dry cottage cheese
½ pint heavy cream
Pinch salt
1 teaspoon vanilla
2 tablespoons flour

Mix grated zwieback with 1 cup sugar and cinnamon. Pour butter over mixture and mix well with hands. Remove 1 cup and reserve. Line bottom and sides of buttered 9-by-13-inch baking pan with crumb mixture.

Beat eggs; beat in remaining sugar. Add cheese, cream, salt, vanilla, and flour and mix well. Pour into crust and sprinkle top with reserved crumb mixture. Bake at 300 degrees for 1 hour or a little longer, until done.

Submitted by Susanne Marie Williams-Brown, Clintonville.

Other recipes for Cheese Torte (or Cheese Cake) called for Holland rusk or graham crackers instead of zwiebach.

MÁKTORTA (Hungarian)

¼ cup butter
½ cup sugar
6 eggs, separated
½ cup fine bread crumbs
¼ cup melted semi-sweet chocolate
⅓ cup ground poppy seeds
Strawberry or apricot jam

Cream together butter and sugar. Beat egg yolks until thick and lemon colored; beat in creamed mixture and crumbs. Fold in chocolate and poppy seeds. Beat egg whites until stiff and fold in. Spread in 2 buttered, paper-lined pans and bake at 325 degree for 30 minutes or until a light touch leaves no depression. Turn out cakes and remove paper at once. Cool.

Put layers together with jam, and frost with a chocolate cream frosting.

Submitted by Darlene Kronschnabel, Greenleaf.

DOLLY CAKE (Scottish)

½ dolly cup butter
1 dolly cup sugar
1 bantam egg
2 dolly cups flour
2 dolly spoons baking powder
¼ dolly spoon nutmeg
½ dolly cup boiling water

Cream sugar and butter. Beat egg and add. Sift flour with baking powder and nutmeg; add to creamed mixture. Add water, beating batter as it is added. Bake in a small tin until done.

Submitted by Jean Bunker (Mrs. Felix) Schmidt, Siren, who added that "this is delicious for little girls and their dollies." Her Scottish aunt gave her recipe after the family acquired two bantam chickens.

KIRSCH TORTE (German)

1½ cups flour
¾ cup sugar
1 teaspoon baking powder
10 tablespoons butter
2 tablespoons brandy
6 eggs, separated
1 quart fresh pitted red cherries *or* 1 cup
   canned pitted sour red cherries, drained
¼ teaspoon cream of tartar
¼ pound grated almonds (unblanched)
Rind of 1 orange, grated

Combine flour, ¼ cup sugar, and baking powder. Cut in butter as for pie crust. Beat together brandy and 1 egg yolk and add. Stir until particles cling together. Place dough in a spring-form pan and pat dough on bottom and up the sides almost to the top. Cover with cherries. Bake at 350 degrees for 20 minutes.

Beat egg whites with cream of tartar until frothy; gradually add remaining sugar and beat until stiff and glossy. Fold in almonds, orange rind, and remaining egg yolks, beaten. Pour mixture over cherries and return to oven for 45 minutes more.

Submitted by Phyllis Trimberger (Mrs. Roger J.) Schwartz, Milwaukee.

HICKORY NUT CAKE

½ cup butter
2 cups sugar
1 cup milk
3 cups flour
3 teaspoons baking powder
1 cup hickory nuts
4 egg whites

Cream butter and sugar. Add milk. Sift flour with baking powder and stir in nuts; add to creamed mixture. Beat egg whites until peaks form and fold in. Bake in a 9-by-13-inch pan at 375 degrees 30 or 35 minutes. Frost with a chocolate boiled frosting.

Submitted by Margaret Rose Hart, Milwaukee. This was one way her grandmother used up the nuts that grew on the hickory trees on their farm near Eureka, north of Berlin.

Hickory trees grew widely in Wisconsin and numerous recipes using hickory nuts were submitted. Other similar cake recipes suggested finishing off a cake with powdered sugar, cream cheese, or thin white frosting.

PIERNIK (Polish)

1 cup honey (strongly flavored like buckwheat honey)
1 cup sugar
½ cup corn oil
3 eggs
1 teapoon cinnamon
1 teaspoon cloves
1 teaspoon baking soda
1 cup boiling strong black coffee
3½ cups flour
3 teaspoons baking powder
1 cup raisins
Peel from 1 orange, chopped
1 cup walnuts or almonds, chopped

Combine honey, sugar, corn oil, and eggs and mix well. Add cinnamon and cloves and mix. Dissolve baking soda in coffee; cool. Sift flour and baking powder together and add alternatingly with coffee to honey mixture. Stir in raisins, orange peel, and nuts. Pour into a greased and floured tube pan and bake at 350 degrees for 45 minutes.

Submitted by Mrs. Waclaw Soroka, Stevens Point.

CRUMB CAKE (English)

½ cup shortening
1 cup sugar
2 cups flour
2 teaspoons baking powder
1 teaspoon nutmeg
1 teaspoon cloves
1 teaspoon cinnamon
1 egg
3 tablespoon molasses

1 teaspoon baking soda
1 cup sour milk

Mix together shortening, sugar, flour, baking powder, nutmeg, cloves, and cinnamon. Measure out ½ cup and reserve. Add egg, molasses, baking soda, and sour milk. Mix well. Pour into a greased 8-by-12-inch pan. Sprinkle over reserved crumb mixture. Bake at 350 degrees for about 1 hour.

Submitted by Nancy (Mrs. Robert) Cushman, Elkhorn.

CHOCOLATE CAKE

½ cup butter
1 cup sugar
1 egg
1 square bitter chocolate, melted
1 cup sour milk
1½ cups flour
1 teaspoon baking soda
½ cup currants or raisins
½ cup walnuts

Cream butter and sugar together; beat in egg. Stir in melted chocolate. Add milk alternately with flour and baking soda. Add currants and nuts, and stir well to blend. Bake in a greased 9-by-13-inch pan at 350 degrees for 25 to 30 minutes. Frost with your favorite icing.

Submitted by Mrs. Claude Sorenson, Manitowoc.

DANISH DARK CAKE

3 cups flour, browned
½ cup butter
1 cup sugar
1 cup molasses
1 teaspoon baking soda
1 cup strong coffee, cold
½ teaspoon salt
½ pound chopped raisins
12 pounds currants

Brown flour in a shallow pan in a moderate oven (350 degrees), watching carefully; cool and set aside.

Cream butter and sugar; add molasses and beat well. Dissolve baking soda in coffee and add to creamed mixture alternately with browned flour and salt. Stir in raisins and currants and blend well. Pour into greased and floured bread pan and bake at 350 degrees for 1½ hours or until done. Cool and wrap well and store for a few days to mellow the flavor.

Submitted by Mrs. Jean S. Hesse, Sheboygan. Her grandmother's recipe was also known as Poor Man's Fruitcake. "Years ago," she explained, "thin slices of this cake were often served with strong cups of tea, diluted as Danes like it with milk and sugar."

CHOCOLATE COOKIE-SHEET CAKE

2 cups sifted flour
2 cups sugar
½ teaspoon salt
½ pound butter
1 cup water
3 tablespoons cocoa
2 eggs, well beaten
1 teaspoon baking soda
½ cup buttermilk
1 teaspoon vanilla
1 teaspoon cinnamon (optional)

Quick and Easy Chocolate Frosting (see Frosting section)

Sift together flour, sugar, and salt into mixing bowl. In a saucepan, combine butter, water, and cocoa and bring to a boil. Pour over dry ingredients, and mix. Beat together eggs, baking soda, buttermilk, vanilla, and cinnamon, if desired; add to batter and mix well. Bake in a greased 15½-by-10-by-1-inch baking pan at 350 degrees for about 20 minutes.

Make frosting about 5 minutes before cake is done, and frost as soon as it is removed from oven.

Submitted by Augusta (Mrs. Adolph) Miller, Montello.

BREW CAKE (Irish)

1 cup butter
4½ cups sifted cake flour
2½ cups brown sugar
¼ teaspoon or more spices as desired
4 eggs, beaten
2 cups warmed beer
1 teaspoon baking soda
3 cups raisins
1½ cups white raisins
1 cup candied cherries
1 cup blanched chopped almonds

1 cup candied citrus peel (citron, lemon, and orange), cubed
Juice and grated rind of 1 lemon

Cut butter into flour. Add brown sugar and spices. Mix well. Beat together eggs, beer, and baking soda. Mix into dry ingredients. Fold in fruits and nuts and lemon juice and rind. Pour into a well-greased and floured 9-by-13-inch baking pan and bake at 275 or 300 degrees for 3 to 3½ hours. Cover with waxed paper until the last 30 minutes of baking.

Submitted by the Reverend Cormac Dwyer, Milwaukee.

PORK CAKE

1 heaping teaspoon baking soda
2 cups boiling water
1 pound ground, fat, salt pork
1 cup light molasses
2 cups sugar
1 tablespoon cloves
2 tablespoons cinnamon
7 cups flour
2 cups raisins

1 pound currants
½ pound diced citron or yellow raisins

Dissolve baking soda in boiling water and pour over ground salt pork. Add molasses, sugar, cloves, cinnamon, and 5 cups flour. Mix well. In another bowl combine raisins, currants, citron, and remaining flour. Stir into first mixture. Bake in small loaf pans at 275 or 300 degrees for 1 to 1½ hours or until done.

Submitted by Jane (Mrs. Edward) Rikkers, Madison.

BLITZ TORTE (German)

4 eggs, separated
1½ cups sugar
½ cup butter
1 teaspoon vanilla
1 cup sifted cake flour
¼ teaspoon salt
1 teaspoon baking powder
⅓ cup milk
Custard (see below)

In a medium bowl, beat egg whites, slowly adding 1 cup sugar to make a meringue. Beat until thick peaks form. Set aside.

In another medium bowl, cream butter; add remaining sugar, egg yolks, and vanilla. Beat well (beaters do not need to be washed from beating meringue). Slowly add flour, salt, and baking powder, which have been sifted together, alternately with the milk. Beat until well mixed. Divide into 2 greased and floured 9-inch cake pans (layers will be thin). Spread meringue evenly over cake batter. Bake at 350 degrees for about 25 minutes. Cool.

Remove carefully, meringue up; assemble on a cake plate with Custard between layers and over the top.

Custard:

½ cup sugar
¼ teaspoon salt
1 tablespoon cornstarch
1 tablespoon flour
2 cups milk
1 egg yolk
1 tablespoon butter
1 teaspoon vanilla

Combine sugar, salt, cornstarch, and flour; stir into milk in a saucepan. Cook over low heat, stirring constantly until thick. Beat egg yolk in a cup with a fork; add a little of the hot mixture, then blend into custard. Cook a little longer. Remove from heat and add butter and vanilla; stir well. Cool.

Submitted by Mrs. Norbert La See, Marshfield.

SCHAUM TORTE (German)

6 egg whites
2 cups sugar
1 teaspoon vanilla
1 teaspoon vinegar

Beat egg whites until peaks form. Add sugar gradually, beating well after each addition. Beat in vanilla and vinegar. Bake in a greased and floured 9-inch spring form pan at 225 degrees for 1 hour.

Submitted by Miss Edna. L. Timmel, Oconomowoc. Shaum Torte is usually served with strawberries or other fruit and whipped cream, with flavored whipped cream alone, or with ice cream.

A novelty recipe widely circulated at the turn of the century was for Scripture Cake; the ingredients were to be found in the cited verses from the Bible.

SCRIPTURE CAKE

1 cup Judges 5, verse 25
3½ cups I Kings 4, verse 22
3 cups Jeremiah 6, verse 20
2 cups I Samuel 30, verse 12
2 cups I Samuel 30, verse 12
1 cup Genesis 24, verse 17
1 cup Genesis 43, verse 11
6 Isaiah 10, verse 14
1 teaspoon Judges 14, verse 18
Pinch Leviticus 2, verse 13
To taste I Kings 10, verse 10
2 teaspoons I Corinthians 5, verse 6

Follow Solomon's advice in Proverbs 23, verse 14 for making good boys and you will make a good cake. Or proceed as in the ordinary rules for cake baking, putting in the fruit and nuts last of all. The raisins should be seeded, the figs chopped and the almonds blanched and sliced; all of these well floured to prevent sinking to the bottom.

From a recipe submitted by Mrs. Lucius Fairchild in the Capital City Cook Book, *third edition, published by the Grace Church Guild, Madison, 1906. Lucius Fairchild was governor of Wisconsin from 1866 to 1872. For those whose Bible is not close at hand, the ingredients, in the order given, are: butter, flour, sugar, raisins, figs, water, almonds, eggs, honey, salt, spices, and baking powder.*

Frostings

QUICK AND EASY CHOCOLATE FROSTING

¼ pound butter
3 tablespoons cocoa
6 tablespoons milk
1 pound confectioners' sugar
½ cup chopped nuts
1 teaspoon vanilla

Mix butter, cocoa, and milk in a saucepan and heat over low heat, but do not boil. Remove from heat and add sugar, nuts, and vanilla. Mix well.

Submitted by Augusta (Mrs. Adolph) Miller, Montello.

HICKORY NUT FROSTING

1 cup sugar
1 cup sour cream
1 cup hickory nuts

Combine sugar and sour cream and cook until thick. Beat in nuts.

Submitted by Virginia Roe, Whitewater.

CAKE FROSTING

1 sheet coopers isinglass dissolved in small teacup boiling water. Stir into 2 pounds pulverized sugar and flavor to taste.

From a notebook kept by Frances Kimberly Babcock of Neenah. Her husband, Havilah Babcock, whom she married in 1872, was one of the four men who founded the Kimberly Clark Paper Company. Submitted by Mrs. Henry Babcock Adams, Neenah. Isinglass is transparent, pure gelatin made from the bladder of fishes such as sturgeon.

CARAMEL FROSTING

1 cup cream
¾ cup brown sugar
Vanilla to taste

Combine cream and sugar in a saucepan and bring to a boil over high heat, stirring constantly. Reduce to simmer and cook until of a rather thick consistency, stirring frequently. Remove from heat, add vanilla, and beat with a spoon until cool. Frost cake and sprinkle with chopped nuts if desired.

Submitted by Romona (Mrs. Courtland) Sperger, Waupun.

STRAWBERRY FROSTING

¾ cup butter
½ cup confectioners' sugar
Strawberries

Beat together butter and sugar until creamy. Add strawberries, whole or sliced, as needed to make a frosting.

Submitted by Mrs. Rosalie Franckowiak, Cudahy.

COOKIES

PROBABLY THE TWO MOST UNIVERSAL MEMORIES of childhood in old (and even new) Wisconsin were the smell of cookies baking and the filled cookie jar always at the ready for snacking. Of course, cookies and Christmas are as inseparable as salt and pepper, and have been so for many generations.

Cookies were an important and permanent part of daily menus where hard physical work was performed: in logging camps, on construction sites, at threshing time. Their versatility contributed to their ubiquitousness. They were portable and nourishing; they could be baked up dainty or hearty to fit the occasion; and they were usually simple to make—an undoubted attraction to the novice, the hurried, or the busy cook.

The following recipes illustrate the kinds of cookies that were baked by a wide variety of Wisconsinites for hungry working men as well as for holiday celebrants and pleading schoolchildren.

LOGGER'S GINGER COOKIES
1 cup molasses
2 teaspoons baking soda
1½ cups shortening
1 cup sugar
2 eggs
1 teaspoon water
Pinch salt
2 teaspoons ginger
2 teaspoons cinnamon
2 teaspoons cloves
2 teaspoons allspice
About 4 cups flour

Bring molasses to a boil; remove from heat. When cool, add baking soda, shortening, sugar, and eggs. Mix well. Add water, salt, ginger, cinnamon, cloves, allspice, and enough flour to roll out thinly. Cut and bake at 400 degrees for 8 to 10 minutes.

Elizabeth Meating Proctor, Appleton, submitted this family-sized version of the cookies her grandfather baked as a cook in northern Wisconsin lumber camps.

AUNT NELLIE'S DROP COOKIES

1¾ cups melted lard
4 cups sugar
6 eggs
2 pounds raisins
7 teaspoons cinnamon
5 teaspoons cloves
7 teaspoons salt
7 cups flour
2 teaspoons baking powder
1 cup buttermilk
2 teaspoons baking soda

Combine melted lard and sugar. Beat in eggs. Stir in raisins, cinnamon, cloves, and salt. Sift flour and baking powder. Mix buttermilk and baking soda. Add flour to first mixture alternately with buttermilk. Drop by spoonfuls onto greased baking sheets and bake at 375 degrees for about 10 or 15 minutes. Makes enough for a threshing crew.

Cookies that Nellie Kedzie Jones, who lived on a farm in Marathon County, recommended in her column in Country Gentleman *as ideal to make at threshing time. No directions were given in the original; she simply noted that the cookies should be stored in an earthenware jar.*

MARZIPAN COOKIES (Norwegian)

2 cups very finely ground almonds
1 cup extra-fine granulated sugar
1 cup confectioners' sugar
½ teaspoon almond extract
4 egg whites

Mix together almonds, sugar, and confectioners' sugar. Add almond extract and blend well. Add egg whites and beat vigorously until creamy. Drop by teaspoonsful onto buttered baking sheet 2 or 3 inches apart. Bake at 350 degrees for 15 minutes. Remove from baking sheet quickly and carefully.

Submitted by Helen Collins, Montello, who noted that these are very much like macaroons.

A similar cookie, called Zimpt Hippen in German, is seasoned with cinnamon instead of confectioners' sugar; after baking, the cookies are rolled around a wooden spoon handle into a cigarette shape.

CRY BABIES

1 cup lard
1 cup sugar
1 cup molasses
1 egg
1 teaspoon baking soda
1 cup boiling water
5 cups flour
1 teaspoon salt

Cream lard and sugar together. Beat in molasses and egg. Dissolve baking soda in boiling water and add alternately with flour and salt. Drop by teaspoons on greased baking sheet, allowing room to spread. Bake at 400 degrees for about 10 minutes.

Submitted by Mrs. Glenn Daigle, Neenah.

CRACKLING COOKIES

1 cup brown sugar
2 cups sugar
2 eggs
2 cups cracklings (fried out crisp)
1 cup chopped nuts
1 cup ground raisins or dates
2 teaspoons baking soda
½ cup hot coffee
Salt to taste
Cinnamon to taste
Nutmeg to taste
4 cups flour

Combine sugars and beat in eggs and cracklings. Stir in nuts and raisins or dates. Dissolve baking soda in coffee and add along with salt, cinnamon, and nutmeg. Stir in flour. Form dough into balls and flatten on baking sheet with a fork. Bake at 400 degrees until done, about 10 minutes.

Submitted by Mrs. M. Burleton, Oakfield.

Many ethnic groups had a molasses cookie specialty similar to this one, with variations in flavorings.

MOLASSES CRUMB COOKIES

2 cups dry grated bread crumbs
½ cup molasses
½ cup shortening
1 cup sugar
1 egg
1 teaspoon baking soda
1 teaspoon baking powder
½ teaspoon ginger
1 teaspoon cinnamon
2 tablespoons cream
1½ cups flour

Mix bread crumbs and molasses. Add shortening creamed with sugar. Beat in egg, baking soda, baking powder, ginger, cinnamon, cream, and flour. Mix well. Form into balls with fingers. Bake on greased baking sheet at 375 degrees until done, 8 to 10 minutes.

Submitted by Frances W. (Mrs. Robert J.) Booker, Milwaukee.

HICKORY NUT COOKIES

1 cup lard
1 cup butter
1 cup brown sugar
1 cup sugar
3 eggs, well beaten
Vanilla to taste
About 5½ cups flour
1 teaspoon baking soda
½ teaspoon cinnamon
1 cup or more chopped hickory nuts

Cream lard and butter together. Cream in brown sugar and then sugar. Beat in eggs and vanilla. Combine baking soda with some of the flour and then add with enough flour to make a firm dough. Stir in nuts. Form into rolls or loaves; chill overnight.

Cut in thin slices and bake at 375 degrees until done, about 8 or 10 minutes.

Submitted by Alice (Mrs. H. E.) Johnson, Racine.

LARK'S NESTS (German)

½ cup butter
1 cup sugar
3 eggs, separated
About 3 cups flour
2 teaspoons baking powder
Cinnamon, nutmeg, or grated lemon peel to
    taste
Raspberry jam (optional)
Filling (see below)

Cream butter and sugar; add beaten egg yolks. Combine flour and baking powder and add desired spices or flavoring. Beat egg whites and add to dough. Roll out and cut into rounds large enough to fit into small cupcake tins. Put a layer of jam, if desired, into bottom of cookie cups and add filling. Bake at 400 degrees about 15 minutes or until done.

Filling:

6 eggs
½ pound chopped almonds (unblanched)
3½ cups confectioners' sugar
½ teaspoon cinnamon
Pinch nutmeg

Beat eggs well. Add almonds and sugar. Stir in cinnamon and nutmeg.

Submitted by Elinore L. Loveland, Platteville.

CHRISTMAS FORM COOKIES

1 cup shortening
1 cup sugar
3 eggs, lightly beaten
2 teaspoons cream of tartar
1 teaspoon baking soda
1 teaspoon salt
3 cups flour
1 teaspoon vanilla
Frostings and decorations as desired

Cream shortening and sugar; beat in eggs. Sift together cream of tartar, baking soda, and salt. Add to creamed mixture with flour. Stir in vanilla. Chill several hours or overnight.

To bake, roll a little out at a time and cut with cookie cutters. Bake on greased baking sheets at 300 degrees until done, about 15 or 20 minutes. Frost and decorate.

Submitted by Joan (Mrs. Willian) Fancher, Racine, who remembered that as a child, the best part of the holiday baking for her brother and herself was decorating the Christmas cookies. "The trees were sprinkled with green colored sugar and decorated with cinnamon candies. Also made wreaths, stars, and Santa Claus forms. My daughter and I have branched out to include Halloween cookies . . . . It has also led me to an interesting hobby: collecting cookie cutters."

CANNOLI (Italian)

1 cup flour
1 teaspoon cocoa
2 teaspoons sugar
1 teaspoon baking powder
2 teaspoons butter, softened
Semi-dry white wine
Oil for frying
Filling (see below)
Pistachio nuts, crushed
Jimmies

Mix together flour, cocoa, sugar, and baking powder. Add butter and mix until a dough is formed. Add wine slowly until it becomes a pliable dough that can be rolled out.

Divide dough into 4 or 8 portions and roll each separately on a floured board until dough is paper thin. Using a very sharp knife, cut into 4-inch squares. Roll each square on an aluminum cannoli tube, corner to corner, forming a cylinder. Seal the tip with a finger moistened in water.

Deep fry shells in very hot oil (375 degrees) no more than 2 minutes or until bubbly and golden brown. Slide off tube carefully and let drain on absorbent paper. Repeat until all dough is used up.

Shells may be made as long as a week in advance; store in airtight containers with absorbent paper between layers. After 3 days, change paper.

When ready to serve, fill shells with filling. Dip ends in crushed pistachio nuts and/or jimmies. Makes 25 Cannoli.

Filling:

8 tablespoons cornstarch
2 cups sugar
2 cups milk
2½ pounds ricotta cheese
1 tablespoon vanilla
1 pint heavy cream, whipped
1 1-pound bar chocolate-almond candy
1 tablespoon canned citron (optional)

Mix together cornstarch, sugar, and milk. Cook over low heat, stirring constantly, until mixture comes to a boil and is thick. Set aside and allow to cool 3 or 4 hours.

Whip ricotta cheese with electric mixer until fluffy. Fold in milk mixture and add vanilla. Fold in whipped cream. Cut chocolate bar into tiny pieces and fold in. Add citron, if desired.

From the files of the International Institute of Milwaukee County.

DATE PINWHEEL COOKIES

2¼ cups dates, chopped
1 cup sugar
1 cup water
1 cup chopped nuts
1 cup shortening
2 cups brown sugar
3 eggs, well beaten
4 cups flour
½ teaspoon baking soda
1 teaspoon baking powder
Dash salt

Combine dates, sugar, and water. Cook about 10 minutes over low heat. Add nuts and cool.

Cream shortening and add sugar. Add eggs. Sift together baking soda, baking powder, and salt. Add to creamed mixture and mix well. Chill thoroughly.

Divide dough into two parts. Roll out each ¼-inch thick. Spread with date mixture and roll as for jelly roll. Chill overnight.

Slice ¼-inch thick and bake at 375 degrees for 10 to 12 minutes.

Submitted by LaVerne Hogan (Mrs. A. A.) Koeller, Ashland.

CINNAMON FLOP

2 cups flour
1 teaspoon baking powder
1 tablespoon or more lard
1 cup sugar
1¼ cups milk
3 tablespoons or more melted butter
Cinnamon
Brown sugar

Combine flour and baking powder and rub in lard well. Add sugar and mix. Add milk and mix well. Pat dough 1-inch thick into pie pans and spread with melted butter. Sprinkle thickly with brown sugar and cinnamon. Bake at 350 degrees for 15 to 20 minutes or until nicely browned. Watch carefully as this burns easily.

Submitted by Mrs. Clyde Zahn, Shawano.

PRINCESSCHEN (German)

4 eggs, well beaten
1 cup sugar
Pinch salt
1 cup flour
1 teaspoon vanilla
Sugar
Slivered almonds

Combine eggs and sugar and beat until sugar is dissolved. Stir in salt and flour. Blend well. Stir in vanilla. Spread in greased baking pan or pans so batter is ½ to ¾-inch thick. Sprinkle over the top sugar and slivered almonds. Batter should be covered, but topping should not be too thick. Bake at 350 degrees about 30 minutes or until done.

Submitted by the Reverend Frederick W. Ringe, Mukwonago.

Norwegian, Scottish, Irish, Bohemian, German—just about every ethnic group that settled Wisconsin had some version of the sugar cookie.

SUGAR COOKIES

2 cups sifted flour
½ teaspoon baking soda
½ teaspoon cream of tartar
¼ teaspoon salt
½ cup shortening
½ cup butter
1 cup sugar
1 large egg
¼ teaspoon nutmeg

Sift together flour, baking soda, cream of tartar, and salt. Cream shortening, butter, and sugar until light. Add egg and cream well. Stir in nutmeg and blend in flour mixture. Cover dough and chill.

Roll dough into small balls, place on lightly greased baking sheet, and press flat with the bottom of a glass that has been dipped in sugar. Bake at 375 degrees for 10 minutes. Makes 5 or 6 dozen.

Submitted by Florence Rice, Oconto Falls.

SWISS KRABELI

2 eggs
1 cup sugar
1½ teaspoons anise seed
¾ teaspoon grated lemon peel
1½ cups flour
¼ teaspoon baking powder

Beat eggs until foamy; add sugar and beat until light. Add anise seed and lemon peel. Thoroughly blend together flour and baking powder and stir into egg mixture. Chill thoroughly.

On lightly floured surface, roll out a sixth of the dough at a time into a rope ½-inch in diameter. Cut into 3-inch pieces. Place on a well-greased baking sheet, curving to form crescents. Bake at 350 degrees about 10 minutes or until lightly browned. Remove to a rack immediately. When cool, store in tightly covered containers. Makes 3 dozen.

Submitted by Miss Kathleen M. Bauer, Knowles.

CARAWAY SEED COOKIES (Cornish)

1 egg
1 cup sugar
2 tablespoons lemon juice
½ cup butter, softened
1 tablespoon caraway seed
2½ cups flour
½ teaspoon baking soda
½ teaspoon salt

Beat egg and gradually beat in sugar. Add lemon juice, butter, and caraway seed. Sift together flour, baking soda, and salt, and stir into egg mixture. Roll out and cut. Bake on greased baking sheets at 400 degrees until lightly browned. Makes about 60 cookies.

Submitted by Fay S. (Mrs. Orr) Dooley, Marinette. This recipe was handed down from her great grandmother, who homesteaded a farm with her husband about 5 miles northwest of Peshtigo around 1860. She was one of the 1,200 victims of the great Peshtigo Fire in 1871. Her married daughter, Mrs. Dooley's grandmother, survived by spending the night in the Peshtigo River, and made these cookies regularly when Mrs. Dooley was growing up.

DEW DROPS

½ cup butter
1 cup sugar
3 eggs
1 cup sour milk
1 teaspoon baking soda
1 tablespoon cinnamon
1 teaspoon cloves
1 teaspoon nutmeg
About 2 cups flour
1 cup chopped nuts
1 cup raisins or currants

Cream butter and sugar until light and fluffy. Beat in eggs, one at a time. Dissolve baking soda in sour milk. Sift together cinnamon, cloves, nutmeg, and flour; add to creamed mixture alternately with milk, mixing thoroughly. Stir in nuts and raisins. (Dough should be stiff.) Drop by tablespoon onto greased baking sheets, 2 or 3 inches apart. Bake at 350 degrees for 15 minutes or until golden.

Submitted by Florence Baker (Mrs. J. A.) Riegel, St. Croix Falls.

BAVARIAN SEEDCAKES

1 cup sugar
1 cup butter, lard, or rendered chicken fat
  (scant measure if using chicken fat)
3 eggs and 1 cup sour cream *or* 2 eggs and ⅓
  cup sour cream
3 cups flour *or* 2 cups flour and 1 cup corn
  starch
1 teaspoon baking soda (scant measure if no
  cream is used)
2 teaspoons cream of tartar
1 teaspoon salt
1 teaspoon nutmeg
1 teaspoon vanilla or lemon or almond extract
Caraway seeds

Cream sugar and butter. Beat in eggs. Combine well flour, baking soda, cream of tartar, salt, and nutmeg; mix into creamed mixture. Stir in vanilla. Chill slightly.

Flour board lightly and sprinkle with sugar. Roll out dough very thinly; cut with large scalloped cutter; sprinkle with sugar and caraway seeds and press lightly. Bake on greased baking sheets at 375 degrees about 10 or 12 minutes.

Submitted by Pat Gottschall (Mrs. B. A.) Schuknecht, Lodi.

LEBKUCHEN (German)

1 cup honey
¾ cup brown sugar
1 egg, beaten
1 tablespoon lemon juice
Grated rind from 1 lemon
About 2½ cups flour
½ teaspoon baking soda
1 teaspoon cinnamon
¼ teaspoon cloves
½ teaspoon allspice
½ teaspoon nutmeg
⅓ cup citron
⅓ cup almonds, very finely chopped
Almond halves
Citron
Glaze (see below)

Bring honey to a boil; cool. Add sugar, egg, lemon juice, and rind. Sift together flour, baking soda, cinnamon, cloves, allspice, and nutmeg; add to honey mixture. Stir in citron and chopped almonds. Chill in refrigerator overnight.

On a floured board, roll out dough (which will be sticky) to ½-inch thickness. Cut with round or scalloped cutter. Place on greased baking sheet and press a piece of citron in center and three almond halves, like daisy petals, around it. Bake at 350 degrees until lightly browned. Glaze immediately; allow to set.

Glaze:

1 cup sugar
⅓ cup water
1 tablespoon lemon juice
¼ cup confectioners' sugar

Boil sugar, water, and lemon juice until syrup forms threads from a spoon. Stir in confectioners' sugar. If glaze thickens while using, add a bit of water and heat again until all cookies are covered.

Store in air-tight containers with waxed paper between layers. Put a piece of apple in the container and allow to ripen at least 2 weeks.

Submitted by Ione R. Gadow, Oshkosh, who remembered that her grandmother stored the Lebkuchen *in stone crocks with a plate on top.*

BARAVYKAI (Lithuanian)

5 cups flour
½ teaspoon cinnamon
¼ teaspoon nutmeg
¼ teaspoon cloves
¼ teaspoon cardamon
¼ teaspoon dried lemon peel
¼ teaspoon dried orange peel
1½ teaspoons baking soda
1 cup honey
1 tablespoon brown sugar
2 tablespoons sugar
½ cup butter, creamed
2 tablespoons sour cream
2 eggs
Icing (see below)
Poppy seeds (optional)
Coconut (optional)

The Lithuanian name means "mushroom-shaped cookies."

Sift together flour, cinnamon, nutmeg, cloves, cardamon, lemon and orange peel, and baking soda. Heat honey to lukewarm; add sugars and mix well. Add flour mixture, alternating with butter and sour cream. Add eggs and blend well. Let dough rest for a few minutes.

Cut about 2 dozen pieces of waxed paper 2 by 5 inches; roll into cones.

From two-thirds of the dough, form about 1-inch balls; flatten to ½-inch thickness. These will be the mushroom "caps". If you wish to assemble some of the mushrooms upright, make several balls larger to form a base. Place on an ungreased baking sheet 1 inch apart. Bake at 325 degrees until center springs back when touched, about 15 minutes.

Roll remaining dough into a long roll and cut ¾-inch pieces (these will be the "stems"); place in the paper cones. Place on baking sheets and bake at 325 degrees about 10 minutes.

Icing:

1 cup sugar
½ cup water
1 egg white
5 drops lemon juice or corn syrup or ¼
   teaspoon cream of tartar
Food coloring

Boil water and sugar until thread spins from the spoon. Beat egg white, then quickly add sugar mixture. Beat at high speed. Add lemon juice and beat until mixture is like thick cream.

If you wish to have the caps a brownish color, remove some of the icing and color with food coloring. For upright mushrooms, color some of icing green.

To assemble, make an indentation in the cookie cap to fit the narrow end of the stem. Ice stem and bottom of mushroom cap and place stem into identation. Let dry.

Poppy seeds may be used to simulate spores on the bottom of the cap and end of mushroom. Ice top of cap using brown colored icing. Let dry. For upright mushrooms, frost base pieces with green icing, place assembled mushroom on top and support with a stand or toothpicks. Colored coconut may be used to simulate grass.

Submitted by Mrs. Theresa Balciunas, Kenosha, who explained that these elaborate cookies were used as decoration for the Christmas table. "The mushroom is quite prevalent in Lithuania," she wrote, "and do look very attractive as decoration." Other cookies were made to look like birch branches, porcupines, or oak branches, and were often given as Christmas gifts.

DUSE CONFECT

1 pound butter
2 cups sugar
1 pound (about 4 cups) flour
½ pound finely ground almonds
Currant jelly
Confectioners' sugar

Cream butter. Cream in sugar, flour and almonds until smooth. Roll out as thinly as possible and cut in 1½-inch rounds. Bake on baking sheets at 325 degrees until just "sugar cookie color." While still warm, spread with jelly and put 2 cookies together into a sandwich. When cool, roll in confectioners' sugar.

Submitted by Jane (Mrs. Edward) Rikkers, Madison, who noted that these are the first to disappear from her family's Christmas cookie platter.

PUMPKIN BARS

4 eggs
2 cups sugar
¼ cup butter, melted
2 cups canned pumpkin
2 cups flour
2 teaspoons baking powder
1 teaspoon baking soda
¼ teaspoon salt
½ teaspoon cinnamon
1 cup chopped nuts

Mix eggs, sugar, butter, and pumpkin together. Sift together flour, baking powder, baking soda, salt, and cinnamon; add to pumpkin mixture and mix well. Stir in chopped nuts. Pour into a well-greased and floured 15½-by-10½-by-1-inch jelly roll pan. Bake at 400 degrees for 25 minutes. Cut into squares when cool. Frost with a confectioners' sugar icing. Makes about 35 cookies.

Submitted by Mary Gillis, Oconto Falls.

PFEFFERNÜSSE (German)

1 cup lard
1 cup molasses
¾ cup brown sugar
2 eggs
¼ cup warm water
1½ teaspoons baking soda
5 cups flour
½ teaspoon nutmeg
1 teaspoon cinnamon
½ teaspoon cloves
½ teaspoon allspice
¼ teaspoon salt

¼ teaspoon freshly ground pepper
½ teaspoon ground anise
¼ cup finely chopped almonds (optional)

Cream together lard, molasses, brown sugar, and eggs. Dissolve ½ teaspoon baking soda in warm water and add. Blend and sift together remaining baking soda, flour, nutmeg, cinnamon, cloves, allspice, salt, pepper, and anise. Gradually mix dry ingredients into creamed mixture. Stir in almonds if desired. Knead down until dough can be molded into small balls, ½ to ¾-inch in diameter. Bake on greased baking sheet at 350 degrees for 10 to 12 minutes.

Submitted by Marion Philippi (Mrs. John A.) Urich, Madison.

CHRISTMAS COOKIES (German)

1 quart honey
4 cups sugar
½ pound butter
1½ cups milk
1 pound mixed candied fruits
½ pound walnuts
½ pound almonds
2 teaspoons cardamon
2 teaspoons baking soda
5 eggs, slightly beaten
About 13½ cups flour

Heat honey and sugar until sugar is dissolved. Add butter and 1 cup milk; let cool. Add candied fruits, walnuts, almonds, and cardamon. Dissolve baking soda in remaining milk and add with eggs. Stir in flour. Chill overnight.

Roll out and cut as desired. Bake on greased baking sheets at 350 degrees until lightly browned, about 8 or 10 minutes. Store and season 4 weeks.

Submitted by Leone (Mrs. Elmer) Mielke, Janesville.

In Norway and elsewhere in Scandinavia, a more seasoned fried cookie is served at Christmas.

FATTIGMAND (Norwegian)

6 eggs, separated
1⅛ cups sugar
6 tablespoons heavy cream, whipped
1 cup butter, melted
¼ teaspoon cinnamon
1 teaspoon cardamon
1 teaspoon baking powder
About 4½ cups flour
2 teaspoons lemon extract
1 tablespoon cognac (optional)
Fat or lard for frying
Confectioners' sugar

Beat yolks and sugar for about 12 minutes. Add whipped cream. Stir in butter, cinnamon, and cardamon. Combine baking powder and flour and sift several times; add to batter. Add lemon extract and cognac. Beat egg whites until stiff and fold in well. Turn dough out onto a board. Taking a small portion at a time, roll out thinly using as little flour on the board as possible. Cut into diamond shapes 5 by 2½ inches. (Make a pattern as a guide for cutting with a floured knife.) Make a lengthwise slit in the center of the diamond, pulling one tip end through it and tucking back under. Deep fry in hot fat or lard until light brown, turning once. Do not crowd *Fattigmand* in kettle. Drain on absorbent paper. Sprinkle with confectioners' sugar.

Submitted by Agnes E. Norem, Antigo, who added that, like her mother, she believes these are more flavorful if you grind or finely crush the cardamon seed fresh. She uses a 200-year-old heirloom Norwegian mortar and pestle for the job when she makes them.

Some version of a light, fried cookie is found in numerous cuisines in middle and northern Europe. Many traditionally served them on Shrove Tuesday as well as at Christmas time. They are called *Chruscik* in Polish, *Listy* by Bohemians, *Fastnach Kuechli* by Swiss. This Czech version, which translates as "Celestial Crusts," is representative of the type.

BOŽÍ MILOSTI (Czech)

4 egg yolks
1 tablespoon sugar
1 tablespoon brandy or wine
3 tablespoons cream
2 or 3 drops vanilla
About 1½ cups flour
Lard for frying
Confectioners' sugar

Cream yolks with sugar; add brandy, cream, and vanilla. Work in enough flour to make a stiff dough, not quite as stiff as for noodles. Work until smooth. Roll out on a lightly floured board until thin. Cut into squares and prick each with a fork. Deep fry in hot lard, a few at a time. Drain on absorbent paper. When all are fried, put on a plate and dust with confectioners' sugar.

Submitted by Blanche Mendl, Deerbrook.

ROSETTES (Swedish)

2 eggs
2 teaspoons sugar
1 cup milk
1½ cups flour
¼ teaspoon salt
¼ teaspoon vanilla
Shortening for frying
Confectioners' sugar

Beat eggs; add sugar, milk, flour, salt, and vanilla and beat until batter is consistency of thick cream. Heat rosette iron by dripping into heated shortening for 10 seconds. (Shortening should be 350 to 375 degrees.) Dip heated iron into batter, so that batter is even at the top; dip into hot shortening so top of iron is covered. As soon as batter starts to expand from the iron, gradually lift iron until rosette drops off. Remove cookie from fat and drain on absorbent paper and sprinkle with confectioners' sugar.

Mildred O. (Mrs. Willett S.) Main, Milwaukee, submitted her Scandinavian aunt's recipe. Her aunt, like her mother, always served afternoon coffee along with rosettes or other cookies: "I can remember coming home from school and being greeted by whiffs of delicious coffee made the old-fashioned way with egg. . . ."

SAND BAKKELS (Norwegian)

1 cup butter
1 cup sugar
2 egg yolks
½ teaspoon vanilla
2½ cups flour

Cream butter; beat in sugar. Add egg yolks and vanilla and beat well. Gradually stir in flour and work dough until well mixed. Chill several hours.

Spread dough as thinly as possible in Sand Bakkels pans. (See note below.) Bake at 375 degrees about 15 minutes or until golden brown. Cool and remove from pans.

Submitted by Mrs. Robert Smart, Muskego. Lacking a Sand Bakkels pan, the dough may be rolled out thinly and baked on cookie sheets. Some recipes call for topping the baked Sand Bakkels with chopped nuts, after brushing with egg whites.

KRINGELN (German)

½ cup sugar
¾ cup shortening (½ of it butter)
1 egg, beaten
2 cups flour
½ teaspoon baking soda
½ teaspoon salt
½ teaspoon cardamon
Cinnamon
Sugar

Cream sugar and shortening together. Beat in egg. Combine flour, baking soda, salt, and cardamon and mix in well. Roll out thinly, about ⅛-inch. Cut with doughnut cutter (so there will be a hole in the center). Place carefully on lightly buttered baking sheet. Sprinkle with cinnamon and sugar. Bake at 350 degrees about 8 minutes; watch carefully so they do not burn. Cool slightly, then place on a rack until cool. Store in airtight containers in a cool place (not the refrigerator).

If dough is too stiff to roll out easily, beat an egg and use as much as needed. A little more beaten egg may also be necessary to roll dough left from the first rollings.

Submitted by Ruth Jochimsen (Mrs. John) Mattke, Sheboygan. The shape specified for these Christmas cookies represents the halo of the Christ Child.

SCOTCH KUMFITS

1 pound butter, at room temperature
¾ cup sugar
½ cup confectioners' sugar
4 cups sifted flour

Work butter until creamy. Sift sugars together and beat in. Add flour, one cup at a time, mixing well. Divide dough into 3 parts. Knead on a floured board working in about ⅓ cup more of flour to each portion. Roll out about ⅓-inch thick. Cut with diamond-shaped cookie cutters; place on baking sheets and prick with a fork several times. Bake at 325 degrees about 30 minutes or until very light brown. Watch carefully as these burn easily. Makes about 55 cookies.

Submitted by Irene Jones (Mrs. Leon A.) Pratt, Edgerton. These improve with age and can be frozen. "In making the recipe, our grandmother made it into 4-by-6-inch cakes ½-inch thick. Pieces were broken off and served," she wrote. "Sometimes the shortbread was made with part butter and part pork drippings."

Cookies baked in a special iron similar to a waffle iron are made in a number of European countries. After baking, they are rolled up. In Norway, they are known as *Krumkage*. This is a Swiss version.

BRETZELS (Swiss)

2 eggs
2 cups sugar
⅓ cup butter, melted
⅔ cup lard, melted
¾ cup cream
½ teaspoon salt
About 5 cups flour
2 teaspoons vanilla

Beat eggs. Add sugar, butter, and lard. Stir in cream. Mix in flour and salt and blend well. Stir in vanilla. Roll into small balls and place in a hot Bretzel iron. Bake until light brown. Remove from iron and roll around wooden spoon handle while still warm.

Submitted by Mrs. Edith H. Gotz, Pittsville.

DESSERTS
and DESSERT SAUCES

THE SWEET TOOTH IS UNIVERSAL. IF NOT satisfied with pie, cakes, or cookies, its demands have always been met with some other sort of dessert.

Wisconsin's repertoire of recipes included meal endings or treats of great variety in taste and complexity of preparation. These could be as simple as fresh-picked fruit or berries eaten in garden or orchard. Only slightly more complicated was the dish called *A Beurrée* in the French-Canadian family of Mrs. Henry R. Bowers of Marion: "One generous slice of bread on a plate. (Homemade bread works the best.) Spread with jam or sprinkle with brown sugar. Pour over heavy cream generously. Eat hearty!"

Indeed eat hearty was the usual procedure for this sampling of the state's dessert cart.

BREAD PIE DESSERT

Fresh fruit, for example 4 big apples, *or* 2 pints berries, *or* 5 or 6 peaches
Sugar
Flour
Bread slices
Melted butter

Prepare fruit as necessary—wash and hull berries; core and slice apples, peel and slice peaches, etc. Sprinkle with sugar and flour lightly. Fill a deep pie plate with the fruit. Brush bread on both sides with melted butter and cut into 1-inch strips. Cover fruit with bread strips. Sprinkle about ½ cup sugar (more if fruit is sour or tart) over top. Bake covered in 350 degree oven until the fruit is done, then uncover to brown.

Serve with pudding sauce or whipped cream.

Submitted by Mrs. Cecil A. Fisher, Milwaukee.

BREAD MERINGUE

1 pint of bread crumbs, 1 quart sweet milk, 1 cup brown sugar, yolks of 4 eggs, grated rind of 1 lemon, piece butter the size of an egg. Bake until stiff. Put over it the whites of eggs beaten stiff with a teacup of the juice of lemon. Brown lightly.

From the notebook of Frances Kimberly Babcock of Neenah. Submitted by Mrs. Henry Babcock Adams, Neenah.

SLIP EASY PUDDING (English)

3½ cups whole wheat bread crumbs
3½ cups fresh rhubarb or any fruit
1½ cups sugar
Salt
Butter
2 cups milk
Sauce (see below)

Put 1 cup crumbs in bottom of a baking dish. Cover with one-half of the rhubarb, ½ cup sugar, and a few grains of salt. Top with half the balance of the crumbs, then the rest of the fruit, ½ cup sugar, and a bit of salt. Cover with remaining crumbs and sprinkle over remaining sugar. Dot with butter and pour milk over all. Bake at 325 degrees until golden brown. Serve with sauce.

Sauce:

1 cup brown sugar
1 tablespoon flour
1 cup hot water
1 tablespoon vinegar

Combine sugar and flour; add water and vinegar and boil until creamy.

Submitted by Mrs. S. G. Corey, Wisconsin Rapids.

BIRDS NEST PUDDING

2 cups dried peaches, apples, or berries
2 or 3 cups water
1 cup sugar or syrup
1 scant cup buttermilk or sour milk
½ teaspoon baking soda
Pinch salt
Flour

Wash fruit well. Simmer in water for 20 minutes. Sprinkle with sugar or syrup. Combine buttermilk, baking soda, salt, and enough flour to make a very firm dough. Drop batter over fruit. Cover tightly and place over very low heat for 20 minutes. Serve with a generous sprinkle of sugar and cream.

Submitted by Dorothy (Mrs. Clarence) Proksch, Stoddard, who explained that her great-aunt told her this dessert got its name from the fact it is made the way birds' nests are—"with whatever you can get a hold of."

APPLE FLOAT

Take one pint of green apple sauce, made smooth by passing through a sieve or colander; the whites of three eggs beaten to a stiff froth; and sugar and lemon to suit the taste. Beat all well together, then send to the table, dish out and eat with rich, cold cream.

From "The Household" column, Milwaukee Sentinel, *August 24, 1877.*

APPLE PUDDING

Sliced apples
1½ cups sugar
1 teaspoon nutmeg
1½ cups cream
2½ cups milk
½ teaspoon salt
2 cups flour
2 teaspoons baking powder
Vanilla to taste

Put enough sliced apples in a 10-by-13-inch pan to make a layer about 1 inch deep. Mix with 1 cup of sugar; sprinkle nutmeg over top. Combine cream, ½ cup milk, salt, flour, and baking powder into a thin batter. Spread over apples. Bake at 350 degrees about 30 minutes. Combine remaining milk, sugar, and vanilla to taste. Cut pudding in squares and serve (apple side up) with the flavored milk.

Submitted by Mrs. Claire Bennett, Endeavor.

APPLE ELDERBERRY DUMPLINGS (Cornish)

1½ cups sweetened elderberry juice
¼ teaspoon cinnamon
¼ teaspoon nutmeg
3 tablespoons butter
Crust for 2 pies
Apples, peeled and cored
Sugar
Cinnamon
Nutmeg
Butter
Cream

Make a syrup by combining elderberry juice, cinnamon, nutmeg, and butter.

Roll out pie crust. Cut into 6 squares. Place 1 peeled, cored apple in center of each square. Sprinkle each apple with sugar, cinnamon, and nutmeg. Dot with butter. Moisten edge of crust, bring together with corners at top, pinking or fluting edges. Place 1 inch apart on baking sheet. Pour syrup over dumplings and bake at 375 degrees until apples are done. Serve warm with cream.

From the Shullsburg Methodist Womens Cornish Recipe Book, *Shullsburg. Submitted by Hila (Mrs. Robert) Hefferman, Kewaunee, who added that she has used jam—gooseberry, strawberry, etc.—in place of elderberry juice. "Tartness counts."*

INDIAN PUDDING

2 quarts milk (skim milk is best)
1 cup cornmeal
Salt
1 cup brown sugar
⅓ cup molasses
Raisins (optional)
Pinch ginger (optional)

Scald 1 quart of milk; add cornmeal. Cook until mixture thickens. Add salt to taste, sugar, molasses, remaining cold milk, and raisins and ginger if desired. Bake at 325 degrees about 1½ to 2 hours.

Submitted by Florence Baker (Mrs. J. A.) Riegel, St. Croix Falls.

BAKED HUCKLEBERRY PUDDING

One quart of ripe, fresh huckleberries or blueberries; half a teaspoon of mace or nutmeg; three eggs well beaten, separately; two cupsful of sugar; one tablespoonful of cold butter; one cupful of sweet milk; one pint of flour; two teas-poonsful of baking powder. Roll the berries well in the flour, and add them last of all. Bake half an hour and serve with sauce. There is no more delicate and delicious pudding than this.

From The White House Cook Book, *1891, used at Old Wade House, Greenbush.*

These two Finnish recipes mean, respectively, "Apple Snow" and "Apple Souffle." Both are well suited to the Wisconsin table.

OMENALUNTA (Finnish)

1 cup thick apple sauce
Sugar to taste
4 egg whites, beaten stiff
Whipped cream

Sweeten applesauce to taste with sugar. Add egg whites. Serve in sherbet glasses with whipped cream.

OMENAKOHOKAS (Finnish)

2 cups apple sauce
Sugar to taste
4 egg whites, beaten stiff
Whipped cream

Sweeten apple sauce with sugar to taste. Fold in egg whites. Bake at 325 degrees for 25 minutes. Serve with whipped cream.

Submitted by Mrs. Milton M. Mandelin, Greenfield, who reported that these "were always our 'extra special' desserts when I was a child on the farm (where we had our own apple trees)."

RIS KREM (Norwegian)

4 cups water
2 cups milk
½ teaspoon salt
1 cup rice, washed
½ cup sugar
¾ cup heavy cream
1 teaspoon vanilla
Crushed pineapple or chopped almonds
    (optional)
Fruit juice thickened with cornstarch
    (optional)

Bring to a boil water, milk, and salt. Add rice and sugar and cook over low heat until rice is soft and fluffy, stirring gently once or twice. Chill.

Whip cream and add vanilla. Mix with the rice just before serving. Crushed pineapple or almonds may be added. If desired, pour a circle of cooled thickened fruit juice on each serving.

Submitted by Mrs. Selma Casberg, Holmen.

CITRONGELE (Norwegian)

5 large eggs
7½ tablespoons sugar
Juice and grated rind of 1 lemon
1 pint heavy cream
About 2 tablespoons lemon extract
2 tablespoons unflavored gelatin
Raspberry-Juice Sauce (see below)

In the bowl of an electric mixer, combine eggs and sugar; beat until lemon-colored and light, about 12 to 15 minutes. Add lemon rind and juice.

Whip cream and fold in gently until well blended. Add lemon extract and taste, adding more extract if necessary for sufficient lemon flavor.

Soften gelatin in a small amount of cold water in a measuring cup; add boiling water to make about ¾ cup; stir to dissolve.

Holding the cup about a foot above the egg mixture, gradually pour a small stream of dissolved hot gelatin into the bowl, blending gently with a rubber spatula. (It is important to pour gelatin in a little at a time, and very gently, or it is apt to form a firm custard layer at the bottom.) Pour mixture immediately into a large serving bowl and store in refrigerator. (This may be made the day before.)

To serve, spoon onto plates and pass Raspberry-Juice Sauce.

Raspberry-Juice Sauce:

Clear raspberry juice, preferably home-made
Potato starch flour

Heat juice and add enough potato starch flour to thicken. Chill.

Submitted by Agnes E. Norem, Antigo.

A DELICATE DESSERT

Lay half a dozen crackers in a tureen. Pour on enough boiling water to cover them. In a few minutes they will be swollen to three times their original size. Grate loaf sugar & a little nutmeg over them and dip on enough sweet cream to make a nice sauce.

From the handwritten recipe collection of Ann Eliza Tenney Jackson, begun January 3, 1864, and preserved in the archives of the State Historical Society of Wisconsin.

RICE PUDDING (Yankee)

1 quart milk
6 tablespoons rice
9 tablespoons sugar
Pinch salt
1 teaspoon vanilla
1 egg, if necessary
Nutmeg (optional)

Pour milk into a lightly buttered baking pan. Stir in rice, sugar, salt, and vanilla. Bake at 325 degrees for 3 hours or more, stirring 2 or 3 times during baking. The longer this is baked, the thicker it becomes, sometimes thick enough to cut into squares. If it doesn't thicken enough, beat egg and gradually add to hot pudding as soon as it is removed from oven. Sprinkle on nutmeg, if desired.

Submitted by Mrs. Twylah Kepler, Richland Center. She remembered that her "grandmother would bank the fire in her range with a large piece of wood and the rice pudding would bake for many hours in a slow oven along side a pork roast."

ROMME GROT (Norwegian)

4 cups soured cream
3 cups flour
9 cups milk
2 teaspoons salt
Sugar
Cinnamon

Bring cream to a boil and simmer 10 to 20 minutes. Sift in half the flour, stirring continuously. (Fat will begin to separate.) Remove from heat, cover, and let stand 3 minutes. Remove fat and reserve. Bring milk to a boil. Add or sift rest of flour into cream mixture and add hot milk gradually, stirring constantly to keep it smooth. Simmer 10 to 20 minutes, stirring frequently to keep from scorching. Serve in soup bowls; make a well in center and add reserved fat. Sprinkle with sugar and cinnamon.

Submitted by Selma (Mrs. Harry) Thewis, Cochrane. Other recipes for Romme Grot, *which was a staple in Norwegian households, mentioned that this pudding is traditionally stirred with a* tvare, *a long wooden stick hand that has five fingers carved from branches. It was also served with honey or maple syrup for breakfast.*

HIMMEL FUTTER (German)

2 eggs, beaten
1 cup sugar
1 teaspoon vanilla
2 heaping tablespoons flour
2 teaspoons baking powder
1 cup chopped dates
¾ cup chopped walnuts
2 bananas, diced
2 navel oranges, cut into pieces
Whipped cream

To beaten eggs, add sugar, vanilla, flour, and baking powder; mix well. Stir in dates and walnuts. Pour into 2 greased 8 or 9-inch cake layer pans. Bake at 350 about 25 minutes or until golden brown. When cool, break into small pieces and add bananas and oranges. Serve with whipped cream.

Submitted by Mrs. Edith Haertl, Fond du Lac. Other verions of Himmel Futter, *which means "heavenly food," called for crushed pineapple instead of oranges, and added marshmallows and maraschino cherries.*

EGG-A-DUCE (Norwegian)

4 egg yolks
4 tablespoons sugar
1 egg white
4 teaspoons brandy

Combine egg yolks, sugar, and egg white; beat until *very* stiff. Spoon into 4 cocktail glasses and add 1 teaspoon brandy to each serving; stir well.

Submitted by the Charles R. Amacker family, Madison. This has been a special part of their Easter dinners since a great-grandmother brought it from Norway in 1870.

If the number of recipes submitted is any measure, the single most treasured dessert memory of Wisconsinites is of Plum Pudding—or as some call it, Suet Pudding. Most of the recipes came from people of English background, but other ethnic groups had their versions: German, Danish, Swiss, Welsh, Scottish, Yankee.

On the basic theme of ground suet, currants, and spices, mixed into a pudding and steamed, were woven all sorts of harmonious variations: raisins, dates, nuts, apples, candied fruit, mashed potatoes, grated carrots, to name only some. The mixture was variously steamed in molds, coffee tins, or flour sacks sewn or tied into bags. (The version with the mashed potatoes and grated carrots called for baking rather than steaming.)

In some households, the Christmas Plum Pudding was served with flaming brandy poured over it; in others it was embellished only with a sprig of holly. Either way, is was usually served with a sauce, the exact kind determined by family tradition and tastes. One widespread custom connected with the Plum Pudding was to have every member of the family, or anyone who came to visit during the preparation of the pudding, give it a stir; it brings good luck.

The following illustrates the typical Christmas pudding set out on Wisconsin's tables.

PLUM PUDDING (English)

2½ cups currants
2½ cups raisins
2½ cups flour
½ teaspoon baking soda
1 cup milk
1 teaspoon baking powder
1 tablespoon cocoa
1 teaspoon nutmeg
2½ cups brown sugar
2½ cups coarsely ground suet
2½ cups fine bread crumbs
2 tablespoons molasses
3 eggs, beaten
½ cup candied lemon peel, cut fine

Mix currants and raisins with a small amount of the flour. Dissolve baking soda in milk. Sift flour with baking powder, cocoa, and nutmeg.

In a large bowl, combine brown sugar, suet, bread crumbs, raisins, currants, and flour; mix well with hands. Add milk, molasses, eggs, and lemon peel, and mix well. Pour into greased molds, about ⅔ full to allow for expansion. Cover and steam 3 to 4 hours. Serve hot with a sauce.

Plum pudding keeps indefinitely frozen and wrapped in foil. To serve, cut off a piece and steam until hot.

Submitted by Mrs. Harvey M. Johnson, Milton.

Directions for steaming a pudding in a cloth were included in the recipe submitted by Linda L. Leake, Burlington: "Wring cloth (clean dish towel or flour sacks) out of hot water and sprinkle with flour. Pour pudding into cloth (or cloths depending on size desired) and tie. It is important to tie the sacks only with cloth, preferably the same material as the sacks. [Allow room for expansion when tying.] Steam. . . in a covered kettle. I set a small container of water in the bottom of my kettle, then prop the sacks around it—but NOT IN IT!. . . After the pudding is steamed, it can be served immediately, or cooled, then frozen. Frozen pudding should be thawed, then heated through by steaming again—about 20 minutes—when you're ready to serve it. . . . "

See the end of this section for Plum Pudding Sauces.

The making and eating of old-fashioned ice cream is another memory that sticks with many state residents. Ice cream was always a part of old-time Fourth of July celebrations, and taking turns at turning the hand crank of the ice cream freezer was a task willingly assumed, no matter how hot the day.

VANILLA ICE CREAM

5 eggs
3 cups sugar
2 teaspoons vanilla
Pinch salt
4 cups heavy cream
5 cups milk

Break eggs into a large bowl and beat well. Add sugar, vanilla, and salt and stir well. Stir in milk and cream. Pour into freezer container and place in ice cream freezer. Put in dasher and cover. Pack salt and ice in layers around the container. Turn crank slowly at first, and faster as it gets harder to turn. (If the crank is turned too fast at first, the ice cream may have butter-like lumps in it.) Be careful that salt and ice do not get into the ice cream mix. Ice and salt may be added as needed. When crank can no longer be turned, remove dasher, cover hole in the container lid with a cork or cup, and pack ice around and cover the container. Let stand at least 1 hour before serving.

Submitted by Mrs. Robert Sanford, River Falls, who reported that she freezes water in milk cartons or plastic containers to obtain the ice, which is then placed in clean burlap sack or pillow case and pounded into usable chunks. Six 1-gallon cartons of ice are enough to make one recipe of her ice cream.

The making of the ice cream produced memories as sweet as the eating. One Oshkosh resident remembered being chosen to sit on the ice cream freezer to keep it steady during the freezing process,

GRAPE JUICE ICE CREAM

3 cups Welch's grape juice
3⅓ cups sugar
1 cup freshly squeezed lemon juice
4¾ cups heavy cream

Combine grape juice, sugar, and lemon juice; mix and stir until sugar is completely dissolved. Place cream in a large bowl and pour grape juice mixture *into the cream.* (Caution: do *not* pour cream into the grape juice mixture as it will curdle!) Stir thoroughly until well blended, then turn into a 1-gallon container in ice cream freezer. Crank until frozen. Pack in ice to ripen before eating.

Submitted by Mrs. Clayton R. Stannard, Oshkosh, who noted: "No substitutes, please, for the ingredients. This recipe was found in a very old printed cook book left in a house into which our family moved: Atlanta, Georgia, 1912. So old was this book that it crumbled to pieces in 1914."

WINTER ICE CREAM

2 cups heavy cream
2 eggs, separated
¾ cup sugar
Pinch salt
Flavoring extract as desired
Crushed fruit (optional)

Whip cream. Beat egg yolks and add to cream and beat again. Add sugar and salt and beat well. Beat egg whites until stiff and fold into cream mixture along with flavoring. Add crushed fruit if desired. Place in a can with well-fitting cover, leaving room for expansion. Set outside until frozen.

Submitted by Mrs. Arthur Johnson of San Francisco, California, who was 4-H baking champion of Wood County in 1933 and 1934. This recipe was used in the days before the family had electric refrigerators or freezers.

Dessert Sauces

RAZZLE DAZZLE (Yankee)

1 quart gooseberries
1 quart currants
1 quart sour cherries
Water as needed

Combine ingredients and cook slowly to desired consistency.

Submitted by Mrs. Raymond J. Koltes, Madison.

MAPLE CREAM

1 cup maple syrup
2 tablespoons butter
¼ cup cream

Combine maple syrup and butter and boil for 3 minutes. Cool and stir in cream. Serve over ice cream with pecans.

Submitted by Minnie Reynolds, Boscobel.

RASPBERRY SAUCE

2 10-ounce packages frozen raspberries, thawed
½ cup sugar
2¼ teaspoons cornstarch
Peach liqueur or Kirsch (optional)

Force raspberries through a sieve to remove seeds. Combine raspberries, sugar, and cornstarch; mix well. Cook slowly, stirring constantly, until slightly thickened. Add liqueur as desired. Serve over baked custard.

Submitted by Florence Buckner, Antigo.

Sauces for Plum Pudding

HARD SAUCE

4 cups water
2 cups brown sugar
½ teaspoon salt
1 teaspoon vanilla
About 2 tablespoons cornstarch
2 tablespoons butter
Brandy to taste

Combine water, sugar, salt, vanilla, and cornstarch. Boil until smooth, clear, and thick. Stir in butter and brandy if desired.

Submitted by Mary E. (Mrs. Edward A.) Mathwig, Waupaca.

WINE SAUCE

1 egg
1 cup sugar
½ cup butter
½ cup sherry

Cream together egg, sugar, and butter. Cook until thick. Stir in wine, adding more if necessary to achieve desired consistency. Pour over individual servings.

Submitted by Mrs. Charles A. Sims, Antigo.

BRANDY SAUCE

3 or 4 eggs, separated
⅓ cup sugar
Brandy

Beat egg whites until stiff; gradually beat in sugar. Beat yolks and fold into whites with 3 tablespoons brandy.

Before serving Plum Pudding, heat ½ to ¾ cup brandy and pour over hot pudding. Light brandy and carry flaming to table. Cut into servings and pass sauce.

Submitted by Dorothy S. Cole, Baileys Harbor.

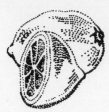

LEMON SAUCE

½ cup sugar
2 tablespoons flour
¾ cup cold water
2 tablespoons butter
Grated rind and juice of 1 lemon
1 egg yolk

Mix together sugar and flour. Add water and stir until smooth. Add butter and lemon rind. Bring to a boil and boil, stirring constantly, until thick, about 5 minutes. Add lemon juice and slightly beaten egg yolk. Cook 2 minutes longer. Serve warm or cold. Makes 1 cup.

BUTTER SAUCE

½ cup butter
½ cup sugar
½ cup brown sugar
½ cup cream
1 teaspoon vanilla

Combine all ingredients and bring to a boil; boil 2 minutes. Serve warm.

Submitted by Mrs. Harvey M. Johnson, Milton.

SUGAR SAUCE

½ cup sugar
½ tablespoon flour
1 tablespoon syrup
¼ teaspoon salt
½ tablespoon vinegar
½ teaspoon nutmeg
1 tablespoon butter
¼ cup boiling water

Combine all ingredients and cook until clear and smooth.

Submitted by Miss Louise Keiner, Greenwood.

CANDY and CONFECTIONS

IN SIMPLER TIMES, CANDY MAKING WAS OFTEN AN occasion for socializing. Old diaries and memoirs contain numerous references to gay evenings spent pulling taffy and making fudge, and spring in Wisconsin was marked by "sugaring off," the treat connected with the hard work of making maple sugar. As Cecilia Ellarson Nieman of Muskego described it, " 'Sugaring off' was when hot syrup was placed on clean snow, and was enjoyed by everyone. It was a warm maple candy mixture cooled by the snow."

Just as it is today, Christmas in the nineteenth century was a time for stirring up large batches of sweet confections to give as gifts and to serve at various holiday festivities.

SALT WATER TAFFY (English)

1 cup sugar
3 tablespoons cornstarch
Few grains salt
½ cup water
⅔ cup honey

Mix dry ingredients. Add water and honey. Cook to hard ball stage or 265-270 degrees. Pour into well-buttered pan. Cool. Pull until porous; cut into 1-inch pieces.

Submitted by Mrs. Roger Helms, West Allis.

NORWEGIAN SUGAR KNUP

3 cups brown sugar
4 tablespoons water

Combine sugar and water in a heavy frying pan. Bring to a boil, stirring constantly with a wire whisk. Cook 2 minutes after a good boil starts. Score into small pieces at once. Break apart and store in a tightly covered glass jar.

Submitted by Mrs. Selma S. Casberg, Holmen, who confided that these are "very nice with a cup of coffee."

BADEN KAFFEE BONBONS (German)

1 cup strong black coffee
1 cup heavy cream
6⅔ tablespoons unsalted butter
1½ cups plus 2 tablespoons sugar
2 teaspoons vanilla

Combine coffee and cream. Brown 3⅓ tablespoons butter and sugar, stirring constantly. Add remaining butter, coffee-cream mixture, and vanilla. Cook to firm ball stage (247 degrees). Pour quickly into a metal plate or pan and cool. Shape into hickorynut-size balls and wrap in waxed papers.

Submitted by Ms. Elizabeth Meating Proctor, Appleton.

SWISS CREAM CANDY

1½ cups cream or evaporated milk
3 cups sugar
½ cup corn syrup
1 teaspoon vanilla

Combine cream, sugar, and syrup. Cook, stirring constantly, to very firm ball stage; it must become a light brown color. Watch carefully as mixture burns easily. Remove from heat and add vanilla. Pour into buttered 7-by-10-inch pan and cool. Mark into squares with a buttered knife.

Submitted by Mrs. Edith H. Gotz, Pittsville.

POTATO CANDY (Irish)

1 cup warm, unseasoned mashed potatoes
½ teaspoon salt
2 teaspoons vanilla or rum
About 2 pounds confectioners' sugar

Combine potatoes, salt, and vanilla in a mixing bowl. Sift sugar over potatoes, about 1 cup at a time, stirring constantly, until mixture is like a stiff dough. Knead well, adding more sugar as needed. Cover with a damp cloth and chill until small spoonful can be rolled into a ball. Shape into small balls. Makes about 2 pounds.

Submitted by the Reverend Cormac Dwyer, Milwaukee.

COCONUT CANDY (Vietnamese)

1 medium coconut
1 cup sugar
½ cup water

Remove meat from coconut and grate or shred. Boil water and add sugar; boil until sugar is dissolved. Add coconut and cook over very low heat, stirring very frequently until syrup has cooked away and coconut is dry, about 2 hours.

Eat while hot or cool. Candy stored in a very dry place will keep indefinitely.

From the files of the International Institute of Milwaukee County.

BUTTERY TOFFEE

2¼ cups sugar
1¼ cups unsalted butter
½ cup light cream
¼ cup light corn syrup
1 teaspoon salt
2 teaspoons vanilla
6 ounces milk chocolate or semi-sweet
  chocolate, melted
1 cup chopped nuts

Combine sugar, butter, cream, corn syrup, and salt in a large, heavy saucepan. Bring to a boil over low heat, stirring frequently. Continue cooking and stirring until syrup reaches hard crack stage (300 degrees). Remove from heat and stir in vanilla. Pour into buttered 9-by-13-inch pan. Cool until firm. Spread melted chocolate evenly over top and sprinkle with nuts. Cool; break into bite-sized pieces.

CHOCOLATE TRUFFLES

8 ounces milk chocolate, cut in pieces
8 ounces semi-sweet chocolate, cut in pieces
1 egg
2 egg yolks
2 tablespoons unsalted butter, softened
½ cup multicolored candy decoration

Melt chocolates in double boiler. Remove from heat; add egg and egg yolks, one at a time, beating smooth after each addition. Add butter and beat smooth. Chill mixture until firm enough to hold its shape. Shape into 1-inch balls, then roll in multicolored decoration. Refrigerate until ready to serve. Makes about 3 dozen.

Or candy may be pressed into a greased pan. Cover the top with multicolored decoration and press into chocolate mixture. Cut into squares when cooled.

Submitted by Kathleen M. Bauer, Knowles, who reported that these two recipes are among the fifteen to twenty Christmas candies that are traditional in her family.

WHITE DIVINITY

3 cups sugar
1 cup boiling water
1 cup light corn syrup
3 egg whites
½ teaspoon vanilla
Few grains salt
Chopped nuts (walnuts or butternuts)
Chopped dates or candied cherries

Combine sugar, water, and corn syrup and boil to the soft ball stage (234-240 degrees). Beat egg whites until they hold their shape; add vanilla and salt. Carefully pour sugar mixture in a thin but steady stream over the egg whites, beating constantly, until the candy holds its shape when dropped onto a buttered surface. Add nuts and dates. Drop by spoonful on buttered baking sheet or waxed paper.

LIGHT BROWN DIVINITY

1½ cups light brown sugar
½ cup cold water
1 teaspoon vinegar
1 egg white, beaten
½ cup nuts, broken into pieces
½ teaspoon vanilla

Boil sugar, water, and vinegar to firm ball stage (244 to 248 degrees). Pour into beaten egg white. Add nuts and vanilla. Drop onto buttered baking sheet or spread into buttered pan.

Submitted by Miss Margaret I. Gibson of White Plains, New York, formerly of Madison.

PRESERVES, PICKLES, and EMBELLISHMENTS

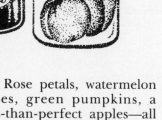

JAMS, JELLIES, PICKLES, AND THE LIKE WERE ONCE made at home quite as much to use and preserve the produce of garden and orchard as to provide variety of taste and texture to everyday meals. In a time when frugality was a creative art, nothing was wasted. Rose petals, watermelon rind, green tomatoes, green pumpkins, a bumper crop of less-than-perfect apples—all could be converted into sweet or sour condiments of one kind or another.

HOMEMADE APPLE PECTIN

4 pounds tart, hard, ripe apples
Water

Remove bruised spots on apples, but do not peel or core. Cut into thin slices and place in a large enamel kettle. Add 9 cups water and bring quickly to a boil. Cover and boil rapidly for 20 minutes. Strain through 4 thicknesses of cheese cloth. When juice stops dripping, press pulp lightly with a spoon; *do not squeeze out.* Reserve juice.

Measure out the pulp and combine with an equal quantity of water. Boil again for 20 minutes as before. Strain. Combine the two juices extracted. It should measure about 3 quarts. Place juice in a wide enamel dish pan so the liquid is not more than 2 inches deep. Boil rapidly 30 to 45 minutes, or until liquid is ½-inch deep or reduced to 1½ pints. If not used at once, pour into sterilized bottles and seal. Bottle should not hold more than ½ cup.

Submitted by Jane Steinhorst Lyons, Greenfield.

CORNCOB JELLY (German)

20 large, freshly shelled red corncobs
Water
Sugar
Lemon juice
Fruit pectin
Beet juice or red food coloring

Rinse cobs well to remove all loose bits. Place in a kettle and cover with water. Bring to a boil and simmer for 30 minutes or more, adding more water as needed to keep cobs covered.

Strain 3 cups of cooking water into a saucepan; add 3 cups sugar, ½ cup lemon juice, and 1 box powdered or 1 bottle liquid fruit pectin. Boil several minutes or according to directions on box or bottle. Add ½ cup beet juice or a few drops of red food coloring to give a rosy hue. Skim and pour into hot, sterilized jelly glasses and seal with 2 thin layers of melted paraffin. Cool, cover, and store in a dark, dry place. Repeat in 3-cup batches with remaining cooking liquid. Makes about 6 pints.

Contributed by Mrs. Virginia Kraegenbrink, Menomonee Falls.

WATERMELON JAM (Pennsylvania-Dutch)

Remains of 1 watermelon "after it has been cut
and ate"
1 or 2 lemons, sliced paper thin
Sugar

Collect rinds of melon. If children have eaten too close to rind leaving no pink pulp, discard that rind. Cut off green rind sparingly. Dice remaining melon rind into ¼-inch cubes. Cover with spring water and simmer on back of stove until suppertime.

For each pint of rind and cooking liquid, add 1 cup sugar. Add lemon and again simmer while range is hot with suppertime stoking. The jam will be done when it has formed a thick golden syrup and the melon pieces are mottled with white bubbles. (This may take several mealtime-firings of range.) Put in jars and seal or cover well with paraffin and cloth squares tied securely over top of jars, or in earthenware crocks. Serve over Pan Haus or buckwheat pancakes.

Loretta Holmes, Beloit, submitted her great-great-grandfather's recipe as it came to her. The original added: "The syrup when mixed with horehound drops or oil of wintergreen is good for quinsey, whooping cough, or catarrh of the throat."

PRESERVED STRAWBERRIES

Put ½ cup hot water in a kettle. Add 2 pounds sugar. Boil up, then add 3 pounds strawberries. Cook slowly 5 minutes. Take whole up and put in platters or shallow dishes. Place in hot sun for 3 days, taking in at night, and if very hot, move in shade at noon. Third day color will return and berries become plump, the syrup like jelly. Put in jelly glasses or can without reheating.

Mrs. Frederic La Croix, Milwaukee, submitted this very old, hand-written recipe from the Daniel Wells family papers. Wells was an early Milwaukee landholder and businessman who served in Congress from 1853 to 1857.

MARMALADE (Scottish)

4 oranges
2 lemons
1 grapefruit
Water
Sugar

Cut up fruit and rind into slivers; save any juice; place seeds in a separate dish and cover with water overnight. To each quart of fruit and juice add 2 quarts water. Let stand overnight. In the morning, add liquid from seeds to fruit and water. Boil for 2 hours. For every pound of fruit and liquid, add 1¼ pounds sugar. Boil for 30 minutes more or until it jells. Pour into sterilized glasses and seal with paraffin.

Submitted by Elizabeth McMillan Wood, Appleton.

ROSE SYRUP

1 pound rose leaves
1 quart water
4 pounds sugar

Pick over fresh rose leaves. Wash in cold water and drain well. Bring water to boiling; add leaves. Remove from heat and let stand overnight, well covered.

Strain through a jelly bag. Pour liquid into a double boiler, add sugar, and let boil until syrup is clear. Cool and bottle in sterilized bottles.

Submitted by Jane Steinhorst, Lyons, Greenfield.

GREEN PUMPKIN SAUCE

1 medium green pumpkin
2 tablespoons drippings or shortening
4 tablespoons flour
About 2 cups water
Salt to taste
½ teaspoon caraway seed or to taste
½ tablespoon vinegar (optional)

Peel and seed the pumpkin and grate as for shoestring potatoes. Salt and set aside.

Combine shortening, melted, and flour; brown slowly to golden color; add enough water to make a medium sauce. Simmer 20 minutes.

Squeeze excess liquid from pumpkin. Add pumpkin, salt to taste, and caraway seed to sauce and simmer slowly about ½ hour or until pumpkin is tender. Add vinegar if desired.

Submitted by Mrs. Anne Shoberg, Milwaukee, who added that more of the medium sauce may have to be made depending on the size of the pumpkin: "It should have the consistency of thick apple sauce."

Making apple butter was a harvest ritual for many Wisconsinites that took the better part of three days. Most often it was cooked outdoors in huge batches; since many folks had at least one or two apple trees growing in the kitchen garden, the basic ingredient was not hard to come by. These two recipes illustrate both the outdoor and the indoor method of cooking. One makes up the old-fashioned, huge batch; the other is family-sized.

APPLE BUTTER

You need a 36-gallon copper kettle, slung by a heavy chain from a tripod. Arrange three large rocks for the kettle to rest on, high enough to have a good fire under it. The kettle should be scoured thoroughly with vinegar and salt to remove any trace of verdigris. Then scrub, and boil a few minutes, 12 or 15 stones about the size of a silver dollar, and put them in the bottom of the kettle. (The stones will help to keep the butter from sticking.) You will also need a long-handled wooden paddle to stir with. Ours was a long handle with a paddle set at right angle to the handle; make sure the paddle part is as long as the depth of the kettle.

Have ready:

60 gallons fresh cider
3 bushels sweet apples
3 bushels mild-flavored apples

The first day, boil the 60 gallons of cider down to 20 gallons. Cover closely at night so no foreign substance can get in the kettle. The second day, peel and core the apples and keep adding them during the day. From now on, the mixture must be stirred most of the time, to avoid sticking and burning. Towards night the apples should all be cooked to a marmalade consistency.

Then add:

1 pound sugar for each gallon of apple butter
2 rounded tablespoons each cinnamon and
  cloves for each 20 gallons of apple butter

Stir until thoroughly mixed and cook about another ½ hour. Cover it again for the night. In the morning, heat apple butter in kettles in the house before putting it in jars and sealing.

Submitted by Mrs. Ardis D. Boynton, Beloit, who helped make this apple butter on occasion. Her grandmother, whose recipe it was, told her that before moving from Ohio to Wisconsin in 1850, "they made a big cask of apple butter and one of apple sauce, and kept them frozen in the winter, out of doors, on the porch. When they needed a fresh supply, during the winter, they would chip it out of the cask and thaw it. In Wisconsin, they always canned it."

APPLE BUTTER II

1 gallon apple cider
2½ quarts peeled, cored, sliced apples
1 cup brown sugar
1 cup sugar
¼ teaspoon whole allspice
1 3-inch stick cinnamon
3 or 4 whole cloves

Boil down cider to two quarts. Add apples and cook rapidly until apples are soft; reduce heat and cook slowly until the mixture begins to thicken. Stir constantly to prevent burning. Put in earthenware crock and add sugars. Tie allspice, cinnamon, and cloves in a cheesecloth bag, and add. Cook slowly on top of the stove or bake slowly in the oven until the apple pulp is smooth and thick enough to spread. Remove spice bag.

Submitted by Ila (Mrs. Fred A.) Meyers, Humbird, who added that plum butter was made with the same spices and cooked the same way. "The aroma was pleaant," she remembered from her childhood, "and we as children enjoyed the apple butter spread on toast made of homemade bread toasted on top of the wood range."

SULFURED APPLES

1½ gallons freshly gathered apples
1 teaspoon Flowers of Sulfur U.S.P. (available in drug stores)

Wash, peel, quarter, and core apples. Remove bruises or other parts that may cause spoilage. Place apples in a clean, 3-gallon crock with tight fitting cover. (Paper held down tightly with a board makes a suitable cover.) Place a piece of cotton, 2 or 3 inches square and about ½ inch thick, on a small plate. Sprinkle Flowers of Sulfur on the cotton. Place the plate in the crock on top of the apples and light the cotton. Be sure the cotton is burning so as to completely ignite the sulfur and form the necessary gas. Quickly cover the crock to hold in all the fumes. (Live coals may be used in place of the burning cotton.)

After 3 hours remove the cover and the plate. Put a scalded plate on top of the apples and a clean, close cover on top of the crock. Store in a dry, cool place. More apples, sulfured in another crock, may be added to this one for storage. Apples may also be stored in clean canning jars fitted with covers.

When removing apples for use, scoop them out with a clean dish and quickly replace the cover. Rinse the sulfured apples in cold water in a colander before using. Then use as you would a fresh apple for pie or sauce.

Submitted by Mrs. Robert Swartz, Kenosha. "It is important," she noted, "to use U.S.P. grade Flowers of Sulfur, as a less refined sulfur may cause arsenic poisoning."

DRIED CORN

Cut kernels of sweet corn off the cobs. Spread in a single layer on flat pans or drying racks. Set on a sunny screened porch to dry, or on the back of the wood-burning range. When dry, store in cloth bags in a cool, dry place.

To serve, soak overnight. Cook in a small amount of boiling, salted water; drain. Season with salt and pepper; add warmed cream. The corn is deep golden brown and has a nutlike flavor.

Submitted by Jane (Mrs. James L.) Roeber, Milwaukee.

DRIED APPLES OR PEARS

Peel and core good solid apples. Cut into ⅛-inch slices. Drop in a salt water bath of 4 to 6 tablespoons salt to 1 gallon of water; keep slices in salt water until all are prepared. Drain. Blanch in steam for 10 minutes. Place on drying racks in the oven at 130 degrees. After 2 hours, increase heat to 150 degrees. Leave the oven door open at least 8 or more inches to control heat and allow moist air out. Dry until apples are leathery and when cut in half are no longer moist in the center.

Store in moisture-proof containers in a dark place.

Treat pears the same as apples. When dry, pears have a springy feel and when cut in half are no longer moist in the center.

Submitted by the Reverend Cormac Dwyer, Milwaukee.

SPICED CURRANTS

5 quarts currants (measured when picked from stems)
3 pounds sugar
1 cup vinegar
1 teaspoon cloves
1 teaspoon cinnamon
1 teaspoon allspice

Combine all ingredients and boil for 1 hour. Put in sterilized jars and seal.

Submitted by Mrs. Henry Babcock Adams, Neenah.

MINCEMEAT

2½ pounds beef, boiled, cooled, and put through a food chopper
1½ pounds raw suet, ground
5 pounds apples, chopped
2 pounds raisins
2 pounds cranberries, chopped
1 pint apple jelly
1 teaspoon cinnamon
1 teaspoon cloves (optional)
2½ pounds sugar
1 tablespoon salt
Apple cider

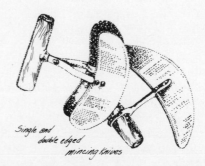

Single and double edged mincing knives

Mix together all ingredients; add enough apple cider to make mixture very juicy. Cook over low heat, stirring often, about 2 hours. Freeze or can in sterilized pint jars 60 minutes at 10 pounds pressure.

Submitted by Azalea L. (Mrs. Alvin) Engbertson, Spooner.

GREEN TOMATO MINCEMEAT

1 peck green tomatoes
2 tablespoons salt
1 pound raisins
1 pound currants
½ peck apples, peeled, cored, and chopped
¼ pound suet, chopped
5 pounds dark brown sugar
1 tablespoon nutmeg
1 tablespoon cinnamon
1 tablespoon cloves

Put tomatoes through a food chopper. Measure and add equal amount of hot water; add salt. Cook 15 minutes; drain very well. Add fresh boiling water and cook 20 minutes more. Drain thoroughly. Add remaining ingredients and cook over low heat until thick. Can while hot in sterilized glass jars.

Use for mince pie or turnovers or tarts. Serve with hard sauce or hot honey sauce.

Submitted by Frances Stiles (Mrs. William M.) Lamont, Aberdeen, South Dakota, whose husband's family emigrated to Dakota Territory from Lodi, Wisconsin in 1883. This was a way, she noted, to use up green tomatoes which might be lost in an early frost.

KOSHER DILL PICKLES

Kosher salt
Pickling cucumbers
Garlic
Fresh dill
Pickling spices
Hot pepper

Make a brine of 1 cup kosher salt to each gallon of water. Mix and heat in a glass or enamelware pot until salt is dissolved. (Use kosher salt only; table salt *cannot* be substituted.)

Wash and scrub cucumbers, as freshly picked as possible. Into sterilized 1-or-2-quart jars, place 1 peeled clove garlic, a head of dill, and whole cucumbers. Repeat layers of dill and cucumbers. Each jar should have a total of 3 dill heads. Add 1 hot red pepper and 1 heaping tablespoon pickling spices. Add brine covering cucumbers and to within ½-inch of top of jar. Seal jars with screw-top lids.

After two weeks, tighten lids. Allow pickles to season at least 4 weeks, but the longer the better.

Submitted by Charlotte (Mrs. Irvine Y.) Stein, Madison.

CHERRY DILL PICKLES

Pickling cucumbers
Cherry leaves
Dill
White vinegar
Salt
Pickling spices
Powdered alum
Sugar
Celery seed
Mustard seed

Wash pickles well. Wash cherry leaves. Place a layer of cherry leaves in a stone jar or crock. Add a little fresh dill, then make a layer of pickles. Repeat layers until crock is full, ending with a generous layer of leaves on top.

Make a brine of 8 cups cold water, 1 cup white vinegar, 4 tablespoons salt, 2 tablespoons pickling spices, 1 tablespoon powdered alum. Make enough to cover well the pickles in the crock. Place a plate on top of mixture and weight with something heavy. Let stand for 2 weeks.

Remove cucumbers, wash, and cut in chunks. Pack tightly in sterilized jars. Combine 2 cups sugar and 1 cup white vinegar. Tie 1 tablespoon celery seed and 1 tablespoon mustard seed in a cheesecloth bag and add to sugar mixture. Boil until syrupy; remove spice bag and pour hot syrup over pickles in jars. Seal tightly.

Submitted by Walter G. Wight, Greenbelt, Maryland, whose family came from Baraboo.

CARROT PICKLES (German)

18 medium carrots
1 cup water
2 cups vinegar
1½ cups sugar

Wash, scrape, and cook carrots until tender. Cut in 3 or 4-inch slices and place in an earthenware jar. Combine water, vinegar, and sugar; boil well for 3 minutes. Pour over carrots and let stand at least 24 hours before eating.

Submitted by Bernice Wilsnack Prochnow, Markesan, who remembered her grandmother always had an earthenware jar of these carrot pickles in her cellarway: "I delighted in sampling them whenever I visited her."

SWEET GREEN TOMATO PICKLES

1 peck green tomatoes
6 large onions, sliced
1 cup salt
2 quarts water
2 quarts vinegar
2 pounds brown sugar
2 heaping tablespoons ground mustard
2 tablespoons cloves
2 tablespoons cinnamon
½ teaspoon cayenne pepper

Sprinkle onions with salt and let stand overnight. Drain.

Combine tomatoes, onions, water, and 1 quart vinegar. Bring to a boil and simmer 5 minutes. Drain.

Combine remaining vinegar, sugar, mustard, cloves, cinnamon, and red pepper; pour over tomatoes and boil together 3 or 4 minutes. Put into sterilized jars and seal.

Submitted by Mrs. Henry Weddig, Kewaskum, who added that "these are very sharp and good with fried potatoes."

SHIPPLE BEANS

Green beans
Sugar
Canning salt

Wash and slice in long thin strips homegrown green beans. For 8 quarts of pickled beans, you will need 2 pecks. Place the beans in a large punch bowl or ceramic crock (do not use metal container); container should hold beans to within 2 inches from the top. Sprinkle the beans with a scant cup each of sugar and canning salt. Mix well and cover. In about 24 hours, juice will form and usually will cover the beans. If it doesn't, uncover the container and add ½ cup each of sugar and canning salt and mix. Recover and let stand until juice covers the beans.

Pack beans and juice into sterilized jars; pack down with a wooden mallet as tightly as possible. Seal with rubber rims and lids. Use at Thanksgiving.

To cook:

1 pint beans
1 small onion, finely chopped
3 tablespoons sugar
2 tablespoons vinegar
Pepper
2 tablespoons bacon fat
Cooked crumbled bacon

Cover beans with cold water; bring to a boil slowly. Stir and simmer 30 minutes. Drain well. Add onion, sugar, and vinegar and pepper lightly. Mix and taste; generally no additional salt is needed. Set aside at least 1 hour.

Just before serving, drain and place on low heat; pour over bacon fat and heat until hot; do not bring to a boil. Turn into serving dish and sprinkle with crumbled bacon. Serves 8.

Submitted by Mrs. William Sachtjen, Waunakee.

CUCUMBER RELISH

Cucumbers
3 tablespoons salt
2 tablespoons celery seed
2 tablespoons mustard seed
2 cups vinegar
2 cups sugar

Pare, seed, and grind enough large cucumbers to make 5 pints. Add salt and let stand 1 hour or more. Drain.

Combine celery seed, mustard seed, vinegar, and sugar and bring to a boil. Add drained cucumber and cook for 10 minutes. Place in sterilized jars and seal.

Submitted by Mrs. Art Manthey, Waunakee.

LAKE GARDEN CUKES

8 cups unpeeled cucumber chunks or slices
1 tablespoon salt
1 cup coarsely chopped onion
1 cup red or green peppers, cut up and seeded
1 cup vinegar
2 cups sugar
1 teaspoon celery seed
1 teaspoon mustard seed

Sprinkle salt on cucumbers; let stand 1 hour. Drain, but do not rinse. Add onion and pepper. Combine vinegar, sugar, celery seed, and mustard seed; blend well. Pour over cucumber mixture. Refrigerate 2 or 3 days, stirring occasionally.

Place in desired containers and store, continuously refrigerated, for as long as 5 months.

Submitted by Roma E. (Mrs. Harry) Rabe, Kiel.

SWEET PEPPER RELISH

12 red peppers, seeded
12 green peppers, seeded
12 small onions, peeled
2 pints cider vinegar
3 cups sugar
1 tablespoon salt

Put peppers and onions through a food chopper; mix well. Pour over 1 pint boiling water. Let stand 5 minutes; drain.

Bring 1 pint water and 1 pint cider vinegar to a boil; pour over peppers mixture and let stand on back of wood stove, but do not boil for most of the day. Drain.

Make a syrup of sugar, salt, and remaining vinegar. Add to pepper mixture; boil for 5 minutes. Place in sterilized jars and seal.

Submitted by Joan (Mrs. William) Fancher, Racine, who suggested keeping the mixture hot but not boiling by placing it on the lowest heat of an electric stove.

CRANBERRY RELISH

1 pound fresh cranberries
2 cups sugar

Grind or finely chop cranberries. Mix well with sugar.

Variations:

For *Cranberry-Apple Relish,* add to basic relish 2 apples, ground, and ⅓ lemon, ground.

For *Cranberry-Orange Relish,* add to basic relish 2 oranges, including rind, ground.

Recipes distributed at the Warrens Cranberry Festival.

TOMATO CATSUP

1 peck very ripe tomatoes
2 or 3 onions
4 tablespoons salt
1 cup sugar
1 cup vinegar
2 teaspoons allspice
2 teaspoons cinnamon
½ small red pepper, seeded and cut up
2 teaspoons celery seed

Cut up unpeeled tomatoes and cook, without water, until tender. Put through a colander or sieve to remove seeds and skin, then boil for 20 minutes longer. Add onions, salt, sugar, vinegar, allspice, cinnamon, pepper, and celery seed. Boil until reduced about in half. Bottle in sterilized jars and seal while hot.

Submitted by Donna (Mrs. Dale I.) Hanson, Stevens Point.

HOT BEER MUSTARD

3 ounces ground mustard
2 tablespoons brown sugar
4 tablespoons cider vinegar
2 teaspoons salt
Beer

Combine mustard, sugar, vinegar, and salt. Add enough beer to make a paste of desired consistency. Let stand for 2 days to blend flavors.

Submitted by Hope C. (Mrs. R. H.) Loveland, Cassville. The recipe was given her by a friend, the late Mrs. Dorothy Dewey Peart of Cassville, whose father and mother operated an inn and boardinghouse in Iowa on the Old Galena Road. This mustard was served in the inn. Her father, James Dewey, was related to Nelson Dewey, first governor of Wisconsin, whose home was in Cassville and is now part of Stonefield, which is operated by the State Historical Society of Wisconsin.

CHRZAN (Polish)

2 cans beets
4 ounces uncreamed horseradish
1 tablespoon vinegar
½ teaspoon sugar

Drain beets and grate them. Combine with horseradish, vinegar, and sugar. Mix well. Place in sterilized jars and let flavors blend for 2 or 3 days. Serve with ham or kielbassa.

Submitted by Eleanor (Mrs. Anthony) Yankowski, Neenah, who added that this is delicious on a ham sandwich on rye bread.

BEET VINEGAR

Wash beets and discard greens. Place beets in a crock and cover with cold water. Place in a warm spot and let stand for 3 or 4 weeks or until mixture becomes sour.

Submitted by Jane Steinhorst Lyons, Greenfield.

BEVERAGES

CAFE AU LAIT (French-Canadian)

1 pint strong hot coffee
1 pint hot (not boiling), rich milk

Put coffee and hot milk in separate pots. Grasp a pot in each hand and pour milk and coffee simultaneously into coffee cups. Add sugar if desired

Submitted by Mrs. Florence M. Vint, Springfield, Virginia.

HOT SPICED CIDER

2 quarts apple cider
½ cup brown sugar
12 whole cloves *or* 1 teaspoon ground cloves
4 small sticks cinnamon *or* 1 teaspoon ground cinnamon

Put cider in a kettle; add sugar, cloves, and cinnamon. Simmer 3 to 5 minutes. Let mixture cool and stand several hours to blend flavors. If using whole spices, remove; reheat and serve hot. Makes ten 6-ounce servings.

Submitted by Mr. and Mrs. Bay. Sprengel, New Berlin.

GINGER WATER

½ cup sugar
2 quarts water
½ cup vinegar
½ teaspoon ginger

Mix ingredients and shake well. Refrigerate.

Submitted by Mrs. Ernest Bartels, Peshtigo, who noted that this very old recipe was used a lot during haying time as it is very thirst-quenching.

[329]

POTATO CIDER (Lithuanian)

5 gallons potato juice
15 cups sugar
Lemon or orange peel

Save the juice expressed from potatoes when making potato dumplings or pancakes. Fill a clean 5-gallon jug with juice and some of the starch if available. Add sugar and lemon or orange peel. Close tightly with a cork fitted with a glass tube that lets air out but not in. Add water periodically to the bubble of the glass tube. Let ferment for 3 months.

Transfer to clean bottles and set aside for one year. The cider is then ready to be served or used in chicken, meat, or sauce recipes.

Submitted by Mrs. Theresa Balciunas, Kenosha, who added that the same method can be used with berries, apples, or other fruits.

DANDELION WINE

1 gallon fresh dandelion blossoms (packed full)
16 cups sugar
4 quarts boiling water
2 lemons, grated rind and all
2 oranges, grated
2 cakes compressed yeast

Discard all dandelion stems; use freshly picked blossoms only. Combine blossoms and sugar. Put into a stone jar and pour boiling water over to cover well. Let stand until lukewarm. Add lemons, oranges, and yeast. Stir well and let stand in a warm place for 24 hours.

Strain through a fine cloth and let stand in a cool place for 3 days or so. Strain again and let ferment in a wooden keg or crock. After fermenting stops, the wine may be bottled.

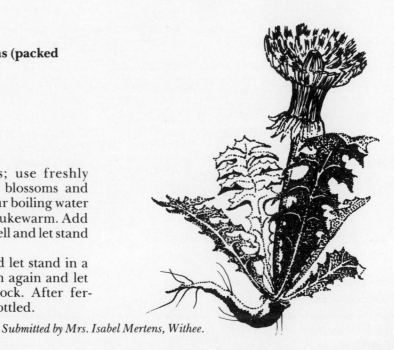

Submitted by Mrs. Isabel Mertens, Withee.

ELDERBERRY WINE

9 pounds elderberries
4¾ pounds sugar
Cold water

Pick over elderberries, discarding all stem pieces. Place elderberries and sugar in a 2-gallon container. Cover with cold water. Cover with a cloth and keep in a warm place, stirring twice a week for 6 weeks. Strain and let stand 2 weeks longer. Strain and bottle.

Submitted by Mrs. Edith Gotz, Pittsville.

SIMA (Finnish)

2 or 3 lemons
3½ pounds light brown sugar
10 quarts water
5 tablespoons hops *or* **12-ounce can beer**
1 teaspoon active dry yeast
Raisins
Sugar

Peel lemons; discard white part of peel. Slice lemons and remove seeds.

Combine sugar and water and bring to a boil. Remove from heat and add lemon slices, rind, and hops. When mixture has cooled to lukewarm, add yeast and stir. Cover tightly and let brew overnight at room temperature.

Place some raisins in liter bottles and add ½ teaspoon sugar to each bottle. Pour in liquid and cap tightly. Store in a cool place. The Sima is ready when the raisins have risen to the top. Serve chilled.

From the files of the International Institute of Milwaukee County.

BLACKBERRY SYRUP

To 2 quarts of the juice of blackberries add 1 pound of loaf sugar, ½ an ounce of nutmeg, ½ an ounce cinnamon pulverized. To this add ½ an ounce of cloves, and ¼ of an ounce of allspice pulverized. Boil all together for a short time, and when cold add a pint of Brandy. This beverage is said to be a cure for the summer complaint.

From a handwritten recipe collection, whose earliest entry is dated 1816, in the Jackson Kemper Papers at the State Historical Society of Wisconsin.

OLD MADISON NEW YEAR'S PUNCH

40 lemons
3½ gallons whiskey
1½ gallons brandy
2 ounces whole cloves
1 ounce mace
½ ounce nutmeg
½ ounce whole cinnamon
1 gallon sherry
1 gallon black currant wine, or substitute
2 quarts sweet grape juice
2 quarts champagne
Sliced oranges

Thinly slice lemons, removing seeds. Arrange in three layers on a platter and let stand for 6 to 8 hours.

Mix whiskey and brandy. Simmer for 1 hour. Add lemons and continue simmering 5 minutes. Skim off lemons and set aside. Thoroughly grind together cloves, mace, nutmeg, and cinnamon and place in a linen bag. Add bag to simmering liquor for ½ hour.

Combine sherry and black currant wine and simmer for 30 minutes; add to whiskey mixture with grape juice. Place in a punch bowl with sliced lemons and some sliced oranges. Add champagne.

From A Taste of Old Madison, *by Lynne Watrous Hamel, 1974. This punch was served when neighbors and friends came to call on New Year's Day at the home of F. W. Montgomery, president of the Madison Street Railway Company during the early part of this century.*

KRUPNIK (Polish)

1 cup dark honey
1 cup water
4 cloves
1 1-inch cinnamon stick
Dash nutmeg
½ to 1 teaspoon vanilla
3 or 4 small pieces orange peel
2 cups 80-proof alcohol or vodka

Combine honey and water and bring to a boil; skim well. Add cloves, cinnamon, nutmeg, vanilla, and orange peel. Bring to a boil several times, then set aside to cool and absorb flavors. Strain. Bring to a boil and carefully pour in alcohol; do not let it burn or ignite. Serve hot in small cups.

Submitted by Mrs. Catherine Ellingboe, Milwaukee. Other recipes call for igniting the alcohol after adding to the honey mixture, then smothering immediately by covering.

GRAPE JUICE CORDIAL

Wash the grapes & pick them from the stems. Cover them with water and put them up to boil, stirring from time to time until the seeds are free. Pour into a cheese cloth bag & press out the juice. To each cup of juice allow ½ cup of sugar. Heat again and when at the boiling pour, pour into *hot* bottles, cork & seal. Serve Ice Cold with water, ¼ c. juice, ¾ c. water.

Bottle Wax:
Equal parts of beeswax & Rosin. Melt together & dip the corked bottles into the hot mixture until the corks are covered. Boil the corks.

From Lizzie Black Kander's lesson for the cooking class at The Settlement in Milwaukee, November 4, 1900. Her classes later led to the publication of the celebrated Settlement Cookbook.

SELECTED BIBLIOGRAPHY

Correspondence with contributors of recipes, their cookbooks, memorabilia, and reminiscences, together with the author's research notes, a more complete bibliography, and various drafts of her manuscript, are in the files of the Editorial Division of the State Historical Society of Wisconsin. Eventually they will be deposited with the Society's Archives Division.

American Heritage. *The American Heritage Cookbook: An Illustrated History of American Eating & Drinking.* New York, 1964.

Ames, Jesse Hazen. Reminiscences. SHSW Archives.

Anderson, Anna Magnuson. Reminiscences. SHSW Archives.

Anderson, Hans A. Autobiography. SHSW Archives.

Anderson, Thomas G. "Narrative of Capt. Thomas G. Anderson." *Wisconsin Historical Collections,* 9:137–206 (1909).

Atwood, Cora S. "A Wee Bit of New England in Wisconsin." SHSW Archives.

Baird, Elizabeth Therese. "Reminiscences of Life in Territorial Wisconsin." *Wisconsin Historical Collections,* 15:205–263 (1900).

Baldwin, Norman S., Saalfeld, Robert W., Ross, Margaret A., and Buettner, Howard J. *Commercial Fish Production in the Great Lakes.* Great Lakes Fishery Commission, Technical Report No. 3. Ann Arbor, Michigan, 1979.

Baron, Stanley Wade. *Brewed in America: A History of Beer and Ale in the United States.* Boston, 1962.

Bauer, Joyce. "History of Kohlsville, Wisconsin." SHSW Archives.

Bentley, Mrs. Charles R. "Pioneers of Edgerton." SHSW Archives.

Bertrand, Achille H. "Recollections of Old Superior." SHSW Archives.

Better Homes and Gardens Heritage Cook Book. Des Moines, 1975.

Birkeland, Ole A. O. Autobiography. SHSW Archives.

Bremer, Fredrika. *The Homes of the New World: Impressions of America.* Translated by Mary Howitt. 2 vols., New York, 1853.

Bridgman, Charles. Papers. SHSW Archives.

Brown, Charles E. Papers. SHSW Archives.

Burmester, Ruth Seymour, ed. "Silas J. Seymour Letters." *Wisconsin Magazine of History,* 32: 188–199, 328–338, 456–471 (1948–1949).

Burnham, E. H. "Wisconsin Lumber Camp Names and Amusements." Charles E. Brown Papers, box 5. SHSW Archives.

Carver, Jonathan. *Three Years' Travels Throughout the Interior Parts of North America for More Than Five Thousand Miles . . . .* Walpole, New Hampshire, 1813.

Cate, Jennie D. "My Memories of Pioneer Days in Wisconsin." SHSW Archives.

Ceresco Community Papers. SHSW Archives.

Clark, John Garretson. *The Grain Trade in the Old Northwest.* Urbana, Illinois, 1966.

Cochran, Thomas C. *The Pabst Brewing Company: The History of an American Business.* New York, 1948.

Coe, Edwin Delos. "Reminiscences of a Pioneer in the Rock River Country." State Historical Society of Wisconsin. *Proceedings,* 55: 189–203 (1907).

Cooke, Warren W. "A Frontiersman in Northwestern Wisconsin." *Wisconsin Magazine of History,* 23: 281–303, 406–426 (1939–1940).

Coryer, Albert Eugene. Tape recording (February 20, 1951). SHSW Archives.

Crane, Ellery B. A History of the Settlement of Beloit. SHSW Archives.

Current, Richard N. *The History of Wisconsin. Volume II: The Civil War Era, 1848–1873.* Madison, 1976.

Dart, Richard. "Settlement of Green Lake County." State Historical Society of Wisconsin. *Proceedings*, 57: 252–272 (1909).

Delgado, Jeanne Hunnicutt, ed. "Nellie Kedzie Jones's Advice to Farm Women: Letters from Wisconsin, 1912–1916." *Wisconsin Magazine of History*, 57: 3–27 (1973–1974).

Densmore, Frances. *Chippewa Customs.* Smithsonian Institution. Bureau of American Ethnology, Bulletin 86 (1929). (Republished by the Minnesota Historical Society, 1979.)

Diederichs, John Frederick. Journey of the Joh. Fr. Diederichs family. SHSW Archives. (Published in part as "Letters and Diary of Joh. Fr. Diederichs." Translated by Emil Baensch. *Wisconsin Magazine of History*, 7: 218–237, 350–368 [1923–1924].)

Doudna, Edgar G. Papers. SHSW Archives.

Duerst, Mathias. "Diary of One of the Original Colonists of New Glarus, 1845." Translated by John Luchsinger. *Wisconsin Historical Collections*, 15: 292–337(1900).

Ebling, Walter H., et al. *A Century of Wisconsin Agriculture.* Wisconsin. Department of Agriculture. Crop Reporting Service, Bulletin 290 (1948).

Ellis, William S. *Wisconsin's Door Peninsula: "A Kingdom So Delicious."* Washington, D.C., 1969. (Reprinted from *National Geographic* [March, 1969].)

Fifield, Elbridge Gerry. Some Pioneering Experiences in Jefferson County. SHSW Archives.

Fonda, John H. "Early Wisconsin." *Wisconsin Historical Collections*, 5: 205–284 (1907).

Fox, Mary Theresa Dodge. Blueprint of the Dodgeville home of . . . Henry Dodge . . ., including typewritten description. SHSW Archives.

French, Mrs. Bella, ed. *The American Sketch Book.* 5 vols., La Crosse, 1874–1882. (Cataloged as Swisher, Mrs. Bella French.)

Gilmore, Melvin R. *Indian Lore and Indian Gardens.* Ithaca, New York, 1930.

Glover, John George, and Cornell, William Bouck, eds. *The Development of American Industries: Their Economic Significance.* New York, 1933.

Grignon, Antoine. "Recollections of Antoine Grignon." State Historical Society of Wisconsin. *Proceedings*, 61: 110–136 (1913).

Halasz, Emma Rendtorff. Diary. SHSW Archives.

Hartwig, Theodore E. F. Letters. SHSW Archives.

Haygood, William C., ed. " 'God Raised Us Up Good Friends': English Immigrants in Wisconsin." *Wisconsin Magazine of History*, 47: 224–237 (1963–1964).

Hibbard, Benjamin Horace. "Indian Agriculture in Southern Wisconsin." State Historical Society of Wisconsin. *Proceedings*, 52: 145–155 (1904).

Hine, Ruth L. "The Wildlife Resource of Wisconsin." Wisconsin. *Blue Book*, 1964: 91-112.

Hintzman, A. J., Estes, C. W., and Morris, W. W. *Wisconsin Cranberries: Production, Varieties, Utilization, and Markets.* Wisconsin. Department of Agriculture. Bulletin 322 (1953).

Holand, Hjalmar Rued. *Old Peninsula Days: The Making of an American Community.* Ephraim, Wisconsin, 1946.

Johns, Mary Schaal. Reminiscences. SHSW Archives.

Kelly, Mrs. Jane. Diary. SHSW Archives.

Keyes, Elisha W. "Early Days in Jefferson County." *Wisconsin Historical Collections*, 11: 416–434 (1888).

Kolehmainen, John I., and Hill, George W. *Haven in the Woods: The Story of the Finns in Wisconsin.* Madison, 1965.

Krohnke, I. O. Diary. SHSW Archives.

Kroll, Wayne L. *Badger Breweries, Past and Present.* Jefferson, Wisconsin, 1976.

Kuhlmann, Charles B. *The Development of the Flour-Milling Industry in the United States, with Special Reference to the Industry in Minneapolis.* Clifton, New Jersey, 1973.

Lampard, Eric. E. *The Rise of the Dairy Industry in Wisconsin. A Study in Agricultural Change, 1820–1920.* Madison, 1963.

Leiser, Fred O. "Sauk Farming in the 1880's." SHSW Archives.

Martin, Morgan L. "Narrative of Morgan L. Martin." *Wisconsin Historical Collections,* 11: 385–414 (1888).

Martin, Xavier, "The Belgians of Northeast Wisconsin." *Wisconsin Historical Collections,* 13: 375–396 (1895).

Merk, Frederick. *Economic History of Wisconsin During the Civil War Decade.* Madison, 1916.

Messerschmidt, William H. Autobiographical notes. SHSW Archives.

Meyer, Leona K. "Pioneer Agriculture in Town of Ashford, Fond du Lac County." SHSW Archives.

Miner, John. "Yesterday's Delhi." *Wisconsin Magazine of History,* 32: 41–48 (1948–1949).

Monroe, Charles E. Letters, SHSW Archives.

Mould, M. H. "Recollections of the Indian Days." SHSW Archives. (Transcribed from the *Baraboo Republic,* July 18 and 19, 1918.)

Murray, Mrs. Robert. "From Boston to Wisconsin in 1838." SHSW Archives. (Transcribed from the *Waukesha Freeman,* May 15, 1913.)

Neal, Robert M. "Pendarvis, Trelawny, and Polperro, Shake Rag's Cornish Houses." *Wisconsin Magazine of History,* 29: 391–401 (1945–1946).

Nesbit, Robert C. *Wisconsin: A History.* Madison, 1973.

Neville, Ella H., Martin, Sarah G., and Martin, Deborah B. *Historic Green Bay, 1643–1840.* Green Bay, 1893.

Oakes, Elinor F. "A Ticklish Business: Dairying in New England and Pennsylvania, 1750–1812." *Pennsylvania History,* 47: 195–212 (1980).

Ogden, George W. Papers. SHSW Archives.

Olsen, Lars, and Olsen, Marie. Letter. SHSW Archives.

Owen Family. Correspondence with relatives in America and Wales. SHSW Archives.

Pellett, Frank C. *History of American Beekeeping.* Ames, Iowa, 1938.

Peltier, George L. *A History of the Cranberry Industry in Wisconsin.* Detroit, 1970.

Puchner, Rudolph. "Early History of New Holstein." SHSW Archives.

Ragatz, Joseph, ed. and trans. "Memoirs of a Sauk Swiss." *Wisconsin Magazine of History,* 19: 182–241 (1935–1936).

Raney, William Francis. *Wisconsin: A Story of Progress.* New York, 1940.

Reinhard, David G. Reminiscences. SHSW Archives.

Remeeus, John. Record of a Voyage from the Netherlands. SHSW Archives.

Rodenkirch, Michael. Letter (unprocessed). SHSW Archives.

Root, Waverly, and de Rochemont, Richard. *Eating in America: A History.* New York, 1976.

Runals, E. L. "Story of the Mascouten Nation and Their Massacre." SHSW Archives.

Russell, E. E. "A History of Ogdensburg and Vicinity." SHSW Archives.

Schafer, Joseph. *A History of Agriculture in Wisconsin.* Madison, 1922.

Schafer, Joseph. *The Wisconsin Lead Region.* Madison, 1932.

Schlebecker, John T. *Whereby We Thrive: A History of American Farming, 1607–1972.* Ames, Iowa, 1975.

Schoenfeld, Sophia Ehrhardt. Diary. SHSW Archives.

Schuette, H. A., and Ihde, A. J. "Maple Sugar: A Bibliography of Early Records. II." Wisconsin Academy of Sciences, Arts and Letters. *Transactions,* 38: 89–184 (1946).

Schuster, Peter. Autobiography. SHSW Archives.

Sherman, Simon Augustus. Papers. SHSW Archives.

Sherman, William. Reminiscences. SHSW Archives.

Skinner, Alanson Buck. *Material Culture of the Menomini*. New York, 1921.

Smith, Alice E. "Daniel Whitney: Pioneer Businessman." *Wisconsin Magazine of History*, 24: 283–304 (1940–1941).

Smith, Alice E. *History of Wisconsin. Volume I: From Exploration to Statehood*. Madison, 1973.

Smith, Huron H. *Ethnobotany of the Forest Potawatomi Indians*. Milwaukee. Public Museum. *Bulletin*, 4: 1 (1923).

Spies, Margaret Agnes (Seitz). "The Story of Anton Seitz and His Wife Katherine Haas." SHSW Archives.

[Sproat, Florantha Thompson]. "La Pointe Letters." *Wisconsin Magazine of History*, 16: 85–95 (1932–1933).

Stare, Frederick Arthur. *The Story of Wisconsin's Great Canning Industry*. Baltimore, 1949.

Stevens, Neil E., and Nash, Jean. "The Development of Cranberry Growing in Wisconsin." *Wisconsin Magazine of History*, 27: 276–294 (1943–1944).

Stickney, Gardner P. "The Use of Maize by Wisconsin Indians." *Parkman Club Papers*, 63–87 (1897).

Streissguth, Wilhelm. Report to Peter Jenny on the Colony of New Glarus, Wisconsin. September 12, 1850. SHSW Archives.

Taube, Edward. "Wild Rice." *Scientific Monthly*, 73: 6 (December, 1951).

Taylor, Clare, ed. *From Wales to Wisconsin: Selections from the Plas Yn Blaenau Papers*. Aberystwyth, Wales [?], 1973.

Taylor, Rose Schuster. "Peter Schuster, Dane County Farmer." *Wisconsin Magazine of History*, 28: 277–289, 431–454 (1944–1945).

Thomas, Daniel. Diary. SHSW Archives.

Thompson, John Giffin. *The Rise and Decline of the Wheat Growing Industry in Wisconsin*. New York, 1972 ed.

Thompson, Mrs. Sarah Schoyen. Reminiscences. SHSW Archives.

United States. Agriculture, Department of. *Agricultural Statistics*, 1936–1979.

United States. Agriculture, Department of. *Annual Reports*, 1849–1876, 1879, 1890.

United States. Census, Bureau of the. Compilations of agricultural and manufactures statistics for the United States and Wisconsin for the decennial censuses, 1840 to 1970, plus special censuses of agriculture (1925, 1935, 1945, 1954, 1959, 1964, 1969, and 1974) and manufactures (1905, 1914, 1947, 1954, 1958, 1967, and 1972).

United States Brewers Association, Inc. *Brewers Almanac*, 1953, 1975.

Walsh, Margaret. *The Manufacturing Frontier: Pioneer Industry in Antebellum Wisconsin, 1830–1860*. Madison, 1972.

Weber, Peter Dale. *Wisconsin Honey: Production and Marketing*. Wisconsin. Department of Agriculture. Special Bulletin 61 (1956).

Weber, Peter Dale. *Wisconsin Maple Products: Production and Marketing*. Wisconsin. Department of Agriculture. Bulletin 335 (1956).

Whitehouse, J. L. "A History of Wolf River." SHSW Archives.

Wisconsin. Administration, Department of. Executive Services Division. Demographic Services Center. *Wisconsin Statistical Abstract*, 1979.

Wisconsin. Agriculture, Department of. Statistical Reporting Service. *Wisconsin Agricultural Statistics*, bulletin 200, 1965–1978.

Wisconsin. Horticultural Society, State. *Transactions*, various volumes, plus *Index*, 1859–1918.

Wisconsin Then and Now. [A serial publication of the State Historical Society of Wisconsin. See especially the issues of December, 1956; February, 1968; January, 1972; July, 1975; April and October, 1976; and July, 1977.]

Wright, William W. Diary and unfinished memoirs. SHSW Archives.

CONTRIBUTORS

*The author and compiler of this book,
as well as The State Historical Society of Wisconsin,
would like to thank the following persons
whose contributions were used, as
well as all those who sent in material,
for making this book possible.*

Mrs. Henry Babcock Adams, *Neenah*

Mary L. Albrecht, *Auburndale*

The Charles R. Amacker family, *Madison*

Mrs. Mary Anderson, *Wisconsin Rapids*

Helen F. Andruskevicz, *Green Bay*

Jeanne Cragin (Mrs. Lawrence) Atkinson, *Superior*

Mrs. Gordon Austin, *St. Francis*

Mrs. L. P. Baerwolf, *Madison*

Mrs. Theresa Balciunas, *Kenosha*

Verna Jensen Barnes, *Darlington*

Mrs. Ernst Bartels, *Peshtigo*

Mrs. Carl T. Barth, *Coleman*

Miss Kathleen M. Bauer, *Knowles*

Mrs. Claire Bennett, *Endeavor*

Roscella Berdal, *Montello*

Mrs. Jean Beyer, *Appleton*

Mrs. John Blathers, *Milwaukee*

Frances W. (Mrs. Robert J.) Booker, *Milwaukee*

Mrs. Jack Boone, *Appleton*

David J. Borth, *Bayfield*

Mrs. Henry Bowers, *Marion*

Mrs. Ardis D. Boynton, *Beloit*

Coral (Mrs. John) Brahm, *West Allis*

Carolyn C. Brown, *Milwaukee*

Florence Buckner, *Antigo*

Mrs. Eugene Bukowski, *Wisconsin Rapids*

Mrs. R. J. Burgoyne, *Plymouth*

Mrs. M. Burleton, *Oakfield*

Mrs. Robert Burmeister, *East Troy*

Genevieve (Mrs. John) Butenhoff, *Milwaukee*

Dr. Lois Byrns, *Dane*

Mrs. Ruth V. Calvin, *Elkhorn*

Mrs. Selma Casberg, *Holmen*

Mrs. Ruth Bunker Christiansen, *Frederic*

Mrs. Ruszella Christensin, *Freeport, Illinois*

Mrs. Harold Clumpner, *Ogdensburg*

Mrs. Verne Cluppert, *Markesan*

Dorothy S. Cole, *Baileys Harbor*

Helen Collins, *Montello*

Mrs. S. G. Corey, *Wisconsin Rapids*

Nancy (Mrs. Robert) Cushman, *Elkhorn*

Maya Presber Custer, *Marshfield*

Mrs. Ronald Daggett, *Madison*

Mrs. Glen Daigle, *Neenah*

Rev. Lloyd C. Denzer, *Wild Rose*

Mrs. Beatrice Durand Derrick, *Webster*

Ms. Virginia M. Derridinger, *Appleton*

Mrs. John Desris, *Kenosha*

Mrs. Byron Dolgner, *Pardeeville*

Fay S. (Mrs. Orr) Dooley, *Marinette*

Mrs. Wencel F. Dufek, *Manitowoc*

Rev. Cormac Dwyer, *Milwaukee*

Mrs. Catherine Ellingboe, *Milwaukee*

Azalea L. (Mrs. Alvin) Engbertson, *Spooner*

Joan (Mrs. William) Fancher, *Racine*

Ada (Mrs. Gust) Federman, *Sauk City*

Mrs. Lewis G. Fedyn, *Wauwatosa*

Rich Felsing, *Manitowoc*

Elizabeth Fischer, *Stockbridge*

Mrs. Cecil A. Fisher, *Milwaukee*

Mrs. Bernice Forrer, *West Allis*

Mrs. Rosalie Franckowiak, *Cudahy*

Mrs. Daisy Frase, *Eau Claire*

Ione R. Gadow, *Oshkosh*

Mrs. F. J. Gall, *Eagle River*

Ade (Mrs. Stanley) Garvin, *Janesville*

Gladys Gauthier, *Oconto Falls*

Mrs. Norma L. Gedamske, *Milwaukee*

Mrs. John Gehler, *Ladysmith*

Mrs. J. Gericke, *Appleton*

Miss Margaret E. Gibson, *White Plains, New York*

Rebecca Trumpy Gillings, *Redgranite*

Mary Gillis, *Oconto Falls*

Mrs. Edith H. Gotz, *Pittsville*

Mrs. Leon Grimm, *Arpin*

Roger W. Gunnerson, *Waukesha*

Mrs. Edith Haertl, *Fond du Lac*

Betty and Mrs. Sanford Hanson, *Sturgeon Bay*

Donna (Mrs. Dale I.) Hanson, *Stevens Point*

Mrs. Elmer Hare, *Dalton*

Mrs. Betty Harnack, *Janesville*

Lynora Jean Harnack, *Janesville*

Priscilla Kay Harnack, *Janesville*

Elva Hart, *Milwaukee*

Margaret Rose Hart, *Milwaukee*

Mrs. E. R. Hasselkus, *Madison*

Mrs. Emma Heesakker, *Appleton*

Hila (Mrs. Robert) Hefferman, *Kewaunee*

Mrs. Roger Helms, *West Allis*

Charles Hendricksen, *Milwaukee*

Mrs. Jean S. Hesse, *Sheboygan*

Mrs. Freida Hirsch, *Wisconsin Dells*

Mrs. Edward Hoffman, *Pewaukee*

Mrs. Ernest F. Hochstetter, *Waunakee*

Mrs. Stanley Holland, *Mineral Point*

Loretta Holmes, *Beloit*

Agnes A. (Mrs. Oscar) Hoyer, *Milwaukee*

Ruth Weber (Mrs. Harlan) Huebner, *Oconomowoc*

International Institute of Milwaukee County

Mathilda Jadin, *Green Bay*

Mrs. Ruth L. Jaeger, *Brown Deer*

Ruby Jane Jenkins, *Marshfield*

Vivian M. Jenkins, *Marshfield*

Mrs. Arthur Johnson, *San Francisco, California*

Alice (Mrs. H. E.) Johnson, *Racine*

Mrs. Harvey M. Johnson, *Milton*

Mrs. Leslie N. Jones, *Holcombe*

Gwendolyn Kaltenbach, *Potosi*

Mrs. Darwin Kamke, *Seymour*

Myer Katz, *La Crosse*

Miss Louise Keiner, *Greenwood*

Margaret Keizer, *Platteville*

Patricia (Mrs. Ronald J.) Kelly, *La Crosse*

Mrs. Twylah Kepler, *Richland Center*

Mrs. Edward Kisser, *East Troy*

Carlyne M. (Mrs. Otto) Klein, *Burlington*

Lydia Catherine Phillips Kleinschmidt, *Milwaukee*

Mrs. F. Knurr, *Mukwonago*

Mrs. Alice Knutson, *Iola*

LaVerne Hogan (Mrs. A. A.) Koeller, *Ashland*

Mary K. Koestler, *Cudahy*

Mrs. Marcia Smith Kolar, *Westminster, California*

Mrs. Raymond Koltes, *Madison*

Norma J. Kolthoff, *Madison*

Patricia (Mrs. Ronald K.) Kolwitz, *Menomonee Falls*

Eva Koopikka, *Calumet, Michigan*

William E. Kostka, *Algoma*

Mrs. Virginia Kraegenbrink, *Menomonee Falls*

Ms. Marion I. Kraemer, *Merrimac*

Darlene Kronschnabel, *Greenleaf*

Mrs. Mae A. Krueger, *Kaukauna*

Mrs. Joe Kucera, *Cudahy*

Chris Kuehl, *Milwaukee*

Maria Kulawik, *Stevens Point*

Mrs. Frederic La Croix, *Milwaukee*

Frances Stiles (Mrs. William M.) Lamont, *Aberdeen, South Dakota*

Mrs. Albert Larson, *Manitowoc*

Madelyn Lee (Mrs. Arne V.) Larson, *Clintonville*

Mrs. Norbert La See, *Marshfield*

Marion Lawson, *New York City*

Linda L. Leake, *Burlington*

Mrs. William Lindauer, *Dodgeville*

Mrs. C. W. Loomer, *Madison*

Elinore L. Loveland, *Platteville*

Hope C. (Mrs. R. H.) Loveland, *Cassville*

Irene I. Luethge, *Kiel*

Jane Steinhorst Lyons, *Greenfield*

Mrs. Koidula Maeste, *Milwaukee*

Mrs. Jean Schoch Magarian, *Milwaukee*

Mrs. Rosella Mallory, *Milwaukee*

Mildred O. (Mrs. Willett S.) Main, *Milwaukee*

Mrs. Milton Mandelin, *Greenfield*

Mrs. Art Manthey, *Waunakee*

Mrs. Bess Mantuefel, *Green Bay*

Lillian A. Marsh, *Chilton*

Emma L. Marshall, *Gillingham*

Mary E. (Mrs. Edward A.) Mathwig, *Waupaca*

Ruth Jochimsen (Mrs. John) Mattke, *Sheboygan*

Rosalie (Mrs. Oscar) Mayer, *Madison*

Edith (Mrs. Francis) McConnell, *Wisconsin Rapids*

Trudie Meixner, *Milwaukee*

Mrs. Joseph Meinholz, *Eau Claire*

Blanche Mendl, *Deerbrook*

Mrs. Isabel Mertens, *Withee*

Edna Meudt, *Dodgeville*

Mrs. Alex Meunier, *Sturgeon Bay*

Ila (Mrs. Fred A.) Meyers, *Humbird*

Leone (Mrs. Elmer) Mielke, *Janesville*

Marjorie V. O. (Mrs. Alfred) Miley, *Sheboygan Falls*

Augusta (Mrs. Adolph) Miller, *Montello*

Mary L. Monisen, *Wauwatosa*

Mary Anna (Mrs. Peter) Mowat, *Waukesha*

Mrs. Charles Mowbray, *Janesville*

Mrs. Floyd Myron, *Milwaukee*

Leone Nelson, *Cobb*

Ruth (Mrs. C. E.) Nelson, *Manitowoc*

Virginia Nelson, *Middleton*

Cecelia Ellarson (Mrs. George F.) Nieman, *Muskego*

Dagmar P. Noel, *Waukesha*

Miss Anges E. Norem, *Antigo*

Ethel J. Odegard, *Whitewater*

Mrs. Eleanor Van Putten Oelstrom, *Waukesha*

Mrs. Flroence Paczkowski, *Milwaukee*

Mrs. Francis Palma, *Greenfield*

Kathyrn Parkinson, *Madison*

Mrs. Zane Pautz, *Milton*

Stefanija Pelanis, *Kenosha*

Mrs. R. W. Peterman, *Wauwatosa*

Pamela Pier, *Potosi*

Victoria (Mrs. Ralph C.) Pierce, *Racine*

Mrs. Wilfred Posbrig, *Muskego*

Irene Jones (Mrs. Leon A.) Pratt, *Edgerton*

Bernice Wilsnack Procknow, *Markesan*

Ms. Elizabeth Meating Proctor, *Appleton*

Dorothy (Mrs. Clarence) Proksch, *Stoddard*

Mrs. Edward Pudas, *Iron River*

Roma E. (Mrs. Harry) Rabe, *Kiel*

Gladys M. Randall, *Hustisford*

Mrs. Doris Reichert, *West Allis*

Minnie Reynolds, *Boscobel*

Florence Rice, *Oconto Falls*

Vera (Mrs. Meredith) Richter, *Janesville*

Mrs. Jerome L. Riedy, *Fort Atkinson*

Florence Baker (Mrs. J. A.) Riegel, *St. Croix Falls*

Jane (Mrs. Edward) Rikkers, *Madison*

Rev. Frederick W. Ringe, *New Berlin*

Ruth H. (Mrs. Thomas A.) Roberts, *Brown Deer*

Virginia Roe, *Whitewater*

Jane Roeber, *Madison*

Elizabeth J. Rojahn, *Oshkosh*

Mrs. Albert Rokus, *Vesper*

Mrs. Claire Rood, *Shawano*

Mrs. Janice Runge, *Merrill*

Elsia Ruselink, *Milwaukee*

Mrs. William Sachtjen, *Waunakee*

Miss Marie T. St. Louis, *Shorewood*

Mrs. Robert Sanford, *River Falls*

Mrs. Paul W. Sawyer, *Racine*

Pamela J. Schalk, *Milwaukee*

Jean Bunker (Mrs. Felix) Schmidt, *Siren*

Pat Gottschall (Mrs. B. A.) Schuknecht, *Lodi*

Violet Fendry Schumacher, *Franklin*

Viola (Mrs. Felix) Schuster, Menomonee Falls

Phyllis Trimberger (Mrs. Roger J.) Schwartz, *Milwaukee*

Mrs. Clarence Schwebke, *Beloit*

Hedwig A. (Mrs. Victor) Semran, *Milwaukee*

Mrs. Linda Rajala Sereno, *Montreal*

Mrs. Hugh Severson, *Greenwood*

Marlyne Schantz (Mrs. William L.) Seymour, *Elkhorn*

Marian Sheko, *Loyal*

Charles Shetler, *Madison*

Mrs. Raymond Shirek, *Junction City*

Mrs. Anne Shoberg, *Milwaukee*

Anne Short, *Madison*

Mrs. Charles A. Sims, *Antigo*

Mrs. Robert Smart, *Muskego*

Mrs. August Sommerfield, *Chippewa Falls*

Mrs. Claude Sorenson, *Manitowoc*

Mrs. Waclaw Soroka, *Stevens Point*

Romona (Mrs. Courtland) Sperger, *Waupun*

Mrs. Charles Spitzbarth, *Fennimore*

Mrs. and Mrs. Bay. Sprengel, *New Berlin*

Mary Staj, *Neenah*

Mrs. Clayton Stannard, *Oshkosh*

Mrs. Martie Steele, *Fond du Lac*

Charlotte (Mrs. Irvine Y.) Stein, *Madison*

Mrs. Warren Stevens, *Kenosha*

Mrs. Ann Strathman, *Waterloo*

Mrs. Frank M. Suess, *Luxemburg*

Hilda Hillman (Mrs. Sulo) Sukanen, *Marengo*

Mrs. Manfred Swarsensky, *Madison*

Mrs. Robert Schwartz, *Kenosha*

Mrs. Mary Symanek, *Beloit*

Mari Taniguchi, *Appleton*

Magdalena W. Tank, *New London*

Georgya Tatreau, *Platteville*

Mrs. Daniel E. Taylor, *Oconomowoc*

Mrs. Ora P. Taylor, *Drummond*

Pat (Mrs. William) Taylor, *Whitefish Bay*

Selma (Mrs. Harry) Thewis, *Cochrane*

Mrs. Rosemary Thielke, *Milwaukee*

Mrs. Veva Thill, *Potosi*

Alice Thorpe, *Stanley*

Celia M. (Mrs. Clarence) Thorson, *Cedarburg*

Miss Edna. L. Timmell, *Oconomowoc*

Mrs. Theodore Toepel, *Howards Grove*

Mrs. Louis Tornowske, *Patch Grove*

Mrs. Herman Tuchman, *Milwaukee*

Mrs. Spencer W. Turner, *Rice Lake*

Mrs. Walter Turnquist, *Eagle River*

Marion Philippi (Mrs. John) Urich, *Madison*

Mrs. Julia Vanderschaegen, *Iron Belt*

Mrs. Florence M. Vint, *Springfield*, *Virginia*

Mrs. Walter H. Waite, *Clinton*

Mrs. Margaret Weber, *St. Nazianz*

Mrs. Wencil Weber, *Whitelaw*

Florence (Mrs. Charles) Weckerle, *Milwaukee*

Mrs. Henry Weddig, *Kewaskum*

Mrs. Leo Wesolowski, *Oconto Falls*

Betty and Susie Westra, *Waupaca*

Walter G. Wright, Greenbelt, *Maryland*

Susanne Marie Williams-Brown, *Clintonville*

Mrs. Forrest Wilms, *Neenah*

Elizabeth McMillan Wood, *Appleton*

Delta (Mrs. Herbert) Woinowsky, *Madison*

Mrs. B. E. Wrensch, *Brookfield*

Eleanor (Mrs. Anthony) Yankowski, *Neenah*

Alexa Young, *Madison*

Mrs. Clyde Zahn, *Shawano*

Mrs. Ervin Zahn, *Shawano*

Mrs. Irving W. Zirbel, *Elm Grove*

ACKNOWLEDGMENTS

WHEN IT COMES TO WRITING ABOUT FOOD, AS opposed to preparing it, there is no such thing as too many cooks. And certainly many people were figuratively beside me, contributing important ingredients, seasonings, relishes, and food lore to this varied spread.

First off were the more than 900 Wisconsinites and former state residents who contributed recipes and reminiscences. Only a fraction of their material could be included in these pages, but each and every contribution helped immeasurably to enlarge my knowledge of Wisconsin's culinary past and attain a broader feeling for its flavor. I thank them all. (Those whose recipes *were* selected for inclusion are listed elsewhere.)

I am grateful, too, for the work of Rosalie Mayer of Madison, liaison with the Women's Auxiliary of the State Historical Society of Wisconsin, and the committee of home economists and food experts that she organized and supervised to screen the almost 1,600 recipes submitted. They were: Edith Bangham, Lillian Fried, Ava Jones, Joanne Kelsey, Helen F. Killingstad, Phyllis Lovrien, Marge Meier, Louella Mortenson, Iva Mortimer, Dorothy Strang, and Dorothy Traisman.

This project would have been even longer in the doing without the help and expertise of numerous members of the staff of the State Historical Society of Wisconsin who were always ready to supply encouragement, clarify a murky historical point, or chart the correct path for research. Among them were Joan Freeman, Peter Gordy, Marilyn Grant, Sara Leuchter, Mary McCann, Christine Schelshorn, Joan Severa, George Talbot, and the late Raymond S. Sivesind. I am indebted to Paul Hass, head of the Society's editorial division, whose unfailing good humor and refined diplomatic skills kept this project on track, and most especially to John O. Holzhueter, associate editor of the *Wisconsin Magazine of History*. I found it convenient and expedient to have Jack easily available during both the organization and the writing of this book; if he could not readily come up with a requested historical fact from his remarkable encyclopedic memory, he knew just where to find it in the written record. I am particularly appreciative of the improvements to the manuscript that resulted from his careful scrutiny of facts and figures throughout the book, and especially Chapter 8, "The Corporate Kitchen."

The student assistants I had at various times over the years were exceedingly important to this undertaking: researcher Elizabeth Hachten, who spent many hours one summer in the Society's archives deciphering spindly nineteenth-century handwriting, and Linda Levendusky and Mariann Goss, who tied up numerous loose ends. Most important of all was my project assistant for two years, Timothy N. Walters, now assistant editor of *Horizon* magazine, who organized the research, did the lion's share of it, and revealed to me the efficacy of the 4x6 index card as a research and writing tool.

Finally, I wish to acknowledge the valuable support and assistance provided by my husband William A. Hachten, professor of journalism in the University of Wisconsin–Madison. He is unexcelled as a coddler of a writer's ego, as an implacable setter of deadlines, and as an exciser of clichés. I doubt even he knows how important were his insights and sure editorial sense before, during, and after I set words to paper.

H. H.

GENERAL INDEX

XYZ

INDEX TO RECIPES

About the author

HARVA HACHTEN is a journalist and author
and editor of several books, including
Kitchen Safari, an African cookbook. She
directed the research and began the writing
for *The Flavor of Wisconsin* while serving as
public information officer for the State Historical Society of Wisconsin. A resident of
Madison, she writes regularly for *Madison*
magazine and for *Insight* magazine of the
Milwaukee Journal.

This book was designed by
JUDITH PATENAUDE
who also did the drawings

Typography by
A-R EDITIONS, INC.
Madison, Wisconsin